THE MOTLEY FOOL
UK INVESTMENT GUIDE

The following Motley Fool books are also published by Boxtree:

THE MOTLEY FOOL
UK INVESTMENT GUIDE

DAVID BERGER

WITH AN INTRODUCTION BY DAVID AND TOM GARDNER

NEW INTRODUCTION TO SECOND EDITION BY DAVID BERGER

First published 2000 by Boxtree

This updated and revised edition with new introduction by
David Berger and new appendices published 2000 by Boxtree,
an imprint of Macmillan Publishers Ltd
25 Eccleston Place, London SW1W 9NF
Basingstoke and Oxford

www.macmillan.com

Associated companies throughout the world

ISBN 0 7522 1901 4

9 8 7 6 5 4 3

A CIP catalogue record for this book is available from
the British Library.

Designed and typeset by Keystroke, Jacaranda Lodge, Wolverhampton
Printed by Mackays of Chatham plc, Chatham, Kent

Contents

What You've (Maybe) Already Got

Bits 'n' Bobs

Rounding Up

Acknowledgements

Foolish Glossary of Investment Terms

Appendices

Introduction to the Second Edition: Of Books and Web Sites

There's something paradoxical about writing a book at the same time as running an Internet publishing operation like the Motley Fool. In the one, the content is updated many times daily, errors corrected in seconds and much of the written content on the Web site is submitted, not by the staff, but by the users, posting their thoughts, ideas, questions and analyses twenty-four hours a day. That gives it an immediacy and vibrancy it's impossible to match in any other medium. With a book, on the other hand, content is submitted once, it takes two years (in this case) to update it, no immediate user input is possible and, in contrast to the Web site, *it costs money to read it*.

Looking at the bare facts of the matter, you'd conclude both that we were insane to continue publishing books and you were insane to continue buying them. As ever in life, though, bare facts are less than half the story. We're creatures of habit. Books have been hallowed objects for thousands of years, even more so before the widespread adoption of printing in the fifteenth century. We could wonder for hours why this is and it's the kind of lazy speculation that goes so well with a fridge full of ice-cold beers or a bottle of Chardonnay on a sun-drenched terrace, somewhere where English isn't the native tongue. (*Mmmm . . .*) For now, though, we can probably wrap it up by saying that, for whatever reason, books are wonderful things to own, read and behold. A much-loved book encapsulates a body of knowledge or an experience that we would love to call our own, even for just a short time; and it's much easier to assimilate large bodies of information from a book, which we read as, when and where we want to, than it is from a screen. The Internet is not going to replace books any time soon (let's remember that Amazon, the best-known Internet retailer, started life as a bookstore) and that's why I'm writing this introduction to the second edition of the *Motley Fool UK Investment Guide* and you're reading it.

While the Internet can't replace books, however, it can and does complement them. In the case of the Motley Fool, the Internet provides a forum for discussion and an opportunity to plug into the corpus of information and ideas that has generated the book in the first place – to tap into the energy source. In this, the Internet offers another, entirely new dimension to the experience of reading a book. Just how revolutionary this is is brought home to us here at the Fool every day as we take part in and observe the daily interchange of ideas and information that unites a community of investors on the Internet.

A lot has changed since this book was published back in November 1998 and even more has changed since the inception of the Fool UK in September 1997. From small beginnings and a tiny public awareness of the potential of the Internet, the Motley Fool UK now has hundreds of thousands of visitors each month. This growth in the Internet, which really started with the launch of Freeserve as a free Internet Service Provider in 1998, has proved phenomenal, and the advent of the wireless Internet in the next five years could prove even more far-reaching. A short-lived boom in the prices of Internet and other technology shares in the early part of 2000 resulted in a spate of British press headlines like 'DOT COM MANIA', 'DOT COM FRENZY', 'DOT BOMB', 'DOT GONE?' As ever, the British press was taking a short-term, sensationalist viewpoint, something we talk about later in the book in relation to investing. Well, the 'dot' hasn't 'gone' and it's here to stay. It always takes a while to view new developments in a mature light, particularly when they threaten to upset a comfortable and long-lived status quo, and the wild swings in press opinion and in the stock market in recent times are probably a reflection of that.

Viewing the Internet as a threat, though, just isn't helpful and taking that attitude carries within itself the seeds of one's own destruction. In our experience here at the Motley Fool, the Internet is a tremendous leveller. That is to say it is an extraordinary discriminator of value, in whatever terms, financial or personal, one cares to define it. If someone or something is not providing value – and the traditional practices of the financial services industry are a graphic example – the Internet will blow the whole game wide open. Similarly, the Internet can also be a tremendous provider of value in its own right and also a complement to traditional sources of value. All those people who say that the Internet is a poor substitute for books are right. They're also right when they say sitting in front of a computer screen is a poor substitute for life. Of course they are. But what the Internet can do is provide a complement to them. The Motley Fool UK Web site provides a complement to this book. A newly struck-up e-mail correspondence with long-lost cousin

Edward in the Australian outback provides a tremendous complement to the life of your family. (Well, it may do, depending on why you decided to ship him out there in the first place.)

Having spent all this time musing on why we're still writing books — basically cos we love 'em and think they're great — what have we actually changed in this second edition? In some ways quite a lot and in some ways not so much. The basic ethos of the Fool remains unchanged, many individual passages and indeed some whole chapters remain fundamentally unchanged, but much of the treatment of individual investing issues in this book represents, we think, a more solid approach, and some chapters have been entirely transformed, incorporated into others or dropped as being no longer relevant. We've updated numbers, updated our thinking where it needed it, beefed up some of the most important bits and inserted secret Masonic catchphrases where we think they'll be most effective.[1] In short, the world has moved on, the Fool has moved on and we've tried hard to reflect that.

In terms of specifics, readers of the first edition will notice the most major changes in:

- The Obviously Great Investments chapter, where we've looked at what went well with our companies from the first edition and what went badly, and thrown in some more companies for consideration. We've also made a couple of changes to the Obviously Great Investment criteria. The old 'Repeat purchase' criterion has been folded into 'Have They Built a Strong Brand?', and a new criterion, 'Is Their Position Easily Defended?', has been added.
- Our treatment of pensions, endowments and ISAs. These have all been updated to reflect the current situation and current thinking.
- The Mechanical Investing chapter (formerly Beating the Footsie). It's become apparent that mechanical investing, while attractive for some, requires a greater diligence and commitment than it's possible to instil in a single chapter of a book. We've therefore broadened the chapter out, making it much more about mechanical investing in general than a single strategy, and pointing the interested reader to our Web site where much more in-depth treatment is available.

There's always a fine line to be trodden in any second edition. This is between writing a stand-alone volume in which new readers aren't irritated by constant

---

1 Not actually true.

references to 'In the first edition . . . ', while at the same time paying due homage to what went before, both for reasons of intellectual rigour and to give readers of the first edition a sense of continuity. To serve these twin masters, we have therefore adopted a deliberate policy, beloved of generations of British politicians, known as 'fudging it'. Hopefully, though, the fudge has allowed us to achieve a middle ground which will satisfy both camps. I think and hope it has. On the one hand, we hope this edition represents a totally new, stand-alone volume for people who may never have heard of the Motley Fool and on the other it is a worthy successor and inheritor of the first edition, providing a useful refresher and update.

Inestimable thanks are due to the thousands who wrote in and commented on the first edition. We can't say we've incorporated all your suggestions and feedback, but an awful lot has found its way in. We'd love to hear what you thought of this book, too – where we could have made it clearer, bits we should have put in, bits we should have left out and anything else you think of. Tell us what we ought to do to make personal investment in Britain easier to understand. In fact, tell us how to improve our business – we're always on the look-out for bright ideas and bright people. One thing, though: if you ask us to give you directive, individual advice about what to do with your own money, we'll neatly sidestep the question. Britain already has more than enough financial advisers.

You can send an e-mail with any and all feedback to us at **foolukbook @fool.co.uk**, or else post a message on the UK Investment Guide discussion board, which you'll find at our Web site – **www.fool.co.uk**. You can even write:

Motley Fool UK
6th Floor
The Media Centre
3–8 Carburton Street
London W1W 5AJ

And if you're in the area and feel like seeing what goes on in Fool HQ, please drop in.

Viva il Fool!

DAVID BERGER
LANGTREE, DEVON
SUMMER 2000

Introduction to the First Edition: Welcome to the Age of Foolishness

David B.

Who isn't a little anxious about money? Who doesn't worry that they're not saving enough or that their savings aren't growing fast enough? Who has a total and utter, rock solid, unshakeable faith in their financial adviser and in the financial professions as a whole? If none of these questions worries you, then you should probably put this book back on the shelf and leave very quietly the way you came in. Our bet is, though, that most people picking up this strangely named volume have at least some doubt in their mind on one or other or all three of these questions. It's only natural. After all, who amongst us was taught anything whatsoever about personal finance at school? Who amongst us has ever understood, *really* understood, what a financial professional was going on about? Yes, we bet the answers are pretty doubtful to these questions too.

There's a dark void in many people's lives when it comes to finance, a feeling that 'Here be dragons', that it's best not to meddle in what you can never hope to understand. Well, tosh, piffle and rubbish! We don't believe that's so at all and in this book we plan to show why. We'll show you how the financial professionals and the City are out to keep the public as ignorant as possible, how they sell investment plans which eat up 80 per cent or more of the first two years' contributions in charges and take a full seven years to break even, how they sell other plans which perform worse than even the average in over 90 per cent of cases. We'll take you on a tour of all those TESSAs, PEPs, PPPs, ISAs and BAPs (one of these is a type of filled roll, no prizes for guessing which). We'll show you what they all mean – in very simple, easily understandable terms – and then we'll show you just how you can beat the professionals at their own game. And beat them roundly. You don't need GCSEs, 'A' levels or a degree for this. Just a smattering of common sense, your feet on moderately firm ground and a willingness to challenge the orthodoxy, to rise against convention. In fact, as usual, Winnie the Pooh puts his finger right on the spot. Here he is summing up his friend Owl:

> *'Owl hasn't exactly got Brain, but he Knows Things.'*

Knowing Things, not very many things, is one of the keys to this whole business.

The final quality you'll need is a sense of humour. In contrast to the financial professionals, we don't believe that learning about investment has to be worthy or turgid or boring. We believe it should be fun. We have got a lot of enjoyment out of writing this book and from working to promote a sound understanding of basic financial principles, both offline and on and we hope you'll come and share in our spirit of lightheartedness. But please don't think us flippant. We understand how deadly serious is the issue of financial security; we, however, simply don't buy into the mock awe and very real pomposity with which it is invested by the ranks of the professionals.

So who are we, these three strange-looking characters in silly hats? For that, we must go back to 1993, when David and Tom Gardner sat down and took a long, hard look at the investing orthodoxy that prevailed in the United States of America. The wisdom seemed to be that Mr Joe Average, as the common punter is termed in the United States, was a hopeless case when it came to understanding anything about investing; one step removed from a flatworm in fact. His only hope lay in finding a benevolent professional who would take over the burden of managing his savings and steer it through the financial minefield which, alone, he had no chance of negotiating without losing a leg at the very least. In return for this limb- and possibly even life-saving help, the professional would take a modest commission. The result? Mr J. Average could go home and sleep at night, secure in the knowledge that his savings were in good hands and the professional would make a fair living, returning to his family every evening and basking in the satisfying glow of an honest job, well done.

It was fairyland, but in this prosperous nation, with its sunstruck coasts, purple mountains, gun-toting crazies and pizzas the size of tractor tyres, all was not quite as it seemed. Mr Average was ignorant all right, but it wasn't because money and finance were impossible, or even difficult to understand. It was because he had never been *taught* anything about them at all. Simple concepts like pensions, price-to-earnings ratios, stock market indices and execution-only brokers were not just unknowns, they were terrifying, shadowy concepts, the very mention of which might unleash malign powers. Nowhere in the entire educational system was provision made to teach this basic and vital information.

Without education, it was true that the average investor (read: 'Everybody who ever hoped to save any money for their future') had no chance of understanding what was going on and had no choice but to hand over his or her hard-earned dollars to the professionals. That was a shame in itself, because actions based on ignorance of any kind cannot be auspicious for the future. But that was far from the end of the story.

You see, the professional money managers of the United States were not stepping into the breach of ignorance and delivering a solid, dependable service as part of a public service commitment. It turned out that it was in their interests to keep the level of ignorance and confusion about money as high as possible, because the foundation of their industry was based on some very unstable bedrock indeed. It was an extraordinary but true fact that 90 per cent of the returns on offer from America's professional money managers were lower than the returns that could be made off simple, low-cost investments, easy to purchase, requiring no skill to pick and with negligible charges attached to them. With a tiny amount of time and even less effort, Joe Average could outperform the professionals, precisely by being average. He just didn't know it yet. Another thing he didn't know was that in itself the stock market is not a dangerous place to invest, but is in fact one of the *safest* kinds of investments. With the financial media constantly harping on potential short-term losses in the stock market, the long-term story of reliable, outperforming growth was totally lost. Of course, short-term panic stories are what sell newspapers and lure television viewers.

America was being duped and neither its financial professionals nor its media had any real interest in the spread of mass education about their subject. They had it very cushy, which was how it had been for a long time and that's how it might have stayed. Then something happened, something which this writer, with characteristic vision, welcomed with open arms:

'What's it called? The Internet? You can talk to other people with your computer? You can get hold of information? Why on *Earth* would you bother to do that?!'

Yes, really, and at about the time that the Oracle of Bournemouth (where David hails from originally) was dismissing the greatest revolution in mass communication since the invention of moveable type, David and Tom Gardner were transferring their print publication *The Motley Fool*, started a year earlier in 1993, onto America Online, otherwise known as AOL. A small, subversive movement had begun.

The name alluded to Shakespeare's Fool – Touchstone in *As You Like It* – who had an unnerving habit of demonstrating that truth often lay beyond the bounds of conventional wisdom. Fools in the olden days were about the only people who could tell the King how it really was without getting their heads lopped off for their pains. In its print incarnation, *The Motley Fool* ('Ye Olde Printed Foole', as it is now fondly remembered) had a terribly small audience, mostly of family friends, we are told, who wanted to support the boys' attempt to make a living. (And about time too, their mum was probably saying.) Things soon took off, though, with the move to the mass medium and by the end of 1995 they were the most popular site on AOL, they had added a website and were publishing a book which went on to become a best-seller. Soon, the Fool was on the lips of everyone in America who had any interest in finance, the Fool's newspaper column was syndicated in over 160 newspapers around the country and the website was registering 20 million visits a month. As the Wise grew more disdainful, so the Fools were growing ever more popular, helping people to help themselves out of financial bondage.

It was about at this time that I, a jobbing British doctor, sometime of Bournemouth as we've heard (Three cheers for Bournemouth! Hello, Mum!), stumbled across the Fool on the Web. Humour? Down-to-Earthness? A willingness to engage with the world and do something novel? And all this in a site about investment? Very strange.

So strange in fact that I got hooked and, well, you know, one thing led to another and while initially I only needed five or ten minutes a day of the Fool online to keep me satisfied, pretty soon I was doing cold turkey without three, four or even more hours plugged in every day. Yes, the Fool had snared another unsuspecting innocent. It was pitiful to see. And then this happened:

One day, after many hours' surfing, I found myself moving through a deep, inner sanctum of the online area, a place I had never visited before. The cavernous walls of the chamber echoed with the clicks of my mouse. It smelt damp and musty and of a sudden the stillness was broken by the distant sound of breaking glass and a woman's high-pitched scream. Then all was quiet once more. On the muted, darkened screen there was now just one gently flashing icon and it said 'Click here if you wish to become a Fool'. I hesitated, awestruck and barely comprehending the step I was about to take. There was no going back now, that at least I knew. I clicked. A message came up: 'Please Wait.' Then: 'Please be still while we upload your brain. Click here to proceed.' I clicked and sat motionless, as bidden. Suddenly, the screen became busy with activity and it was clear that something extraordinary was about to happen. And then I felt it – as if someone had pulled the plug out of the bath at the base of my skull. My brains were leaving me and being *uploaded to the Motley Fool*! I sat still, a curious sense of ease washing over me. After a few minutes, another dialogue box sprang up through the misty haze of well-being: 'Please click here to download a test version of a Mark 1 Foolish brain.' As the Foolish brain was downloaded, I felt my skull filling up once more and my consciousness returning to clarity. I had become a card-carrying Fool.

All right, it didn't happen *quite* like that, but the brain-sucking, Boris Karloff imagery was too tempting to forgo. What actually happened was that I composed an e-mail one wet Tuesday afternoon in April to David and Tom Gardner. 'It's just the same here, you know,' I said. 'We pay outrageous charges for underperforming investments, just like you,' I said. 'No-one knows anything about this stuff and when the professionals come and sell it to us, we just gawp and nod blindly and believe it, like you do,' I said. 'How about a British Motley Fool? And soon!' I said. To their credit – and this says something about the accessibility this new medium provides, as well as their openness to new ideas and innovation – they didn't do the high-tech equivalent of screwing up my e-mail and lobbing it at the basketball hoop they have poised over the wastepaper bin.

Again, one thing led to another and by the autumn of 1997, five months after the first e-mail, the Motley Fool UK Online was launched on AOL UK (keyword: FOOLUK), followed in February 1998 by the Web site **www.fool. co.uk**). With what we hoped was a similar blend of humour and irreverence, we set ourselves the same Foolish task of pointing to the Emperor and revealing that those new clothes he thought he was wearing weren't such a bargain after all.

In the very birthplace of Folly, the United Kingdom, the Wise spin doctors had kept the upper hand for more years than anyone could remember: 'It's too complicated for you. Trust us. We'll look after your financial future. We have your *best* interests at heart.'

But as the Emperor paraded the streets on his magnificent charger, collecting tributes and dispensing blessings as he went, already there were rumblings of discontent and not a little merriment: 'That fellow might believe he's wearing a new suit of clothes and he's certainly been telling us that for more years than we can remember, but it looks almost as if he's got nothing on at all, as if he's been having us on all these years! He still believes it, though. Amazing!' With sentiments like this already circling on the peasants' rumour-mill, the soil was ripe for the Fool to sow even more seeds of revolution and, yes, even treason.

The bloke on the horse, you see, really does have nothing on. Not a stitch.

Bombast, bamboozlement, overcharging, investment underperformance, longer words where shorter ones would do: it's all here. The truth, though, is that you don't have to put up with paying through the nose to investment managers, *90 per cent* of whom, as we've heard, will perform worse than the average. You don't have to smile gratefully as you slip most of your first two years' worth of pension contributions directly into your financial adviser's pocket. You don't have to weep tears of thanks as it takes seven years or more for your endowment policy to even *start* to show a positive return on your money.

None of what we are going to discuss in this book is complicated or intimidating or impenetrable to the average person. It's all totally simple and totally Foolish and it will give you the key to unlock the sinister mystery which investment remains for so many of us. It will also show you how, with no skill whatsoever, you can beat the professionals at their own game. And what's more, it will show you how you can do this with as little as half an hour of effort each year. Or even less.

Does that sound a trifle unrealistic? Really, it shouldn't. You see, your motivation and that of the financial professionals are very different. While your first priority is to make money for you, *their* first priority is to make money *from* you. Their second priority is to make money for you, but it comes a long way down the line. As a savvy individual, you can cut out the middle-man, head straight for the best value, lowest-cost investments bringing in 'average' returns and outperform 90 per cent of the pros. Jim Slater, who has written some excellent books on investment himself with a highly down-to-Earth take on the subject, had this to say about the *Motley Fool Investment Guide* (the US version) in his January 1998 newsletter:

> *One of its main contentions, with which I agree wholeheartedly, is that ordinary private investors are in many ways much better placed to make consistently good returns from shares than highly paid professionals in the City and on Wall Street.*

And if all this is starting to sound just a little too suspiciously easy, rest assured you won't find any get-rich-quick schemes between these pages. You won't even find anything controversial or risky. All you will find is the investment good sense we should all have been learning since we were in secondary school explained in simple terms and without huge amounts of jargon. We hope that by the time you have finished this volume (a weekend of frippery and delight or eighteen weeks of tooth-grinding misery, depending on your constitution) the black cloud of guilt and unease which hangs over you as you contemplate the need to do something for your financial future will have lifted. We hope you'll feel free and light and knowledgeable and . . . Foolish.

Before I make way for David and Tom G., I'd like to hark back a few years. Some of you reading this will have spent the early 1980s as enthralled as I was by *The Hitch Hiker's Guide to the Galaxy*, the book, radio and television series that followed the adventures of one Arthur Dent to the ends of the universe after the Earth had, regrettably, been demolished to make way for a hyper-spatial express route. Printed in large, coloured, friendly letters on the snug plastic cover of the *Guide* – the most remarkable book ever to come out of the publishing corporations of Ursa Minor and containing an alarming recipe for the best drink in existence, the Pan-galactic Gargle Blaster (see Appendix 6) – was the most useful piece of advice in the universe:

DON'T PANIC

We can't pretend that *The Motley Fool UK Investment Guide* has even an atom's worth of the brilliance of the *Hitch-Hiker's Guide*. But the advice? Surely, surely no Fool can do without it.

David and Tom G.

Something had to be done about this situation.

Ah, but there we go again, starting *in medias res*, 'in the midst of things', as was Homer's inclination in the *Iliad* and the *Odyssey*, and now ours too (in a desperate attempt to appease the Homeric Society we have offended in the past). So we should back-pedal. And be brief.

A few years ago, we two brothers stayed up past midnight for a few months running, in order to pour our souls into a literary product – that's what the book salesman called it, 'product' (had to get used to that) – designed to revolutionize thinking about money in our home country. It needed to be done. Despite the tremendous prosperity of the US stock market, studies showed that the distribution of wealth was growing more and more skewed. Of course, the haves have *always* had, and the have-nots have always had not, but the situation was growing more distressing. We deduced (correctly, we still believe, despite what the haves tell us) that one of the primary reasons for the *status quo* was the almost complete lack of education about money in the United States of America. No standard study of the subject has ever been made mandatory for American ankle-biters, something which would teach them the subtly destructive power of credit card debt, something which would teach them to understand just how much better the stock market had done than any other competing investment over the entire century. It was ironic to us that we had studied quadratic equations and binomial coefficients, and yet our own schools had never taught the far more important facts about compounded financial returns. It was incredible that the example of Anne Scheiber was not shouted from the rooftops of our educational institutions. This humble New Yorker died at an advanced age in 1995, leaving a fortune of over $20 million to charity, a fortune accumulated, from a starting point of $5,000 in the closing years of the Second World War, entirely through investments in common stocks such as Coca-Cola and Gillette.

Swooping in to redress these wrongs, *The Motley Fool Investment Guide* was published in January of 1996 to some critical acclaim, went on to earn that *sine qua non* label 'best-seller', and continues to sell well several years later . . . in the United States. We checked our sales in Great Britain, and discovered we'd sold seventeen copies. That's as best we can tell – there's some question as to whether that seventeenth copy was in fact purchased or used as wrapping at Billingsgate fish market, but we'll leave that to the accountants.

Something – we repeat – *something* had to be done about this situation.

(That one was for you, Homer, and please be more understanding now, gentle Society.)

Enter David Berger. This British junior hospital doctor had been playing the voyeur for several months, peeping into our US website (http://www.fool.com) from his perch in the pastoral setting of North Devon. He grew gradually braver, to the point of contributing occasional scribblings to our communal effort. Indeed, his written stuff was sufficiently sassy that we felt we must meet the fellow. Without really even being able to afford it (we're an 'Internet startup company', after all, a phrase synonymous with 'unprofitable'), we flew David across the Atlantic Ocean to spend a week with us at Fool Global HQ. We discovered among other things that he was far funnier than we, and (as it turned out) more intelligent, and better-looking, too. (He had hair, for instance – hey, why do you think we wear the caps?) We also discovered, with his help, that the lack of education about money in the UK was at least on par with the situation in our own country, if not even a little bit worse (!) . . . and that a book speaking in plain and entertaining terms about the subject might be a valued contribution to the British literary scene.

In addition to those revelations, we spied further evidence that he could write, which mattered to us most of all. We then asked him to draw up a series of *Steps to Investing Foolishly* for a proposed UK Fool site. In typical Bergerish (his own language), Step Five began like this:

> **Editor's Note:** *Welcome to a short treatise on the importance of shares, which also happens to constitute the Fifth Step in the Ten Steps to Investing Foolishly. You can find the fornicating monkeys about halfway through, but*

we suggest you read the entire article slowly from the start to allow the suspense to build.

If that doesn't read like winning material to you, return this book to the shelf right now, as you are the proud possessor of better taste than will be on offer here. From our point of view, though, any writer capable of using fornicating monkeys to make an important point about shares was our chap.

Something therefore *has* been done about this situation.

You see, as funny as we once wanted to hope we were in our own country, we were clearly neither amusing, nor useful, nor interesting in even a superficial sense in the United Kingdom. Our answer is thus to tag along with the fellow on the cover photo of this book, figuring that he might be.

In closing, all the blame for the appearance of this subversive text or its contents must fall on David's head (his e-mail address is **foolukbook@ fool.co.uk**). Any spontaneous overflows of emotion, recollected in tranquillity, that tilt toward the 'praise' end of the spectrum are, however, still best addressed to TheGardners@fool.com. Bless you and thank you, Dear Reader.

How to Use This Book

Chaos often breeds life, when order breeds habit.

— Henry Brooks Adams, *The Education of Henry Adams* (1907)

Many people reading this book *will* like to start at the beginning and read all the way through and that's fine. It's even how we initially planned it would be. Others, though, will start at the end and read it backwards. Others still will skim back and forth through the text, eyes alighting here and there on a different spot of interest on each pass. Yet others will read only the one or two chapters that interest them and a few, a very few, will be so aghast at what they read in the first few pages that they will fling themselves in front of a bus in protest against the unfair practices of the financial professionals before they even get to any of the really juicy bits. While it doesn't really matter how you come at the book, we'd prefer you not to plump for the latter option as the liability implications make our jumpy lawyer even jumpier.

Most of the chapters in the book can more or less stand on their own, although we do think they add up to a coherent story in which the total is greater than the mere sum of the parts. The way you tot up that total is down to you, but above all we hope your journey to understanding the basics of investment will be not only liberating, but fun. Please promise us, therefore, that as soon as you find yourself glazing over, and certainly as soon as you find yourself re-reading paragraphs in a desperate and increasingly frantic attempt to understand just what we're banging on about, that you'll take a break. Make a sandwich, listen to some music, hitchhike to the South of France, do anything as long as you're not breaking your head over something you don't understand. We don't actually think there's anything very complex in here – in fact, there is nothing in this book a twelve-year-old couldn't understand; in fact, we hope there *are* a few twelve-year-olds reading this – but eventually any brain which has dealt with a single subject for too long seizes up. When that happens to your brain, be kind to it and give it a rest. When you come back, things will seem much clearer.

How the Book is Structured

In the first section, we look at how and why you should invest for your future and how to go about it simply and Foolishly. Then we have a short interlude where we depart on a couple of tangents for light relief before embarking on the second section which gets into the juicy stuff about investing in shares. The third section, 'What You've (Maybe) Already Got', dishes the dirt on pensions and endowments. The last main section, 'Bits 'n' Bobs, is where we've stuck all the, er, bits and bobs. Finally, we round things off with a summary (of sorts) and a glossary.

Finally, there's a glossary. Oh *yeah*, a *glossary*, you say. Well, don't! We went to a bit of trouble putting it together and we think it's a useful reference.

At the end are a number of useful appendices.

In fact, that's enough of an introduction. Now it's up to you to read this book and decide if it's any use or not.

Starting Out

1

Why You Should Invest

I am a Millionaire. That is my religion.

— George Bernard Shaw, *Major Barbara*

Think about it: Monday matinées, Saga holidays to Scarborough, trips to the shops in a Mini Metro at 18 miles an hour. You're going to have to finance all these somehow. The money that you are earning today is going to have to pay for what you hope will be — and is increasingly likely to be — a long retirement. Whether it will be happy or not is down to you and will depend at least partly on whether you have to worry about where the next box of teabags is coming from.

That's one very important reason to think deeply about investment.

Maybe you're a bit ashamed about the other reason. Maybe you want to make some money, some *real* money, by investing. That's OK, you can admit that here and, yes, you've come to the right place. It is possible, genuinely possible for you, Arthur Smallridge of Chorlton-cum-Hardy, to take a portion of your regular income, invest it and watch it grow to monumental proportions. We've already seen how Anne Scheiber did it in the United States, but just the same is possible here. You don't have to know exactly what you'll do with the financial freedom you are going to buy for yourself in years to come, but our guess is that something will come to you. As we see it, money is like fuel. Most of us have to work fairly hard to bring in enough logs to feed the fire we need to keep us warm in our daily lives. And the curious thing is, the fire just seems to get hotter the more fuel you throw at it. One day, though, with a stockpile of enough logs to feed a reasonable-sized fire, perhaps you'll have the time to turn your creative attentions elsewhere. Jean-Jacques Rousseau, the Swiss philosopher, and incredibly enough one of the first people to point out in the eighteenth century that the Alps were in fact beautiful, had this to say of money:

Money in one's possession is the instrument of liberty.

3

Even today in Britain, with all the hoo-hah that surrounds the Lottery, many of us feel that setting our caps in pursuit of a large sum of money is at the very least a trifle vulgar and at worst obscene. Seeing money as opportunity, however, *we* don't subscribe to this view at all. Things have changed a lot in the last fifty years and the idea of a secure job for life isn't with us any more. Since we're all likely to change jobs and careers many times in our lives, we don't see anything wrong with earning yourself the opportunity to do what moves you. You might want to write the history of the Darlington marshalling yards, compose a masterpiece, devote your entrepreneurial skills and your fortune to working on behalf of others or maybe you'd just like to take the time to walk in the woods and hear, really hear, the wind rustling the leaves and the birds calling to each other in the upper branches. Whichever you choose, you're going to need the resources to sustain yourself while you do it.

By picking up this book, buying it and reading this far you are soaring ahead of most of your contemporaries, the majority of whom are already guaranteed to know less about investment than you do. Your future wealth is assured. So sit back, relax, make yourself another cup of tea and have a biccy – you've broken the back of it.

What Investing Means

Investment is something we do every day, consciously and unconsciously. We invest in our relationships, our jobs, our hobbies, and our lives. (We hope you've just invested £12.99 in this book and if you haven't, if you've stolen it, put it back this instant.) If we didn't invest in these things, we wouldn't get anything back, or at least nothing back of very much worth. And investment is all about 'getting back'. We invest something, whatever that may be, in the hope of a return over and above the original input. It seems so pathetically simple that you're probably wondering why we're going on about it at such length. What is interesting, however, is that while we put a lot of effort and time into, say, investing in our relationship with our partner – flowers, surprise weekends away, not screaming and stamping our feet when they smash Grandma Flo's prize fruit bowl – so often we put pitifully little thought or effort into investing for something as vital as our financial future. Oh yes, many of us are paying into some plan or other, sold us by some adviser or other, but *time, effort, interest, energy*? 'Fraid not. There are quite a few reasons for this and we'll look at some of them later on, but the purpose of this book is not to turn you into an investment geek, an anorak who is barely able to converse with their fellow human beings except in terms of earnings per share and cash flow analysis. No, instead we hope to awaken more than a spark of excitement in this thrilling and very Foolish business of investing. The business of managing your own money and guiding your financial ship towards its ultimate destination is as fulfilling as it can be simple and as enjoyable as it can be lucrative.

A Very Crafty Move and a Little Bit of History

Time was when you could expect to work all your life, retire at sixty-five and drop dead shortly after. The advantage of this system was that it meant there was no need for investment by the state to provide a wage for the country's pensioners. The number of people in work so far exceeded the number of OAPs that incoming taxes were more than able to cover the outgoings, a reasonable-ish pension was provided and everyone was happy. Pensioners marvelled at the enlightened, beneficent nature of the newborn welfare state, while looking back on a hard life, well lived. The welfare state paid up every week with a smile, while at the same time crossing its fingers and counting on the pensioners' imminent demise.

Now, though, the population is becoming less and less obliging and not only are people living longer and longer, they are retiring earlier and earlier. Whereas there were around five employees per pensioner in the 1950s, there are likely to be closer to two per pensioner in the second decade of the twenty-first century. 'Not much dosh coming in to pay for all those pensions,' you whistle. Yes, but Mrs Thatcher was there before you. In 1981 or thereabouts.

In 1981 a crafty thing was done. We don't want to get into politics here, but whatever you think of the Lady Who Was Not For Turning, this was a crafty thing, a very crafty thing, to do. Up until 1981, the old age pension was linked to average earnings. This meant that as average earnings went up each year, so the pension increased by the same percentage amount, an arrangement which seems equitable enough. The only problem was that this was costing an awful lot of money, more money in fact than the Government could afford. There was no investment fund out of which pensions were paid, a fund that was growing with time. Instead, pensions were paid – and are still paid – out of the National Insurance contributions of people in employment, and those in the know could see that one day soon it was all going to prove just a dash too expensive. The solution? Clearly it was impossible to simply cut pension payments – there would have been an outcry and this, you will remember, was a Britain still smarting from the deprivations of the 1970s. No, there had to be a better way and it was this: instead of linking the pension to average earnings, link it to the Retail Price Index ('the rate of inflation' to the rest of us). This sounded all right in principle, but the fact is that the Retail Price Index appreciates on average at around 2 per cent less per year than average earnings. Effectively, this means that the state old age pension is now depreciating at 2 per cent per year in relation to average earnings. (If you don't think 2 per cent per year sounds like much, then wait until you have read the next chapter.) The result today is that the Government is making a saving of nearly £10 billion a year. This is great news for the Treasury, but at the time of writing, the single person's basic state pension is £3510 per year and average earnings currently stand at about £24,000. Taking the one as a percentage of the other, we end up with . . . not very much.

Something, then, had to be done about the future destitution of the nation's pensioners and, you will not be surprised to hear, the onus was put on to the individual to save for themselves. This took the form of savings incentives like the Personal Equity Plan, introduced in the late 1980s, and the Personal Pension Plan, introduced shortly after. We won't go into detail here about just what these consist of – that comes later – but they are both tax-efficient means of saving that have had quite a degree of success. This success, however, has only really been among those who could afford to pay, and that includes paying for the charges they carry. A report by the Association of British Insurers reveals that even people who pay personal pension contributions for thirty years can see a quarter of their final investment fund eaten up by charges.

Cough! Splutter! Gasp!

Please excuse us, tales of Wisdom always have this effect on us, but – pass the smelling salts, will you? – we are feeling better now.

This is loadsamoney and someone, somewhere, is laughing all the way to the proverbial bank. Just how hard they're laughing will be revealed later in the book.

It is fair to say – whatever pups the financial services industry has sold us to date – that governments now and in the future will have to continue to encourage personal saving in a big way, because pictures of pensioners in soup queues don't do much for the image of 'Cool Britannia'. All this, of course, is splendid news for investors.

A Foolish Investor

We hope that having read this far you realize not only how much of an investor you already are, but how much of an investor it is necessary to be in modern Britain. Some people reading this will already know a fair amount about the basics of personal finance, while others will not. Whichever is the case, most people who have a pension plan or investment plan of one sort or another do not think of themselves as 'Investors'. They just think of themselves as someone who has a pension plan or investment plan.

'So what, Fool?! You're nit-picking!'

Well, we beg to differ. If you consider yourself an Investor, rather than just simply someone who pays into a pension plan, this changes the mindset, broadens the outlook and, crucially, it puts a level of responsibility on you to look after your investments. 'Looking after your investments' means ensuring maximum return with minimum cost in terms of charges and tax and within the limits set by your own attitude towards risk. By calling yourself an Investor, whichever investment vehicle you choose to use is simply that – a vehicle. Whereas in the other case, investments are potentially fragmented into a pension plan, ISA and a host of other things, each in its own encapsulated world. The Investor, or rather the Foolish Investor, is able to take an overview and to think in terms of Total Return. As long as an investment is pulling its weight in the Total Return scheme of things, then that's fine. If it isn't, then Out It Goes.

Total Return is (almost) all that matters. By 'Total Return' we are talking about the return of the sum of an individual's investments, after all taxes and charges have been accounted for. Very little else is relevant. Whether an investment is sold as a School Fees Plan, a Personal Pension Plan or a Put Your Dog Through Obedience Training Plan is irrelevant. Does it bring in the rate of return you expect, at a cost you are prepared to bear? It's very simple, but it involves being prepared to sweep through the suffocating layers of humbug that envelop much of what the financial services industry (hereinafter known as 'the Wise') is busy peddling to the British public. By doing this, you will soon find it simple to distinguish between contributing to the Send A Pension Fund Manager To The Bahamas Plan, and the Retire At A Young Age And Breed Racing Pigeons/Collect Stamps/Take Up Freefall Parachuting Plan (delete as appropriate). Sadly, many more people are contributing to the former than the latter types of plan.

Think of yourself, then, as an Investor. Look[2] you're a person, you have thoughts and ideas and opinions about all kinds of things. You can have them about investing too. Once you've been through this book (and perhaps visited the Fool online), you will have the basic knowledge necessary to cut away the confusion and hype of so many of the investment products being marketed in Britain today. We will even make a promise. Before you are halfway through this book you will know how to beat most of the financial professionals (that's the Wise, again), with the expenditure of just a few minutes each year.

The world has never looked better for Foolish Investors. The stock markets of the Western world continue to provide the same kind of steady returns as they have done so faithfully for the last eighty years or more, standards of financial reporting and regulation have never been higher and the UK Government is firmly committed to principles of tax-efficient investing for the reasons already outlined. Most importantly of all, perhaps, the Internet is in the process of bringing information and opportunity to the average citizen which was previously the province of only the professionals. Anyone who has ever kept hold of the remote control in the typical British family's Saturday night telly scrummage will testify to the fact that:

(S)he who controls the flow of information controls the flow of life itself.

Increasingly, it is the common person who controls the flow of life and boy, do the Wise not like it.

---

2 Look, we borrowed this habit of saying 'Look' from Tony Blair. It worked for him, didn't it?

2

The Miracle of Compound Interest

Oh wonderful, wonderful, and most wonderful wonderful! and yet again wonderful, and after that, out of all whooping!

— William Shakespeare, *As You Like It*

Not all investment years are created equal. The strange thing is that people who really ought to know this often don't. The *Financial Times* has a 'write in and ask the expert for advice' section in its weekend Money Supplement. In one edition in February 1998, the first question was asked by two parents concerned that their daughter, aged thirty and living in the USA, had no pension provision. They wanted to start her off with a gift of £6000 (what marvellous people!), but where should they invest it on her behalf? A reasonable question from two savvy and obviously loving parents. It is clear from the answer, however, that the expert in question had not the first appreciation of the Miracle of Compound Interest, for he started his answer by saying: 'The age of thirty is not very old, particularly if your daughter is getting valuable qualifications which could lead to high earnings as her career progresses. So, do not worry too much.'

Do not worry too much?! Do not worry too much?! Eeek! The age of thirty is definitely not very old in life-years, but we're not talking life-years here, we're talking investment-years. You calculate dog-years by multiplying human-years by seven (although why Yorkshire terriers and Great Danes have the same exchange rate, we've never quite figured out), but investment-years are altogether more complicated. To investment-years must be applied a complex formula, integrating expected lifespan with current age, shoe size and favourite Sixties rock group into a fractal geometry-based, chaos-driven equation. This is all then fried and served with a sprig of basil and a drizzle of olive oil on a bed of financial advisers. For lesser minds this can be summarized as signifying that, early on, investment years are worth a great deal more than they are later on. A huge amount more, in fact.

Welcome to the Miracle of Compounding! It is the bread, the water, the mead of the investor. It sustains and nurtures in times of famine and exalts in

9

times of plenty. It is the carrot and the stick; it keeps us Playing the Game. Without a firm faith in this particular miracle, Fools are lost souls, doomed forever to bang at the oaken gates of Investment Plenitude, but never to pass those self-same, hallowed portals.

Let us turn back the clock, back to an era you may, or may not, prefer to forget. Already the focus is dissolving, the camera pans to the round window, a trill of gurgling music escorts us through and we burst into . . . into the past!

You are thirteen years old and sitting in Miss Doublebottom's classroom. It is late May, almost lunchtime and you are coming to the end of a double maths lesson. Through the open window wafts not only the gentle scent of spring flowers and the embracing warmth of an almost summer afternoon, but the lazy drone of a lawnmower and occasional disembodied snatches of the groundsmen's conversation. It all seems so peaceful and the soporific voice of Miss Doublebottom so comforting as she rambles on and on and on, that very soon . . . ZZZZzzzzzzzzzz . . .

And that, unfortunately, was your big mistake (and quite possibly also the mistake made by the *Financial Times* expert). In the twenty minutes between your falling asleep and the bell going for lunchtime, Miss Doublebottom dealt with and dismissed the crucial topic of compound interest. Oh, go on, why don't you? Why not blame Miss Doublebottom for it? You can if you want, but it was not entirely her fault. Perhaps she should have stressed it a little more. Perhaps she should have gone over it again, but the truth is that even teachers aren't all that clued up about personal finance and investment and, like the rest of us, they are just a teensy bit frightened of it. Now, this is understandable and the astonishing implications of compound interest are so far-reaching that it is not surprising she wished to gloss over the whole affair. In maths textbooks, interest in general is always looked at in terms of debt: *Johnny buys a motorbike and borrows X amount of money at Y rate of interest, to be repaid over Z years. How much must he repay in total? Answers to be given in the form of $\chi \times 10^y$.* We find questions of this sort are at once tedious and terrifying and it's only natural to want to shy away from the subject as much as possible.

Don't be too hard, then, on Miss Doublebottom. Instead, start to assume some Foolish responsibility – after all, it was you that fell asleep, wasn't it? And, by coincidence, that's just what you're doing: having reached the age of majority you are about to put right the ignorances of the past, a Foolish course of action indeed. You are going to embark on a voyage of mathematical discovery, one of wonderment and awe. You are poised to change the way you look at life and, quite possibly, you are about to become a party bore on the subject of compound interest.

The brave, the foolhardy and the frankly obsessive will find the full ins and outs of the sums involved in compound interest covered in Appendix 1 on page 293. For now, we shall merely derive a few basic principles. So sit back and enjoy the Foolish Laws of Compounding, with inspiration from Mr Hilaire Belloc. Yes, the *Cautionary Tales* of Hilaire Belloc were the moral guides of generations of British children. Who cannot nod sagely at such instructional verses as 'Sarah Byng, Who could not read and was tossed into a thorny hedge by a Bull', 'Charles Augustus Fortescue, Who always Did what was Right, and so accumulated an Immense Fortune' and 'Jim, Who ran away from his nurse and was Eaten by a Lion'. Now we shall hear some modern cautionary tales . . .

The First Foolish Law of Compounding, or *Ferdinand, Who Frittered Away His Twenties and Suffered Dreadful Agonies*

Fay, a Foolish young woman of twenty, decides to save £100 per month from her secretarial salary. She puts this into an investment plan that gives her an average return of 12 per cent per year on her money. She does not give this another thought, but presses on contributing throughout her twenties, year in and year out, all the while living a life of independence, modest excitement and everyday pleasures. At the age of thirty, she meets Ferdinand, a rake who has frittered away his twenties, but who nevertheless captures her heart. Shortly after meeting, the two decide to have children (whether they marry or not in this modern tale we do not know – that is left up to you, the reader, to decide). Fay decides to stop working and bring up the children (again, fearing accusations of prejudice, we would like to affirm that this is a decision she felt free and happy to make). With no income, she must now stop contributing to the investment plan, something she does with a heavy heart. Ferdinand, however, now takes his responsibilities seriously and starts to contribute £100 per month into a similar plan of his own, something he continues until the age of sixty. For the numbers, see the table opposite.

Ouch! Extraordinary, isn't it? Ferdie thought so too. By the age of sixty, Fay has more than twice as much as Ferdinand, although she has not contributed anything for *thirty* years. Now, Ferdinand retires and they both let their nest eggs grow for the sake of their grandchildren. At the age of one hundred, Ferdinand is worth the staggering sum of £28,668,753, but Fay is still worth over twice as much: £62,456,724. And all because she started a paltry ten years earlier, and yet she contributed only a third as much.

	Fay (£100 per month age 20–29)	Ferdinand (£100 per month age 30–59)
Age 20	0	0
Age 30	£22,404	0
Age 40	£69,582	£22,404
Age 50	£216,112	£91,986
Age 60	£671,210	£308,097

We were going to continue this model for another few hundred years, but the numbers became too huge. There was an ear-splitting explosion and smoke started pouring from the Foolomatic supercomputer's overheated main processor. Seconds later, the ground outside Fool headquarters was littered with the groaning, writhing forms of baled-out Fools, begging for mercy from the God of Compounding.

Anyway, this sacrifice was not in vain and neither were Ferdinand's squandered twenties, for from them we derive the **First Foolish Law of Compounding**:

Start early, Fool!

The Second Foolish Law of Compounding, or *A Foolish Female Who Learnt Too Late about the Building Society and Was Burned to Death as a Result*

In this next Foolish example, we follow the fortunes of a Frippery of Foolish *Femmes*, five in all. They all, at the age of twenty, agree on the importance of regular, long-term investment, but they disagree as to which type of investment is the best. Each opts for a different one, ranging in long-term return from a building society deposit account, to a volatile, yet lucrative, share-buying strategy. Some of the investments they choose carry hefty charges. For the sake of argument, the returns range as follows: 5, 8, 12, 15, 20 per cent per year. They each contribute £100 per month from the ages of twenty to sixty – for the numbers, see the table opposite.

What interests us most here is the last line. Look how the return increases at each stage. Now, these women are only sixty and have only been contributing £100 per month, yet some of them have managed to accrue seriously

	Fennella 5%	Felicity 8%	Freda 12%	Faith 15%	Florence 20%
Ground Zero	0	0	0	0	0
5 years	£6,809	£7,341	£8,110	£8,734	£9,870
10 years	£15,499	£18,128	£22,404	£26,302	£34,431
15 years	£26,590	£33,978	£47,593	£61,637	£95,546
20 years	£40,746	£57,266	£91,986	£132,707	£247,619
30 years	£81,870	£141,761	£308,097	£563,177	£1,567,625
40 years	£148,856	£324,180	£979,307	£2,304,667	£9,740,753

alarming amounts of cash. What has made some of their piles double or treble the size of their nearest neighbours is a paltry difference in return of a few per cent.

This leads us, inescapably, inexorably and ineluctably to **The Second Foolish Law of Compounding**:

Small differences in investment return matter. A lot.

They matter far, far more than the uninitiated could possibly think. Two to three per cent simply does not sound like it could matter very much, but it does. It matters so much it hurts. It matters so much that Fools have been known to cut off vital body organs in anguish at the investment return they have lost through heavy investment charges. That's how much it matters.

And while we're on the subject, the Second Foolish Law of Compounding also allows us to conclude that the British Government of 1981 was familiar with the ins and outs of compound interest (well, you'd hope they would be – they were the Government, after all). A lower relative increase of 2 per cent per year in the state pension doesn't sound like much, but as we can now see, over time it most surely adds up. That's why the Treasury now saves nearly £10 billion per year and pensioners are unable to heat their houses. This shows at the same time just how painful and how lucrative a mere 2 per cent can be.

You will be wondering when we are going to get round to the 'Burned to Death' bit. It's only natural and, go on, be honest, that's what's kept you reading this far, isn't it? Aye, 'tis a sad tale, that's for certain and it concerns 'Fennella Five-per-cent'. Labouring under the sad misapprehension that the building society was the place to save her hard-earned cash, poor old Fennella entered retirement ill prepared for what was to come. She found herself with little more to live on than – *frisson* of horror! – the **state old age pension**! Unable to pay her electricity bills, she was forced to live in a single room, huddled up to a one-bar electric fire. One cold day she fell asleep, slipped forward and *whoof!* Within minutes there was nothing left but the charred remnants of a flowery housecoat, some pink, fluffy slippers and the uneasy, cordite-like tang of burnt human flesh.

And that, Dear Fool, is what happens to those who put their faith in the building society.

The Third Foolish Law of Compounding, *or Ffyona, Who Squandered Her Inheritance and Came to Grief*

Now, one final example. Let's take our Foolish gals again, debs one and all, and add another, Ffyona. At the age of twenty each of them has come into £50,000 from an aged great aunt. They are still a sensible crew and each of them decides to invest all the money in their chosen investment vehicle, choosing to continue with their jobs and live off the small salaries they provide. All, that is, except Ffyona, who has decided she is going to live what used to be called, so quaintly, the 'High Life'. Within six months, yes, you've guessed it, there is nothing left. With no money and now no job, poor old Ffyona finds herself a Fallen Woman, earning her living in a way Too Terrible for the ears of Young Children. For the rest of our Foolish friends, however, the future looks like this:

	Fennella 5%	Felicity 8%	Freda 12%	Faith 15%	Florence 20%
Ground Zero	£50,000	£50,000	£50,000	£50,000	£50,000
5 years	£63,814	£73,466	£88,117	£100,568	£124,416
10 years	£81,445	£107,946	£155,292	£202,278	£309,587
15 years	£103,946	£158,608	£273,678	£406,853	£770,351
20 years	£132,665	£233,048	£482,315	£818,327	£1,916,880
30 years	£216,097	£503,133	£1,497,996	£3,310,589	£11,868,816
40 years	£351,999	£1,086,226	£4,652,549	£13,393,177	£73,488,578

Look at the last line again. Ooooh, doesn't it make your eyes water? From this last table we progress naturally and seamlessly to **The Third Foolish Law of Compounding**:

Don't squander your inheritance on sex, drugs and rock 'n' roll. (Unless you want to, that is.)

The Rule of 72

Now consider the Rule, dear Fool. Consider it a labour-saving, convenience aid to modern living. If the Fool is the food processor of investing, then the Rule of 72 is the natty little attachment which grinds the coffee beans. The Rule of 72 lets you estimate with a fair degree of accuracy how long it will take your lump sum investment to double at a given rate of interest, and it couldn't be simpler. Divide 72 by the rate of interest and you have approximately the number of years of doubling of your investment:

$$72 / x\% = \text{years to doubling}$$

Like any rule of thumb this one has its limitations and in this case it is increasingly inaccurate once you get much above 15%, but actually even then it's pretty good. Frankly, if your investments are regularly above 15%, the minor errors here are irrelevant anyway.
Here's an example:
£10,000 invested at 11.4% will take 72/11.4 years to double = 6.3 years

---

The Fourth and Fifth Foolish Laws of Compounding, *or Two Davids and a Tom Skimp on the Numbers, but Are Saved by the Benevolence of a Foolish Public*

Lavish numbers and spreadsheet Foolery were the order of the day for the first three Foolish Laws of Compounding, but now it may seem as if there's precious little to support the final two. A swizzle, says you! Quite possibly, says we, but we hope you will see that the essence of these final two Foolish Laws is encapsulated within the previous three and that by now you will have us down for an honest bunch of fellows. Here, then, without further ado, are our two final Foolish Laws of Compounding, every bit as vital as their predecessors, even if a little shorter on the padding:

The Fourth Foolish Law of Compounding

Over time, regular saving of quite small amounts can build up to an astonishing sum of money.

The Fifth Foolish Law of Compounding

Time and patience are the friends of compounding and, therefore, of investing.

Coming Soon to a Fridge near YOU!

We hope that with the Foolish Laws of Compounding rattling around in your head, you are starting to settle into the mindset of Foolish investing. Maybe you are starting to dream, to realize that you do not need a huge sum of money to begin profitably investing for the future. In short, you're limbering up for what is to come. The key, though, to successful investing is regular saving and keeping your investment objectives in mind. It can be tough to maintain that sort of resolve over a long period, but to aid you in your Foolish quest, you will see that on the next three pages we have duplicated the Laws of Compounding in a super-deluxe, easily digestible form and we've also thrown in the Rule of 72 as a free gift. For no extra charge you can cut out the example on page 18 and stick it up somewhere visible, somewhere where its elegant simplicity and timeless beauty will be a lasting complement to your home. Why not the fridge door? From now on, every time you reach for a pint of milk or the liquefying remains of last Thursday's quiche, the Miracle of Compound Interest will enfold your grey cells with a most gentle and wondrous awe, inspiring you to new heights of saving and investing.

The Motley Fool UK's Laws of Compound Interest

The First Foolish Law of Compounding
Start early, Fool!

The Second Foolish Law of Compounding
Small differences in investment return matter. A lot.

The Third Foolish Law of Compounding
Don't squander your inheritance on sex, drugs and rock 'n' roll. (Unless you want to, that is.)

The Fourth Foolish Law of Compounding
Over time, regular saving of quite small amounts can build up an astonishing sum of money.

The Fifth Foolish Law of Compounding
Time and patience are the friends of compounding and, therefore, of investing.

The Rule of 72
72 / x% = years to doubling

The Motley Fool UK's Laws of Compound Interest

The First Foolish Law of Compounding
Start early, Fool!

The Second Foolish Law of Compounding
Small differences in investment return matter. A lot.

The Third Foolish Law of Compounding
Don't squander your inheritance on sex, drugs and rock 'n' roll. (Unless you want to, that is.)

The Fourth Foolish Law of Compounding
Over time, regular saving of quite small amounts can build up an astonishing sum of money.

The Fifth Foolish Law of Compounding
Time and patience are the friends of compounding and, therefore, of investing.

The Rule of 72
72 / x% = years to doubling

3

All That Glitters Is Not Gold

*It is not that pearls fetch a high price because men have dived for them;
but on the contrary men dive for them because they fetch a high price.*

— Richard Whateley, *Introductory Lectures on Political Economy*

We're moving on, slowly but Foolishly. In the introduction we learnt what the Motley Fool was all about and whence it sprung. In Chapter 1 we learnt why we need to be investors and in Chapter 2 we were thrilled and awestruck by the Miracle of Compound Interest. Now, we're raring to go and, er, invest.

But in what? If you're like most people, you'll have already flicked through the Table of Contents and a few of the later chapters and have figured out that the Fool loves shares. No, it doesn't just love shares, it eats them, it breathes them, it savours them, it caresses their smooth, yielding . . .

OK! OK! That's enough! (Sorry about this, Dear Readers, but some of us get a little carried away at times. Normal service will now be resumed.)

No, shares aren't the only possible investments in this wonderful world of markets and market makers and we'd like to take just a little time now to examine some of the other investment options facing us, before devoting the rest of this book to shares.

Invest in Yourself

Why not? You are your best potential money-making asset. Take the time and the money to invest in yourself. New skills or a new outlook could well propel you into a newer, more highly paying job and one that is more rewarding. If you are running your own business, then investment in that, an enterprise whose value and potential you are uniquely placed to assess, could be your best move. Don't neglect yourself or your talents – it won't pay off in the long run. Of course, if you don't have any talents or you don't think you have much scope to increase your money-making potential, then don't throw good money after bad. Concentrate instead on saving as much as you reasonably can and developing your sense and knowledge of Foolishness as far as you reasonably want to take it. Looked at in that way, your purchase of this book is one of the best investments in yourself you've ever made. Now, who says you don't have any talents?

Britain's Favourite Investment

Is it the chance to watch Dale Winton, Carol Smillie and heavens knows who else on the telly on Saturday and Wednesday nights? Is it the desire to contribute to the good causes? Or is it the opportunity to dally with fate and perhaps, just perhaps find ourselves the grinning subjects of a *News of the World* spread: 'I'll still be going into work on Monday, honest. It won't change nuffink!'? Sadly for the Lottery good causes and the egos of Dale and Carol, we play the National Lottery because we want to win. No matter that the chances against are 14 million to 1, it could, it just could be us.

Ever made acquaintance with Schrödinger's cat? This unfortunate feline has spent the last sixty years since his invention in a sealed box. Inside with him is one bowl containing cat food and one containing poison. Until we open the box and see which one the moggy has chosen to eat, we cannot know whether the cat is alive or dead. It exists in an indeterminate, multi-potential state, neither dead nor alive. Herr Schrödinger invented his cat to illustrate some fairly way-out concepts in quantum mechanics, but he could just as well have been talking about the Lottery. Until the balls start to roll out on Saturday night, each of us who has bought a ticket is neither a winner nor a loser. And it's a thrill!

It's also an investment, just not a very good one. You can tell it's not a very good investment because of what happens to your stake money. Only half of it actually gets paid out in prizes, the other half gets split between the Government, good causes, retailers and Camelot. So, every pound staked generates an average of just 50p in prizes.

However you look at it, with odds of fourteen million to one against winning (and frankly who cares about anything else?), money put on the lottery is not smart money. Granted, the stake is only a pound, but we'd be fools (note the small 'f') indeed to dream too long or hard of what we'll do with the cash when we win. No, if you just want a delicious shiver at the other-worldly possibility that you may win, then play – there aren't many thrills you can get for a pound these days. But if things have gotten out of hand and you spend the second half of every Saturday night punching holes in doors with the soggy remnants of a Lottery ticket protruding from a contorted, foam-spattered mouth, then maybe you need to think again and almost certainly you need to get out a little more often for some fresh air.

History's Favourite Investment

In the last section a poor feline explained, with reference to quantum mechanical theory, why we play the Lottery. In this section, we will be looking at the philosophy of value. Heavy stuff, hey? But don't worry, this isn't going to be too intense. We're just going to wonder why we value one of our oldest commodities as highly as we do. Or did. For gold, store of value since before the Phoenicians were plying the Mediterranean and mincing through the Hanging Gardens, is looking a little tarnished these days.

Since the beginning of recorded history, gold has been the 'gold standard' of value (you see – it's so enshrined in our language that it is now totally synonymous with value). As a mediaeval merchant, you would have taken gold coins with you on your travels. Gold was the only universal currency and was prized for its beauty, malleability and, above all, its quality of remaining untarnished down the years. None of this would have meant much, of course, if the stuff hadn't been scarce as well, but with all these qualities gold was set to be the US dollar – the 'greenback' – of its age, universally convertible and universally valued. Unlike the greenback it's not so easily forged, but that didn't stop a lot of people trying, including our own Sir Isaac Newton who incidentally spent far more time on alchemy than he ever did on classical physics. Tsk, tsk, Sir Isaac.

Today, though, everyone seems to be losing faith in gold. The gold price has fallen from $850 per ounce in 1980 to around $275 today and some of the world's central banks, the national banks of each country, are starting to sell some of their huge gold stores. They reason that they can hold US Government bonds (Treasury Bills) instead and earn interest on them.

Amazingly, the banks can earn interest on gold bullion too – by lending it out – but it's only a tiny amount. As long as the gold price has been falling, it has paid speculators to borrow gold, sell it for dollars and invest those dollars in Treasury Bills. Then, when the time came to give back the gold, they were able to buy the required amount at a cheaper price than they had sold it, making a profit on the deal in that way too. The low rate of interest they received wasn't too much of a bother for the banks, as they didn't have to pay the cost of storing and guarding it. Neat, hey? As long as the gold price keeps falling, that is . . . By 1997, though, even the Australians, one of the world's gold-producing nations, had had enough of this horse trading and sold a large proportion of their gold reserves. The Swiss, too are selling off half their gold. This kind of trading based solely on price speculation obviously worries them. It worries us too.

There we have it then. We say:

1. If the world's central banks want to put their faith in them good ol' boys in the US Government rather than an off-yellow metal of indeterminate value, then we'd be fools to argue.
2. If you're after a store of value when the nuclear winter finally draws in, invest one third in tinned food, one third in petrol and the final third in guns to protect the first two thirds. If things are that desperate, Mad Max probably won't be interested in your gold.
3. No gold bars for these Fools.

The Gee-gees

Got a tip for the 2.30 at Newmarket? No? Oh well, never mind. Like the Lottery, this business is too uncertain for Fools interested in the business of wealth accumulation. Again, you can think about what happens to the stake money. It's not as bad as the Lottery, because with the horses the average punter gets back something like 90p for every £1 staked, but the odds are still stacked against you. It can be fun though and if you're looking for an excuse to wear a dickie bow or a silly hat, this could be your answer.

Banks and Building Societies

How many times have we heard it? 'Put your money in the building society – that'll keep it safe.' It's not true and, as we'll see shortly, 'The Bible of the Long-distance Investor' (see Chapter 4) shows us why. Long-term building society returns just about match the long-term rate of inflation after you've taken tax into account. This means that creaming the interest off and using it to buy a new frock occasionally actually shrinks your money. Putting your money in a building society or bank deposit account is marginally better than putting it under your mattress, but that's about it.

Other than for shortish periods when you need somewhere accessible to put your money, banks and building societies are most unFoolish places to stash long-term cash. Avoid!

National Savings Certificates

'I'm from the Government, I'm here to help you.' Remember that one? It usually comes along with 'The cheque is in the post' and 'Bend over, this won't hurt a bit'. The strange thing about this one, though, is that when we're talking about National Savings Certificates, it's sort of true. The British Government, bless its cotton socks, sells a range of savings certificates, many of them tax-free, that are safe and reasonably good value. Strangely, you can buy these things through your local post office: 'Good morning, Mrs Wiggins, and how are Deirdre and the baby? Oh, how lovely! That'll be a book of second-class stamps and £100 worth of the 17th issue index-linked savings certificates, please. Ta very much. See you next week.'

Simple as that. If you have a granny who, in the parlance of the modern investing world, is totally 'risk-averse' and keeps all her money in the bank or building society, then tell her this:

- She can buy these Government investments in the post office and can put between £100 and £10,000 into them.
- They are currently growing at the rate of inflation plus 2 per cent.
- They are tax-free.
- At the end of five years she'll get her original money back, plus a sum to account for the effect of inflation, plus all that interest at the rate of inflation plus 2 per cent.
- If she sells in the first year, she won't get any interest, but after that she will.
- If she tries washing out the teapot, she may find her tea no longer tastes of five-day-old haddock. (Only add this last if you are on exceedingly good terms with your granny and can truly bear her tea no longer.)

Index-linked gilts work in much the same way as the index-linked savings certificates referred to above, although many have much longer terms than five years. There is still no Capital Gains Tax to pay on the profits, but the price of gilts does fluctuate and if you want to cash them in before their time is up, you may lose money.

One thing, though. Please don't think that the unfair and stereotypical portrayal of the nation's grannies that we have used in describing Government savings vehicles means that they are suitable only for female nonagenarians. No, they can be useful for any old Fool who needs a pot of medium-term cash. As we shall see later on, you must consider stock market investments to be locked away and unavailable for at least five years. Money needed within this time should be stored elsewhere and this isn't such a bad place at all.

For the detailed gen on index-linked savings certificates and gilts, talk to the very helpful people (for they are) at National Savings on 0845 964 5000. If you're super-sweet, they'll even send you a leaflet all about them. Alternatively, stop by their Web site, **www.nationalsavings.co.uk**, which is rather nicely designed.

Corporate Bonds

As we'll see later on, if you buy shares in a company – and here we'll use Swallow & Honk PLC (yard of ale manufacturers, as certified by the Campaign for Real Ale) as an example – then you effectively become a part owner. If one day the market for yards of ale dries up (say, if the world's rugby players are eliminated at a stroke by a mystery virus) and the company goes bust, then you as a part owner will be one of the very last people to see any money back. Everybody the company owes money to will get paid off first and then, if there's any money left from selling off the remaining stock cheap to nurseries and convents, you might get a look in. It's called capitalism – you staked your money directly in the enterprise, it might have paid you back handsomely, but it hasn't and that's just too bad. Not all companies are as risky an investment as Swallow & Honk, of course, but some are.

Being the owner of a corporate bond, on the other hand, puts you in a different relationship to the company whose bond you own. What you have actually done is to lend the company a sum of money to use as they will. They agree to pay the money back to you at a specified date in the future, plus a yearly amount of interest, say 8 per cent. Bonds have different safety ratings, but mostly they are pretty safe. If you wait until the bond's term is up before cashing it in, you will get your money back in full, but if you try to sell it on in the meantime, its value will vary with the prevailing yields on bonds and the time remaining to the redemption date. In the highly unlikely event of the multinational company whose bond you have bought going under, then you, as one of the company's creditors, will have call on the remaining assets long before the unfortunate company's shareholders.

Nothing comes for free, of course, and you have to pay for this extra safety with far lower long-term returns on bonds than you could expect to get from shares. That said, corporate bonds are another Foolish store for medium-term money.

Property

Property as an investment? Well, yes. It's a special case, complicated by the irksome need imposed by the British climate for Fools to keep a roof over their heads. We'll talk about this in much more detail in Chapter 18, 'Be Your Own Landlord'. For now, let's just say that it's pretty good, but a bit awkward.

4

The Bible of the Long-distance Investor

Steady, boys, steady;
We'll fight and we'll conquer again and again.

— David Garrick, 'Heart of Oak'

Welcome to this, the fourth chapter. It may not sound like much to you, but to us it means a great deal, for this fourth chapter isn't just any old fourth chapter. It's more thrilling than *The Compleat Taxidermist*'s Chapter 4, 'Dealing with the Entrails', it's a dimension beyond *A Guide to Icelandic Nightlife*'s Chapter 4, 'Thorvald Sigmundsson's Friday Night Country Music Hoedown' and it has more surprises than *Banking*'s Chapter 4, 'The Cheque Book'. Chapter 4 in the *Motley Fool UK Investment Guide* is the reason we are here and it reveals the truth about shares. It is the heart of our humble book and we can't help but get rather excited about it.

What Many People Think about Shares

Stocks and shares. Equities.[3] The stock market. The Footsie. Wall Street. The Dow-Jones. It sounds impressive, but what does it all mean? What image does it conjure up? For many people who are not familiar with investing in shares (and some who are), it probably looks a little like this:

> *A skyscraper in the City of London with mirrored windows. Black Jaguars swishing back and forth. An immaculate receptionist with razor-red nails and shoulder pads jutting out as far as the Essex end of the District Line. Somewhere in the depths of the building, men in shirt sleeves (stripy ones) and red braces screaming into telephones and tearing out tufts of hair by the handful as they peer intently into television screens: 'BUY!!! SELL!!! Is that*

---

3 Stocks = shares = equities. You can pretty well use them interchangeably.

Tokyo? Get me Higginbotham, dammit! I'll flay him within an inch of his life!' With year-end bonuses of hundreds of thousands of pounds, the Wise never, ever leave their desks at Arrow, Gant and Lowd (motto: 'Profit or Die!') before ten at night. When they do get home to their trophy houses and spouses, they crack open the champagne as they celebrate another evil day in the service of Mammon, before spending the rest of the night torturing small, furry animals on a shrine specially dedicated to the purpose.

If this is the concept you have of investing in shares, and it would not be entirely unreasonable if you did, then odds-on you probably don't think it is something in which you should be dabbling. 'Best leave it to the experts', you've probably told yourself for so many years.

But investing in shares does not have to be like that. It is possible, for Fools, to make a great deal of money in shares without performing regular human sacrifices. Not even when the value of your investments goes for a Burton, as it will do occasionally. Let's examine some of the evidence, and pretty stunning evidence it is, too.

The CSFB and Barclays Capital Equity-Gilt Studies

Despite being two of the most thrilling reads in Britain today, most people have never even heard of the CSFB and Barclays Capital Equity-Gilt Studies, but they should not fret, for this is a good thing and means the delight and frippery of these two tomes still awaits them.

In fact, the kind people from CSFB have made their entire study available for free on the Internet at **www.csfb.com/eqres/eqres_gilt.html**. Barclays Capital, while requiring you to pay £100 for the full version, have put up a useful summary of the main points at **www.barcap.com/egs/**. So, Fools, if you don't believe anything that we say here, and some of it is pretty incredible, you can check most of it for yourselves. Although both studies run to well over a hundred pages, they are worth every little pixel. They look into the returns to be had from shares, cash and Government bonds (commonly known as gilts) since 1918. In fact, they go back even further than this, to 1869 in the case of the CSFB Study and 1900 in the case of Barclays Capital. Getting interested yet?

You would be forgiven for thinking we had temporarily taken leave of our senses. There *is* nothing interesting in the movement of share prices over the last eighty-odd years. OK then, punks, tell us that after you've rolled your eyeballs across this graph:

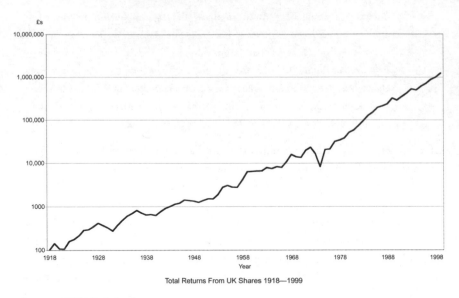

Total Returns From UK Shares 1918—1999

Source: CSFB E-G Study

This graph shows the total return of shares on the London Stock Exchange from 1918 to 1999. Look at it again and notice four things.

1. The scale of returns is logarithmically compressed. If it were not, we wouldn't be able to fit it on the page.
2. Notice the direction it goes.
3. Notice that it doesn't proceed in a straight line of perfectly algebraic proportions.
4. Notice *once again* the direction it goes.

You know, if the financial media and commentators would simply apply this basic 1-to-4 approach to thinking about the stock market, the world would be a much better place. Some of the most experienced financial journalists do their readers a constant, ongoing disservice by causing them to focus on the short term. Talk about not seeing the wood for the trees. This is what we refer to as 'the journalistic approach to the financial markets'.

Although both reports go back further, we Fools reckon that 1918 is as good a place to start as any. Before the First World War, the stock markets were pretty undeveloped and probably the data is not so reliable. Besides, the further you go back, the more you have to ask – When do you stop? You could keep going back as far as the Hundred Years War or the Great Crash of 1066. Nope, as far as possible, we Fools are going to stick with 1918. The CSFB Study tells us that, since then, shares have, on average, returned 12.3 per cent per year (about 8.2 per cent after taking inflation into account). Gilts, which you will remember are Government bonds, have returned 6.2 per cent over the same period (2.3 per cent after inflation), and cash in a deposit account just 5.5 per cent (1.6 per cent after inflation). Barclays Capital comes out with very similar figures, although they make it a post-inflation return of only 7 per cent per year for shares, owing to a slightly different treatment of the period from 1918 to 1934. Anyway, we'll let them argue about the detail, but from both studies there is only one conclusion for a Fool to draw: over the long term, your savings need to be invested in shares.

All roads lead back to compound interest. If we had had a solvent ancestor with sufficient foresight and compassion to invest for his grandchildren back in 1919 and he had decided to invest £100 in the various available options, how would he (or rather we) have fared? The table below reveals all:

	Dec 1918	Dec 1999	Dec 1999 Real terms
Cash	£100	£7,425	£353
Gilts	£100	£13,327	£633
Equities	£100	£1,238,492	£58,835

Source: *CSFB E–G Study*
(NB Real terms = taking into account the effect of inflation)

There is no competition. If only great-grandfather had had a spare thousand or two back in 1919, we can hear you sighing, but let's flip back to reality: no one in 1919 had a thousand pounds to spare. The First World War had just finished, millions were dying in the flu epidemic, the outside privy was standard in much of Britain and the principles of Foolish investing were still several generations distant. It's no good wishing: we're going to have to create our wealth for ourselves, but the example of history gives us strength for the future.

People – misguided people – often say that a building society account or gilts are safer than shares. Long term, very long term, we've just seen that that isn't so. But what about in the shorter term?

This time, we'll look at the Barclays Capital Study. They have worked out that if you take every single two-year period since 1900 (that is, 1900–1902, 1901–1903, 1902–1904, you get the picture), shares have done better than cash in 68 per cent of cases and better than gilts in 71 per cent. For 'rolling' five-year periods, the chances are 77 per cent that shares did better than cash and 79 per cent that they did better than gilts. For ten-year periods the figures are 92 per cent and 86 per cent repectively. It's a shame that they didn't bother to do twenty-year periods, but the results would have been pretty boring since shares did better than cash and gilts in every single twenty-year period in the twentieth century. And this, of course, is a period that includes two World Wars, a couple of major market crashes, a 'great' Depression and a spell of hyperinflation. Wow! They didn't teach you that at school, did they?

The evidence, the incontrovertible evidence, is that the stock market *per se* is not a risky place to put your money. In fact, the evidence is that for long-term savings, the biggest risk is to have too much money in cash. Yet ask most people in Britain whether their savings are 'safer' in a bank deposit account or the stock market and you'll almost be able to see visions of the sort we described earlier (power-dressing secretaries, the torture of small, furry creatures etc.) flashing through their minds. These will be followed by the instinctual memory of the 1929 Crash and investment bankers falling from skyscrapers like tiles off a roof in a high wind and then they'll come out with the supposedly 'obvious' answer: 'A bank deposit account – what do you think I am? Stupid, or something?'

Why is this? Well, take a look at the first line of an article entitled 'A quick guide to market basics' in the Weekend Money section of the *Financial Times* of the weekend 11–12 April 1998: 'The stock market is a dangerous place and small investors may be confused.' If no less a body than the *Financial Times* is telling you the stock market is a dangerous and confusing place, you'd have to be a fool to argue, wouldn't you? Nope, you'd have to be a Fool. Oh, there's danger a-plenty in the stock market alright, if you're going to approach it in a reckless and impulsive manner, but the same goes for the M25 on a Friday night. The thing is that the media, that self-same media that is unable to follow the simple 1-to-4 approach, doesn't find the true story behind the stock market newsworthy. What the financial media wants you to think about is fear and change and specifically what happens NEXT (and 'next' here refers to any time period of up to six weeks). What happens NEXT is what sells newspapers, but the unfortunate result is that many adults are turned off the thought of investing in the stock market because it is *so* risky and *so* volatile and *so* treacherous that they feel they couldn't ever keep up with it.

Look back at the stock market graph. There are groups of several years where it zags more than it zigs. If it zags for deep enough and long enough, (1973–74 springs to mind) then that is called a 'bear' market. Those who sell out during these times, losing large amounts and swearing off the market forever, in most cases deserve what they get. If they're going to take that sort of approach, they're fools, not Fools. Anyone who invests in the stock market with an ultra-short-term time-horizon – less than five and definitely less than three years – is spinning a roulette wheel. Which brings us to a point we want to be extremely clear about:

> *We have no idea where the stock market is heading over the next three years.*
> *Neither does anyone else. DO NOT LISTEN TO ANYONE ON TV, ON*
> *RADIO, OR IN THE PAPERS WHO PRESUMES TO BE ABLE TO*
> *FORETELL THE SHORT-TERM MARKET DIRECTION. THIS PERSON*
> *IS MOST LIKELY AN IDIOT. If you're convinced otherwise, research all his*
> *or her previous market predictions. Compare those to the actual moves in the*
> *market and you will discover we're right. If you discover we're wrong,*
> *immediately e-mail us at* **FoolUKBook@fool.co.uk**. *We'll probably try*
> *to hire this oracle, even though we will almost certainly have lost out to a large*
> *City firm first.*

Interestingly, even if this person were fairly consistently right about the market's short-term direction, it wouldn't be a good move for you to follow along. To play the short-term game involves jumping in and out of a lot of shares. The amount you'd pay in commissions, stamp duty and, potentially, Capital Gains Tax as you jumped hither and thither would most likely leave you with fewer profits (and more headaches) than just buying and holding good companies.

Nope, trying to time the market's short-term movements is definitely not Foolish. In fact, you can cut down on any of the possible dangers of a sudden sharp downturn by saving steadily and regularly, because you will be taking advantage of the downturn by investing your next chunk of savings at the new lower prices.

This point is amply demonstrated by a section in the CSFB Study called 'Consistent investing and market timing'. They only go back thirty years in this section, but bless them for that, because the sums are quite a lot harder. First of all, they work out what would have happened if, instead of just investing a lump sum at the beginning, you had invested £100 at the start of every year since January 1970. Quite predictably, they find that by the end of 1999, investing this money in shares would have generated the biggest pot, worth a healthy £88,315. In contrast, gilts would have got you to £30,328 and cash would have got you to £17,644. As always, after knocking off inflation the figures are just as startling, with equities producing £21,236, gilts £8693 and cash only £5376.

It gets even better, though. Consider the same scenario, of saving £100 per year from 1970, but this time, instead of simply investing it on the first day of each year, imagine that you actually invested it on the worst possible day in each year. In other words, you found the peak of the market in each year and, for some sad and obscure reason, you chose that day to invest your £100. Pretty damn unlucky but, even in this scenario, equities win hands-down over the long term. After five years (ending with the nasty crash in 1974), your equity fund would have stood at £246, with gilts at £407 and cash at £650. After an excellent year 6, though, equities never looked back. From the sixth year onwards, the equity fund was always ahead of cash and gilts and, after the full 30 years, the equity fund would be worth £74,302, the gilt fund £22,921 and the cash fund £17,644. After taking away the effects of inflation, you'd have £17,196, £6709 and £5376 respectively. And this is from investing only once a year. Think what little effect any attempted market timing would have had if you were investing, say, every month.

So, Fools, this shows the power of making regular savings into a broad spread of shares. We'll talk about it again in Chapter 7, 'A Tale of Two Professions', in which we learn how to buy into the market as a whole, follow its ebbs and flows and beat the vast majority of professional investors over time. For many, this type of investment – an index tracker, which aims to 'track' the market's growth over time – will be the beginning and end of your investment career. Nothing further is necessary to ensure a lifetime of Foolish and profitable investment.

Some of you, though, want to beat the average, beat the index trackers, beat that zig-zagging line, and we think we know some ways to do just that. In fact, we take it as a personal challenge to beat the market average, because we believe it can be done by people like you and us.

But let's close with a question, one that is often asked. How far can it go? When will it stop? Is 'growth' eternal? Will the market continue to rise on and on and on, until the ultimate cessation of the human race?

Good question. Please let us know if you have a definitive answer to this. For ourselves, we have a few thoughts on the subject, but which ultimately lead to no firm conclusion, except that we keep coming back and throwing our money into the market.

Over the long term, the market reflects the growth of business. (Over the short term the market moves for an assortment of other, usually far less consequential, reasons.) So, the first question is, will business *always* grow? Now, obviously it doesn't always grow, because there are bad years and good years, but what this question means is could there ever be a prolonged period – say, as long as a human lifetime – in which business and thus the stock market fails to grow, or even shrinks?

Well, what sustains business? A large number of factors, primarily things like population growth, environmental conditions and government stability (and, since we're out-and-out capitalists, we'll also add here 'lack of excessive government interference'). Increasingly, advances in science and technology that are changing the way we live are also fuelling the growth of business. The question now becomes, do you at present perceive conditions that would lead to seventy years of stagnation or decline?

It is very easy to *create* scenarios in which that would happen, but most of those scenarios involve catastrophic events (nuclear war, asteroid impact, alien invasion, lethal airborne flesh-eating viruses – or all four at once). We put it to you that, in each of these situations, gilts and cash are still very unlikely to do any better than shares and, in any event, the investment returns of your portfolio would be the *least* of your worries. Each of these situations could bring about the end of civilization.

Thus, our own best guess is that as long as our civilization is still around, you will continue to see long-term growth in business and in the world's stock markets.

5

You Have More Than You Think

Now is not the time to misuse money.

— Advertising slogan for an Indian insurance company painted on a
rock on the mountain road to Darjeeling, 1993.

Now, we're ready to invest. No holds barred, we are *serious*. Stand back, the
City of London, this is Darren Normal-Bloke of Scrimthorpe and he's coming
through.

But what, Darren, have you got going for you? Who are you, anyway? And
where *is* Scrimthorpe?

Brain

This may come as a surprise to you, but you're pretty well stacked in the grey
matter department. You've picked this book off the shelf, after all. Somewhere
in the depths of your psyche, filed in the 'Dread Department' between cancer,
AIDS, a comet striking the Earth and Mrs Tucker, your moustachioed form
teacher when you were in Class 1A, is the topic of your financial future. Most
people have elected to shut out what they perceive as a far distant era and the
financial demands that may be made on them when the cash flow has dwindled
to zero. Yet you, Fool, have identified the questions of how you're going to
pay the electricity bill and/or the grandkids' bail money in 2030 as issues of
not a little importance and have elected to educate yourself. This is the act of
a supremely rational human being.

'All men by nature desire knowledge', wrote Aristotle. How remarkable
it is, though, that we can elect to cast our essential nature aside when it comes
to something as basic as money. This stuff is important. We do not live in a
barter economy. Trading half a dozen leeks for a knitted woolly hat is not an
option outside of a couple of communes in the west of Wales, and even the
British winter can be distressingly chilly without suitable headgear, as we all

know. We need money and we use money and we think about money many times a day. Why do we allow a steel curtain of despair and panic to drop down (*clang!*) every time we need to think rationally about it? Fear. Gut-wrenching fear. It's only human to want to shut out the unpleasant, but the consequences can be disastrous.

You, reading this, with your Mark 1 Foolish brain, are now going to do a simple sum:

18 − 12 = ?

Now, let's see . . .

This little piggy went to market, this little piggy . . . No, that's not it.

One banana, two banana, three banana, four . . . Nope, not that either.

If you have 18 Motley Fools in a row and you take one away and you do that 12 times, that leaves you with . . .

13?

No.

5?

Warmer.

6?

Now you're talking! Move over, Stephen Hawking, we have a Brain here. Yes, 6 is the answer we've been grappling for. Six is the amount left when you take 12 away from 18. For want of the ability to perform this simple calculation (or else wilful and shameful ignorance), large swathes of the British population have cast themselves into bondage, the bondage of irredeemable debt.

Eighteen is the number of per cent you may pay back every year on the running total of your credit card debt. This is already far more than you pay on your house (around 7 per cent at the moment) or on a personal loan (say, 11–13 per cent). As we saw – nay, as we had rammed down our throats in the previous chapter – the average return from the stock market has been 12 per cent per year since 1918. Now remember that shares are the highest returning of all investments, and then consider that people who are carrying credit card debt, who nevertheless decide to invest in the stock market, are effectively borrowing at 18 per cent to invest at 12 per cent.

We'll come back to credit card debt later, but you don't have to be the winner of Mastermind to realize that the credit card companies have hit on a great money-making scheme. We'll call it the Mushroom Plan because it involves keeping the herd in the dark and feeding them . . . well, you know what mushrooms get fed. The thing about the Mushroom Plan, though, is that it relies on the herd staying in the dark because they like it there and it's warm and it's cosy and it smells right good!

The thing is, we've made up our minds that finance and investments are things that we are not capable of being involved with. We think it's boring, or too complicated, or too much of a gamble and as a result we try not to think too much about it. It's an awe-inspiring prospect. *Moi?* Making decisions on investment? *Mais non*, Sire! Many people with these kinds of feelings turn to the financial advisers we've already talked about, people who work in an industry in which their bread and butter depends on fostering a climate of uncertainty and despair and replacing it with a fug of comforting 'Come to Daddy' warmth. Part of growing up is learning that Mum and Dad don't always have all the answers, and so it is here.

We will see in Chapter 6 ('Be Your Own Financial Adviser') how some of the professionals who advise us operate, and this question should always be in our minds: 'How do *you* make money?' Once we've asked that, we should then move on to the follow-up: 'How do you make *more* money than that?' Most of us have a sense of fair play that does not object to people earning a living if they do a good job on our behalf, but the scales are so stacked in the direction of the finance professional that it is only natural to be uneasy at the business relationship involved.

If nothing else, walk away from these Foolish pages with the simple understanding that:

- Financial advisers working on commission earn their daily bread by selling you endowments, ISAs, Personal Pension Plans and Free-Standing AVCs, and they make more money by selling you the investment plan that pays them the highest kickback.
- Stockbrokers earn commission every time a share is bought or sold on your account and then make more money by trading on your behalf more often.
- Unit trusts take a portion of the funds you give them to manage, and then make more money by attracting as many other people's money as possible.

'Nothing astonishes men more than common sense and plain dealing', wrote Ralph Waldo Emerson. Employ this common sense, this quality so integral to the survival of the human race, and astonish yourself as you reflect on how each of the ways that the entities listed above make *more* money is ultimately by taking as much as possible of it away from you. So, the best way to invest effectively is to give as little of your money away to advisers as possible. Every penny that you pay to an adviser is a penny that you haven't invested. Sometimes the advice might be worth it, but be very careful to remember how these guys make their money. We will talk later and in more detail about financial advisers and stockbrokers and the conflict of interest is obvious.

Briefly, though, let's talk about advisory and discretionary stockbrokers. If you have an advisory or discretionary stockbroking account, this means that you have deposited a sum of money with a stockbroking company and entrusted them with the task of rendering you wealthy. Their aim and your aim, of course, is for them to buy good investments on your behalf. But while simply buying and holding good investments may make money for you, it won't make money for them. The incentive to trade and trade and trade again, earning healthy commissions each time, is hard to resist. Further, this frenetic activity is likely to make the customer think that this is a horribly complicated business which only a *stockbroker* could understand and aren't I lucky to have such a nice man working on my behalf? *Au contraire!*

Unit trusts spend the 5 per cent or so you give them upfront to promote themselves and invite more people to the party, thus giving them more money to manage. It's a bit like one of those backpacker's guide books. No sooner have they written about João DaSilva and his family who run the nicest little guest house on the beach in Goa where three months' stay costs 50p, including three delicious meals and free use of João's motor-scooter, than the place is overrun by hordes of hippie wannabees and the party is spoiled for ever. To put that in financial terms, the more money a unit trust has to invest, the less nimble it becomes; the clumsier it is, the less likely it is to outperform the stock market.

The easiest way to understand things is to ask very simple questions, very slowly and then wait for the answers. Unfortunately, many of us feel afraid to do so, because we worry we may look stupid. In reality, we only look stupid when we try and hide behind presumed knowledge. By contrast, thinking we ought to be able to understand these things, even though we've never really given them much of our attention before – now that *is* stupid!

To return to our theme: we have more than we think. We have the power of reason, our mundane, everyday common sense, and the capability to bring it to bear on what may seem at first to be an intimidatingly complex subject. Reason's simplest tool is the asking of questions, something many financial professionals don't want you to do.

To understand the power of simple reasoning, try this game. There are 132 people entered for this year's men's championship at Wimbledon. How many matches have to be played to find the winner?

Hmmm . . .

OK, so there's 64 matches in round one, plus 32, plus 16 . . .

Stop! There's a much easier way than that. We know that each match produces precisely one loser and we know that, by the end of the two weeks, all but one of the 132 entrants must become a loser. So, there must be 131 matches to play. One less than the total number of players because there has to be one left over at the end (that is, Pete Sampras). So, what if we had a simple knockout darts competition with 587 entrants? Easy, we need 586 losers, so we need 586 matches. And so it is with finance. None of it is very hard, it's just a question of thinking about things in a slightly different way. Faced with this sort of question, the darts promoting equivalent of a financial adviser would probably launch into a Wise discussion about how many rounds would be necessary, how many byes you'd need in round one and the pros and cons of various different seeding structures. You could be left bemused and happy to take his word for it but, by thinking around the problem a bit and using some common sense, you can reach the right answer for yourself in seconds.

Finally, the very act of sitting down to read this book already demonstrates you have taken the decision to move from servitude to freedom. The heart of Foolishness is a fundamental belief in rationalism, in the idea that we can and should bring our powers of reason to bear on financial matters. In fact, the application of reason is the only way to succeed with finances and your employment of your reasoning faculties will mark you out from the majority of other people in the marketplace. If you're not using your brain, you're using something else: someone else's advice, the daily horoscope, or just plain luck. Don't let yourself down. Instead, use your most powerful asset and the cheapest aid to investing yet invented: your brain.

Time

You also have more of this than you think. Even if you don't think you have very much of it, you have more than you think.

In this context 'time' means a couple of things. Firstly, it means the seconds and minutes and hours we cobble together into the daily hullabaloo we call life. We can squander these through precipitate action, or we can husband them and cherish them and use them – Aha, you think we're going to say 'wisely', don't you? – Foolishly. Use time to your advantage. Do not, ever, agree to anything immediately, particularly if it's an investment that someone else wants you to buy. Stall, stammer, feign an epileptic fit if you must, but don't get bullied into signing anything the first time around. This also goes for people who are allegedly on your side, like your financial adviser. Use time to your advantage by deferring any decision and researching it and any possible alternatives. If you do that, you may find yourself calling your financial adviser back and saying: 'Felicity, I see the unit trust ISA you want me to buy has a

5 per cent initial charge and has significantly underperformed the market average over the last five years. Now tell me why I should buy it.'

It's funny. If you've scanned the cover of this book, you'll have figured out that two of the authors are American and one British. It was George Bernard Shaw who referred to us as 'two nations separated by a common language' and we can attest that it is true. Only, the difference isn't just in language, it's in approach and style as well. Here in Britain, we nurture a reticence, a desire not to rock the boat and above all not to create a scene, which seems, at least to the British author's eyes, to be lacking across the water. Cultural stereotypes are a dangerous thing to bandy about as we enter the new millennium, but what we're trying to say here is that this kind of challenging approach seems to us far less natural for a British person than an American. A British friend of one of us, a doctor, was on the verge of being sold a clutch of high-commission products by a financial adviser. Following some discussions of the type you have read here, she returned to the adviser fully armed with a series of questions concerning the performance of these investments as compared to the stock market index, their flexibility, alternatives at lower cost, etc. Unfortunately, she was not able to get past the adviser's secretary. On hearing the kind of thing our newly Foolish doctor was going to be asking, she rolled her eyes and said, 'Oh, he's going to love talking to you. I'll get him to phone you with an appointment.' And that was it. She never heard from him again. The point is that this kind of approach was not something she felt comfortable with and she had to steel herself to do it. When she finally got over that hurdle, her attitude cut through the layers of obfuscation and blather like a knife through warm butter. It is so important to train yourself to take a hard-headed and firm line. Practise polite but emphatic refusal and delaying tactics in front of the mirror. This is your future you're dealing with, after all.

There are also other ways to use time when you decide to start investing on your own, as we hope you will by the time you have finished this book. At all costs, do not rush headlong into the stock market, convinced you are going to make a killing. That kind of attitude leads to large stakes in aggressive shares and big gambles. It is far more likely that *you* will be killed, lose a significant amount of money and be turned off investing forever, with sad consequences for your financial future.

Instead, practise. Just practise. Create a paper portfolio (or a practice online portfolio at one of the many sites offering this facility) which you go on to track, leaving your stack of crisp fivers safe and sound in the bottom drawer of the freezer (you didn't know we knew, did you?). Follow the ups and downs of the shares you would have invested in. Rejoice as they plummet and groan as they rocket skywards – it's the exact opposite of what you'd be doing if you'd staked real money in them and it's all the more useful for that. Do it for a year if you like, or longer. This may sound like it contravenes the First Foolish Law of Compounding ('Start early, Fool!'), but it doesn't. Compound interest is your friend and it's an especially good friend if you hug it to your bosom early enough, but compound depreciation can have as devastating an effect on your investments as compound interest a miraculous one. So, start early on the Foolish investing ladder and don't squander time with unFoolish investments. Use that time instead to set up the habits for a lifetime of savvy investing. You have years and years to invest – don't spoil it all right at the beginning.

The other obvious thing 'time' means is the years (hopefully) you have left before the band starts to play and St Peter's asking if you'll be taking the full board or demi-pension option. We touched on this in Chapter 2, where we saw the effect of time and compound interest demonstrated before our very eyes. It was inspiring, was it not? Salt away your stash, make a regular contribution to it and turn up in thirty years to collect the abundant proceeds. But time alone isn't enough – you need to combine it with patience. And faith.

Over the years, the stock market produces a reliable return, but there are times, such as in 1973–74, when it loses ground: a lot of ground. If you lose faith at times like this, you will scupper all the hard work and patient effort you have put into your investments thus far. One person who had patience was Anne Scheiber who we mentioned in the introduction. This was the humble New Yorker whose $5000 investment in shares on the New York stock exchange in 1944 grew, by the time of her death in 1995, to $22 million. She left all her money to Yeshiva University, also in New York, and the resulting media splash was the only reason we ever heard about her. Through good times and bad, Ms Scheiber plugged away, her investments growing all the while at a steady 18.3 per cent per annum, far above the average of 11 per cent per annum for the US stock market as a whole during that period. Some years, the value of her portfolio doubled. Others, it halved. When she woke up in the morning and, we presume, read headlines in the newspapers about doom and gloom and bursting bubbles, she just plugged on regardless. What was running through her mind as she left the Wall Street professionals gasping in the far distance behind her? We will never know, but we can hope that she spent many of those years bathed in a quiet satisfaction. The reasons for her ascent to such heights were that she had patience a-plenty, she bought common, well-known shares, she held onto them and held onto them and she had confidence in her approach. If anyone knew the value of time, it was Anne Scheiber.

What about the eighty-year-olds reading this? All this talk of time means this can't be a party they're invited to, surely? No, we think the points we're making apply to everyone. These days, you probably *do* have more time left than you think. Even if you don't, you will likely be looking to pass your invested pile on to your descendants in your bid to obtain Most Favoured Ancestor status. Of course, if you really want to leave them a worthwhile legacy, you will not only be investing Foolishly on your and their behalf, but encouraging them to learn about the subject for themselves. As we see it, if you get up in the morning and despite careful scrutiny of the obituaries column fail to find your name, you are set for another day of Foolish investment.

Other People

As with our brain power and the time we have, so we often overlook the value of other people to us.

Sadly, not all people are valuable to us all the time. When your flatmate throws out your twenty-year (*twenty-year!*) collection of *Motor Sport* magazine, because he thought those were the recycling boxes, he loses value to you pretty quickly. (I've been waiting over ten years to make this confession in a national medium. Sorry, Kirk. D.B.) Or how about when your toddler pours Ribena into your computer keyboard? Or you discover years later that your financial adviser has sold you one of the worst-performing, highest-charging pensions there is? Sometimes it's enough to make you want to declare the Republic of MacFool on a rocky Hebridean outcrop and repel all invaders with clods of peat and solidified porridge.

But don't do it.

Turn the tables. *Learn* from other people. Learn from older brother Arthur's venture into Venezuelan coffee futures. Profit from Aunt Dora's experience with the cowboy plumbers (£800 for an hour's work on a blocked pipe at a weekend – it got a full page spread in the *Sun*). Reflect on the poor financial planning of your friend Ted ('Lend us fifty quid till the weather breaks'). If you lecture them from a tone of high financial rectitude, you'll get the come-uppance you deserve, but try showing them some of the numbers from this book.

There will be other people in your life who you can turn to for positive lessons in how to look after money and make it grow. Perhaps another friend has negotiated a cheap mortgage deal or you have an uncle who has always been a sound investor. Take him out to dinner, pump him for information – it's an investment that may repay itself many times over. (It may not, but you'll have healed the rift in the family dating back to when your dad pushed him down the stairs for pinching his tricycle.)

You can't make use of any of this huge repository of financial experience, though, unless you and they are prepared to talk about the subject. It's strange how in our age when just about anything else is fair game for general conversation, money and investment is still a taboo topic. Loosen up and try and get your immediate circle to do so too. The professionals are out there to profit from our ignorance and the best weapon we have is ourselves and our pooled experience. Let's use it.

If you like, we'll help you. Start a dining club of half-a-dozen friends or so who meet once a month to discuss money and investment strategies. Put on jester caps, call yourselves the Motley Fool UK Dining Club (Hartlepool Chapter) – we're always on the lookout for licensing deals.

You might want to go even further and start an actual investment club. These are groups of friends, neighbours, business partners and a sprinkling of very smart gerbils, who invest a pooled sum of money in shares and track their performance over time, buying and selling according to the conclusions of the regular group meetings. Some clubs seriously outperform the professionals and many investment club members actually find the club's investments outperform the ones they hold on their own. It's something to do with the centring effect of a group of Foolish people discussing investment, or the effect of rhubarb crumble and custard on the decision-making centres of the hypothalamus – scientific opinion remains divided. Whatever the explanation, it's a real effect and an organization called ProShare, whose aim is to promote share ownership in Britain, has a sheaf of information on the subject. Details of how to contact them are in our Foolish Glossary under 'Investment Club'. We've even written a cheap, short book ourselves on the subject, the *Fool's Guide to Investment Clubs*, available from a good bookshop near you (or the book bin of your local charity shop if you're reading this in 2010).

The universe of investing knowledge does not end, though, with friends and family. There are other people out there who have something useful to say and some of them are people who write books on investing. Naturally, we think you've bought the most important book on investing already, but there are many other books on finance and investment worth reading. Authors such as Graham, Buffett, Lynch and Fisher all have useful things to say and of course there are a number of other Motley Fool books too (you'll find these listed in Appendix 6, 'Other Fool Books').

Finally, we would not be Fools if we left this section without mentioning our online world. Without it, the Motley Fool could never exist. It's people who have made the Motley Fool and who continue to make it what it is. Out there, on the Web, is a community of people who are interested in the same subject as you are: how to increase their savings and have an enjoyable time doing it. Only, this isn't one or two people getting together for a chat occasionally, this is hundreds of thousands of people, all with specialist knowledge of one sort or another, stopping by regularly and helping each other out with advice and suggestions. Any mistake you're about to make, someone else will have made before you and will be prepared to give you the benefit of their experience. It's a community like no other. If you like what we've been saying here, then come and visit – it could be the most profitable and enjoyable free thing you've ever done.

That you're prepared to mention in public, anyway.

Money

We reckon that the people reading this book are perfectly capable of deducing that if they give up smoking forty cigarettes a day they'll have plenty of money left over for investment, or that if they cycle instead of taking the bus the pennies saved will soon add up. Mrs Thatcher told poor people not to go shopping when they were hungry and obviously thought she was dispensing pearls, but the fact is we all have to figure out for ourselves where we can make economies in our lives. Most of us, if we look hard enough, will have some cash-draining activity or other we could happily live without and may even be the better for it.

A lot of this money thing is down to priorities. Investment isn't such a priority for most of us, because it's not something we *want* to do. It's something we *have* to do, something we feel compelled to do. As long as investing isn't fun, as long as it remains a remote, incomprehensible business, then figuring out how to save more money to put away isn't going to be high on the List of Enjoyable Things to Do This Month. Simply having a little knowledge about the basics of investing, though, and knowing the awesome might of compound interest can alter the whole way you look at investment and make it a lot more real.

We all need targets of some sort and quite a good one to start with is to aim to save 10 per cent of your income. This may be way too much or way too little for your personal circumstances. It doesn't matter – it's just a tool. Take a look at your finances, ask yourself if you're saving 10 per cent of what you make and if you aren't, look at the reasons why. It might be illuminating.

We won't present you with a series of money-saving ideas here, but we are going to mention just one. Consider very carefully whether you want to spend fistfuls of cash on a brand new car. A friend of one of us bought a new MG sports car with borrowed money. Within a year it had depreciated to just over half its initial value and she was now carrying more in debt than the car was even worth. Spending large amounts – and, worse, borrowing large amounts – on a new car is one of the surest ways to savings penury for the majority of us who don't have unlimited incomes. These things are expensive! There are some out there whose life aim since the age of twelve has been a Ferrari sports car with leather seats and the acceleration of a Saturn V rocket. That's fine, but to the rest of you, we say: take a critical look at what you're paying for your wheels and you may find you want to spend some of that money more fruitfully elsewhere.

6

Be Your Own Financial Adviser

Never give a sucker an even break.

— W. C. Fields

'Wait a minute!' you're saying, 'this is getting out of hand. You people – Fools, you call yourselves – are making some pretty outrageous claims here and you tell me there are more to come. I'd like to hear what the professionals have to say about you upstarts.'

Look, this is fine with us, it really is. In fact, the urge to seek independent, impartial advice could hardly be considered anything but Foolish. Entering the world of investment is an intimidating step. It is intimidating because, firstly, the Wise like to make it so. There is seemingly a large amount of information to be digested, jargon to be deciphered and swish brochures with impressive-looking graphs to be waded through. The Wise like it this way because it gives them the drop on the punter. (That's you.) Secondly, it is intimidating because it quite obviously is, dummy! Look, you're taking on the sole responsibility for investing for your and your family's future. You are effectively saying that you will invest your available funds more effectively than a highly trained professional. By your own efforts your retirement will be spent either living on bread and dripping in the one room you can afford to heat, or snapping your fingers at the waiters in the Grand Hotel in Cannes. Scary stuff, indeed.

By reading this far, though, you have proved yourself to have some Foolish mettle. You're not the run-of-the-mill punter, you like to ask questions and are prepared to engage with life. You'll take on responsibility, but are also aware that by doing so you may reap benefits and satisfaction far higher than if you hand over this most important aspect of your life to someone else. Watch out, you're turning into a Fool!

Now, where are you, a Fool, going to go for impartial, independent advice? Good question. There are two basic types of financial adviser: tied financial advisers, and those who style themselves 'independent'. Tied financial advisers are employed by a particular company and can only sell you the financial

45

products – pensions, endowments, ISAs, unit trusts – of that company. They may work on a salaried or a commission basis, but they cannot be independent or impartial. When your bank phones you up to ask if you'd like to see one of their advisers, this is probably the type of person they want you to see. They are salespeople, whose brief is to sell you a product they think you need. Avoid them as if your life depended on it. Which in a way, it does.

The second type are independent financial advisers, or IFAs. Independent by name, independent by nature? Not necessarily. IFAs work for themselves or as part of a larger corporation. They have all had to take and pass financial planning exams and their activities are now far more regulated than ever they used to be. However, there is one small fly in the ointment: your hopes and aspirations and theirs do not absolutely, 100 per cent coincide. As long as this is the case, it is hard to see how you can both move in the same direction. You wish to invest for your future in as profitable a way as possible, while remaining as flexible as possible and incurring the smallest costs possible. They, on the other hand, have to make a living. They also have to make sure they don't 'mis-advise' you, which means they are likely to keep more or less within the boundaries of financial Wisdom and conservative investment planning.

Let's take a look at how they make a living, first of all. Mostly, they pay their household bills through regular remittances from you. When you buy an investment product from them, a portion – sometimes a very, very significant portion – of the payments you make over the first couple of years and beyond will go into the pocket of the IFA. As we shall see later, there are significant differences between the sizes of commissions that the various types of investments pay IFAs, and it is a fact, a not particularly surprising fact, that those charging the highest commissions tend to perform the worst. We'll see in the very next chapter that managed unit trusts – pooled investments in shares – carry far higher charges than those that simply mimic the average, known as index trackers. Strangely enough, they also tend to underperform those trackers by the amount of their extra charges. So, the IFAs will probably do better by selling you a managed unit trust, whereas you will almost certainly do better by buying an index tracker. With IFAs only being human and us being suspicious Fools, we suspect that there is just a teensy conflict of interest here.

Stop the book! Fade the focus! We're going on a fantasy journey . . .

You're an IFA. A client, Mr Alan Average, sits in front of you. You lean back, feet resting on your imitation mahogany desk with leather writing pad and muse that two types of investment might be suitable for him, both of which you can justify as being appropriate. One pays pitiful commission, the other a hefty whack over the first two years, followed by a healthy trailing commission over the next twenty. They're much of a muchness, you think, so you'll sting him with the heavy commission, you think. He won't be too disadvantaged and I have to make a living. Is this so wrong? Well, is it?!

Change the scene slightly. The hefty commission-paying investment isn't quite as good as the other one (which, in fact, is generally going to be the case for similar products). The trouble is you've got the Child Support Agency on your tail for maintenance payments for your children, Doris and Edna. Also, Edna wants a pony in the way only a twelve-year-old can and Doris wants to go on the school ski trip this winter. Which are you going to choose now, given that you're only a human being?

It's obvious that the potential conflict of interest is very great indeed. If you then consider the incentive a commission-based IFA has to sell you an investment in which you are financially penalized for leaving early (thus keeping you in and paying commission), the plot thickens.

Some IFAs do work on an upfront, hourly-fee basis, while others will undertake to rebate a percentage of the commission they receive from any company whose investment they sell you. Some of these people will even recommend the index trackers we have just talked about. There *are* good IFAs about and engaging one at an hourly rate is far more likely to avoid any conflict of interest.

Many IFAs will offer you the choice of paying with an upfront fee or with a commission but, unfortunately, there are even problems with this. If an IFA is recommending one product for their commission-paying customers, then they will potentially have a lot of explaining to do if they offer a different product to a fee-paying customer in a similar position. In other words, the conflicts of interest experienced in the commission-paying side of the business can pollute the seemingly innocent fee-based side of things.

Even if you find a purely fee-based IFA, he or she will suffer from the paradoxical disadvantage of being accountable. If you are given misleading advice, or sold a totally inappropriate product, you have redress. You can go to the Financial Services Authority (FSA) and complain and are likely to get a satisfactory result. Isn't Britain an enlightened place, compared with, say, Chechnya or Sierra Leone? How can this be a disadvantage? Well, it can. For the majority who wish to place their trust entirely in another's hands, it is obviously crucial that the people in whom they place that trust are highly regulated. The effect, however, on those who are being watched over, is to make them conservative and conformist, prepared to choose between the stale clutch of products on offer by the Wise, but not prepared to step outside those narrow confines into a wider world. By offering the control of your finances to someone whose horizons are already limited, you are closing down the spectrum of your investment universe before you've even started. More, these people are slick-talking, charming, convincing and compelling. They have to be – their survival depends on it. Don't expect to convince them of your point of view either. It's as hopeless as Galileo trying to convince the Pope that the sun doesn't go round the earth and can attract just as violent a response. As a Fool, you are accountable to no one but yourself. That sets you apart from the teeming masses, giving you independence of action and an invaluable edge. Take advantage of it.

While we will make the point once more that there *are* good independent financial advisers out there, we'd like to propose a name change for the group as a whole. You see, 'adviser' somehow implies impartiality, and what we've seen is that the nature of the commissions business means that it is extremely hard for them to be that. For the rest of this book, we will refer to them as independent financial advisers (salespeople) or IFAs (salespeople). We don't mean to cause any offence, but since that's clearly what they are, let's call a spade a spade.

So, if you wish, seek independent, impartial advice and do your utmost to verify that it really is. Do so, however, in the awareness that the only person who truly shares your aims, hopes and aspirations is yourself. By reading this book and devoting just a small amount of time to learning about Foolish investment, you are setting the scene for a lifetime of fulfilment, Folly and wealth. In short, get educated, get Foolish and be your *own* financial adviser!

7

A Tale of Two Professions and Basic Foolish Investment

All professions are conspiracies against the laity.

— George Bernard Shaw, *The Doctor's Dilemma*

Tales of Amateurism

In the nineteenth and early twentieth centuries, there was a strong tradition of amateurism in Britain. It was generally reckoned that being a professional was somehow underhand, that it was a trifle vulgar and that there was really nothing a professional could do that an amateur couldn't do better and with more aplomb. Sometimes this was true. The early Everest mountaineers thought training was for cissies and that smoking cigarettes was a cure for the altitude sickness caused by the lack of oxygen at great heights. In 1924 Mallory and Irvine puffed their way to the stupendous height of 28,000 feet and were last seen alive going strong for the summit. Maybe they reached it. Nobody knows for certain, because they never returned and the discovery of Mallory's frozen body in May 1999 seems only to have added to the confusion. It wasn't for another thirty years that Everest was finally climbed, a stunning testament to the stamina and endeavour of these amateurs.

In the nineteenth century, many of the greatest linguistic works were compiled by amateurs. One of the major contributors to the forerunner of the *Oxford English Dictionary* was a Dr W. C. Minor, an inmate at Broadmoor with a persecution complex and a conviction for murder. When you look up a word in the *OED* today, you may well be reading an entry penned by an insane, Victorian murderer.

So, don't knock amateurs because they can sometimes turn in surprising performances.

Let's see how amateurs fare against a couple of professions in the late twentieth century – the heart surgeon and the investment fund manager. How

49

well can the 'know-nothing' hope to perform against these two groups of professionals, each of whose jobs is highly skilled and requires years of training? The answers may surprise you.

A Tale of Two Professions

The heart surgeon

You gasp at *Your Life in Their Hands*. You're a *Casualty* and *ER* groupie. You've been studying these programmes for a long time now, you've picked up the terminology and you're starting to say to yourself that it really doesn't look that difficult. Thoughts like this are starting to arise more and more frequently in your mind: 'I've got a 'C' in biology O level. I could do that.'

Come up close and we'll let you into a secret – it isn't that difficult and you don't even have to be very good-looking or drive a red sports car. Heart surgery is a hobby you can develop in your own garage, at your own pace. If it takes off – and there's no reason why it shouldn't – you could find yourself with a part-time job that is more lucrative than selling water filters door to door and so much more satisfying. Interested? We think you should be. Here, let's show you how to get started.

First, clear out the accumulated junk of lifetimes from the back of your garage and take it down to the car boot sale. The proceeds from the sale of jam jars full of nuts and bolts with Imperial threads and Great Aunt Doris's collection of Victorian thimbles will fund the next stage of your self-improvement programme. Next, scrub down the inside of your garage with a hard bristled broom and a bottle of Domestos. (We consider the importance of antisepsis in surgical procedures to have been overplayed, so this is not strictly necessary, but the smell does impress future customers, er, sorry, 'patients'.) Next, cover over the inspection pit with some planks, borrow your neighbour's Black and Decker Workmate and, with your own, place them together end to end on the planks. The operating theatre and operating table are now ready for use. Some Fellows of the Amateur Cardiothoracic Society of the Royal College of Surgeons (FACSRCS) do advocate soundproofing the garage to mask the screams of ungrateful clients, but we have found Radio 1 played at full volume works just as well and is much cheaper.

Now you are ready for a trip to the DIY Superstore. Load the kids in the car, leave the dog in the garden and off you go. You're looking for a pair of garden shears (go for a good make, as these do tend to work loose otherwise), a large cool box (the purpose of which will become clear), a length of garden hose (five metres should do it) and a pair of bellows (you may have to make a side trip to the ironmonger's for these). Oh yes, and you'll need a pig, a bucket, some bailer twine and a pair of jump leads (you may have these already, in which case, so much the better).

Back home again, turn the pig loose in the garden and cut your hose up into two equal lengths, one of which you now insert into a hole you have cut in the side of an empty, plastic lemonade bottle. Now, make a hole in the bottom of the bottle and plug your other length of hose into that. This can be a bit fiddly, but do make sure the seal is tight, as otherwise you will have blood running all over the garage floor and seeping down into the inspection pit, which is a nuisance. Into the top of the bottle, insert the bellows. Your basic, but functional, cardiopulmonary bypass machine is now ready.

It remains only to fill the cool box with six packets of frozen peas and tether the pig to a convenient spot and you are ready for action.

If no prospective patient has turned up by word of mouth, then an advert in your local paper will usually bring in a number of possible punters. Be sure to peg your rates at around half of what the local private hospital is offering to ensure a good response.

Greet your client at the front door and offer them a glass of sherry. This always breaks the ice as they may be feeling a little nervous. After some small talk to put them at their ease, escort them through to the operating theatre and invite them to lie down on the operating table, all the while keeping up the flow of chit-chat. If you think you may be disturbed by screams and wild flailings as you operate, take the opportunity at this point to disable your patient with a swift but clean blow to the head with a trolley jack.

The scene is now set for operation. Open the chest with the shears directly through the sternum. This should be the work of just a few moments and now part the ribs to expose the heart (you can identify this as it is the only thing moving). Identify the inflow and outflow tracts of the heart – it's worth mugging up on this beforehand – and, cutting small holes in them, insert the lengths of garden hose. Again, make sure the seals are tight. Now, instruct your youngest child to commence pumping the bellows. The patient is on cardiopulmonary bypass.

You will have noticed that there is a fair amount of space within the thoracic cavity and into this you empty the frozen peas, thus slowing the heart down and eventually stopping it.

At this point, send your next youngest child out to slaughter the pig and get them to bring back the heart in the bucket, while you open the patient's own heart and extract the diseased heart valve. Then, exchange the pig valve for the patient's valve, sewing it in with the bailer twine.

You are now ready to restart the heart. Disconnect the patient from the bypass machine, sew up the holes and, connecting one end of the jump leads to the battery of your car which your teenage child has started in the driveway, apply the other end to the heart. This should, usually, start it beating again.

Finally, scoop out the peas and sew up the chest wall. (If you don't manage to locate all the peas, it doesn't matter too much.) The operation is now over and by this time the patient should be waking up from the blow on the head and a strong cup of coffee is indicated.

It is only courteous to call a taxi to take the patient home, as they do not generally feel like taking the bus. We usually pay for this from our own funds and add it to the bill later.

Some budding amateur heart surgeons worry about the legality of garage cardiac surgery, but we can genuinely assure you after enquiring at the Royal College of Surgeons of London that it is entirely legal. As long as you do not label yourself as something you're not and the patient gives their consent, the law of the land takes no position on operations carried out by people without officially recognized qualifications. The same is not true for animals, however, and since, in this instance, a licence from the Home Office will be required for the pig, we suggest you consider starting off with coronary artery bypass surgery instead. Simply become competent at sewing together two pieces of soggy macaroni without any leaks and you should be all set.

Having mastered the intricacies of DIY heart surgery, you are now set to become your own investment fund manager.

The investment fund manager

While we have to admit that you will be doing well at amateur heart surgery to outperform the majority of professional cardiac surgeons, we are confident that as an amateur fund manager you will be able to achieve this level of expertise. Not only that, but the degree of preparation required is less, as is the clearing up afterwards.

How so? How can the amateur, 'no brain' (no offence intended) investor hope to outperform the majority of the professional unit trust fund managers who have spent years training for their jobs and spend twelve hours a day or more living, eating and breathing shares? They earn hundreds of thousands of pounds, drive fast cars and wear flashy suits. It is hard to imagine how Alan and Cynthia Average in their suburban semi in Middlesex are going to better them. This is a complicated business, after all, and not one the lay person should really get involved in. Not unless they want to lose their shirts, that is! (Guffaw! Guffaw! Guffaw!)

Not.

To understand the true situation, you need to understand, just a little, about how the the stock market works. First of all, consider that almost all of the share trading in the stock market involves one highly paid fund manager buying shares from another highly paid fund manager. At a given price, one of them is buying and the other is selling. They can't both be right, yet they are paid lots of money to be right. Let's imagine two of our fast-car-driving, flashy-suited fund managers. One is called Ingrid, and the other, Dexter. They both manage standard UK equity unit trusts with an initial charge of 5 per cent and annual management charges of 1.5 per cent per annum. They have both taken the same investment exams and read the same newspapers. They also both speak to the same stockbrokers' analysts (and get taken on the same freebie jaunts). They are both supported by huge marketing organizations telling everyone how wise they are, yet they both spend their days buying and selling shares from and to each other and others like them. They just can't all be right. In fact, overall, for every decision that is made, someone is right and someone is wrong. Therefore, there are as many wrong decisions being made as right ones. Despite this, the fund managers are all being paid highly to get it right more often than not. It is not possible, *on average*, for this to be achieved. Just in the same way that it is not possible for people, *on average*, to be above *average* height. *On average*, people must, of course, be the *average* height and weight and, *on average*, fund managers must provide *average* returns (that is, *average* returns **before we take away their charges**).

Both Ingrid and Dexter will try to convince you that they will be right more often than each other. They will each have plenty of apparently good reasons why this might be the case. So, who do we believe? If they're so Wise and they disagree about the best approach to selecting shares, what chance do *we* have of deciding which of their approaches is best? Well, we can do something rather sneaky. Since we know that the performance of all the Ingrids and Dexters will average out between them over time, we may as well simply buy the market average. That is, a sort of combination of all the Ingrids and Dexters mushed together. OK, you know it's been coming: we'll buy the 'index'. This way, we can let Ingrid and Dexter fight it out between themselves, knowing that it doesn't matter to us which of them is right. Effectively, we hedge our bets between them, so we don't run the risk of picking the wrong one.

But here's the really clever part: by buying the market average (that is, an index tracker), we can significantly reduce our charges. We can entirely dispense with the initial charge so that we've got about 5 per cent more money working for us straight away. On top of this, we can reduce our annual charge by around 1 per cent, so that we have a statistical expectation of doing

1 per cent a year better than Ingrid and Dexter on an ongoing basis. Over the long term, an advantage of 1 per cent a year can make a very big difference. Going back to our height analogy, imagine that we take a group of people who happen to be exactly the same height *with their shoes on*. Now, we tell everyone to take their shoes off. The people who had the biggest heels on will now be the shortest. In these terms, the highest charging fund managers wear four-inch stilettoes. Index trackers wear flip-flops. When we take away everyone's charges, index trackers will, *on average*, stand head and shoulders above the crowd.

Be warned, Ingrid and Dexter don't want to be put out of a job, so they will tell you that buying an index tracker is very foolish. Dexter will tell you how confident he is of outperforming Ingrid and Ingrid will explain how Dexter's style of fund management is past its sell-by date. They will also both tell you that they will be able to outperform an index tracker in 'difficult market conditions', because they will see it coming and move some invest- ments into cash. **Don't believe it, it's absolute twaddle**. They might see the crash coming, but they might not: and who's to say that they will switch the cash back into shares in time for the upswing? *On average*, they just can't do it. Whatever they tell you, there is one inescapable fact. Their charges are like a leak in the portfolio. Money is dripping out of it year after year and, over the long term, this will make a big difference to performance. They are both going to have to do **extremely** well to overcome their high charges and beat the index over the years and, quite frankly, it's very unlikely that either of them will manage it. In fact, the longer the time period that you take, the harder it becomes.

Research conducted by the WM Company in 1999 backs this theory up. They analysed data from managed funds and index trackers over twenty years to the end of 1998. If you have access to the Internet, you can see the research findings for yourself at **www.index-tracking.co.uk**. The basic conclusions that they reached were as follows ('active funds' means the funds managed by people like Ingrid and Dexter, 'passive funds' means index trackers):

Active and passive funds compared

— Active funds naturally had a much greater range of returns than passive funds.
— Passive trusts performed in line with the index but slightly below it due to management costs.
— Over three-year periods, the average passive fund was in the second quartile of overall performance.

— Over longer periods, passive funds maintained their performance relative to the index while that of active funds fell away.

Consistency of performance

— Over five years, the chance of an active fund beating a passive fund is around one in four. The issue is how much this can be used to predict the fund's future performance.

— Overall, the probability of a trust achieving top quartile performance in a five-year period and repeating this in a subsequent period was no better than random.

— There was stronger evidence that investing in a bottom quartile fund would give a better than random chance of achieving top quartile in the subsequent period.

— The key to benefiting from active management is the identification of superior managers before their superiority shows. Past performance figures would appear to have a limited role in this process.

The first bit, 'Active and passive funds compared', stands to reason — it simply flows from what we've been saying about averages and charges. We think the really interesting bit is the 'Consistency of performance'. After all, if there was a way of picking the funds that would perform above average, then we'd be laughing. The WM Research shows that this can't be done. Think of the typical fund management company. It has, let's say, ten or fifteen funds in operation. At any one time, most will be underperforming. However, there's always one or two that will be doing OK, perhaps a bit more than OK. Which funds do you think they'll be concentrating their marketing effort on? You've guessed it. But there's no reason at all to think that the decent performance can be sustained. In fact, there's every reason to think that it can't be. To be fair, an update of the WM Report found that 'there was evidence of a shorter-term persistence with a defined top quartile of trusts in any one year continuing to out-perform as a group in the subsequent year *but this information cannot be used as the basis for a profitable trading strategy after costs*' (our italics). What this means is that there is some chance of picking a fund that will keep performing for one more year, but the costs of changing funds frequently to invest in these more than erodes any possible benefit.

All we have to do, then, is invest in the market average. Is that complicated? Nope. It's very simple.

Index-tracking unit trusts have as their sole aim the mimicking of the stock market index, the market average. The index in question may be the FTSE 100 or the FTSE-ASI (the All Share Index), but it doesn't make too much difference as they return similar rates over the longer term. In Appendix 2, in which we explain how they work in a bit more detail, we try to zap them up a bit, but it's an uphill struggle and it hasn't really worked, because index trackers are dull things. There is no flair to them. Their sole *raison d'être* is to be average, to be unremarkable. In fact, the more unremarkable they are, the better they are. The closer they mimic the performance of the market average, the more successful they become. The last thing you want is an index tracker that posts returns *greater* than the index, as this shows a high degree of error in following the average and implies they may be even further *under* in future. By the very fact of being unremarkable, index trackers shine as beacons to the investor who wants to outperform the professionals with the expenditure of precisely no cerebral calories and almost as little effort.

Average is best? Run-of-the-mill rules? Standing out from the crowd ain't chic? Yup, it's a topsy-turvy world.

Below, you'll see what the return of an index tracker looks like, as compared to the average return of the market. This example uses the Gartmore Index-tracking Unit Trust, first started in February 1989. The straight line follows the dotted line pretty closely, which is the idea. In fact, the FTSE All Share

Gartmore UK Index Unit Trust returns relative to the
FTSE All-Share Index - February 1989 to June 2000

Source: Gartmore

Index gave an average annual return over the period (to 1 June 2000) of 13.3 per cent and the Gartmore index tracker of 12.7 per cent.

Now see below how the average British unit trusts – the ones where fund managers are buying and selling shares as they try to *beat* the index – compare over the same period. This shows what would have happened back in 1989 if you had invested £1000 into unit trusts now contained in the UK All Companies sector and the Gartmore index tracker.

Gartmore UK Index Unit Trust returns relative to the
UK All Companies Sector - February 1989 to June 2000

Source: Gartmore

To us, this graph is one of the most remarkable sets of statistics in modern investing. We have to keep pinching ourselves to make sure it's real. It is so hard to believe that all that fire and fury which goes into active fund management really counts for less than nothing. The Emperor's shivering in nothing but a pair of shoes here as we reflect that the average return of UK All Companies unit trusts over this period was 11.8 per cent. This was almost *1 per cent* behind the index tracker. How much more does the average unit trust charge than the Gartmore index tracker? Well, funnily enough, it's pretty close to 1 per cent. Think back now to the Second Foolish Law of Compounding: *Small differences in investment return matter. A lot.*

Let's have a look at how being average in performance (but lower than average in costs) works out in terms of real money. *Money Management*, effectively the industry magazine for those in financial services, has performance figures for the unit trusts in the UK All Companies sector. These are the ones that are most closely linked to the fortunes of the UK stock market. They include the UK trackers (although there are only a few of these so they don't really affect things) and the figures can be compared to the average performance (that is, the FTSE All Share). We'll look at the performance of the average fund, the Gartmore UK Index Tracker and the FTSE All Share. The figures show the effect of investing £1000 (with income reinvested in each case). Going backwards from April 2000 for five and ten years looks like this:

Figures for April 2000

	Five-year performance (total of 193 funds)		Ten-year performance (total of 157 funds)	
	Value of £1000 invested in April 1995	Annual growth rate	Value of £1000 invested in April 1990	Annual growth rate
Average fund	£2,164	16.7%	£3,251	12.5%
Gartmore UK Index Tracker	£2,246	17.6%	£3,632	13.8%
FTSE All Share	£2,348	18.6%	£3,881	14.5%

Notice that there are more funds that have been around for five years than there are funds that have been around for ten years (193 against 157). It's interesting to think about why this is. Naturally funds that are doing well tend to stay around. The ones that are doing badly tend not to. They tend to get closed down or absorbed into other funds. So these figures exclude, to a large degree, the performance of the very worst funds.

The performance of the Gartmore Index Tracker put it in 34th place out of 157 funds over ten years and 51st place out of 193 funds over five years. In other words, over ten years, only 21 per cent of funds were able to beat it and, over five years, only 26 per cent of funds were able to beat it. This backs up the findings of the WM Company. And, remember, there's no reliable way of picking, in advance, the few funds that actually manage to outperform.

These seem like amazing findings – probably sufficient in themselves to fill a whole investment book (we tried to pull that one on our publishers, but they insisted we pad it out a bit, hence the other three hundred-odd pages).

Yet, if you think about it a bit, it's not at all surprising and the fact is that the Wise fund managers don't like it when we think about it a bit. They'd be much happier if we continued to pay for their lavish lifestyles without batting an eyelid. Well, sorry, guys and gals, but we have batted an eyelid and we're not too happy with what we see. All the effort and money that goes into running your underperforming unit trusts is totally wasted. You could have done a better job by not having tried to beat the market at all and merely put your efforts into mimicking it. All your snazzy offices, with their complimentary coffee and tea dispensers, hordes of staff and latest computer systems, expensive research materials and daily meetings – it's all a complete waste of money.

No, we had better correct ourselves here. The money is not totally wasted, it is only wasted from the point of view of the hapless investor who is paying through the nose for a service which he or she could get better and more cheaply elsewhere. You see, it doesn't really matter to the unit trusts how well they perform as long as the money keeps rolling in. Of course, they all want to do well, because that's a draw to new investors, but as long as people can be bedazzled by glittering prospectuses and cleverly reported statistics, then just how well isn't crucially important. It is a fact that few unit trusts report their results as compared to the performance of the market average. You don't have to be a rocket scientist to realize that it sounds much more impressive to say '74 per cent growth over five years' than to say '74 per cent growth over five years, versus market average growth of 125 per cent over the same period'.

So, the Foolish lesson to draw from all this is that the only way that you can give yourself an edge in performance terms is to keep your charges low. On the whole, the cheapest, and therefore the best, funds are index trackers. Index trackers also give you a benefit in terms of risk since their returns necessarily track the growth in the stock market. Remember, the stock market has returned, on average, 12.3 per cent every year since 1918. Since the Second World War it has been around 13.5 per cent and in the last ten years even more. If you take out yearly management charges of around 0.5 per cent and allow for a degree of inaccuracy in tracking the index, you may be looking at an average return of around 13 per cent per year or more from an index tracker.

Can it really be so simple that all you have to do is to make regular contributions into an index tracker, keep breathing for thirty or forty years and you'll come out at the end with a bulging pile of cash, for which you have paid very little? Yes, indubitably it can be and that is why in a single week in May 1998, Unilever, Zeneca and Sainsbury's took over £2000 million away from the various active fund managers who had been managing the money on behalf of the companies' pension funds – and doing a shockingly poor job of it – and placed it into index trackers. (One of the greatest *Financial Times* front pages of 1998 had the announcement of Unilever sacking Mercury Asset Management, sitting directly next to an almost quarter-page advertisement for – you've guessed it – Mercury Asset Management!)

It will come as no surprise to learn that others have seen the potential of this kind of investment before you. Richard Branson, the bewhiskered, balloon-piloting, retiring self-publicist of Virgin fame is one. It was he who brought index trackers to the forefront of the public imagination with the launch of his Virgin UK index-tracking unit trust in 1995, although the idea is not new at all. Gartmore have been running one since 1989 and the Vanguard 500 fund in the US has been in existence since the early 1970s. The numbers below show just how impressive a mere £100 per month can be if it grows at a rate of 13 per cent every year:

After 5 years	*£8,787*
10 years	*£24,977*
15 years	*£54,806*
20 years	*£109,764*
25 years	*£211,020*
30 years	*£397,578*
35 years	*£741,299*
40 years	*£1,374,583*

To reiterate: there is no catch to this. We're not suggesting you send us five pounds and then write letters on to twenty of your friends telling them you've got a great new money-making scheme and why don't they do the same? (Although, if you do have a spare fiver, you can always send it our way.) No, this is kosher, bona fide, straight up. Anyone can do it. If you stop at this point in the book and read no further, you have set yourself up with the only investment information you will ever need (besides having been pointed in the direction of a lucrative and fulfilling new hobby).

Fear Not a Falling Market

And as if that wasn't enough, there's even more to this amateur exercise. Perhaps you have followed the steps to be outlined in the final section to this chapter and have gone out and started investing in an index tracker. Perhaps you're feeling pretty good about yourself and are even starting to be a bit of a loudmouth at parties: 'Oh yah, I'm in trackers, actually.'

Well, hang on, you don't even know just how clever you are. Take a look at this:

You contribute £100 per month into an index tracker. At the time you start, each unit of the index tracker costs £1, buying you 100 units a month. Then the market falls after six months to half its value, cutting the cost of the units in half to 50p. After twelve months – six with units costing £1 and six with units costing 50p – what is the average price of the units you have bought? Common sense would tell you that half the time you bought the units at £1 and half the time at 50p, so the answer is 75p. Common sense – and why did you know we were going to say this – is leading you up the garden path. The real answer is 66⅔p. How?

For 6 months at £1, £100 will buy 600 units. Total cost £600.

For 6 months at £0.5, £100 will buy 1200 units. Total cost £600.

Over 12 months, therefore, 1800 units have been bought at a total cost of £1200.

Cost per unit = £1200 ÷ 1800 = £0.666666 = 66⅔p

By putting a regular pound amount into the index tracker, you have bought into the index over twelve months for an average price of 66⅔p, when the *actual* average price of the units was 75p (half the time at 100p, half at 50p, giving an average of (100 + 50) ÷ 2 = 75p). Magic? Yes, in a way, and it's called *pound-cost averaging*.

In this example, we assumed that the index dropped in value by half from one six months to the next, but it would have worked just as well if the index had instead been highly *volatile*. If the units of the index tracker had instead fluctuated from £1 to 50p on alternate months, the effect would have been just the same – six months buying at £1 and six months buying at 50p. Pound-cost averaging isn't just relevant in a market that is turning down, but also in a market that is simply volatile. Look back at the first graph of the Gartmore UK Index Tracker against the index to see what we mean. It's volatility – the fluctuations in share price from day to day and thus in the value of the index – which often scares people out of the market. They can't bear the thought of their holdings darting up and down in value from week to week, but as long as they're net purchasers of shares – and most of us are, since we don't yet need to live off our holdings – pound-cost averaging means that they need have no fear of a stock market that either looks like it is falling or which is highly volatile. Radical, very radical.

In fact, all this talk of pound-cost averaging is making us a bit peckish, putting us in mind of hamburgers. How so? Warren Buffett, ace long-term investor, wrote the following on hamburgers in the 1997 Letter to Share-holders of his Berkshire Hathaway investment company in a section entitled 'How We Think About Market Fluctuations':

> A short quiz: If you plan to eat hamburgers throughout your life and are not a cattle producer, should you wish for higher or lower prices for beef? Likewise, if you are going to buy a car from time to time but are not an auto manufacturer, should you prefer higher or lower car prices? These questions, of course, answer themselves.

> But now for the final exam: if you expect to be a net saver during the next five years, should you hope for a higher or lower stock market during that period? Many investors get this one wrong. Even though they are going to be net buyers of stocks for many years to come, they are elated when stock prices rise and depressed when they fall. In effect, they rejoice because prices have risen for the 'hamburgers' they will soon be buying. This reaction makes no sense. Only those who will be sellers of equities in the near future should be happy at seeing stocks rise. Prospective purchasers should much prefer sinking prices.

It's a funny old world.

Getting Started

But how do you actually go about buying an index tracker? How do you physically do it? Where do you start?

Relax, we're nice guys, we've made it easy for you.

If you're connected to the Internet, then probably the easiest thing to do is pop along to the Trustnet Web site. The address is **www.trustnet.com**. There you can search a huge range of UK and overseas unit and investment trusts. Go into the unit trusts area and narrow down the field of the search to 'indexed funds', click 'select' and, Bob's your uncle, around fifty UK index trackers pop up from nowhere. It gets better than this, though, since you can get details (including charges) for most of the funds (the bigger ones anyway) just by clicking on their name in the list. If you're not connected to the Internet, then we've included a selection of index trackers in Appendix 3, together with their contact details.

With this in hand, or with your own selection from the Trustnet Web site, sit down in your most comfy chair with a cup of tea, the telephone and a stout heart. Start at the top of the list and dial the number of Company A. The exchange will probably go something like this:

VULTURE FUND MANAGEMENT. Hello, Vulture Fund Management, 'Carrion is our game', how can I help?

YOU. Umm, hello. Can you tell me about your index tracker, please?

VULTURE FUND MANAGEMENT. Ah, you mean our Vulture Index Fund?

(*They often have a fancy name for it and you may have to ask a couple of questions to make sure it really is their index tracker you're both talking about.*)

YOU. How long has the 'Vulture Index Fund' been in existence?

(*If they give a time less than three years, say 'thank you very much' and hang up. You can't really assess the accuracy with which an index tracker follows the market over such a short period.*)

THEY. Five years.

(*Excellent.*)

YOU. Can you give me the annualized return on an offer to bid basis since it started? And also the percentage tracking error?

(*Hey, impressive, Fool.*)

THEY. Certainly. It has returned an average of 13.8 per cent per year, with an average tracking error of 0.4 per cent.

(*Reasonable enough.*)

YOU. Right, and how much are the annual charges?

(*If they're much more than 0.5 per cent and certainly if they're more than 0.75 per cent, think carefully.*)

THEY. 0.5 per cent, with no initial charge.

(*Fine.*)

YOU. Uh-huh. And what about an exit charge?

THEY. No exit charge.

(*That's good, because some companies have a sliding scale of exit charges if you withdraw your money in the first five years. We are long-term investors, yes, but we don't tie our hands unnecessarily.*)

YOU. And is it possible to hold this investment within an ISA? If so, how much will it cost me?

(*To tell the truth, they will probably have mentioned this by now, but if they haven't, then ask at this point.*)

THEY. Of course and it costs no extra.

(*It shouldn't cost extra.*)

YOU. Is it possible to make regular monthly savings into it and what is the minimum amount?

THEY. Certainly, you can save upwards of £50 per month.

(Obviously the minimum needs to be below the amount that you're planning to save.)

YOU. Well, that sounds very interesting. I wonder if you'd send me all your bumf?

THEY. Of course, what's your address?

(Etc. etc.)

By the time you've been through the list, you'll have eliminated a goodly proportion of the candidates. Now, sit back and wait for the A4 envelopes to start clogging up your letterbox. (Strike from your candidate list any companies that take more than five days to send you a brochure: if they're not prompt and efficient at responding to potential customers, do they have the acumen to manage your money over the next half-lifetime or so?)

Once you've got all the prospectuses in front of you, draw up a table covering all the points we have talked about and make your selection. If you really have a stomach for detail, there's more on how to pick them in Appendix 3, but we've probably gone a bit over the top (we do like trackers a lot, after all). Also, you could visit our Web site and see the thoughts and selections of other Fools, with their reasoning, on our index trackers discussion board. Once you've made up your mind, it is simply a matter of filling in the form and sending off a cheque (or signing the standing order from your bank) to get the ball rolling.

At this point, you can sit back and breathe a sigh of relief as the nagging guilt that has plagued you – for oh so long! – with the knowledge that you really ought to tidy up your financial affairs and learn something about this whole bally business starts to lift. It is a blissful feeling and one to be savoured.

As you sit and bask in this warm glow of a job well done and an onerous task completed, perhaps you'd also like to give a thought to other Fools around the country. If you'll permit us another plug, why not come along to our Web site and post the information you have gleaned about the various index trackers to one of the message boards? That way, others can take advantage of your endeavours and the net sum of Foolishness and co-operation in the world can be increased. A noble aim, we think, and hope you do too.

Finally, you will have noticed that the book does not end here. Far from it. There is still a good half inch to go. What will we be talking about from now on? A hint: we think index trackers are an excellent first step on the path to Foolishness, but Foolish investors with an interest in the subject often want to try to do better than the mere average, impressive though that average may be. Most of the Foolish activity you'll find online revolves around this aspiration, so read on for a diverting interlude and then an introduction to the exciting and Foolish world of single company investing.

Interlude
(Two, Actually)

8

A Foray into Some Very Foolish Futures

Fortune's a right whore:
If she give aught she deals it in small parcels,
That she may take away all at one swoop.

— John Webster, *The White Devil*

You may be thinking that our copy-editor has slipped up and failed to capitalize the 'f' on 'foolish' in the title to our interlude. You know by now what a wealth of difference there is between 'foolishness' and 'Foolishness' and you're thinking we should sack our publishers for doing a sloppy job.

You're wrong, though. This is most definitely a 'foolish Futures Foray' rather than a 'Foolish Futures Foray'. Mark Kelly wrote to us in the early days of the Fool UK with a story which he has courageously offered to the world. We think it shows very eloquently why a Fool turns his back on any sort of trading that involves forecasting of short-term market trends. In this case it was index derivatives that turned Mark's world upside down for a short period, but it could just as easily have been share options or simply day trading in shares — buying and selling on the basis of what you think the share price will do that day, or afternoon, or minute.

Before we let Mark tell his story and once more praise his courage and candour for doing so, we must issue a health warning. This is not for the faint-hearted, those recovering from major operations or psychiatric breakdowns. Have a box of tissues handy and if these do not prove sufficient, trained operatives are on hand twenty-four hours a day at our Web site and AOL online areas to provide counselling and trauma support.

Mark, the floor is yours:

> *The news from the front line of idiocy is that a fool and his money continue*
> *to enjoy a short acquaintance. Only a few months ago I was reading a* Sunday
> Times *article about spread betting on sports events. A throwaway line there*

suggested that spread betting on the financial markets was best left to the experts. I recall feeling certain that I knew better. I had, after all, been paper trading the FTSE 100 Index for all of a month, using as my guide the live prices published on the City Index Web site. Out of twenty-five trading days I had shown a profit on all but two. Betting £10 a point, I was already £10,000 ahead. On paper, that is.

I don't know what rush of blood to the head or hormonal imbalance led me to believe that I could turn that notional paper money into the folding, bankable variety. The impulse was strong enough, however, for me to resign a well-paid, if boring, career to risk my Christmas bonus on the pursuit of serious riches.

Equipped with a futures pager and a mobile phone, and with accounts opened with two financial spread betting companies, I was ready to start throwing my money at the market. I had no clear strategy — merely an unshakeable belief that I could spot the trends at an early stage, jump on to their coat tails and ride them to a quick profit. I laughed at the very idea of using the limited risk products offered by both companies, namely traded options and limited risk futures. The cost of the option premiums or additional futures spread looked like so much wasted money.

The outcome was sadly predictable. I could have foreseen it myself had it been anyone else who was approaching the business this way. On Day 1, I was late into the market on the morning of a huge rise in the FTSE 100. I bought near the top, over-committed by betting £20 a point and spent all day sweating it out to come out only £80 in front. A late surge by Wall Street saved my bacon. Even at this stage the numbers were frightening. Around £500 down in the UK market and £580 up in the US. A lot of money had been at risk for the eventual paltry reward.

Day 2 was somewhat better, with another strong finish by Wall Street leaving me up by around £350. Again I had taken a pounding in the FTSE contract and was beginning to doubt my innate ability to read market directions. I was also beginning to see how misleading paper trading could be. Both of the financial spread betting companies set their quotes not at the current level of the index, but rather at where they think the index is heading. The result was that by the time I thought I had spotted a trend, they were ahead of me by 10 or 20 points. Adding that to the normal spread between buying and selling prices of between 6 and 8 points meant that there had to be a substantial market movement just for me to break even.

On Day 3 it all began to come apart, with me giving up almost all of the previous day's gains. Again I was pacing the floor until the close of the US markets at around 9pm. This time Wall Street didn't come to the rescue. Even at this stage it didn't occur to me that maybe I wasn't cut out for the life of a trader, this knife-edge balance between elation and despair. Nor did I think of starting to use limited risk products. Instead I simply thought that tomorrow would be the crunch day and I would have to make up for my dismal performance to date.

I was right that the crunch would come on Day 4. The market was waiting for the latest interest rate pronouncement from the Bank of England and I correctly guessed that it would stay unchanged. As a result, by ten o'clock in the morning I was showing a profit of £580. At this stage I should have gone back to bed. Instead a greedy notion came over me that the London market might be given an extra boost by any early gains in Wall Street, which were indicated by the direction of the futures markets. I hadn't exactly played a cautious game up until this point, but now I really lost the plot. By using up my credit limits with both companies I was able to place a total of £40 a point on both the FTSE 100 and the Wall Street Dow-Jones index. Within minutes of opening, Wall Street had indeed soared to new heights. However, perversely, the London market seemed to be slipping. Unknown to me, Merrill Lynch was taking advantage of the market conditions to offload a large number of March FTSE futures. As the effect of this selloff took hold, first the FTSE, then the Dow began to slide down, with me on the wrong side of the market. At this stage I should have panicked and sold, taking the loss on the chin. Instead I calmed myself down, reassured myself that the market would turn around and watched it plummet for the next five hours. A kind of fear-induced paralysis came over me. I was terrified to close my positions, because it would mean taking the losses. At the same time a residual optimism was telling me that the markets must surely turn around again and that I could still end up with a handsome profit on the day.

Head in hands, I bowed to the inevitable at around 8pm, with just an hour left of trading in the USA. I started ringing around, closing positions and counting the cost. Which was huge. To close out all of my positions left me with a net loss of just over £8000, wiping out a large portion of my bonus and completely annihilating any illusions of my possessing the ability to trade in the futures markets.

Bizarrely, one of the people whom I instructed to close my account, who had just told me that I owed his company £6000, asked me whether there was any particular reason why I was closing the account. I guess they must have people throwing money at them like this on a regular basis. And coming back for more. I told him that I had passed my personal pain threshold by a sizeable margin and didn't want to have the mechanism open for me to repeat the experience.

So four days into my career as a financial speculator, I resigned. I wouldn't say that it's impossible to make money in that way. What it does take is a certain discipline to know when to let your profits ride and when to cut them, when to take an early loss to avoid a later larger loss. A sensible approach to the management of risk, including the use of the range of limited risk products available. And a lack of naïve optimism.

Ah well, back to the grind. Anyone know of any vacancies for an unexpectedly available senior audit manager, with extensive experience in derivatives risk management?

9

This Online World

How much a dunce that has been sent to roam
Excels a dunce that has been kept at home.

— William Cowper, *The Progress of Error*

c. 55,000 years ago, Tunbridge Wells, Kent

Hew and his brother, Blok, are out hunting deer in the forest. The forest covers almost the whole of that part of the peninsula that will one day be called 'Angle-land', for no better reason than that 53,000 years later a people from Germany called the Angles would sail up, show themselves to be the most frightful boors and thenceforth behave as if they owned the place. What Hew and Blok called it, history does not record.

Ignorant of the momentous events to come, Hew and Blok were concerned only with catching a deer, but were not having much success. Every time they came close, Blok would sneeze, or stumble, or snap a twig and off the deer would go, tails bobbing through the undergrowth. Hew became increasingly exasperated and Blok, sensing this, grunted and whined in apology, for Hew and Blok did not have the gift of language.

By the third time this had happened, it was starting to get dark and Hew knew if they did not return with meat by nightfall there would be trouble at home. He became more and more angry and frustrated until, instead of the enraged grunt and blow on the back of the head that he had intended to deliver to Blok, he came out with this: 'Look, dunderhead! If you can't keep quiet, then at least go up to the head of the river, make a noise and drive the deer down towards me. I'll hide behind this tree and spear one as they go past. Now, move!'

Well, Hew was as surprised as Blok and clasped his hand to his still open mouth in horror at what had come out. Blok, by now picking up the general drift of what was required and having been thinking along the same lines himself, decided it might be wiser to absent himself up to the head of the watercourse. In due course, down came the deer, followed by Blok. Hew took aim at a plump doe and the rest, as they say, is history.

Hew and Blok returned to camp, where they deposited not only a month's worth of deer meat, but also the gift of language. Before long, they had set themselves up as itinerant language teachers, giving lessons in basic and advanced Cro-Magnon and Neanderthal for the price of a week's board and lodging. Their invention was taken up across the whole of Europe and soon people were discussing everything from the state of the market in wild boar futures to the latest fashions in sabre tooth tiger jewellery.

c. 5500 years ago, 42a Hanging Gardens Terrace, Babylon, Mesopotamia

Tetiphet is one of the entrepreneurs of his age. It was he who supplied the pot plants for the Hanging Gardens and he holds the state-wide monopoly on amphora production. Recently, he has started a bread delivery service, running twenty-four hours a day and delivering slabs of unleavened bread, topped with optional olives, tomatoes or curd cheese. An idea that was over 5000 years ahead of its time, it has taken off in a big way among the elite of ancient Babylon. Tetiphet is thinking not only of a new chariot and team for his wife, but perhaps an executive reed boat which he plans to moor on the Euphrates and with which he'll take his more important business clients on cruises.

Things are generally going well, but there is a fly in the ointment. Shrewd businessman that he is, Tetiphet is worried by all the unpaid bills that he fears are eating into his profit margins. Every time he says to one of his more troublesome customers, 'You haven't paid,' they say, 'Yes, I have,' and he has no means of proving it one way or the other.

He goes home and thinks. And thinks and thinks. Finally, he has it. The clay he uses in his factory to make amphoras – when it's wet you can scratch the surface. He will scratch marks in wet clay to show who has paid and who hasn't. Then there'll be no argument.

Tetiphet's scheme is a roaring success and soon all the businesses in Babylon are using a similar system. From there, the news spreads around the known world and it's not long before even the bards and storytellers are writing their stories down so they don't forget them.

c. 500 years ago, Germany

Johannes Gutenberg, a metalworker, has diversified into the Bible-copying business. The hunger for Bibles in Christendom is insatiable and Johannes has twenty-five scribes copying away in his scriptorium, night and day. Yes, Johannes makes reasonable money, but the rate of production is so painfully slow, the scribes have such large, expensive appetites and they make so many mistakes. He tries to hurry them up by increasing the speed at which the head scribe dictates to the rest, but it backfires and first one, then another, and another, leaves. Before long they're all gone, leaving their manuscripts torn into shreds on the desks of the scriptorium. Johannes wanders through the now silent room and, sighing, is about to start scooping them into the bin, when he notices that this is no random pattern. His departing employees have torn the pages up letter by letter and rearranged them into rude messages directed at him and his mother and . . . what's that . . . his donkey? (The exact content need worry us no further here; suffice to say that Middle German of that period was rife with choice expletives and insults.)

Hang on, thought Johannes, I'm on to something here. Suppose instead of wood block printing, which is a time-consuming, irritating business, I was to make letters out of metal and then move them about to make the words I wanted? Just like this shower of no-goodniks has done. Hmm, it could just work . . .

Soon, Johannes was devoting the entire output of his metalwork shop to moveable type and printing presses and before the decade was out, a Bible wasn't a Bible if it wasn't a printed, *Gutenberg* Bible.

And what of the dissident scribes, without whom the printed word may have been delayed by another hundred years or more? Certainly Johannes never mentions them again.

c. 75 years ago, Edinburgh, Scotland

John Logie Baird has had enough of sitting in the 'three and nines' to watch the British Pathé News every day. It would be all right if the children who were waiting for the main feature would just sit down and be quiet while the adults catch up on what's happening in the world. No discipline these days, that's the problem. In fact, wouldn't it be splendid if you could watch the news in your own home, just as you listen to the wireless? muses Mr. Baird.

Shock! Another aniseed ball thrown by MacDonald minor, the notorious delinquent from 24 Stirling Street, bounces off his balding pate. 'Right, that's enough! I'm going home to sort this out once and for all!'

For weeks he doesn't come in for meals, sometimes working continuously for twenty-four hours at a time. Mrs Baird peeks anxiously through the net curtains. From the garage comes the sounds of banging, crashing and curses. Occasionally, the door flies open and aerials, valves, cathodes, rays, tubes are ejected, before it closes again and the ferment continues.

Finally, a dishevelled Baird, red hair in wild disarray, the fire still in his eyes, storms back into the kitchen, sweeps his wife's embroidery to the floor and plonks down in its place a wooden box, with a dirty window at the front and an aerial on top. 'Aye, Morag, this is the answer to those pesky brats!'

And we've been watching the news at home ever since.

1996, Bill Clinton's acceptance speech following re-election to the White House, Washington D.C., US

'When I entered office in 1992, only nuclear physicists were surfing the World Wide Web. Now, my cat Socks has its own Web page.'

The Internet is about Communication

Five pivotal shifts in the way human beings communicate. Five turning points in history, and the last of these we are living through right now. As products of the Internet age ourselves, perhaps you'll forgive us our embarrassing enthusiasm for a few moments and let us show you what we think this astonishing new medium has to offer. (If you're already an Internet enthusiast, whether you're using it for the odd bit of serious research or are spending the wee small hours with your face basking in the blue reflected glow of your computer screen, then please bear with us. By all means, read on for a spirited and light-hearted account of what you already know, or else skip to the next chapter.)

As with many things, Internet usage in the United States has taken off far more rapidly than in the UK, but we are fast catching up. Most people have some idea of what the Internet is in physical terms – a network of computers around the world linked up through the phone lines – but don't necessarily know what it has to offer them personally. Obviously, the best way to find out what it is all about is to go and have a look yourself and if you have a friend or relative who is online, then ask them to budge up and let you have a gander. (One Foolish bit of advice: ask them to let you wield the mouse. Otherwise, they'll zap around all over the place and, apart from feeling a bit sick, you won't quite know what's going on.) We hope that by the time you've finished this book you'll have decided that one place you *must* be is online.

When you hear people talking about the Internet, you often hear them talking about 'information' and the 'Information Superhighway'. You would have thought 'information' was the last thing we would have needed more of in our lives. It sounds so unattractive, doesn't it? What are you going to do with this 'information' you've just received, anyway? File it away in the recycling pile with all the other 'information' that comes through the door? Add it to all the other 'information' that is beamed at you night and day through the television and radio? Perhaps this is the image you have of the Internet: 'Oh, bother! Looks like we're running low on information again, darling. It really is the most terrible nuisance. Hey ho, off to the computer to stock up.'

Banish these thoughts from your mind. The Internet is not just a hypersonic *Encyclopaedia Britannica*, set to come flooding out of your computer screen at the touch of a button. It is first and foremost a means of communicating and is a natural successor to the endeavours of Hew and Blok, Tetiphet, Johannes Gutenberg and John Logie Baird that have so shaped human history.

Words, words, words. What are we actually talking about? Let's have an example, one totally unrelated to investing. (Come to think of it, we're already 1500 words into this chapter and not a word on investing yet. Yikes!)

One of us (D.B.) is an enthusiastic Telemark skier. 'A what?' Indeed. A Telemark skier. Unless you are yourself a Telemark skier, a disciple of the arcane art of skiing in the style of the original skiers from Telemark in Norway, you are unlikely to know much about it and there aren't all that many of them around. Not in North Devon, anyway. But you can find them on the Net and they are talking. Phew, are they talking! It was November 1997 and D.B. had £500 burning a hole in his pocket, one hundred crisp fivers that he was going to spend on a new pair of Telemark skis and bindings. So far, so good, but how on Earth to decide just what equipment to buy?

Bring on – you've guessed it – the Internet. A quick search on the Internet revealed a Web site devoted entirely to Telemark skiing, called Telemarque. com[4] and describing itself as a 'Resource for the Telemark skier'. Besides articles, listings of Telemark events across the world, listings of suppliers of Telemark equipment and information (Ugh! that word again) about Telemark races, there was a large section devoted to 'Discussion'. This section contained areas where, among other things, people were swapping hints of good places to ski, hair-raising stories of Telemark derring-do and the ins and outs of Telemark gear. Getting warmer.

A click on the Telemark gear discussion folder and D.B. was soon immersed in a world where people were buying, using, testing and manufacturing the very equipment he was thinking of buying. In response to a few initial questions left at the discussion board, replies were received from people who had bought the skis and bindings that D.B. was interested in and were skiing on them every day. Their advice – not always agreeing – was noted, as were the thoughts of people using different equipment, but who felt they had better ideas about what might suit this lonely British Telemarker. Finally, a tentative decision was made to purchase a particular ski and binding combination. Then, in reply

---

4 Unfortunately, since the first edition of this book Telemarque.com has mysteriously slunk back into the Internet ether whence it came. However, in the unlikely event you still want to find a Web site on Telemarking with a thriving discussion forum you could try **www.telemarktips.com** or even **www.tele-skiers.co.uk**, a UK-based site. RIP, Telemarque.com!

to a question about suitable ski length, the very person who had *designed* the skis replied with what he felt was appropriate and in reply to a technical question about mounting the bindings, the very person who had *designed* the bindings came up and offered his advice. Finally, another British Telemarker passing by the site dropped off the link to the Web site of the only shop in the UK selling these particular brands of equipment.

Now, *that's* information!

But that's not all. Over the next few days, D.B. was able to offer advice to another person on a particular ski boot/binding combination he had experience of, and joined in a useful debate on the prevention of injury among Telemark skiers, directing other respondents to a Web site run by a physician with a special interest in the subject and who was conducting an online survey of Telemark injuries. He also gave advice from his own experience to people coming to the Alps to ski and advanced some rather forceful opinions on the advisability of using safety bindings when Telemarking. There then followed an interesting discussion with a skier in Alaska on Telemark skiing in America's last frontier, which eventually turned into a more private exchange of e-mails and heralded the birth of an Internet friendship.

So, it's not just information we are talking about here: this is interacting and engaging with your fellow human beings for mutual benefit. The group of people congregating at Telemarque.com was a community of people united by a single, great enthusiasm − for Telemark skiing. Only, this wasn't a community that could exist in any other sphere beyond the virtual one. Even if you could have gathered together, say, half-a-dozen people in the whole of Devon who were interested in Telemark skiing, you'd still have been reduced to meeting on the third Thursday of each month at 7.30pm under a single 60-watt light bulb and a leaky roof in the 14th Sea Scouts Meeting Hall in Exeter. Telemarque.com had over *10,000* visitors every day. You were able to join in the comings and goings of the community as and when you wanted and − if you had a laptop computer − from wherever you wanted.

Now are you starting to see where we're heading? Contrary to how it may seem, you have not stumbled on a 'How to' manual for Telemark skiing, cunningly disguised as an investment guide. There is rhyme and reason and rhythm to our musings, for while there may not be many Telemark skiers in the green fields of Devon, there aren't many investors either. Let's put it another way. There are a great number of investors − all those with personal pensions, ISAs, endowments and what-have-you − but relatively few who are actively investing in shares on their own behalf. If you wanted to stage a get-together of these active investors, you'd be looking at a relatively small club which would meet, perhaps on a regular basis, to talk things over. In fact, we favour these

sorts of gatherings, whether they are informal dining clubs or actual investment clubs, where the members pool a sum of money and invest it in shares
they have researched. However, they still involve relatively small numbers of
people – ten or twenty at the most – and can hardly be termed a community.

Enter the Fool!

Ever since its inception in 1994 in the United States, the Motley Fool
has been bringing investors together and forging its own, unique online
community. Now its offshoot, the Motley Fool UK, is bringing the same spirit
of Foolishness to Britain. If you come and visit the Motley Fool UK, as we hope
you will, you will find not only interesting articles, ideas and musings on
Foolish investing, but useful reference material and one of the most enjoyable
parts of the site – the discussion boards. In the same way as Telemark nuts at
sites like Telemarque.com swapped advice and information and knowledge
about Telemark skiing, so the Fool UK discussion boards are teeming with
Fools jawing about investing.

They're not talking about skis and bindings, but companies, managing
directors, whether Laura Ashley has a future or is nothing more than a brand
name, the ins and outs of endowments and ISAs, investment strategies, painful
(and wonderful) investing experiences they have had, whether Pizza Express's
pizzas are really good enough to justify such a phenomenal expansion . . .
the list goes on. Instead of the people who designed the skis and bindings
responding to others' queries, it's the people who work in the different
industry sectors who are coming on to give the world (or at least Fooldom)
the benefit of their unique experience. Instead of ski owners coming on to tell
you how they give a 'great ride in the powder, man', you have purchasers and
users of companies' services coming online to tell you where they shine
and where they need to pull their socks up. You have professional share
analysts from the City giving their opinion on a potential investment and
steel importers, doctors, accountants, teachers all giving their unique points
of view. Independent financial advisers (salespeople) – yes, they grit their
teeth and stop by too – will provide useful perspectives on endowments,
Personal Pension Plans and tax, among other things. Others will interject
pithy comments and witticisms into ongoing discussions and the feel is one of
a hurly-burly of ideas and opinions and advice erupting around you. Every
level of investing skill and experience is represented, from the total novice
asking what 'ISA' stands for, to seasoned investors of many years' standing
discussing the sustainability of a company's business model. Whatever level
of investing experience people have, we hope they will feel free to ask or
comment on anything they like, or, if they're feeling shy, to lurk awhile, not
saying anything and simply lapping up the atmosphere and Foolish good sense.

So, the Internet brings together communities of like-minded people, but is that all? No, not on your nelly. It is the most responsive of all media to individuals' ideas and beliefs. Remember all those science fiction stories from the 1950s and 60s? Some of them were pretty strange, but in any collection of short stories you'd always be able to find one in which there was not only personal transport by aerocar or gyrocopter, but democracy via the television: they were voting every five minutes from their living rooms for something or other. (You don't remember? Believe us – there were loads of these stories.)

Well, it's here. It's the Internet. We've tried it. We've tried putting up articles on our site that weren't entirely correct (for that, read: 'contained stupid errors') and it wasn't a pretty experience. Within minutes the e-mails and discussion board posts started flooding in to tell us just where we'd gone wrong. While this may be momentarily uncomfortable for us at times, we actually welcome it. There is no other sphere in which the relationship between the people doing the writing and the people doing the reading is so equal or so fluid. It's not like a newspaper where there are journalists and readers and the two seem separated by a barrier as impenetrable as the Berlin Wall – before it came down. At our site (ours is by no means unique in this), the readers are writing – on the discussion boards and often formidably well – and the writers are reading what the readers have to say. Confused? You soon will be.

Most of our writers here at the Fool were actually recruited from among active participants on the discussion boards. We are always talent-spotting, because we understand that no one understands this new means of communicating as well as the people who are using it all the time and who are enthusiasts for it. That doesn't mean professionals or journalists, but you, sitting in your bedroom in Accrington Stanley and tapping away on your computer keyboard. The Motley Fool UK itself came into being as the result of an e-mail one wet April afternoon from David B. to David G. and Tom G.

Being connected to the World Wide Web (the part of the Internet most of us use most of the time) brings us all together and puts us all on the same footing. Reading a posting from someone, you cannot tell what they look like, what sort of house they live in, what accent they speak with and often even what part of the world they're in. It's a great leveller, giving everyone the same opportunities to advance themselves on their merits.

Another example of Internet democracy. In the United States, large companies have what they call 'conference calls'. In these calls, companies give briefings to the analysts who monitor them on their current performance and expectations. Mostly, these companies will now allow members of the general public to participate. After all, if the professionals can have a slice of this information, why shouldn't we? The stocks we hold are just as valid as the stocks they hold. You will note that we said 'mostly'. One day in 1996, Starbucks, the coffee shop company, was holding a conference call and refused to allow a representative of the Motley Fool to participate. This information was put up on the Motley Fool's Web site and within minutes the company had relented.

OK, OK, here endeth the lesson on the Internet meritocracy. We'll stop harping on about it lest you think we're a trio of dangerous zealots.

Anyway, having talked about how the Internet isn't about information, it's about communication, we reckon you're now sufficiently indoctrinated to be able to cope with what comes next.

The Internet *Is* about Information

We admit it: it is about information as well. There is loads of it, unimaginable expanses of the stuff, everywhere you look and on every subject you can ever think of. Everything those scaremongers have told you is true: you can overload yourself with information via the Internet, but equally there are resources available out there that will make you gasp in wonderment.

As an investor connected to the Internet, you'll be able to access company news as it breaks, read company reports, obtain share quotes, buy and sell shares, consult the financial press, set up a portfolio of shares, with their prices updating automatically so that you can keep track of your investments and, of course, have the resources of the Motley Fool at your disposal.

All this information is there on your desktop immediately. There's no penning of letters — 'Dear Sir/Madam, I would be very grateful if you could send me your latest . . .' — and no licking of stamps. There's just raw, useful data — as much or as little of it as you like.

Information is often wielded in surprising ways on the Web. Take Amazon.com, for instance. This American company began life as as 'The World's Biggest Bookstore', with literally millions of titles available to order. These days, you can buy anything from cordless drills to porcelain on their Web site. Go and visit them when you get online (the Web addresses of the US and UK sites are in Appendix 5) — it is an extraordinary experience. Not only will you find summaries of the books sold on the site, but readers are encouraged to write reviews of books they have read and to e-mail them in. It works like this. You read *Shares for Dogs: a simple guide to equity investing for the genus Canis*, and you like it, so you write in 'An excellent starter book, although goes into a little too much detail on financial analysis at times. Enjoyed the section on "Buy What Everyone Knows: buy dog food companies". Arf! Arf! John D. Pinscher, Barking, Essex'. This review then appears below the book on the Web site, along with other readers' reviews, which may strike a chord with you or not. Finally, when you decide to buy the book, you are presented with a list of books bought by those other dogs who bought this book: *Rubber balls 1945–95*, *The History of the Dog Collar*, *Sniffs and Smells of an Alsatian's Life: a career with the Metropolitan Police*, and so on. Neat marketing trick this may be, but it is also very useful and is another way of narrowing down the amount of information you have to sift through to find something relevant. If you like this book and so do they and they also liked the other books in the list, then there's a good chance you may do so too.

Some people are worried by what they might find out on the Web and it is true there are weirdos out there, but if you don't bother them, they won't generally come and bother you. A few Web sites are pretty nasty, but to be honest the really nasty ones aren't easy to find. If you reckon that 99 per cent of the stuff on the Web is harmless and you have to go out and actively search for the other 1 per cent, you won't be far wrong.

More on Information

Remember the Wright brothers, the two bicycle mechanics who flew the world's first controllable aircraft? Of course you do. Some of you will even remember the name of their aircraft – the Wright Flyer. But do you know the name of their next aircraft, or their next? Chances are you don't.

The Wright brothers first flew in December 1903 and then retreated from the public eye for the next two years. Partly, this was to perfect their invention, but partly it was because they were afraid of others stealing their ideas before they had them adequately patented. The only place they would allow coverage of their machine was in a not surprisingly little-read journal run by a friend of theirs entitled *Gleanings in Bee Culture*. During this time, countless other people around the world were trying to fly, but having very little success. One or two made uncontrolled hops of a few tens of metres, but for the most part they ended up on their noses in ploughed fields, lakes and what have you.

When the Wrights did finally emerge and started giving flying displays in the United States and in Europe, they were still streets ahead of their contemporaries, but they were getting more and more obsessed with their patents. As time went on, they were putting less and less of their creative energy into their machines, and were instead spending a large part of their time fighting lengthy lawsuits. Even as early as 1910 the Wrights' aircraft were practically obsolete.

So what's the point here? The point is that they were on a futile mission from the start. There was no way they were going to be able to patent the process of flying, which was essentially what they wanted to do. By trying to keep a tight hold of information that was so powerful it was destined to change the world irrevocably, they lost their lead. Perhaps, just perhaps, if they had said to the world 'Mimic us if you will, but we don't care for *we are the Wrights*!' then we would be crossing the Atlantic today on the Wright Flyer Mark 86.

So what's the *real* point here? The real point is that we're seeing a similar phenomenon today with the Internet. For a long time, a lot of people have made a lot of money from hanging on to large masses of information and letting little bits out at a time. (For a handsome consideration, of course.) Now, though, information is losing its value as a commodity, because there is so much of it about and it is so easily accessible. The old guard knows something's up and is looking distinctly anxious, but as yet isn't quite sure exactly what's going on or how to react to it.

Information as a marketable commodity is dying and the people who rely on selling information for their livelihood will have to adapt or watch the world pass them by. *That's* what's meant by the information technology revolution.

The Written Word: The Sequel

The written word has never left us since Tetiphet decided to rationalize his accounting procedures back at the dawn of civilization. Thanks to the industrial action of his scribes, Johannes Gutenberg gave it quite a boost with his remarkable invention of moveable type. Of late, though, it has lost a little of its impact. The invention of the telephone by Alexander Graham Bell and our very own John Logie Baird's contraption to allow him to watch the news in peace have, let's say, knocked it from the pedestal it once occupied in the life of the Western world. These days, you tend to pick up the phone rather than write a letter. You slip in a video rather than read the latest instalment of the *Pickwick Papers* to the family in the parlour. Imagine telling the kids they can't watch *Terminator 2* tonight and are going to have a sing-song around the piano, followed by reading aloud. They'd drop to the floor and hyperventilate to death.

All that is changing. Now people love to write e-mails, which is a little like writing letters, but not entirely and is almost, but not quite entirely, unlike a telephone conversation. We believe that the Internet signals the resurgence of the written word and that characters, words, sentences and paragraphs are a superior medium for teaching and learning than the moving image. It is less easy to savour and digest and reflect on the moving image. It is hard to refer back to, even with a video, and when you do, it seems curiously lacking in depth and context. There's an adrenalin hit there, that's for sure, but something lasting? Uh-uh.

The written word is an ideal medium for learning and when the Internet combines it with the snappiness and dynamism we've come to expect from the moving image, then that's a winning combination.

Which leaves you wondering why we're writing a book. Well spotted, but you didn't seriously think we were going to leave ourselves wide open on this one, did you? It's down to aesthetics. Books are enjoyable things to wield. When was the last time you saw someone lounging for hours on the sofa with a laptop computer flipped open? You can't take a computer to the beach or to bed and there is something pleasing about simply holding a book and knowing that in your hands you have a snug capsule of knowledge. The Internet will never replace the book, it will only complement it. After all, one of the most successful Internet businesses, Amazon.com, which we've already discussed, started life as a book retailer. Books are here to stay and it's a jolly good thing, too.

A Final Note

One day soon the Internet will be delivered to people via their mobile phone or a digital television set, or via cable TV or all three. It's all changing so fast that some people say there's no point wasting money on buying a computer at the moment when it's all in such a state of flux; far better to wait until you can see which way things are going.

Ignore these people, for they are dangerous. We say:

One year in Internet time is like seven years in snail time.

Get online!

Now.

Moving On

10

When Not *to Invest*

He that diggeth a pit shall fall into it.

— Ecclesiastes 10: 8

That graph of the performance of UK shares over the twentieth century is pretty compelling. The value of public business has forged ahead at a rate of over 12 per cent a year and the companies that have fuelled that growth have poured rewards into the widening pockets of their shareholders. It's a story that passes so many people by. Consider that if, in a given year, shares on average rise 11 per cent, they'll actually have turned in an *under par* year. Yet, that 11 per cent return marks the outperformance of the historical average of every other investment vehicle out there, from unit trusts to property, from gold coins to gilts. Slow years on the stock market are fast ones off it. The enduring direction of the stock market is upward; investments in shares since 1918 have doubled on average every six years.

What does all this say? What have we been saying throughout the book so far? We've been saying 'Invest in the stock market, for it will not disappoint.' And that's quite true, it won't, as long as you are ready for the challenge. If you're not ready for it, on the other hand, and you lose faith at the critical moments which will come upon you in years to come, or else you start to invest when you shouldn't even have been considering it, then things could get to look very ugly indeed.

So, when *shouldn't* you invest in shares, Fool?

When You Owe Money

Harry's in debt. He's already lost a fortune at Honest Ed the Turf Accountant, but he's got some acquaintances who've made a few bob on the stock market. The light dawns. Why not borrow more money, invest it in shares and pay off the debt in a few months? It's *so* simple!

If the year ahead is like 1993, when shares rose by 28 per cent, or the early part of 2000 when technology shares rocketed, then it'll be drinks all round at the Dog and Duck and everyone who wanders into range will be regaled with the share-picking prowess of this Buffett of Ilford. 'Mmm, interesting, Harry. And how are the ferrets these days?' yawns the hapless citizen, before slinking off surreptitiously to the other end of the bar.

But, if the market clocks in a year like 1973, always a possibility, those self-same ferrets might just start to look like a succulent substitute for Sunday's roast. In 1973, shares fell by 29 per cent, turning £100,000 into £71,000 in twelve months. Worse, much worse, was to come: 1974 brought a breath-taking 52 per cent decline, shrinking the £71,000 into £34,000. (Excuse us while we pause here for some fresh air and a gallon of hot, strong coffee. *Fifty-two per cent* – did we say that?! OK, the following year they rose by 152 per cent. That makes us feel a bit better.)

That 1974 was a bad year all right, but while the losses were painful for anyone investing their savings money, they were calamitous for debtors banking on quick profit. Betting against your debt is simply ludicrous *and it doesn't make mathematical sense.*

Fire up your Mark 1 eyeballs, Foolish investor, and spy the numbers with us. Below sits an investor with £2500 in cash and £2500 in credit card debt, who decides not to pay off that debt, but to put that cash into shares:

What happens with £2500 concomitantly in shares and debt			
	Shares (12%)	*Debt (18%)*	*Difference*
At Launch	£2,500	£2,500	£0
Year 1	£2,800	£2,950	−£150
Year 5	£4,406	£5,719	−£1,313
Year 10	£7,765	£13,085	−£5,320

A decade later, his debt has grown to over £13,000, while his investments have only grown to just over £7700. Though he started the experiment with enough money to eliminate the debt, he's now in a £5000 hole and things are looking mighty black down there. 'Loadsamoney', as a well-known comic of the 1980s used to say. In fact, loadsamoney to the tune of several hundred copies of this book, one restricted view seat for the Men's Final at Wimbledon, or a private hip replacement and half a knee thrown in for luck.

Now, had he capped himself in bells and donned motley, he would have paid down the debt first, and later begun a savings and investment plan.

Nobody in their right mind lets debt pile up on their credit cards and nobody in their right mind likes to be lectured to either. Credit card debt isn't Foolish, and long term it will scupper your chances of investing success, sure as too many chip butties are a direct route to the coronary care unit. Anyway (flourish of trumpets, Fool heraldic banner unfurled) . . .

We promise to largely drop that point for the remainder of this book.

Before moving on to the next situation that would cause you not to put new money into the market, let's digress briefly and ask, 'What sort of debt can you be carrying as a stock market investor?' There are myriad types of debt, but here's a Foolish rule of thumb: *Any debt at interest rates much greater than 2 per cent above the Bank of England base rate will prove enduringly unbeatable.* What kind of debt do we classically carry at around this level? Yup, mortgage debt, Fools, and we will see in Chapter 18 ('Be Your Own Landlord') how we can get this kind of debt to work in our favour. But those flexible friends, those springy bits of plastic – they will suck your lifeblood if you let them. Oops! We said we'd drop it, but we got carried away, so important is the point. So we're only human, OK? For the last time, the message is: pay down your non-mortgage debt *before* you start investing. That will bring you one giant step closer to building broad and enduring wealth. There, we're finished.

The first time you shouldn't be investing is when you owe money. The second?

When You'll Need to Spend Your Savings

Now that you've bid adieu to the misery of liability, and have squirrelled away, say, £2500 to invest, are you ready to get right into shares? There's a stockbroker two doors down from your office. United Kingdom PLC, powerhouse of Europe, is waiting to reward you. You've had a few tips from Uncle Sidney. And Russell Grant says your star is in the ascendant: *Now is the time!*

Just a minute.

Not every penny of your savings is created equal. That's especially true when you may need to use some of them to buy a sandwich for lunch tomorrow, another handful for new clothes, a few thousand for car insurance, thousands more for travel and entertainment, and a half-million or so for the deposit on your dream house. In fact, much of your savings money will be eaten up by immediate concerns. A little preparation and planning, really, no more than a few hours of thought, will go a long, long way here. You cannot be investing what you'll need shortly, because over the short term the market can get hammered, devastated, annihilated. Remember 1974? If you lose 50 per cent of the money you will need to live on in the year ahead, you may try and put a brave face on it, look at it as an emotional growth experience perhaps, but cornflakes three times a day for a year? Not pretty.

Sadly, far too many 'investors' have been flattened by a marketplace that has no mercy on those who would chance their savings on a single year. Buying shares with money you'll need next month or next June will have you anxiously pacing a moonlit living-room floor. The miracle of compounding takes time to work its magic. Warren Buffett, the greatest investor of the twentieth century – of all time, possibly – has earned more in the past five years than in the previous thirty. Let's think about that for a second – the thirty years from 1963 to 1992 earned him less than the five years from 1992 to 1997. So how much time can you give to your latest amount of savings? Answer that question honestly and it will help you decide where to put them.

We don't think you should invest in shares any savings you will need within the next five years. Why five years? Because since 1900 shares have out-performed cash in a bank account in 77 per cent of consecutive five-year periods. In fact, the longer you plan to invest in shares, the more likely you are to come out on top: shares outperformed cash in 92 per cent and 100 per cent of ten-year and twenty-year periods respectively. Still, the odds are pretty good for five-year periods and we think that you should think of this as the minimum.

Short-term money, then, should be placed in a high-interest bank account. You are aiming to use this as you or your family need it, whether that's for a replacement car, holiday, dental treatment or to pay the rent. Spend it, don't gamble with it.

When else shouldn't you invest?

When You Don't Yet Know Enough

You've clawed your way out of debt. You've hived off money you won't need for four or five years. Hi-ho, let's get it into shares!

Brrrrrrrrrrring!

Now just hang on one cotton-pickin' minute. Again. There are two things to think about here: first, do you really, really know what investing in the stock market means and, secondly, does it feel like you're making share selections on the back of a guess and a hope, a wing and a prayer?

You have to be sure you've understood the nature of the stock market beast before you throw money at it. It's a frisky mare and if you're going to take fright every time that it bolts or rears, then you don't yet know enough. Stick outside the market and watch its daily antics a while longer. Similarly, if you're looking at individual companies and can't get over that uneasy feeling that you don't really feel comfortable making a decision about this one or the other one, it's Not Your Time.

Thomas Huxley, described at the time as Charles Darwin's 'Bulldog' and the man who publicized and fought for the theory of evolution against a hostile and sceptical Victorian establishment, had this to say on knowledge: 'If a little knowledge is dangerous, where is the man who has so much as to be out of danger?' Now, none of us can ever be totally out of danger, but we can all achieve a level of knowledge where we feel comfortable with the risks. That level is different for all of us and Foolishness is about finding that level out for ourselves.

Right, so you don't owe anything, you have some money earmarked precisely for stock market investment that you won't have to touch for five years and you know what you know, so when *else* can't you invest, for Pete's sake?

When You Are Dead

The fourth and final reason not to invest is if the blood has stopped moving through your veins and your lungs are no longer drawing in oxygen. When the background sopranos strike up, and you see that flash of bright light through a tunnel of clouds, and the Giant Hand reaches down to pull you into the next life, that's about as good a time as any to stop flicking Teletext on and off to check your share prices.

Once you're settled at the Gates of Paradise Holiday Inn, you've unpacked your suitcase, tested the bed and the shower and cleared out the mini-bar, we hope you'll spare a thought, just once, for what went before. Raise your Martini and toast yourself as you recall that before your departure, you paid down all your debts, set aside some inheritance for those who would invest after you and even conferred some useful investment principles for your descendants to mimic. The wealth that you have left to trickle down through your family tree – mere earthly riches though they be – will go on to support the scholarship, creativity and daring of your offspring. Certainly, it'll allow a few ne'er-do-wells to flit around the honeypots of Europe, quaffing champagne and cavorting licentiously wherever they go, but your financial gifts will be a big fat positive in the lives of many others and to all your descendants you will be their Most Favoured Ancestor. And while you're in the vicinity, perhaps you'd have an otherworldly whisper in the ear of the management on behalf of all the Fools still toiling down here. We'd all appreciate it.

11

A Share Primer

There is less in this than meets the eye.

— Tallulah Bankhead, quoted in Alexander Woollcott's
Shouts and Murmurs

You need never go to the trouble of buying an individual share. If you wish, you can invest directly in the stock market without using a stockbroker by buying into something known as a unit trust. This is essentially a portfolio of shares bought and sold by a management team into which you can buy a stake. If you have good share-pickers in the team, you'll do well; if not, you won't. Mostly, unit trusts don't do very well and the vast majority of them, as we have already seen, fail to beat the average. We do, however, advocate one particular type of unit trust as a first Foolish investment and that is the index-tracking unit trust we talked about in 'A Tale of Two Professions' (see Chapter 7). These worthy animals aim to mimic the movements of the market as exactly as possible and are the first plank in our investing philosophy. If you think you'll be bored by learning just what shares are about and how they are traded, but still want to become a Foolish investor, then skip the rest of this chapter, fly onward to 'Be Your Own Landlord' (see Chapter 18) and that's you sorted out. Don't worry, you're not doing your financial prospects irretrievable damage. In fact, you're still setting yourself up to be in far better shape financially than most of your contemporaries, but you may want to come back at a later date and finish off here. Alternatively, if you know all this stuff already, then purse your lips into a long 'Beeep', as you would if you were beeping over the names in a Russian novel, and we'll see *you* later too.

We're going to start with an overview of what companies are all about and how the stock exchange came to be. Incredibly, by the end of this section you will be bandying about terms like 'Articles of Association' and 'PLC' like nobody's business and actually enjoying it. Don't believe it? Read on . . .

Companies and Shares

Enterprise is the foundation of the modern economy. By setting up and running businesses, people generate jobs and wealth. It's not surprising, then, that the Government is pretty keen for people to be enterprising. The trouble is that setting up a business and taking on obligations to suppliers and staff can be risky. If you set yourself up as a straightforward trader, then the obligations of your business are yours personally. If the business goes bust, then those people who are owed money can come after you to get it back. Your personal assets are likely to be seized to repay the debts. Not surprisingly, this is not a great incentive for people to be enterprising. Starting way back in the seventeenth century, successive governments have developed the notion of a limited company to try to solve this problem.

As its name suggests, the obligations of a limited company are limited to the company itself, rather than to the people who have invested money in it. This means that if the company goes bust, then those people who are owed money can only get back what there is in the remains of the company. Other than in very unusual circumstances (which needn't concern us here), what they can't do is try to get any money back from the investors. This is fair enough, since when these people (the *creditors*) decided to do business with the company, they were aware that it was the company, and not the individual investors, that they were dealing with. The flip side of all this is that limited companies have to go to the trouble of getting their accounts checked (by *auditors*) and published to the world. That way, the theory goes, everyone can make their own assessment of a company's creditworthiness themselves and decide, for instance, whether (and at what rate of interest) to lend it money.

Companies are therefore created and governed by a long list of statutes. These are now mostly condensed into the Companies Acts of 1985 and 1989. They run to a total of about 600 pages, most of which are written surprisingly clearly. Amongst other things, they set out the basis for a company's constitution. A company has two main contitutional documents called the Memorandum and Articles of Association. The Memorandum is fairly boring, just setting out a few things like the name, how many shares there are and what the company is going to set out to do. The Articles of Association is a much more interesting read. It goes into how the company is to be managed. This involves giving the directors a series of rights and obligations and, importantly, saying when the shareholders are entitled to call their own meetings to do things like check on the performance of the directors (and, if necessary, to vote them out). The important thing to note is that when you buy a share in a company, you are basically buying the rights to which that share is entitled according to the Articles of Association, a few statutes and a bit of company law.

Private and Public Companies

In the United Kingdom there are two main types of company: private companies and public companies. You can spot private companies because they have the word 'Limited' or 'Ltd' at the end of their names. Public companies are denoted by the words 'Public limited company' or 'PLC' at the end of their name. The difference is that Public companies have to follow a few more rules, designed to show that they are particularly creditworthy. This is supposed to inspire a bit more confidence in those who deal with these companies, and indeed it does.

All the large companies that you see around the UK will tend to be PLCs, because in business you need to inspire confidence in people (such as your bank and your suppliers) and the little extra work that's involved in being a public company is generally well worth it. However, both public and private companies have shares and these shares are owned by individual people, pension funds or financial institutions such as banks. Whenever anyone owns shares, they are in possession of something that can be bought and sold. However, unless a company's shares are 'listed' or 'quoted' on a stock exchange, it is going to be very hard to find buyers for them. Indeed, a buyer of unquoted shares should certainly do things like read the company's Articles of Association, so that they know what they are actually buying. The uncertainty involved in buying into unquoted companies and the difficulties in matching buyers and sellers mean that the buying and selling of unquoted companies is inefficient and there is clearly a need for a more user-friendly way of going about it. Enter, the Stock Exchange.

The Stock Exchange

The London Stock Exchange grew out of informal meetings of investors in the coffee houses of seventeenth-century London. Here, bewigged gentlemen with, incidentally, accents far closer to the contemporary American accent than the English one, would haggle with each other to buy and sell portions of likely-looking companies. As the volume of trading grew, they eventually moved to their own premises in Threadneedle Street, renaming it the Stock Exchange in 1773. The Industrial Revolution of the nineteenth century and the need this created for companies to raise large amounts of capital fuelled the growth of the exchange, and at one point there were about twenty provincial exchanges dotted around the country. Now they are all concentrated into one – the London Stock Exchange.

In 1995 a smaller, subsidiary market was created, the Alternative Investment Market (AIM). This was to give smaller, more speculative companies the opportunity to be listed on the stock market. The requirements for entry to the AIM are not so stringent and the volumes of shares traded much smaller. We're all for opportunity but, for the most part, we don't advocate investing in shares on the AIM. They can be risky, difficult to trade and often not worth the heartache.

Many of us are intimidated by the City and the Stock Exchange, but really it's just a big market. It's bigger than it was when it was an assembly of gents swapping tall stories and shares in East Indian trading concerns over cups of coffee, but that's all. It's a giant shopping centre, offering shoppers the partial ownership of around 2000 British businesses. Instead of buying a jumper from Marks & Spencer, you buy a portion of M & S itself. Instead of filling your car with £20 of BP's petrol, you buy some of BP Amoco itself.

As we saw above, buying a share makes you a part-owner of that company. This means that you have a share in the profits and can vote in major company decisions. If the company does well, then the share price will go up as other people start to look interested in buying into this promising enterprise and earning some profits themselves. Conversely, if the world decides it isn't yet ready for a combined television/microwave/refrigerator ('Never take your eyes off the telly!'), then your shares in MicroWatch PLC are likely to decline in value. The people who buy and sell shares on your behalf are called stockbrokers. As we shall see later in this tome, some charge more and some less for the privilege.

The to-ing and fro-ing of share prices as people value companies differently at different times is what makes up the 'market', and we'll be talking a little more about this idea of the market later, too. The major share prices from the previous day can be found in all the major daily newspapers, and most of the shares listed on the London Stock Exchange can be found in the *Financial Times*. If you're hooked up to the Internet (and if you've not been convinced to do so by the time you finish this book, we've failed), then you can get the current share prices (delayed by a mere twenty minutes) for free at many places on the World Wide Web.

Quoted Companies

If a company wants investors to be able to buy and sell its shares on a stock exchange, then it must apply for its shares to be added to the list of companies whose shares are quoted on that exchange. Not surprisingly, stock exchanges tend to be a bit sniffy about which companies' shares are added to its list. This doesn't mean that there aren't any bad companies on any particular stock exchange (anybody who's been investing for a while will probably have a few to tell you about, ourselves included). What it does mean is that for a company to be quoted, it must follow the rules of the particular exchange on top of all the rules of law that we mentioned above. These rules cover a range of things like having a reasonably standard set of Articles of Association (so people know roughly what their rights are without having to check a company's Articles every time they invest), disclosing a certain amount of extra information (so that investors can judge how a company is doing) and giving shareholders extra rights to vote on certain major transactions. Oh, we almost forgot, as far as the London Stock Exchange is concerned, to be added to its list, you also need to be a PLC.

So, if you want to buy shares in a particular company, you've generally got to hope that it has its shares listed on a major stock exchange. Do you own or have you seen advertised a Dyson vacuum cleaner? You might want to buy shares in this company and we couldn't blame you, because it represents one of the most innovative triumphs of British manufacturing industry of recent years (and it's been pretty skilfully marketed too). Here at Fool UK, we'd love to look into grabbing a piece of this action, but this is one business which isn't for sale because it's a privately owned company. At the moment, anyway. Presumably, Mr Dyson is satisfied with the way things are going and he doesn't want thousands of shareholders breathing down his neck, demanding higher profits every six months. Shareholders are just that, part-owners of the business, and often they think they know what's good for the company. In fact, they often think they know better than the management and large shareholders have to be listened to. Sometimes this can be helpful, but if it's not, it'll be distracting or even downright disastrous.

Also, we have to presume he doesn't need the money.

Money?

Yes, companies go public to raise cash. If a company wants to expand its business, it is generally going to need cash to do it and, broadly speaking, there are three routes to new capital. If Rent-a-Family – 'Ready-made families by the hour or day to busy business executives' – wants to go national, it can do any of the following:

1. It can toddle off to the local bank or building society and get a loan, which will demand regular interest payments.
2. As a private company, Rent-a-Family can look for investment from venture capitalists – investors representing large companies, trusts or just wealthy individuals. Venture capitalists make early investments in rapidly growing companies. They aim to strike it rich on start-up businesses with big stories but not enough cash to do more than simply tell those stories.
3. Finally, it may decide to divide itself up into a few million equal-sized bits and flog most of them off to the highest bidder, while keeping a chunk back for themselves. This will give them a huge cash injection, which they won't have to give back, but it will leave them beholden to a crowd of often impatient shareholders.

Just about every quoted company out there will have gone through some variant of these three financing stages. They started by borrowing money, then perhaps they brought in some venture capitalists and then they worked with an investment firm to get their shares listed on the market. In Britain this is called a New Issue (or, often, a flotation) and in the US it's called an Initial Public Offering, or IPO. Once a company has *floated* on the market, its shares will move up and down depending on the demand for them. If investors feel that the company is doing better than before, then there will be more demand for the shares and the price will move upwards. If investors feel that the company is doing worse, then demand will dry up and the shares will fall until they reach a price at which the demand returns. As we've said before, investors can be a funny bunch, and fast-changing opinions of a company's worth can make share prices very volatile in the short term. However, over the long term, a share's performance will match very closely the actual performance of the underlying business. The great American investor Ben Graham expressed this well when he said that in the short term the stock market is a voting machine, while in the long term it is a weighing machine.

Market Capitalization

Despite all the to-ing and fro-ing, at any one time a company's total value (as far as the overall investing public is concerned) can be calculated from its share price and the number of shares that it has. Take the Magic Umbrella Company, Kilmarnock PLC. You haven't heard of them? Never mind, they are listed on the Highland Stock Exchange under the symbol MUCK, and they make umbrellas that will not only keep a Highland downpour at bay, but will retain their shape in anything up to a Force 11. Not surprisingly, sales of this product are going well, with an overseas factory recently opened in Cherrapunji, India, the world's wettest spot. Currently, the shares are trading on the market at 500 pence (that would be £5 to you or us, but in the world of shares, most things happen in pence; just smile and say nothing). It has 100 million shares (sometimes you'll hear this expressed as 100 million *shares in issue* or *shares outstanding* but it just means that it has 100 million shares). Are you ready for this? Did you pass GCSE maths? If not, fire up your calculator, because the answer is . . . £500 million. At current prices, MUCK is valued at £500 million. Another way of saying this is that it has a market capitalization of £500 million, often abbreviated to 'market cap.'

If MUCK PLC corners the heavy duty umbrella industry, boosts its sales, cuts down its costs, and as a result its profits soar, then more and more people are going to want shares in this dynamic enterprise. More, more, more. The share price will go up – supply and demand operating here: if you really want what I've got, you'll have to pay more for it – and so will the market cap. Everyone will be happy, except those prevaricators who foresaw the huge potential of this product but could never find *quite* the right moment to make their investment in it.

Now, market cap. is used in Britain to subdivide shares into 'indices'. You'll have heard them on the radio and television every morning and evening, sounding like body parts in some strange jig: 'The Footsie's up, the Footsie's down, shake it all around.' What this really refers to is the FTSE indices. There is the FTSE 100 index, the FTSE 250 index and the FTSE All Share index. The FTSE 100 index is simply a list of the 100 shares with the highest market cap. (the UK's hundred largest companies), the FTSE 250 is the next 250 and the FTSE All Share is a list of around 800 of the most important shares on the London Stock Exchange and includes those in the FTSE 100 and the FTSE 250. ('FTSE' stands for '*Financial Times* – Stock Exchange', the two organizations that own the rights to the indices.)

It is useful to subdivide companies according to value in this way because different sizes of companies pose different risks and benefits to the investor. The very largest companies, those in the FTSE 100 and including oil companies like Shell, shops like Marks & Spencer and pharmaceutical companies like Glaxo Wellcome have market caps. in many billions of pounds. These companies all own large amounts of what are called fixed assets – buildings, factories, mineral rights, etc. They employ many people, have very large amounts of sales each year and have strong brand names. In themselves they have a lot of 'value'. If you buy part-ownership in one of these companies you are buying part-ownership of bricks and mortar and of a successful enterprise with a proven track record. It's not quite that simple, because you will also be paying a premium above the sheer monetary value of the company based on its earnings and the projected increase in those earnings over the next few years, but still underlying your investment there is the feel of solidity, of a business which is one of the backbones of the economy. In short, you do not lie awake at night worrying that the company may go bust and you will lose all your money. Far more likely is that you will make a comfortable, steady sum from these sorts of investments. OK, so M&S shares haven't done very well over the last couple of years (and we will, in fact, come on to this later) but the company is still there, it's still selling a huge number of underpants and it is still making a healthy profit from doing so. The company keeps plodding along and, over the long haul, it seems very likely that M&S will continue to participate in the overall growth of the British economy. It is this long-term participation of economic growth that makes shares attractive compared with cash and gilts. By buying into the large companies in the FTSE 100 you buy into businesses that tend to have the strength to continue to participate in this.

Let's contrast this with a small-cap. biotechnology company, which is far off making it into the FTSE 250 and whose total number of shares on the market is worth just £30 million. This company, Flab-o-Zap PLC, has just one avenue of interest and it's called, yup you've guessed it, Flab-o-Zap. Flab-o-Zap, still in the early stages of development, promises to revolutionize the eating patterns of the developed world. One tablet of F-o-Z will cancel out the flab-building effects of up to twelve Big Macs or fifteen Mars Bars, and the company is aiming to market the tablets in sweetie dispensers and at fast-food outlets around the world ('That'll be four Big Macs, three apple pies, a large Coca-Cola *not* diet and an F-o-Z, please.') If it all comes off, this company is going to be big, but F-o-Z is still very early on in the notoriously fraught drug development process. Anything could happen between now and approval by the drug licensing authorities: tumours in rats, hair in human volunteers turning pink, feet falling off, anything. Flab-o-Zap PLC is probably burning £5 million or more every year as it sinks money into its wonder drug and it has no other income. There is nothing else to this company and if F-o-Z does not make it to the marketplace, then your investment will be worth zilch. The other side of the coin, though, is that if F-o-Z changes the eating patterns of a generation, the share price will double, quintuple, centuple, can you say 'go up a very great deal'?

Midway between large-cap. and small-cap., you will find, wait for it, mid-cap. companies, which behave somewhere between the two and which are also a fertile ground for investors. The FTSE 250 is an index of mid-cap. companies.

As a rule, then, small-cap. companies are riskier investments than large-cap. ones, although they may provide much greater returns. These differences in the character and nature of large- and smaller-cap. companies are sufficiently consistent to make it worthwhile separating them out into distinct groups — the indices we have already heard about.

How to Read the Share Tables

With a cup of coffee on the kitchen table, a piece of bread in the toaster and the children still fast asleep, prop this book up against the cornflakes packet and open up the copy of the *Financial Times* you surreptitiously bought yesterday. We're about to do some work.

As confusing as all those numbers may look, they're quite easy to decipher once you know what to look for. In the *Financial Times*, you'll find the share tables in the 'Companies and Finance' section, just inside the back page. You can find the share prices in other major newspapers and at a number of sites on the Internet too, but the Sporting Pink seems like a good place to start.

Have you found them? Good. What do you notice first? That it's all looking just a teensie bit dull and not at all the kind of thing you want to be bothered with? Wrong! That's *not* what you notice. Believe it or not, you may be scanning these pages regularly a few months from now and *enjoying* it. Try again. Aha, you've noticed that the companies aren't arranged alphabetically as one might have thought, but by type of business: Aerospace & Defence, Automobiles, Banks, Beverages, etc. Fool, we knew you had it in you. Splendid work!

Finding the share you want can be a little trying if you don't know exactly what sector it's classified under, but once you have it figured out, this system actually makes quite a lot of sense, as it makes it simple to compare companies in the same industry. In fact, these sectors are placed together into larger industry groupings. You can see a list of these (with the various sectors listed underneath each group) if you have a quick look at the very back page of the paper. Can you see them? Down at the bottom left? Excellent. If you're good, we'll come back to this bit later on. Anyway, we like this system and are prepared to put up with the minor inconvenience of occasionally having to hunt through a number of industry sectors to find the share we're after. It's actually a far better system than in the US papers, where US shares are listed alphabetically.

Let's take Tesco as an example. This is one of the biggest retail companies in the world and a solid, solid FTSE 100 performer. Where you gonna look, Fool? Under 'Food & Drug Retailers', yup, and there it is. No, hang on, there it is. Wait. Grab your glasses. *There it is.* And it looks like this:

Company	Notes	Price	+ or –	52-week high	low	Volume '000s	Yld	P/E
Tesco	✠	208¼xd	+1¼	230	153½	14,547	2.2	20.2

OK, so perhaps it doesn't look exactly like this, but it did when this was written on 27 June 2000. How it looks for you shouldn't be that far different. Don't tell us you've got a copy of the Monday *FT*. If you have, then it might be quite a bit different. As we'll see later, it gives slightly different information about the dividend and, on top of that, it gives the market capitalization, which can be very handy. Anyway, we're going to stick to explaining what happens on the other days. So, starting from left to right, we have the company name. We're OK with that – we found the company, after all. Then come the notes. If you look at the bottom right-hand side of the right-hand of the two share pages, you will see the notes explained and see that this symbol means that Tesco is an 'FT Global 500 Company' for the year 2000. Bully for it. In fact, it's bully for the *FT* too, since it means that they'll charge you £95 for the *FT*'s own detailed analysis of the world's top 500 companies. Well, you'll know by now what we're likely to think about that, won't you? It seems like an awful lot of money to pay when there is so much data and analysis available free on the Internet, both from the companies' own Web sites (like **www.tesco. com**) and various financial Web sites. Anyway, back to business . . .

Now comes the price: 208¼xd. '208¼' is the price in pence at the close of trading (4.30pm) on the previous day. For big companies like Tesco, this will more or less be the last price at which a deal was struck before everyone went home. For other shares (generally the ones that aren't in the FTSE 100), it will be the 'mid-price' of the share, and it falls between the price at which you could have bought it (the 'offer' price, which will be higher than the mid-price) and the price at which you could have sold it (the 'bid' price, which will be lower than the mid-price). It's essentially a fantasy price, used for reference only. Using the mid-price means only one price has to be quoted, saving on time and space. Now, 'xd'. This simply refers to the fact that if you were to buy this share now, you would not be in line for the upcoming dividend payment. This isn't getting any simpler, is it? Think way back to the introduction of this book: DON'T PANIC. Do, however, ask: 'What's a dividend?'

Dividends are simply payments that companies make directly to their shareholders. Companies like Tesco pull some money out of their flow of earnings and use it to encourage shareholders to hold onto their shares for the longer term. They're like a salary to shareholders. The year's dividend is paid in two halves, six months apart. Each dividend payment is payable to people who hold the shares at the close of trading on a certain date (specified by the company when it announces the dividend). This is called the 'ex-dividend date'. As far as Tesco and its next dividend are concerned, that day has passed. If, say, the dividend was for 2p per share then, all things being equal, you would expect Tesco shares to have fallen by 2p in price after 'going ex-dividend'. This would be because the shares have lost their entitlement to an extra 2p and are, therefore, worth 2p less. So, by telling you that the shares have already 'gone ex-dividend', the *FT* is letting you know where you stand. How kind. In truth, though, it's only of much relevance when you're looking at a company that pays a very big dividend relative to its share price – this is measured by dividend yield and we'll come to this in a moment. Onward!

The next column ('+ or −') shows how many pence higher or lower the share price closed compared to the previous day. In this case, it was a mere penny and a quarter up which, when compared to a share price of 208¼p, is not very much at all.

The 52-week high and low of the share comes next. We think this is fairly self-explanatory. One point to make is that at some point later on in the year, the *FT* suddenly switches to giving the highs and lows for the current year, rather than the last 52 weeks. We've never really worked out when it does this, and we're not actually very interested, but it's worth making sure that you know what you're looking at. Over the last year, Tesco shares have fluctuated between 153½p and 230p. This might sound like a lot but, given the way the share prices of some technology companies have gone recently, it's really very steady. You'd expect this from a large food retailer like Tesco. Whatever the economic conditions, you've got to eat, and opinions about Tesco's valuation change less quickly than for companies with less steady (or even no) profits.

It's easy to think that at 208¼p, closer to its 52-week high than to its 52-week low, Tesco is looking expensive. Well, fiddlesticks! While many people are leery of buying shares that are near their 52-week highs, you shouldn't make this your instinctive response. You will come to notice that the shares of truly winning companies score new highs fairly consistently from one decade to the next. Oh yes, they may have a bad three-week run, four-month run or even three-year run, but, if sales and earnings grow, more investors will pile in. Don't be scared off by a share hitting new highs unless you can find something else worrying about the company.

Next, on to the volume of shares traded on the Stock Exchange that day. Fourteen and a half million. Quite a lot, really. With shares worth just over £2, the stock market shifted around £30 million of Tesco shares yesterday. Even so, this only amounts to about 0.15 per cent of the company. Probably about par for the course, with no major news from the company.

'Yld.' Not illuminating at first sight, is it? This actually stands for 'Yield'. Take the dividend that Tesco paid last year, divide it by the current share price and multiply it by 100 to give the percentage. That's the yield, or rather the dividend yield, as it is properly called. If you like formulas, it looks like this:

$$dividend\ yield = dividend \div share\ price\ x\ 100$$
or
$$2.2 = dividend \div 208.25\ x\ 100$$

Knowing all the other parts of the equation, we can, if we wish, calculate the total annual dividend that was paid on each share. And after a little mathematical jiggery-pokery, the answer is 4.6p. Now, we've shown off and calculated the dividend, but if we'd been patient and waited until the Monday edition of the newspaper, we would have seen that it includes the actual dividend. For Tesco, this turns out to be 4.48p which still comes to 2.2 per cent (to the nearest 0.1 of a per cent). The Monday *FT* also shows that the 'Last xd' (last ex-dividend date) was '17.4', or 17 April.

Why do we care what the dividend yield is, anyway? It tells us what percentage return we may expect from the share if it does not rise or fall at all in the year. In this case, it is only 2.2 per cent, which isn't a great deal. It loses to gilts, it loses to a deposit account at the Middle Earth building society and loses to just about anything else you can think of. It barely beats inflation, for heaven's sake. Clearly, investors are not going to buy Tesco for the dividend alone. They are hoping instead that Tesco is going to increase its earnings by selling more food next year, hopefully more efficiently, and that as a result its dividend, and share price, will grow. OK, here comes a fast-paced, pub-quiz starter for ten. Which company do you think investors are expecting more earnings and dividend growth from?

Dividend Yield

Tesco	2.2%
ICI	6.2%

Yes, you're right. They're counting on more growth from Tesco. If neither share price was to move at all in the next year, ICI holders would be happier campers than Tesco holders (assuming ICI managed to keep paying its high dividend, but that's another story). The market is counting on Tesco to achieve more earnings and sales growth over the long term.

Unfortunately, in the wake of a column that demanded some basic calculato-fragilistic expertise, we run into a slightly more complicated beast to its right: the P/E ratio. 'P' stands for the company's share price and 'E' stands for the company's earnings per share. Thus, this ratio compares the company's share price to its trailing twelve months of earnings per share. Gasp. What's that? Forget it, you're never, ever going to grasp this. (Just kidding. Take a deep breath and read on.)

OK, Tesco has a P/E ratio of 20.2 on the day in question. The current price is 208¼p, giving us earnings per share over the last twelve months of 10.3p (20.2 = 208¼ ÷ 10.3). The same numbers for ICI are a P/E ratio of 13.5, a price of 515p and earnings of 38.1p per share. Investors in Tesco are prepared to pay *twenty* times what each share has earned in the past year for their shares while, in the case of ICI, they are only prepared to pay *thirteen and a half* times.

The earnings are what the company actually brings home to investors from its forays out into the wide, wild world of commerce. Investors are prepared to pay more for Tesco's earnings, because they believe that it has the potential to make them increase at a faster rate than ICI. In fact even Tesco has a P/E ratio below the market average of 26.1. This is because there are lots of companies out there from whom investors expect even quicker earnings growth. Vodafone AirTouch, for example, has a P/E ratio of a shade under 65. Vodafone has its work cut out to justify these expectations, but investors clearly think it can do it, because otherwise they wouldn't be prepared to pay this much for the shares.

Going back to ICI, its prospects just aren't that good, as assessed by investors, and all they are prepared to pay is thirteen and a half times earnings. If someone came along and tried to sell his shares in ICI at *fifteen* times earnings, he'd be laughed out of court. This company isn't worth that, he'd be told, it's not going to expand its business quickly enough for us to be prepared to pay that kind of price. Now, begone!

We said earlier that, if you were good, we'd come back and make a couple of points about the bit on the very back page of the *FT* and we think you have been, so here goes. Go to the very back of the paper and look at the bottom left-hand corner. There should be a table full of numbers covering about a quarter of the page. Now we're not going to cover this table in quite as much depth, but we want to draw your attention to a couple of the columns: 'Actual Yield %' and 'P/E ratio'. These are the same figures that we've just been talking about. The difference is that here the dividend yield and the P/E ratios are given for all the different FTSE indices and for all the different sectors of the market. If you look at the row for the FTSE All Share (which should be fairly near the top), you see a figure for the average yield for all the companies in that index. In our paper, it says that it is 2.13 per cent. The average P/E ratio for the FTSE All Share is 26.7. If you think that the presence of investment companies (which are just companies with stakes in all the others) distorts the values, then you can look at the row below called 'FTSE All Share ex Inv Co'. The figures are actually only very slightly different.

Since Tesco has a lower P/E ratio than the market average, we can deduce that investors expect Tesco to grow at a slower rate, overall, than the average company. That's not especially surprising, since Tesco is a food retailer and, despite it being at the forefront of Internet developments in that sector, it's a sector that investors just aren't very excited about. So, instead of comparing Tesco to the average of the whole market, we can have a look at how it compares to the average of the Food & Drug Retailers sector. You can find the row for this listed under 'Non-cyclical services', towards the bottom of the table. The average dividend yield for this sector is 2.93% and the average P/E ratio is 17.93. So, we thought Tesco was a better than average company and that's how it appears. Since its P/E ratio is higher, and its dividend yield lower, than the average of similar companies, we can deduce that investors expect more growth from it.

While we're looking at the 'Non-cyclical services' grouping, we can add a quick warning about how arbitrary the groupings of companies can be. Take a look at the other sector that makes up non-cyclical services. It's 'Telecommunications Services' and it has a whopping P/E of 80. In fact, there is a little sign next to the figure of 80 which indicates that when the *FT* got that far, they stopped counting, so the actual P/E ratio is very likely quite a bit higher. Investors are prepared to pay this much for the earnings of the average Telecommunications Services company because they expect an awful lot of growth from the sector. Anyway, the retailing of food and drugs and the provision of telecommunications services fall into the same grouping, but they are oceans apart in terms of what investors expect from them. So, beware and always have a thought about what it is that you're actually looking at.

There are all sorts of things that investors will look at when deciding how much they expect a company to grow. Perhaps the prime factor is the estimates of potential growth in earnings provided by the analysts who follow the company. These are the people who are paid by the large financial institutions to live, eat, sleep and breathe the company or companies they follow. They assess what the company is likely to earn in the next several years and investors then decide how much of a premium they are prepared to pay for this projected growth. The limitation here is that these analysts only tend to look two or three years ahead. They're a bit frightened of going further ahead than that because they might end up being way off and looking a bit silly. Also, brokers make their money from people changing their minds about shares (and then buying or selling them as a result) and they find it a bit limiting to set out their stall on a company too far into the future. They want results and action now.

Other things, of course, figure alongside the projected earnings estimates when investors decide how much they are prepared to pay for a company: namely, the past history and the current performance. There is more, though, much more, to the P/E ratio and estimates of earnings growth. To learn more about it, a good starting point might be the *Motley Fool UK Investment Workbook* or you might even want to come along to our Web site, where there are a number of articles and endless discussion about this sort of thing.

When you've had a well-deserved break, you can come back and read the next chapter about Obviously Great Investments with confidence, secure in the knowledge that you already know far more about shares than most of your contemporaries ever will.

12

Obviously Great Investments

Greatness knows itself.

— William Shakespeare, *Henry IV*

Buying an index tracker is a sound, Foolish investment and is as far as many people will ever need to go. There are others, though – and we count ourselves amongst this group – who want to be more involved with the growth of their money and who believe that it is possible to actually *beat* the performance of the market as a whole by choosing their own investments. What we're going to consider in this chapter are investments that appear to be such obviously great long-term investments that it is impossible to imagine why in preference anyone would want to invest in an underperforming, overcharging investment scheme such as an endowment policy.

Even so, the jump into investing in individual equities – no matter how 'obviously great' they appear to be – is a big one and not one you should consider making without ample, Foolish preparation. Go back and read Chapter 10, 'When *Not* to Invest'. Particularly go back and read 'When You Don't Yet Know Enough' (see p. 90). If you invest in individual shares before you're ready, what will happen is what happens to anyone who gets out of their depth: they drown. After a few attempts to stay afloat, fairly soon one 'glug' leads to another and they're asking the fishes why the air's so annoyingly thick and wet down here. If you're in shares and the market starts to drop, as it certainly will one day, then you'd better have a sound understanding and faith in the *overall* tendency of the market to rise as the years goes by. If, when the time comes, you panic and sell out as your shares start to drop along with everyone else's, then we're very, very sorry you ever bought this book. We hope we're giving you the bare bones here with which to frame the understanding that long-term wealth is assuredly yours if you will but think with a long-term perspective, but only you can know how well you have really digested it.

Whether it's a first-day skier enticed to the top of the hill with a 'The best way to learn is to start at the top and fall all the way down', or a tyro parachutist looking down and reflecting that it's all looking awfully high up here, the fact is that any pursuit that requires an appraisal of risks and benefits should be approached with circumspection. Now, if you spend too long circumspecting – or whatever the verb may be – you'll never do anything more positive with your life than switch channels with the remote control and issue dire warnings to all your friends and relations. That's it – just issue dire warnings. As long as you have no other aspirations in life than to spend it ingesting a televisual diet of pap and purveying pessimism to anyone who will listen (there won't be many), then that's all right. But we're presuming that if you have read this far, you're some way towards becoming a Fool and have, let's say, slightly higher aspirations. We're hoping, specifically, that you nurture the aspiration to take hold of your fate with your own two hands and, through your own efforts and endeavours, build a future for yourself.

You do? That's great – read on!

Oh, hang on. You didn't go back and read 'When Not to Invest', did you, you eager beaver Fool? We really think you should. Go back to page 87, read those Foolish guidelines again and we'll see you back here in a few minutes. Don't worry about us, we'll take this opportunity to have a well-earned (well, we think so) cup of tea . . .

Tum tee tum tum . . .

Schlurrrrrp!

(Sorry, you didn't hear that, did you? It was terribly hot. Sorry.)

Now, moving swiftly back to our high-tech, thrilling, investment plot: you've returned and you're thinking of making a positive decision to invest directly in some of the powerful companies that make up the UK market. Excellent! Our hope is that in years to come this decision will bring you market-beating returns, something an index tracker cannot, of course, provide. However, reflect yet again that there is no shame, no shame what-soever, in never going any further than investing in the index itself. By doing this, you will beat the vast majority of professionals, leave investments in cash and gilts languishing, assure yourself the most secure future and all this for next to no input or ongoing hassle at all. By stopping at this point and saying to yourself 'I've sorted my finances, I'm not that interested in all this investment stuff, I'd like to devote more time to my family/quilting circle/tired old MG' then you are being a Fool indeed. You are not letting your initial enthusiasm push you into something you may later regret. Well done. We'll see you Fools towards the end of the book in our eloquent closing dissertations. Now go off and enjoy yourselves.

After what seems to have been a lengthy series of disclaimers on our part, but which really represent an attempt to set the right atmosphere, the rest of you are finally deemed to have taken the Fool's shilling. We ask you to spend a moment reading this light-hearted, amusing story of an Old Sea Dog from the Second World War. We think it sets the scene for the kind of contrarian, lateral-thinking mindset we like to use in investing. Look on it as a Foolish limbering-up exercise and a brief respite from this oh-so-serious business of investing:

> Commodore 'Monkey' Brand had been hauled out of retirement to try and lick the British trawler fleet into shape as a minesweeping and anti-submarine force . . .
>
> *One of 'Monkey' Brand's favourite tricks was to speed over to a ship in his motorboat, hustle up the ladder on to the assembled quarter-deck, grab off his gold-braided cap and throw it to the deck shouting: 'There's a bomb — what are you going to do about it?' The ruse never failed to create momentary panic. Until one day, when he tried it out on a trawler. As he flung his cap down in front of the startled company and made his challenge, a rating stepped smartly forward and kicked the cap overboard. The surprised Commodore gazed unbelievingly at his cap floating away on the water. But he was not beaten. 'Good work,' he said approvingly, 'splendid.' Then pointing to the cap, he roared: 'Quick, that's a survivor who can't swim — save him!'*
>
> Paul Lund and Harry Ludlam, Trawlers Go To War

You see, we're not going to think like ordinary investors: we're going to try and think a little like Commodore Brand. We are not going to think short-term profit, we are not going to be looking at the market and trading our shares twenty times a day and, perhaps most importantly of all, we shall not believe what the financial press says about the market. Think of yourself from now on as deeply contrarian. You are going to buck the trend of our short-term, sound-bite, thirty-second-attention-span culture and think in years, tens of years. You are going to invest in strong world-beating businesses. You are going to invest in things you can't imagine yourself, Great Britain or the world doing without. In fact, you are going to 'Buy what you know'.

We'd love to take the credit for inventing this natty little investment aphorism and, believe us, if we thought we could get away with it, we would. Sadly, though, we must give the credit to another: Peter Lynch. Peter was a highly successful mutual fund manager (there are some!) in the US through the 1980s and penned two excellent books on investing: *One Up on Wall Street* and *Beating the Street*. 'Buy what you know' is a simple idea and it's an excellent route into investing.

Understanding the company in which you are about to become a part-owner is vital to success. Do you know much about drilling for oil around the

Caspian Sea? Do you have a detailed knowledge of geophysics and are you equipped to speculate on the potential geopolitical repercussions of a large oil find in this area? Have you been keeping up to date with the progress of organized crime in the republics of the former Soviet Union and are you ready to factor in how much of a cut the Mafia will take of any profits? What are your thoughts on the effect of ongoing wars in the area on the safety of the new oil pipeline from the Caspian to the Black Sea through Armenia and Georgia? We wouldn't be surprised if one or more of these questions drew a blank. What is so much more surprising is how many people are prepared to invest in small companies in these kinds of fields, which are so distant from their everyday lives. Can a small company really hope to make a go of it in this dodgy area or is it only the likes of BP, ExxonMobil and Shell that have a chance of turning out a healthy profit at the end of the day? We simply don't know and neither, we are sure, do most of the investors in these companies.

The world is full of investors with tales of woe concerning often small companies they bought into without knowing anything about them, other than hearing from a 'friend' that they had to jump on board quick or else they'd miss the boat! Penny shares, companies you've never heard of, commodities, options, Venezuelan bean futures. If you find yourself thinking that you could make a quick 200 per cent profit in one of these, switch into another, clear 300 per cent with that one, switch around like this for a couple of years, retire, buy a floating gin palace on the Côte d'Azur and spend your remaining years mixing ever more lurid cocktails and swapping ' . . . and then this old tub of a *sailing* boat almost rammed me as I pootled out of the harbour at 35 knots, can you believe the cheek of it?' stories, then WHOA! It *is* possible to clear huge profits on dodgy investments which you don't understand in a short period. You are more likely, much more likely, to lose all your money in one fell swoop. Don't believe you will be the one to beat the odds, because Sod's Law of Investment says you won't. There's a place for people like you. It goes by the name of Las Vegas and sits in the desert sucking up water and fools somewhere between Los Angeles and the Grand Canyon. Buy a cheap airline ticket, take a thousand pounds and no means of procuring any more and return when you're broke or you've made a million. Dealing with your gambling habit in this way will cost you less in the long run than thinking you will make outrageous returns from investments about which you know nothing. It is also less likely to annihilate any long-term human relationship you happen to have built up over the years.

Consider: one of the richest men in the United States, and therefore the world, is an unassuming Nebraskan called Warren Buffett. We'd tell you exactly where he stood in the richness league tables, but there seems to be something of a tussle going on with postitions changing on a seemingly daily basis. The 'Sage of Omaha' is worth somewhere around $30 billion. How has he done this? Purely and simply by investing in simple, understandable businesses with favourable long-term prospects and which are already efficient at what they do. Using this somewhat mundane strategy, he has returned around 23 per cent annually since 1964 for investors in his Berkshire Hathaway investment company. Let's repeat that: Warren Buffett, the world's greatest investor, has returned 23 per cent a year over the last thirty-six years. It is a phenomenal performance and yet one he calls 'remarkably unremarkable'. By sticking to the basics and investing in companies like Coca-Cola, American Express, Disney and our very own Guinness, he is living proof that the huge investment returns claimed by many investment newsletters and investing schemes are total and utter rubbish, garbage or trash, depending on your linguistic preference. If you buy investing magazines, you will find advertising inserts for investment newsletters falling out all over the place, offering you 20 per cent gains a month or more if you follow their advice (which generally involves stumping up a couple of hundred pounds). These sorts of claims are simply fantastic and we find that the flyers offering them are generally the right size to fit neatly over our corporate Motley Fool dartboard. Buffett has 'only' returned 23 per cent over the long term and this has 'only' made him one of the world's richest men. Fool, if you need a goal, a dream, an aspiration, then 23 per cent every year from easily understandable, reputable companies is sitting slap in front of you. Of course, the mighty Buffett has a knack at being very good at picking the right companies, but the strategy is simple and low risk and has very good odds of at least beating the pros. Verily, look ye not to 'Phcnomcnal profits in just 3 MONTHS!!!!' schcmcs, lcst yc bc burncd most Horriblie.

When you've been Fooling around for a while, you can start to branch out from just buying what you know. The rule, in fact, can be turned on its head. If you feel sufficiently confident, give yourself some leeway by 'not buying what you don't know'. What we don't understand, after all, is what we're really trying to avoid and this mantra gives you a little more scope to find investments in areas that you know well enough, but not absolutely. So what is knowing enough? Well, really it relates to knowing enough about an investment to be confident that it meets the other important elements of a great investment (which we'll come to in due course). You don't need to know the precise chemical processes that go into the manufacture of each (or any) of Glaxo Wellcome's drugs. You just need to understand why their business has, for example, a large element of repeat purchasing (drugs are anything but a one-off purchase), why they add value for the end user (just ask an asthmatic the value of a Ventolin puffer) and why it is hard for other companies to break into their market (patents and brand name drugs). Anyway, we're getting slightly ahead of ourselves, but knowing enough means knowing enough. OK?

If you want to be really Foolish, you can try to think about markets that you have reasons for understanding better than the average investor. Perhaps you are a doctor and have good reason to think that the market underestimates the importance of a new drug. Perhaps you are a software engineer and you understand, better than most, why a particular company's software is likely to become an industry standard because it works so much better than this or that. Be careful, though. Apple Computers is generally regarded as having had a superior product to Microsoft, but look where the two of them have ended up. Although Apple has improved its performance dramatically in the last couple of years, Microsoft still rules the world. Whatever the merits of the two products, Microsoft was better at developing its market position and the rest, as they say, is history. Don't forget, though, that your superior knowledge is only useful in so far as it helps you to recognize whether an investment meets the right criteria. Just because you know a great deal about aeroplanes and flying does not mean that you are going to make a killing by investing in airline companies. It may well be (and probably is) the case that there are no Obviously Great Investments among them.

What Makes an Obviously Great Investment?

As we have already said on several occasions in this book, investing in the stock market is about participating in economic growth. What we're going to consider here are investments that, because of almost unbeatable market positions, are so likely to participate in this growth that they are, to our mind, Obviously Great Investments. Over the short term, their share prices may move up and they may move down but, over the long term, continued profitable growth looks almost inevitable. The emphasis here is on the words 'looks almost inevitable'. Unfortunately, we Fools are not in possession of a crystal ball and we can't predict the future. It would be a wonderful thing if we *knew* which shares would *definitely* do well. Obviously we don't and neither does anyone else. What we can do, though, is build a portfolio of a number of shares that have good chances of doing well. That way, even if we pick a few companies that turn out not to be so obviously great (or even obviously bad), our overall chances of coming up smiling are very good. We'll say more about 'diversifying your portfolio' in Chapter 14, 'The Ten Most Common Investing Mistakes'. For the time being, we just want to be clear that, individually, Obviously Great Investments are not obviously infallible.

In August 1998, Manchester United paid a club record of £12.6 million to sign Dwight Yorke because he was (and is) an obviously great footballer. This doesn't mean to say, though, that he was (or is) infallible. He might have broken a leg in training and never played a single game for the club. At a more mundane level, he might simply have suffered a serious loss of form or just, for whatever reason, failed to produce the goods. Because of this, Manchester United have a large squad of obviously great players. The importance of this was underlined when, on 26 May 1999 in Barcelona, Teddy Sheringham and Ole Gunnar Solskjaer came on as substitutes in the European Cup final to score two late goals, clinching that title and a unique treble. We need to create a portfolio like Manchester United's squad – fill it with Obviously Great Investments while making sure that there is plenty of cover to make up for the few that will fail to perform.

Most invested money is managed by professional fund managers who often have to justify their performance over absurdly short periods. As a result, they are too frequently tempted to throw their money at the latest fashion in the hope of quick profits. The strong and steady performers, frequently rather dull by comparison, tend to attract rather less investment than they deserve. This tends to keep their share prices at attractive levels. It comes back to that thing about woods and trees and not being able to see the former on account of the latter.

So, Foolish investors are able to use patience, and, in particular, the rest of the market's lack of it, to their advantage. However, to let our friend, the miracle of compounding, do its job, we need to find companies that we can rely on to be around, and still showing steady growth, in twenty years' time (or, preferably, even longer).

Fundamentally, what we are looking for in an investment is growth. Now, by this we don't simply mean a growing share price. What we want is a grow-ing business. Without a growing business, a growing share price is ultimately unsustainable. On the other hand, with a growing business, the share price will ultimately take care of itself. Essentially, a growing business generates an increasingly large amount of surplus cash each year. The trouble with cash, however, is that it is a bit lumpy. A company might be spending an extra amount on investment in any one year to reap future benefits, and that may put a dent in their cash flow. This is why accountants like to talk about profits. Profits are designed to smooth out lumpy cash flows and give an idea, from year to year, how much money a company is making. A standard measure of profits is earnings per share (EPS). Remember this? We talked about it a bit in Chapter 11. Basically, it is the profits of a company, after tax has been taken off, divided by the number of shares that there are in that company. This gives a figure for how much profit is being generated for each share. What we like to see is growth in EPS over the long term, although it's important to note that this is really just a proxy for growth in the generation of surplus cash.

Anyway, let's get back to the importance of growth. Indulge us for a moment, Fools, for it is a subject very dear to our hearts. Take a company with its business growing (by which we mean its EPS) at a rate of, say, 15 per cent per year. After twenty years, it will be 16.4 times bigger. Not bad at all. Now let's consider a company that grows at a mere 5 per cent per year. After twenty years, it will be just 2.7 times bigger. If the two companies were the same size to start with, the faster growing company will now be more than six times the size (in terms of EPS). To put it another way, we could have paid a P/E ratio (remember these from Chapter 11?) six times higher for our high growth company and, assuming that their P/E ratios end up the same, you'd still have been better off buying it instead of the slower growing company. Things go really crazy if we look at the picture after thirty years. Our Obviously Great Investment (as it clearly would be), growing at 15 per cent per year, would have increased by just over sixty-six times and would be more than fifteen times the size of the now forgotten laggard. We'll let you do the sums for forty years because the results are a bit messy and this is a family book (have a look at Appendix 1, 'Coping With Compound Interest', to learn how to do this sort of sum).

The point of all this is that it is growth, continued sustainable growth, that makes the real difference to an investment over the long term. It clearly matters how much you initially pay for an investment, but the further you look into the future, the less the price paid matters compared to the actual growth achieved. Take the drugs company Glaxo Wellcome. You could have bought shares in this company (or rather in Glaxo) in 1965 for 2.47p.[5] Since then it has achieved annual EPS growth of 17.4 per cent and its share price is now (in 2000) 1910p, having grown at 20.9 per cent over the last thirty-five years. The slightly higher share price growth is explained by the threefold increase in Glaxo's P/E ratio from 13.7 to 39.0. We could have paid twice as much for our Glaxo shares in 1965 (a P/E ratio of 27.4) and our rate of share price growth since then would only have fallen to 18.6 per cent. We'll repeat

---

5 Data supplied by Datastream.

that. Paying twice as much for our Glaxo shares in 1965 would merely have reduced our annual return since then from 20.9 per cent to 18.6 per cent. The world's stockbrokers would almost certainly have greeted such a sudden doubling in Glaxo's share price at the time with advice to sell to 'lock in profits', while the truly Foolish investor would not have given the matter a second glance. Notice also how close both the figures for annual share price growth are to the rate of annual EPS growth (20.9 per cent and 18.6 per cent against 17.4 per cent). So, if someone comes along and tells you that what matters is how much you pay for a company's shares, then say to them, 'Sure it matters a bit, but what really makes the difference over the long term is how much that company's business actually grows.'

The stock market is full of people who want to make their fortunes here and now. For these poor Wise souls, looking long into the future is a bit of an irrelevance and, not to put too fine a point on it, very frightening. It's like those old maps that, at the edge of the explored world, have pictures of dragons and other unpleasant monsters. Of course, aside from the odd kangaroo, the previously unexplored part of the world (at least it was unexplored by those mapmakers, not the people who actually lived there) has turned out to be pretty much like the explored world. Fools are wary, or rather respectful, of the future too, but we're not frightened of it because as we move forward into it, we're accompanied by our trusty old chaperone, Compound Interest. In short, the stock market tends to undervalue companies that have very solid prospects of good steady growth long into the future. These companies are what we call Obviously Great Investments.

How to Spot Obviously Great Investments

The two most important things about our chosen investments, then, are that they should show solid growth and that they should be able to sustain this growth long into the future. Over time the economy grows and, as a result, most companies that are around at any one time are growing. Over the long term, what happens is that many companies arrive, grow a bit for a while and then disappear. What we are trying to find are the companies that have arrived, have grown a bit for a while, will grow a bit more and then, after that, will just carry on growing. In other words, while growth in companies is everywhere, what isn't everywhere is *sustained and sustainable* long-term growth and this is therefore the supporting plank of any Obviously Great Investment. It's that sustainability that our criteria are designed to seek out.

1. Have they built a strong brand?

This is your first filter for an Obviously Great Investment. Find the businesses that have built at least nationwide or, even better, global brands in their industries. The more world-beating brands a company has, the better. A strong brand gives a company an edge because it represents the faith that the company's customers have built up in a product. It gives the company the opportunity to sell more of the product at the same price as less well-branded competitors. Alternatively, it means the company can charge more and still sell the same amount.

Ideally, a brand should be fixed firmly in the minds of consumers, creating a strong mental association between that brand and the particular product. You know the sort of thing: Hoover and vacuum cleaners, Heinz and baked beans, Gillette and razor blades. Once a company has reached the minds of consumers in this way, it is hard for others to replace it. The perfect brand will be one which consumers buy and use regularly. 'Repeat purchasing' is fantastic and not just because it keeps the profits flowing in, but because it means receiving free daily promotion. When selling products through to consumers, marketing is often the greatest expense and thus it engenders the greatest risk. All over the world, Internet companies are vying with each other for consumer enthusiasm. They are spending money, oodles of it, on their marketing costs. They're in a high stakes game and if their marketing helps build them a global brand, they've won. Companies like Coca-Cola, Heinz and Gillette are getting this promotion gratis millions of times a day. Every time a consumer buys one of their products, it is an opportunity for the company to extend the relationship of trust with that consumer and, without meaning to sound too sinister, an opportunity to get further inside their minds. For this reason, we suggest you study most carefully those businesses that are frequent servants of their global base of customers. These companies aren't just getting their promotion free, they're *making* money as they use the daily sales of their products to promote themselves. Very nifty.

2. Are they the best in their business?

Once we've found our world-beating brands, we need to ask ourselves whether the company is the best in its business. Does it have competitors that are doing a better job? If it does, then it may be that we're looking at the wrong company.

So what exactly is a company's business? It's worth thinking about this on several different levels. Take Tesco for example. At the nub of it all, its main business is food retailing, which it carries out mainly in the UK. So, first of all, we need to decide whether Tesco is the UK's best food retailer. If a company is not the best there is at its 'core' business, then it is unlikely to qualify for obvious greatness. However, it goes beyond this. Tesco is also involved in a certain amount of non-food retailing and it would be nice, although not vital, to see the company being best at this too. The company is also taking on an increasing amount of business overseas. Again, it would be nice to see them being best at this but, since it's a relatively new market for them, we perhaps shouldn't expect too much.

Beyond all this, what we'd really like to see is a company that dominates its entire industry, not just its direct competitors. Consider whether the company you're looking at is the one that makes its industry tick. Generally this comes down to having the brand that the consumer wants, but not always. It might be the company that has a patented widget, which makes it possible to make something twice as cheaply. Everyone in the industry will be at this company's beck and call. So, look at the industry that a company is in. If you find that another company dominates it so comprehensively (whether it is a competitor, supplier or customer) that it makes all the real profits and everyone else is left picking up the scraps, then you're looking at the wrong company. The dominant company is probably making all the money. Ask yourself questions like does Persil need Tesco or does Tesco need Persil? Persil would lose a lot of sales if Tesco stopped stocking it, but Tesco might lose a lot of Persil-loving customers to Sainsbury if it tried something like this. It's probably a dead heat in this case, in the UK at any rate.

More generally, choosing a best over a second best isn't always terribly easy. However, in any given group you can usually distinguish the superior two or three businesses from the rest. We don't think it's a good idea to invest in businesses trying to turn around or trying to become a top-tier competitor after years of slumber. Once you have the top two or three, decide which is the best of the lot, do a few minutes of research into their financial situation (which we'll consider in a bit – honestly, it's not overly complicated) and then buy and hold the strongest among them. Preferably for decades, but at least until they stop matching up to the criteria. If it's too close to call, consider buying the two or three main competitors.

3. Is their position easily defended?

For a company to sustain its growth over the long term, it needs to have some form of sustainable advantage. Commenting on Coca-Cola and Gillette, Warren Buffett had this to say in his 1993 letter to the shareholders of Berkshire Hathaway:

*The might of their brand names, the attributes of their products, and the
strength of their distribution systems give them an enormous competitive
advantage, setting up a protective moat around their economic castles. The
average company, in contrast, does battle daily without any such means
of protection. As Peter Lynch says, stocks of companies selling commodity-
like products should come with a warning label: 'Competition may prove
hazardous to human wealth.'*

It's easy to agree with Warren Buffett and we'd agree that a company's brand
is about the most important protective moat that a company can build around
itself and this is where our criteria began. However, as Buffett also points out,
there are other factors that can keep the competition at bay. Take ARM
Holdings, a designer of microchips. Many of its designs are patented and this
immediately gives it an advantage: if a company wants to make the type of chip
that ARM designs, then it needs to pay ARM, and no one else, to use that
design. In ARM's case, though, it goes further than this. It has established
development partnerships with the majority of the world's large chip manufacturers. This means that it is involved in a daily discourse with these companies
about how the designs can be improved upon or used more effectively. For this
reason, if anybody is going to improve on the design in the future, the chances
are pretty good that it will be ARM itself. As a result, ARM has a series of
moats around it which even the most persistent of competitors will find it
hard to overcome. We'll talk more about ARM Holdings shortly.

4. Are they making a lot of money for their efforts?

The above criteria are designed to find companies that should make a steadlily
increasing stream of profits. In fact, if a company is doing the above things
right, then we'd be very surprised if it wasn't doing this already. So, the best
way to check our thinking is to have a look at its accounts and make sure that
this is the case (don't worry, this is easier than it sounds, it really is). If we look
at the company and it doesn't seem to be making much money, then we need
to ask ourselves why. Generally, we'll have missed something which relates
to its brand or its industry dominance. If you can't find anything wrong, then
go back and keep thinking about what it might be. There may be a good reason
for it but, on the whole, an Obviously Great Investment will be making good,
steadily increasing profits and will have been doing so for some time.

The specific amount of the profits is not what matters. A company can be
as big as it likes, but this doesn't mean that it is financially ship-shape. What
we want to see is a company that makes good profits relative to its sales (also

known as *turnover*). Sales basically corresponds to the money that comes in to the company though the front door. Of course, all the time there is a lot of money leaving a company through the back door (that is, the company's costs). What we want to know is how much money stays in the company relative to how much is coming in. This is called the *margin*.

A company's profit and loss account starts with 'Sales' (or 'Turnover') at the top. It then takes off the 'Cost of Sales'. Cost of Sales basically includes the cost of the things actually used directly to create a particular product: the most obvious example is raw materials. The figure we're left with after taking this off is called 'Gross Profit'. The 'Gross Margin' will be the Gross Profit expressed as a percentage of the Sales. This figure is useful, as it tells you how much value a company is directly adding to the materials it uses in creating its products. The problem is that this can vary hugely depending on what type of business a company is in. For instance, a shop will tend to have low Gross Margins (around 20 per cent) because it only sells things for a little bit more than it costs to buy them. By contrast, a company making something like software, which essentially costs almost nothing, *directly*, to produce, will tend to have very high Gross Margins (perhaps as much as 90 per cent).

The great leveller between these two types of company is what comes in the profit and loss account below the Gross Profit, namely 'Operating Expenses' (or it could be called something else: like 'General or Administrative Costs'). This encompasses all the other costs in a company, things like salaries, wages, paper clips and all those other incidental expenses. It's where most of the costs of a software company will come in, since it has to pay all those clever computer bods large salaries for all the great software that they're creating. By contrast, the extra costs of a retailer at this level are small compared to the Cost of Sales. The figure arrived at by deducting Operating Expenses from Gross Profit is the 'Operating Profit' (sometimes called 'Trading Profit') and you won't be surprised to hear that the Operating Margin is the Operating Profit expressed as a percentage of Sales. So far, so good. Take a look back at these last two paragraphs – you've read them, understood them and even half-digested them. Nice one, Cyril. But we're not quite finished yet . . .

Finally, the cost of paying interest on any debt is taken off to give a figure called Profit Before Tax. You can work out the 'Profit Margin' by dividing this figure by Sales. After this comes the tax, leaving us with, not surprisingly, Profit After Tax (sometimes called 'Earnings'). It is this figure which is divided by the number of shares to leave us with Earnings Per Share. The following is a very basic example of how a company's profit and loss account might look. The company we've chosen is called Leather 'n' Lashes PLC, 'the riding crop of the connoisseur'. Their main line of business is, well, you can guess . . .

Leather 'n' Lashes PLC 1999 Profit and Loss Account

£ million

	Sales	10,000	
(less)	Cost of Sales	6,000	
(equals)	Gross Profit	4,000	Gross Margin = 40.0%
(less)	Operating Expenses	2,400	
(equals)	Operating Profit	1,600	Operating Margin = 16.0%
(less)	Net Interest Costs	150	
(equals)	Profit Before Tax	1,450	Profit Margin = 14.5%
(less)	Tax	450	
(equals)	Profit After Tax	1,000	

Wow. Did you spot the amount of sales? £10 billion. Yikes, that's a lot of whips!

Sometimes companies decide to take both cost of sales and operating expenses away from their sales in one fell swoop, going straight to the operating profit. They're quite at liberty to do that, but this means that we only have the operating profit to look at, and as we saw earlier it is worth splitting out cost of sales and operating expenses as they both give useful information about what it's costing a company to get their product into your hands.

Anyway, however we've got there, we've arrived at the operating margin. We like the operating margin because it comes after all of a company's business costs have gone out the back door and therefore, unlike gross margin, it doesn't depend too much on what industry the company's in. On top of this, since it comes before a company has paid out things like interest and tax, the operating margin is an indicator of the business itself rather than the current financing and tax situation. For these reasons, operating margin is the measure that we tend to concentrate on (after giving the others a quick shufti). If the operating margin is too low, then that's a big black mark for the company even if it is better than others in its industry. In fact, if this is the case, then it's probably a dud industry. At the very least, we like to see an operating margin of 8 per cent, but really you should be aiming for 10 per cent. More than 15 per cent is very good.

It's worth bearing in mind that all sorts of factors can come into play in any one year. If you're really serious about an investment, then you should probably take the trouble to look back at the figures for the last five years and work out the margins for each year (there should be a five-year record with this sort of information towards the back of the accounts). Ideally we like to see stable and strong margins, but don't worry too much if one year is an aberration. It can be interesting and highly instructive, though, to think about why this might be the case.

5. Are they up to their eyebrows in debt?

There's good debt and there's bad debt for companies, just as there is for you. Having a mortgage makes sense because the interest rate you pay on that debt is relatively low and is financing a very necessary thing: your home. Having a mountain of high-interest credit card debt because you can't stop buying Armani shirts isn't so clever. What we really don't want is to find a great company that can't then sustain its position because it is having to spend all its cash paying interest on a large pile of debt. Plenty of companies carry a little bit of debt and this is OK. They borrow a comfortable amount to finance investment, because they are confident that the returns that they'll earn from that investment will outweigh the interest they have to pay. The companies *choose* to be in debt and it is called gearing.

Too much gearing can turn sour. Back to mortgages. Remember what happened to some householders in the negative equity saga of the early 1990s in Britain? In the late 80s, people bought houses with massive mortgages (property was booming, right?), only to watch the market crash. They struggled to pay the loan and meanwhile the asset on which it had been taken out was no longer worth that amount. All this would have been OK if they had been able to live through the downturn and take a long-term view of things. The lesson is to make sure that you don't overstretch yourself. You need to be able to live through a period of rising interest rates and falling house prices. If you can do this, everything should turn out rosy but, if you can't, then you might end up having your house repossessed and sold at precisely the wrong time. All this applies equally to companies. A highly geared (that is, highly indebted) company in an industry with highly volatile or cyclical profits like, say, the building industry, could be asking for trouble. Similarly, a company with too much debt might find its profits dipping rapidly if interest rates start to rise.

One of the simplest ways to look at how much a company is in hock is by looking at how many times over a company's operating profit (skip back to the previous section) will pay the interest on the loans it is carrying. This is called the 'Interest Cover' and, if you want to express it as a formula, it looks like this:

$$Interest\ Cover = Operating\ Profit\ /\ Net\ interest\ Cost$$

Net interest cost is the total amount of interest paid on any debt, less the interest received on any cash (or short-term investments) that the company might be holding. (Your net interest cost would be the amount of money you pay out on your mortgage, credit card and any personal loans each month minus all the interest you receive on the cash in your deposit account, any National Savings certificates you own or what have you.) It's the figure that we subtracted from the operating profit to give us the profit before tax. Interest cover of more than about 10 means that a company can pay the interest on its debt more than ten times over, which is easily comfortable enough. Interest cover begins to concern us when it drops to below 5 or so. Less than this should certainly make you ask a few questions. For companies with very reliable and steady sources of income, it might be OK but, on the whole, it's probably best to stay clear.

6. Have they been a success up until now?

Success breeds success. While past success doesn't correlate infallibly with future success, it is an important indicator. It may be pretty Foolish of us to assert this in a world where ubiquitous legal disclaimers reinforce the idea that past performance is no guarantor of future performance, but we're going to do just that.

Any company that comes into consideration as an Obviously Great Investment should have been a success for many years, and that success will have carved them dominant industry positions which even further ensure their future success. As we have said before, business success, over the long term, will translate into share price success. If we have found an Obviously Great Investment, then it should, almost always, have a good track record of long-term share price growth. It's worth looking at several different time periods. Start by looking at the share price performance over the last ten years or even longer. Ideally, the share price will have grown steadily over the period but, the stock market being what it is, there will be plenty of ups and downs along the way. Although a ten-year price history is preferable, a five-year (or even shorter) period might be relevant where a company has changed greatly in the recent past or where it has only recently listed its shares on the stock market. However, you should always be wary of placing too much emphasis on short-term stock market movements.

The Internet is a good source of information on this type of thing. If you have a look at Appendix 5, you'll see a list of financial Web sites that provide this sort of information. The best ones will automatically give you a chart showing a share's price history over various periods. The Motley Fool Web site will do this for you and, naturally, we'd love it if you came over to our site and had a look. Try some of the other sites too, though, to see what they offer. Just don't forget to come back!

Basically, you're looking for long-term share price growth of about 10 per cent or more per year, on average. If the future were to continue in the same vein, then with our two or three extra per cent a year from dividends, we'd be doing pretty nicely.

Obviously Great Investments from the First Edition

With all this in mind, let's now see if we can apply it to some actual companies. To start with, we can have a look at the companies which, we felt, met our criteria in the first edition of this book back in 1998 to see how they've done. They're set out in the following table.

Taken as a group, then, our obvious greats have done us pretty well, rising by an average of nearly 29 per cent against the FTSE All Share, which has risen only 10 per cent. This average performance of 29 per cent includes, as you'd expect, a wide range of individual performances. These range from fantastic in the case of Ericsson to frankly dismal in the case of Rentokil and it all serves to underline what we said earlier about spreading your investments over a number of different companies.

Company	Price on 1/6/98	Price on 1/6/00	Gain/Loss %
Unilever	670.4p	440p	−34.4
Marks & Spencer	549p	261p	−52.5
Microsoft	$41⅞	$64⁹⁄₁₆	+54.2
Vodafone AirTouch	137.6p	315p	+128.9
Ericsson	$6²⁹⁄₃₂	$21¾	+214.9
Glaxo	1638p	1910p	+16.6
SmithKline Beecham	655p	856p	+30.7
AstraZeneca	2545p	2895p	+13.8
Pizza Express	855p	686.5p	−19.7
Rentokil Initial	418.5p	150p	−64.2
Average			+28.8
FTSE All Share			+10.0

In any event, as you'll have gathered, we'd be the first to say that share price performance isn't very relevant over a period as short as two years. We are still at the stage when what's fashionable will have a greater effect on the share prices than how the underlying business is actually performing. Over the long term, though, business performance will take over as the principal driver of the share prices. So, the question is, are we still happy with the long-term prospects of these companies? Do they still make Obviously Great Investments? Let's have a look at each of them in turn and see what has happened.

Unilever

Unilever owns some of the greatest consumer brands in the world. These include Colman's mustard, Bird's Eye fish fingers, Lipton teas, Domestos bleach, Persil and Omo washing powders, Vaseline care products and Calvin Klein fragrances to name a few. This is what we liked about the company two years ago and it still is. However, when we originally picked them, we had this to say about their margins:

> *To be honest, this isn't where Unilever shines. Over the last few years, before tax they've been making around 8 to 9 pence on every pound, but only about 5 pence after taxes. Yikes!*

and

> *OK, Unilever, rules are meant to be broken. We like your brands and your markets (everywhere), you are consistently profitable and well managed. Your kind of diverse, bulk consumer business is never going to have particularly high margins, but you are expanding aggressively into the huge untapped markets of the developing world. We'll let you squeak through, but we'll be watching your margins over the coming years like hawks. Y'hear?*

Well, we're pleased to be able to report good news on the margins front. Thanks to a process of cost-cutting and a concentration on their higher margin brands, the operating margin has ticked up to around 10 per cent. This is obviously a welcome trend. The process of developing the company's range of brands has continued with the acquisition of BestFoods, a US company, which brings with it such brands as Hellman's mayonnaise, Mazola corn oil and Knorr soups and sauces. All this consolidates Unilever's position as best in business and we're comfortable with the company's status as an obvious great, despite its recently disappointing share price performance.

Marks & Spencer

Marks & Spencer has had a rotten time since we picked them in 1998. Rotten, rotten, rotten. In fact, we'd say that it is an object lesson in what to do when an Obviously Great Investment becomes not so Obviously Great. You can't get it right all the time and if you no longer feel that a company fits the bill, then it's best to get rid of it and find something that does.

The troubles at M&S begin with cheap imports from overseas. In the past, it has benefitted from its policy of 'buying British', but these days it seems that the consumer is becoming more and more concerned about price and less concerned about where the product was made. This has led to extreme price competition on the high street and M&S has unfortunately suffered more than most. On top of this, the company stands accused of resting on its laurels. Many of its clothing selections have been criticized for being dull and, horror of horrors, bad value for money. This has generated a great deal of bad publicity for the company and its loyal customer base has undoubtedly lost some of its faith with a once outstanding brand. Whether or not it can fight its way back from this remains to be seen. Although we expect that it probably will eventually, we don't really see the point in staying around to find out when there are much more Obviously Great Investments elsewhere.

The company no longer matches up, so out it goes. Specifically, its one brand has been considerably weakened and it can no longer necessarily be described as best in its business. Indeed, the power in the overall clothes manufacture and retailing industry appears to have shifted away from the large retailers and towards the clothes designers. That is, if anyone can really be said to wield power in the industry. It seems to us that, more and more, the power is residing with the consumer.

Should we have been able to see this coming back in 1998? Well, with the benefit of plenty of hindsight, there probably were some signals that we should have picked up on. In particular, there were problems with buying and overstocking in the spring of that year. Of course, at the time, the company put these down as mere blips, but Obviously Great Investments shouldn't really have too much in the way of blips. If you see a blip, then wait until it goes away before buying into the company. Remember that we're looking for great companies which should continue to perform well. We are not looking for previously great companies which are now down on their luck and which might turn around. All in all, we'll keep our eye on Marks & Spencer in case things improve in the future but, at least for the time being, it's a case of thanks, but no thanks and a lesson well-learned.

Fare thee well, St Michael!

Microsoft

Since 1998 Microsoft's business has continued to go from strength to strength. It has managed to take its domination of the operating system market into the Internet browser market; and its range of applications software, such as Word and Excel, continues to rule the world. In fact the company has been doing so well that the US justice system has felt the need to intervene. Microsoft stands accused of abusing its strong market positions to undermine its competitors. Now many people would say, 'So what? Isn't this just what any company with a strong brand and market position would do? It's a free world, or at least it should be.' Others feel that Microsoft has behaved in such an underhand fashion that what it has done amounts to breaking a whole range of laws designed to prevent abuse of a monopoly position, and that's certainly the side on which the US Justice Department has come down. The debates at the Motley Fool's discussion boards have been somewhat heated, as you can imagine, especially on the US site but also the UK, and there has been a series of articles on the issue.

Anyway, whatever the rights and wrongs of all this, there is a certain amount of uncertainty attached to Microsoft. At the moment, it looks like the company may have to split itself in two, with the Windows operating system business going into one company and the application and Internet software business going into another. It seems pretty drastic, but you have to ask yourself whether this will make any real difference. The two new companies will still have very important, if not dominant, products and brands in a very attractive marketplace and there isn't much overlap between them. To our Foolish minds, the companies should be able to continue pretty much as before (although without some of the apparent market abuse that Microsoft stands accused of). In terms of defending its position, further problems might come if the computing world evolves away from the desktop computer, as has been suggested by some. Well it might, but there are millions of desktop PCs around the world and it seems hard to imagine that they'll disappear just like that. In any event, in the past Microsoft has shown itself to be quick to spot and capitalize on developing industry trends.

Despite all this uncertainty, we're very happy to stick it out with Microsoft since the problems aren't directly related to its underlying business, which, as we've said, continues to go from strength to strength. Why would we ever want to ditch a company that is being punished precisely because it is *too* successful?

Vodafone AirTouch

Vodafone is another company that has continued to perform well. By buying AirTouch in the United States and Mannesmann in Europe, it has further consolidated its position as the world's biggest, and we would say best, mobile network provider. The Vodafone brand, in a number of important markets around the world, remains almost synonomous with mobile telephony. Meanwhile, the wireless Internet is almost upon us. A recent industry report by the Strategis Group predicts that there will be 1 billion mobile subscribers around the world by 2004, and 'a substantial proportion of the phones sold that year' will have Internet and e-mail capabilities. Quite what people will be doing with these new toys is hard to say, but we're confident that they'll want to be doing something. And a lot of it. There is just so much scope for adding value to our lives by being connected, wherever we are and as much as we want, to the world's electronic neural network (that's the Internet, by the way). Vodafone, as the access point to all of this for a great many people (its various networks currently have about 60 million subscribers around the world), is exceptionally well placed to benefit, however the market develops.

In early 2000 the company paid £6 billion for one of five licences granting the right to run so-called third generation mobile telecommunications services in the UK, which will allow rates of data transfer (that means speed of access to Fools like us) faster than the fixed lines going into many offices today. There will be many more licences that it has to buy around the world and, no doubt, these will cost large sums as well. Some say they paid too much for the UK licence, others consider it a bargain. As the Internet-ophiles that we are, we'll err on the side of the latter opinion, although it's impossible to say for sure, of course. What is sure, though, is that Vodafone is committed to making the wireless Internet a success. As the people who will have a direct connection with the customer, selling them both access devices (aka Internet phones) and a subscription to the service, they have a good chance of dominating the industry. They're also not thinking along strict telecommunications company lines, which is important in such a dynamic market. One example of this is the joint venture they have set up with worldwide media group Vivendi, to run content services over the wireless Internet through an Internet portal to be known as Vizzavi.

Vodafone definitely stays IN.

Ericsson

Ericsson is another company involved with mobile phones. However, instead of operating the networks like Vodafone, Ericsson makes the phones and the actual network equipment that passes the data around. With Vodafone and other network operators currently bidding huge sums for new mobile licences around the world, they will be desperate for the companies that can provide, quickly and efficiently, the infrastructure to make the new networks work. If Vodafone is in a strong position because of its connection with the customer, Ericsson's position is strong because its equipment makes the whole mobile industry work. As a global leader in this field, Ericsson is in a very powerful position.

Putting all this together, Ericsson passes our first three tests comfortably. It has built a strong brand, it dominates the market for mobile network equipment and its lead, together with customers' immediate requirement for equipment, gives it the edge to defend its position. The only concern comes with the fourth test, 'Are they making a lot of money for their efforts?' The operating margin for 1999 was 8.2 per cent. On any basis that's not ideal, but it looks worse when we find that it has fallen from 11.2 per cent in 1997 and 10.4 per cent in 1998 (all this information is available on the company's Web site at **www.ericsson.com**). So, we should ask ourselves why the margin is low *and* falling. To answer this, we need to have a slightly closer look at the profit and loss account. First of all, we can see that it isn't directly the fault of price competition, since the gross margin has been healthy and steady at around 42 per cent. The place where the increasing costs come in is below this level, in operating expenses. Specifically, research and development and selling costs (which we presume to be dominated by marketing) have been increasing rapidly. We would say that for a company like Ericsson, whose markets are near the beginning of a rapid period of growth, this is not only to be expected and forgiven, but it is positively to be encouraged. We'd be far more worried if Ericsson was not taking steps to entrench its market positions.

We're confident that, because of the efforts that are being made now, the money will start to flow in when the markets become more established in a few years' time. If it doesn't, then that will be the time to be worrying about margins. For the time being, Ericsson appears to be doing everything right and that probably explains why the share price has been doing so well.

Glaxo Wellcome, SmithKline Beecham and Zeneca

Well, it's all been happening in the drugs industry. Zeneca has merged with Astra of Sweden to make AstraZeneca, and Glaxo Wellcome and SmithKline Beecham, after a false start, are finally planning to get together later this year. There are several reasons why these companies are merging. First of all, they can make their research and development ('R&D') more effective by sharing resources and cutting out overlapping work. There is also the potential to cut costs in the marketing and distribution of their drugs. Another advantage of being big is that the greater your range of products on sale and in development, the smoother your growth is likely to be.

These companies have some excellent brands, and although most of them aren't really what you'd call 'consumer brands', there's also a sense in which they are. If your life has been saved by Zantac (a Glaxo Wellcome drug), you're unlikely to want to switch (now that Zantac's patent protection has expired) to generic ranitidine, which is the same drug manufactured by someone else and much, much cheaper. That means you're going to kick up a stink when your GP tries to change you from one to the other and (s)he'll eventually give up. Although patents obviously do provide a protected revenue stream for the developing company in the early part of a drug's life, that revenue doesn't simply fade away when the drug comes off patent for the reasons just outlined. And it's not only patients who are emotional and a bit gullible. What about all that trash on your GP's desk? The drug companies spend millions marketing to doctors, who are highly susceptible to their blandishments. In terms of the future, the upcoming science of pharmacogenomics, which deals with the relationship between drugs and genes, holds tremendous promise, both for drug development and also, ultimately, for tailoring drug treatment to individuals.

No, nothing has happened in the last couple of years to take the gloss off these Obviously Great Investments and we'd be more than happy to keep them tucked away in our portfolio for the long term.

Pizza Express

After talking about such global giants as Microsoft, Vodafone and Glaxo Wellcome, it seems a bit odd, at first, to move on to Pizza Express. Let's have another look at whether it fits the criteria. First of all, does it have a strong brand? To this, global giant or not, we have to answer yes. Although the brand is, at present, mostly limited to the UK, it is undoubtedly strong here. Few people in the southeast have not heard of Pizza Express and most have tried their products. Penetration throughout the rest of the country is more limited, but the company appears to be succeeding in extending the brand into other regions without affecting its reputation for quality. What about best in business? Well, at the simplest level, that of pizza restaurants in the UK, Pizza Express stands head and shoulders above the competition. In fact, even if we extend this to include UK restaurants generally, Pizza Express comes out favourably as one of very few chains that give the impression of being masters of their own destiny.

The slightly awkward question for Pizza Express is revealed by the third test – is their position easily defended? Whether they can defend their position depends, primarily, on whether the consistency of the offering can be maintained as the brand is extended throughout the UK and overseas. In the UK the company has an exceptional track record in this respect and we're confident of continued success. However, the requirements of overseas markets are subtly different from the UK and it remains to be seen whether Pizza Express can take account of the differences whilst maintaining its reputation for quality. At the moment the signs are reasonably positive, with the business in Tokyo building up particularly well. However, we accept that this is one that needs watching quite closely and, if you're looking for investments that you can safely tuck away and not worry yourself about, then this might not be one of them.

On the financial criteria, Pizza Express does well. It is certainly making lots of money for its efforts, with operating margins exceeding 20 per cent for each of the last five years (in fact they've got steadily bigger, reaching 22.9 per cent in 1999). It carries very little debt, with interest cover in the year to June 1999 of just less than 100 times, and the share price grew strongly throughout most of the 1990s. Anyway, we'll be keeping an eye on the progress of the overseas operations but, for the moment, we're happy with the company's progress, despite a lacklustre share price performance over the last couple of years.

Rentokil Initial

Rentokil Initial is a 'services company' with activities that now extend well beyond its traditional pest control business. These include Hygiene and Cleaning, Plant and Distribution, and Security and Personnel. Along with Marks & Spencer, Rentokil is the other of our obvious greats to qualify for an unceremonious dumping. Although it still has a very strong brand and in many of its markets still deserves to be called best in business, we now feel that it falls down on the third test – is their position easily defended? In a sense, Rentokil has been a victim of its own success. It has made such a profitable business out of the kinds of services that it supplies that competitors have moved onto its patch. Brand alone has not been enough for Rentokil to sustain a pricing advantage and consequently its margins have suffered. Its growth, meanwhile, has fallen off dramatically and Sir Clive Thompson, the company's chairman, who was famously known in the City as 'Mr 20 per cent' for delivering year-on-year earnings growth of 20 per cent, has had to put up with much ribbing of late.

As with Marks & Spencer, the question to ask is whether we could have spotted this happening in advance. Again, the answer, with lashings of hindsight, is probably yes. The problem for Rentokil is that it is dependent on small businesses as customers for its services. These small businesses are not swayed too easily by a strong brand and they are naturally very keen to get full value for money. The services that Rentokil provides are not significantly better than can be provided by others and, as a result, when the competition moved in, there was nothing they could do but cut their own prices. The lesson that we learn from this is that, no matter how attractive a company appears now, you need to think carefully about whether it is likely to be able to fend off the competition effectively when it eventually arrives.

Back in 1998 we originally termed Rentokil a 'Less Obvious Obviously Great Investment' because we didn't think it struck the average punter immediately as obviously great, not least because it doesn't have much of a consumer brand. In retrospect, we should probably have termed Rentokil an 'Utterly Subterranean Obviously Great Investment'.

We'll return to Rentokil later in the chapter, but for now it's been struck off.

Show Us Some More Companies, Fools

Times have changed, the world has moved on since 1998 and we've had to chuck out a couple of our Obviously Greats. Let's take a look now at some more candidates for obvious greatness and see how they perform.

Diageo PLC

In the first edition, two years ago, we went through something called the Unilever Challenge, in which Foolish readers were invited to do a sweep of their local supermarket without picking up a single Unilever product. Not an easy task. This time, we could do something similar by inviting you to spend an evening in the pub without sampling a Diageo product. If you stuck to wine or beer, you'd have a chance (although you'd have to avoid Le Piat D'Or and Guinness), but if you went anywhere near the spirits, you'd be in trouble. Here, Diageo brands include Bell's, Johnnie Walker and J&B whiskies (as well as a range of single malts), Gilbey's, Gordon's and Tanqueray Gins, Smirnoff vodka and other little titbits such as Bailey's, Pimms and Malibu. (Feeling a bit squiffy yet?)

We eventually decided that, in the best interests of the health of our readers, it would be better not to suggest this sort of challenge, although we did have a trial run at one of the pubs round the corner from Fool HQ (it wasn't easy, we can tell you). Anyway, beyond this remarkable range of tipples, Diageo also boasts several excellent food brands, including Burger King (it's a question of taste, OK?), Green Giant and Häagen-Dazs. Quite typically, since we started thinking about Diageo's credentials as an Obvious Great, the company has announced a number of plans that will change its make-up considerably. First of all, the food businesses are on their way out. Burger King is expected to get its own stock market listing soon and, although Diageo will retain a large shareholding at first, the company has said that it expects to sell these shares in due course. The rest of the food businesses are to be merged with General Mills in the US and, again, it is expected that Diageo will sell its shares in the merged company over time. All this will leave just the spirits, wine and beer operations and the aim is that these will now be brought together into one unit, rather than the more disparate set of businesses that arrived when the company was born out of the merger of Guinness and Grand Metropolitan. We're very happy with these developments, since it was the booze that we wanted to get our hands on in the first place. The cash that is freed up by selling the food businesses should also put the company in a strong position to buy more drinks brands and further consolidate its contol over our inebriation.

Anyway, that's enough of a preamble, let's run 'em through the criteria.

1. Have they built a strong brand?

No prizes for getting this one right. Diageo passes this test with flying colours. It has an excellent range of world-class global brands which, in many cases, create a strong mental association with their product type (Guinness is the most obvious example of this, but several others – like Bell's, Gordon's and Häagen-Dazs – are not far behind). Although excessive repeat purchasing of these products may cause too serious a headache to create a strong feeling of trust with the consumer, it seems that many people just go ahead and repeat purchase anyway. Diageo is truly a king of brands.

2. Are they the best in their business?

After all the shuffling around that we mentioned above, Diageo will emerge as the largest drinks company in the world. Seagram and Allied Domecq are the closest competitors but, recently, Seagram has decided to merge its media interests with the French company Vivendi and, in their own words, the spirits, wines and beverages business will be a 'non-core' asset for the merged group. This is business-speak for saying that this part of the business is up for sale. Possible buyers include both Diageo and Allied Domecq, so it's a case of watch this space. Diageo also arguably dominates its entire industry in several products. Ask yourself whether a pub needs Guinness or whether Guinness needs a particular pub. We'd say that Guinness has become so popular now that many people will go to a pub simply because of the Guinness it serves. It could also be said that a supermarket would be playing a dangerous game if it chose not to stock some of the group's famous spirit brands.

3. Is their position easily defended?

The defence of Diageo's strong position really comes down to the strength of its brands. As we've said, some of the brands seem so strong that they dominate their industries. On top of this, there is plenty of repeat purchasing, point-of-sale marketing and, until the next morning anyway, plenty of opportunity to create a relationship of trust with the consumer. It certainly seems hard to imagine a world without Diageo's products and, with a fair amout of marketing spend, we're confident that they can carry on growing steadily.

Guinness appears to be so strong a brand these days that it has cultural connotations. In terms of its Irishness, it has reached an almost mythical level: people feel Irish just by drinking it. In the US, in particular, many people seem to like feeling Irish and yet Guinness's penetration there is still at a low level. So, if it's not a contradiction in terms, Guinness has both a wonderful brand, but also a relatively low penetration of the world's most important consumer market. This makes its market position easy to defend because it is coming from a relatively low position, but with excellent potential.

4. Are they making a lot of money for their efforts?

Diageo scores highly here as well. For the year ending 30 June 1999, the operating margin was 16.1 per cent. In 1998 it had also been 16.1 per cent and in 1997, it was 15.4 per cent. The small enhancement in margin from 1997 reflects cost savings following the merger of Guinness and Grand Metropolitan, and this should continue as the businesses are brought into one unit. Further margin improvement should come as a result of the sale of the food businesses, since that is a lower margin area of Diageo's current operations (in 1999, the operating margin in the food businesses was 12.7 per cent, whilst for beer it was 12.2 per cent and for spirits and wines it was 19.6 per cent).

5. Are they up to their eyebrows in debt?

Net interest payable by Diageo in the year ending 30 June 1999 was £324 million, compared to an operating profit of £1903 million, giving interest cover of just under six times. We'd say that this is just enough to be comfortable: especially since Diageo's flow of profits is pretty steady. All in all, we could hope for a bit better, but it's nothing to worry about.

6. Have they been a success up to now?

This is the one test that Diageo doesn't score highly on. Following the merger of Grand Metropolitan and Guinness in December 1997, the shares have risen from 552p to 575p, a rise of just 4 per cent. The FTSE All Share, meanwhile, has risen by 32 per cent. So we can safely say that our Wise friends in the City have not been set alight by the merger. Before this, both Guinness and Grand Met had been pretty steady performers over the years, with Guinness having a particularly good run more recently. It has to be said that the overall share price performance has hardly been scintillating, but it certainly hasn't been a disaster. In this category Diageo scores a C minus, but we're prepared to overlook this. The scores in the other tests have been good and, in any event, with the recent and proposed changes to the company's business, the historic share price performance tells us relatively little about Diageo's future.

To us, Diageo clearly looks like an Obviously Great Investment. Do you agree, Fools? We hope so, but if not, let's look at some others.

Tesco PLC

Over the last decade, Tesco has consistently shown itself to be the UK's top-performing retailer. Whether you're talking about loyalty cards or smaller inner-city stores, Tesco is always leading the way. Whenever there is another round of price cuts, Tesco always seems to get the good publicity for it. All in all, Tesco deserves great credit for developing from a 'stack 'em high, sell 'em cheap' retailing model to the premium brand it is today. With all this in mind, it doesn't seem surprising that Tesco is leading the way in Internet retailing, with the largest number of online sales of any grocery company in the world. In fact, Tesco has branched out from groceries and is using its brand to sell an increasing number of financial and other non-food products (such as videos and CDs) online.

1. Have they built a strong brand?

We'd say so. In particular, the brand seems to carry a great deal of trust with the consumer. People feel that Tesco is genuinely keen to serve them and they are happy to assume that the company is giving them as good a deal as they can. There are a couple of drawbacks, though, when compared to others. First of all, though it is an excellent brand in the UK, it is weak abroad. In this sense, there are similarities with Pizza Express. It's all very well for a company to dominate in the UK, but for growth to continue long into the future, it must, at some stage, launch itself successfully into overseas markets. There is evidence that it is already having some success in this, particularly in Eastern Europe, but the jury will remain out for some time yet. The second drawback is that it only really has one brand. It's a good one, but we've learnt from our experience with Marks & Spencer that relying on one brand only can be a bit dangerous. One brand has worked fine for other companies, though, including perhaps the Obviously Greatest Investment of all time: Coca-Cola. To sum up, it's fair to say that we love the Tesco brand, it makes us feel warm inside but, at the same time, we're ever so slightly nervous about it. On this basis, we'll be looking for a particularly strong performance in the other tests.

2. Are they the best in their business?

In the UK, Tesco is certainly the best in its business. Over the last ten years, it has passed Sainsbury to become the country's leading retailer (it now has total annual sales of more than £19 billion) and has always led from the front in terms of marketing initiatives. In the UK, Tesco comes as close to dominating its industry as a retailer can, with over 15 per cent of the UK grocery market. Companies need their products to be in Tesco's stores and only the very mighty suppliers, such as Unilever and Diageo, can hope to stand up to this.

The trouble is that we keep having to say 'in the UK' to qualify our remarks. On a global scale, Tesco comes a long way down the list, in seventh place in terms of market capitalization (remember this from Chapter 11?). The undoubted global leader is Wal-Mart which, at the time of writing, has a market capitalization of around £190 billion and sales of £110 billion. Through its purchase of Asda this giant has now entered the UK market. So, even on its home patch, Tesco's position is far from cut and dried. There are also some seriously big retailers in Europe, such as Carrefour (which has a market cap. of around £40 billion), which will make it very difficult for Tesco to expand into their space. While it seems that Tesco is the undoubted leader in its home market, with annual sales of around £19 billion, it is relatively small on the world stage and it even looks a little bit vulnerable here.

3. Is their position easily defended?

Well, Fools, we've probably already answered this in the first two tests. Tesco's position in the UK must be vulnerable, at the very least, following the arrival of Wal-Mart and overseas, they don't yet have much of a position to defend. Don't get us wrong, we like Tesco – the Motley Fool Staff Investment Club even owns a small slice of it – and we think that its position can be defended. But *easily* defended? Now that's another matter.

4. Are they making a lot of money for their efforts?

Unfortunately, Tesco doesn't do very well here either, with the operating margin for the last five years sticking resolutely in the 5 per cent to 6 per cent range. We have to give it a bit of leeway, because margins are naturally low for a retail company. In fact, a grocery retailer such as Tesco will sell many of their wares before they even pay their suppliers for them, which means they're getting most of their goods on credit. This is excellent for their cash flow and it makes up for a lot. Low margins really become a problem when a company has to have a great deal of stock (which it has paid for but not yet sold) lying around. So, excuses, excuses . . . We'd probably be prepared to let these margins slip by for a retailer if it really scored highly in the other tests, but the way things are going for Tesco, it doesn't look like we should be stretching the rules. Let's keep going.

5. Are they up to their eyebrows in debt?

Here Tesco gets a tick, with interest cover for the year ended 27 February 1999 running at ten times. Perfectly comfortable, especially for a company with such stable profits.

6. Have they been a success up to now?

Another tick. The shares have been deathly dull, but they have outperformed consistently and that, of course, is what we're after. In the ten years to 1 June 2000, the share price increased at an annual rate of 10.7 per cent and in the last five years the growth has been 15.5 per cent. These figures compare with growth in the FTSE All Share of 10.2 per cent and 13.3 per cent over ten and five years respectively. The company's good performance over this decade has therefore clearly not fallen on deaf ears among the suits and braces in the City.

So, Fools, we like Tesco, we think it's a good company and we wish it well. The trouble is that it just doesn't do well enough in the tests to be an Obviously Great Investment. In particular, it struggles when we ask ourselves how easily it can defend its position. It misses, but not by much. Fancy looking at some others?

ARM Holdings PLC

There we are, talking about megabrands such as Guinness and Tesco, when all of a sudden, out of the blue, we come up with something called ARM Holdings. Have you heard of ARM Holdings? We'd certainly forgive you if you hadn't, since we hadn't heard of it either until a few years ago. ARM designs microchips. In fact, it designs 'processor cores'. This is the bit of a computing system that executes instructions. You can think of it as being a bit like the brain. The first thing to note about this is that ARM doesn't actually make chips, it just designs them and leaves the sometimes awkward task of manufacturing them to others. We like this, because it is in designing things that the real value is added: manufacturing chips is a skilled business, but not half as creative or original as actually designing the things.

Where ARM excels is in the design of small, cheap, efficient processors that only need a little power to drive them and which do not get too warm while they're working. Currently, the most obvious place to find this type of chip is in mobile phones. ARM-designed chips are already found in around 70 per cent of new mobile phones and this is likely to rise as we expect more and more functions to deal with things like the mobile Internet. You'll also find these 'embedded processors' in places you wouldn't normally expect to find computers at all, such as in cars. Cars are being made with more and more chips on board, for things such as braking systems, air-bags, information displays, climate control and keyless entry, to name a few. By 2005 a low-end car is expected to have around ten computer chips on board, with a high-end model perhaps having as many as fifty. For these applications, ARM-designed chips offer an unrivalled balance of performance, cost and efficiency. As with mobile phones, ARM already has a large share of this market and this is only expected to increase. There are many other existing and potential markets – 'smartcards', video cameras, microwave ovens, anything where you need a little bit of computing power at a low cost and at low power. Many additional markets have been suggested, from talking toasters to computerized toothbrushes. We're inclined to leave these Arthur C. Clarke-type predictions to the experts and, so far as ARM's credentials as an Obviously Great Investment are concerned, we're happy to stick to the more obvious markets.

And now, having introduced them, let's run them through the sieve.

1. Have they built a strong brand?

This one gets a cautious yes. Although the brand is not well known to consumers, it has become a very strong brand among business customers. After designing a chip, ARM will enter into licensing agreements with customers, who will then set about manufacturing the chip according to the designs supplied. ARM generally receives a licensing fee for the original agreement and it will also stand to receive a small royalty for every chip sold. This can range from a few cents to a few dollars, depending on the particular chip and what it is expected to do (the average is thought to be around 10 cents per chip). Throughout the manufacturing process, ARM remains on hand to tweak the designs, or to offer any advice or help that might be needed. The company has been highly praised for this after-sales service and it has managed to build up some very strong relationships within the industry. ARM licensees certainly include the great and the good of the semiconductor manufacturing industry – Alcatel, Cirrus, Fujitsu, IBM, Intel, NEC, Panasonic, Philips, Samsung, Sharp, Sony, Texas Instruments, Toshiba and Yamaha are on the list, to name a few. It is also undoubtedly a global brand; just looking at that list of partners proves as much. There is clearly a strong element of repeat purchasing although, not being a consumer brand, this isn't such a benefit. Even so, the ongoing relationship with industry partners gives plenty of opportunity to develop trusted business relationships. ARM is particularly assiduous at developing what it terms its 'community' of licensees and developers. By providing a fertile environment in which ongoing development and integration of ARM products is taking place, it is creating a stronger brand, a further lock-in for its customers and a barrier for others attempting to enter the market.

2. Are they best in their business?

It's probably fair to say that ARM has almost created the specialist chip design market, with manufacturers, in the past, generally using their own designs. Several companies have now followed ARM's licensing model with a variety of specialist computer chips, but ARM remains by far and away the leader in the low-power processing chips that are expected to dominate the computing workload in mobile phones and cars.

ARM also dominates its industry. If a mobile phone manufaturer, say Nokia or Ericsson, wants their new phones to have all the fancy gizmos at a low cost and without drawing too much power from the battery, then they have little choice but to use an ARM-designed product.

3. Is their position easily defended?

As far as the current chip market is concerned, patents and licensing agreements mean that ARM doesn't so much have a moat around it as a raging torrent filled with ravenous crocodiles. However, for ARM to be an Obvious Great, we need to be confident that this position will last long into the future.

As far as this is concerned, the main risk to ARM is that another company might come along and design a new and better product. The challenge is therefore to keep its chip designs ahead of the competition. This is where the strength of its industry partnerships comes in. By working closely with the leading chip manufacturers, ARM keeps itself well informed as to what customers want and how its designs can be improved upon or used more effectively. The result of this is that although there is undoubtedly the risk of a revolutionary new design coming along at any minute the chances are more than fair that it will come from ARM itself.

We could worry that most of ARM's competitive advantage comes from the skills and creativity of its employees. What happens if they get enticed elsewhere? Enticed to – *gasp* – Microsoft? That's certainly a risk, but on the other hand if you are a leading professional in the leading company in the world in your area and you're well enough paid, why would you move? ARM has a good working environment, with highly motivated employees, so we're not too concerned about the staff running off.

A final risk to ARM's position comes from the fact that many of the anticipated markets for its chip designs are still in the early stages of development. There is therefore the possibility that they will develop more slowly than expected or that they will develop differently (for example, requiring a more powerful processor). Of course, there is also the chance that these markets will develop more quickly than is generally expected and we actually think this is more likely. Following the huge prices paid in the recent government auction of licences for the next generation of mobile phone networks, it seems that the big phone companies, such as Vodafone and BT, have a very strong incentive to get the market moving as quickly as possible. It brings us back to what we said earlier in this chapter about investors being afraid of the future. When they don't have hard data to go on, they tend to make an overly cautious assessment of things. ARM is not without risks but, given the potential for a better than expected performance, they are risks that we'd be more than happy to take.

4. Are they making a lot of money for their efforts?

Here, ARM gets a resounding yes. As a design company, ARM adds considerable value to its products and it is therefore no surprise to find in its 1999 accounts a gross margin of 84 per cent and an operating margin of 27 per cent. There are very few companies around the world that can beat this and it confirms the good work that the company is doing. On top of this, since an increasing amount of sales are coming through as royalty payments (requiring little or no capital to support them), most of the company's profits come through in the form of cash.

5. Are they up to their eyebrows in debt?

Well, they're not even up to their toenails in debt, because they have no debt. In fact, at the end of the 1999 financial year, the company had a pile of surplus cash lying around worth about £52 million. No problems here, then.

6. Have they been a success up to now?

If you think that ARM strolled through the last two tests, this one's even easier. ARM was set up in 1990 as a joint venture and, for most of the last ten years, the only way investors could easily get a sniff of it was by buying into Acorn Computers, its largest shareholder. Finally, ARM got its own listing in early 1998, since which time its shares have risen about fifteen times. This leaves things like the FTSE All Share standing. However you look at it, ARM has been one of the stock market's greatest success stories of recent years.

Even though ARM doesn't have an obvious consumer brand and even though there are a few risks, we feel that there are plenty of reasons to overlook these shortcomings. In particular, there are good reasons to expect the company's target markets to grow more quickly than most people allow themselves to anticipate, and there are equally good reasons to expect ARM to remain at the centre of this growth, making increasingly large amounts of money for many years to come.

ARM gets the thumbs-up as an Obviously Great Investment. Welcome to the fold.

H. J. Heinz Company

If ARM doesn't have a recognizable consumer brand, here's a company that certainly does. It's an American company, but that's never bothered us before (you can find out more about how you can buy shares in it in Chapter 19, 'Where Else to Invest'). When was the last time you had baked beans? Were they Heinz baked beans? When was the last time you had tomato ketchup? Was it Heinz tomato ketchup? If it wasn't then we're prepared to bet that, deep down, you'd rather wished it was. Try picturing a tin of baked beans or a bottle of tomato ketchup in your mind's eye. If you can't see that famous Heinz label, then we think you're probably cheating.

Not only is the brand strong, it's a solid repeat purchase brand (although we don't recommend too much repeat purchasing of the baked beans). The brand also receives a constant stream of free promotion through the bottles of ketchup often found lying around on the tables of smaller restaurants and in a myriad of other ways. It would certainly be hard to go for more than a few days without seeing the Heinz logo somewhere.

1. Have they built a strong brand?
You bet.

2. Are they the best in their business?
There are others that try to compete in Heinz's main market, but can you actually think of them? Most of the competition that we humble Fools come across is in the form of supermarkets' own brands, which doesn't add up to much. If you don't believe us, check the difference in price between a tin of Heinz baked beans and the own brand baked beans when you're next in the supermarket. Those few pennies are the extra amount that people are prepared to pay to buy Heinz products. If you can charge this much more for your products than your competitors, then you're best in the business.

Heinz also has a degree of industry dominance. If you run one of those small restaurants that has bottles of ketchup on the tables, then you stand a good chance of getting more customers in by associating yourself with the Heinz brand and having bottles of it sprinkled around your establishment. Similarly, if you're a supermarket: we're not saying that Heinz could hold Tesco to ransom, but Tesco could be making a dangerous mistake if it stopped stocking Heinz tomato ketchup.

If we look at the wider picture of food producers generally, then the competition hots up and companies like Unilever appear on the horizon. We're happy to overlook this, though, since in its most important brands, Heinz is best by a country mile.

3. Is their position easily defended?
For Heinz, as with Diageo, this comes down squarely on the strength of its brands. There's repeat purchasing, a relationship of trust with the consumer and a strong product association: all the elements that we like to see for a brand to keep the competition at bay. Can you really imagine a world without baked beans or tomato ketchup in thirty years' time? We can't. Can you really imagine a different leader in these markets in thirty years' time? Again, we just can't see it.

4. Are they making a lot of money for their efforts?
For the year ending April 1999, Heinz made a gross margin of 36.1 per cent and an operating margin of 11.9 per cent. In 1998, the figures were 38.0 per cent and 16.5 per cent and in 1997, they were 31.8 per cent and 8.1 per cent. The first thing to spot here is that the operating margins for the last three years have been all over the shop. So which one do we believe? Like most big companies these days, Heinz has its accounts available for free on its Web site

(**www.heinz.com**). We can find out a bit more about what's been happening to its profits and margins by looking a little more closely at these. Under 'fiscal results', in the overview, there is mention of a couple of restructuring projects called 'Operation Excel' and 'Project Millennia'. These restructurings, and the associated sales of businesses, have given rise to some exceptional (that is, hopefully one-off) items that have been deducted in reaching the figure for operating profit (actually, the Americans call it 'operating income'). These 'exceptionals' amount to a total cost of $562 million in 1997, a gain of $13 million in 1998 and a cost of $544 million in 1999. If you want to get the underlying picture of what is going on behind the scenes (that is, without these *hopefully* one-off costs) then you have to add these figures back to the operating income, before dividing by the sales to get your margin. So, the adjusted figures look like this (with figures in millions of dollars):

	1999	1998	1997
Sales	9,300	9,209	9,357
Operating Income	1,109	1,520	756
Exceptional Loss	544	−13*	562
Adjusted Operating Income	1,653	1,507	1,318
Adjusted Operating Margin	17.8%	16.4%	14.1%

*The exceptional loss in 1998 is negative since it is, in fact, an exceptional gain.

These 'adjusted' margins are pretty good and the fact that they're improving suggests that the restructuring is having a positive effect. There is another section in the accounts called 'Management's Discussion and Analysis' and this includes more information about the restructurings. There is a fair bit of information about both Operation Excel and Project Millennia and here are some snippets:

On Operation Excel

> *In Fiscal 1999, the company announced a transformative growth and restructuring initiative that is expected to generate in excess of $200 million in annual pretax savings and growth in earnings per share of 10 to 12 percent. The initiative, named 'Operation Excel', is a multi-year, multi-faceted program that will result in restructuring charges and implementation costs approaching $1.1 billion over four years . . . The major components of*

Operation Excel include: creating manufacturing centers of excellence; focusing the product portfolio; realigning the company's management teams; and investing in growth initiatives.

And on Project Millennia

During the fourth quarter of Fiscal 1997, the company announced a reorganization and restructuring program named 'Project Millennia'. The reorganization plan was designed to strengthen the company's core businesses and improve profitability and global growth. Key initiatives were focused on process changes and product line rationalizations.

Process change initiatives included:

- *Changing our go-to-market strategies, including the elimination of inefficient end-of-quarter trade promotion practices*
- *Outsourcing certain manufacturing operations and eliminating excess manufacturing capacity, while adding capacity for certain products to support product transfers from closed facilities*
- *Focusing the company's U.S. Weight Watchers classroom business and introducing a new weight loss program (1•2•3 Success™) in the U.S.*
- *Developing a Pan-European category-based strategy in Europe.*

Product line rationalization initiatives included:

- *Divestiture of the Ore-Ida frozen foodservice business*
- *Divestiture of the New Zealand ice cream business*
- *Divestiture of the Weight Watchers dry and refrigerated businesses*
- *Divestiture of the U.S. frozen pizza and pizza topping business*
- *Exiting the Weight Watchers Personal Cuisine business*
- *Exiting the 'dinner' product line from The Budget Gourmet business*
- *Converting all Weight Watchers entrées to the Smart Ones brand and reformulating the product and changing the packaging.*

What you make of all this public relations mumbo-jumbo is largely a matter of judgement, but keep in mind that the default position is that you don't invest your money. If you don't feel very confident about a company's future, then it's not an Obviously Great Investment. The very fact of these two major restructuring projects implies that things have not been going as well as they might have been. It's also a bit suspicious that the second was started hot on the heels of the first. Were things not working out? We will have to wait and see whether the initiatives end up having the desired effect. Until things are clearer then, unless you have very great faith in the company's brands to come good, it might well be worth waiting on the sidelines.

5. Are they up to their eyebrows in debt?

At April 1999 the company had outstanding debt amounting to about $3.3 billion. On this, they had to pay interest of $234 million. Given that the operating profit (after adding back the exceptional charges) was $1.65 billion, we can work out that the interest bill is 'covered' about seven times by the 'underlying' operating profit. So, although they're certainly not up to their eyebrows, they appear at least to be up to their ankles. Even if this level of cover is higher than for Diageo, it concerns us slightly more because of the restructurings that are taking place. These cause some uncertainty in the level of future profitability and thus cause us to be a bit more concerned about the level of debt. So, it's not ideal, but it's just about OK.

6. Have they been a success up to now?

Heinz has been around for 130 years and it's still chugging along, with a market capitalization of around $14 billion. However, the recent performance leaves a lot to be desired. Over ten years, the shares have provided annual growth of just 5.7 per cent against the S&P 500 return of 14.8 per cent. Over the last five years its performance has been even worse, with annual growth of 5.5 per cent compared with 22.1 per cent for the S&P. The uncertainties caused by the restructurings will certainly have played a large part in this.

Heinz is a good-looking company which might have been an Obviously Great Investment a few years ago, and it might be again in a few years' time. However, for the time being, we think that there are just a few too many question marks. We'll be keeping a close eye on it, though.

To Sum Up on Obvious Greats

With the notable exceptions of Marks & Spencer and Rentokil Initial, we're still pretty happy with the companies that we picked out as Obvious Greats in the first edition. On top of these, we'd add a couple more: Diageo, the drinks company, and ARM Holdings, the chip designer. Tesco hasn't quite made the grade, though we like the company, and Heinz might make the leap to obvious greatness in the future but, for the time being, there are a few too many uncertainties for us to feel truly happy.

We'll be watching the progress of the companies we've looked at here on our Web site over the coming years. Come and join us. It beats the hell out of watching 'Newsnight'.

The Six Obviously Not Great Qualities

As well as looking at a number of Obviously Great Investments in the first edition, we also looked at six companies that we felt were just as obviously *bad* investments. The results have been as follows:

Company	Price on 1/6/98	Price on 1/6/00	Gain/Loss %
BICC	166.5p	89.5p	−46.2
J Menzies	512p	346.5p	−32.3
Acatos and Hutcheson	237p	55p	−76.8
Hepworth	261.5p	200p	−25.5
Eurotunnel	74.5p	67.25p	−9.7
Laura Ashley	33.1p	17.25p	−47.9
Average			−39.7
FTSE All Share			+10.0

First of all we must, as ever, point out that it is still early days: two years isn't nearly enough to decide on how well an investment has performed. Having said that, we'll allow ourselves to add that we're nevertheless pleased to have steered clear of this collection of companies. Not a single one has risen and one or two have been positively awful. The reason that we picked these companies out is that they comprehensively failed one (or more) of our tests for greatness. In fact, they failed the tests so badly that, in our eyes, that made them Obviously Bad. So, let's have a look at the tests and see which companies so obviously miss the mark this time. Quite a few of them are still on the list from last time. We promise that this isn't because we're being lazy, it's just that they failed miserably last time and nothing very much has changed. There is at least one surprising new inclusion, though, just to keep things interesting.

No strong brand – Corus Group

If you don't have a strong brand, then you risk falling into the gloomy world of commodity products. These nasty things exist when there is nothing to differentiate one company's products from another's. The result is that all the sellers in a particular market compete with each other only on price. Not surprisingly, it's pretty tough for anyone to make much of a profit in these circumstances. Things like metals and cocoa beans are commodities and, unless you have some reason for thinking that your cocoa beans are so much better than everyone else's (which is unlikely), then you're probably on a hiding to nothing.

In the first edition, we used a company called BICC to demonstrate this point. BICC was a combination of cable-making businesses and the construction company Balfour Beatty. It was the cables businesses that really failed the brand test and, since these have now been sold, we thought a new example was in order. We can think of none better to make the point than Corus Group. Corus is the result of the 1999 merger of British Steel and Hoogovens, a steel producer from the Netherlands. As so often is the case in unattractive commodity markets, the merger was essentially a defensive measure. It cuts the number of competing companies by one and provides the merged company with 'economies of scale'. This just means that by putting the two companies together, some overlapping costs can be removed. The trouble is that you can't make a silk purse out of a sow's ear. Although the task might seem easier if you have a second sow's ear to play with, ultimately that's an illusion. Remember that we're looking for solid long-term growth and, however you view it, one-off cost savings won't give you this. Even after the merger, Corus is merely the fourth largest steel producer in Europe and the sixth largest in the world. It remains a company labouring in a competitive market with nothing to say for its products except that they're pretty much like everyone else's.

We'd say steer clear of commodity products and we'd steer well clear of Corus Group.

Not best in their business – Somerfield

In the first edition, we used John Menzies, the (sort of) newsagents, to make this point. Our complaint was that not only was it clearly not best in its business, but we didn't even feel very sure about what that business was. It seems that we weren't the only ones, since the company has now sold off its shops and is apparently concentrating on the business of distributing magazines and newpapers. Now we could just say that we didn't think it was best at this, but we really don't want to pick on them, so let's have a look at another example.

What about the food retailer Somerfield? Do you ever go there? If you do, you're in a minority, because the company only had a 6.2 per cent share of the UK grocery market in 1999 (according to figures from the research company IGD). This puts in fifth position behind Tesco (15.6 per cent), Sainsbury (11.8 per cent), Asda (8.9 per cent) and Safeway (7.4 per cent). Remember how concerned we were about Tesco's position as best in business when we considered it a few pages ago? Well, if we're worried about Tesco on this score, then Somerfield fails dismally. Scale is important in food retailing, as it can enable a company to get better deals from its suppliers and to get better value from its marketing. With Wal-Mart entering the UK market through its takeover of Asda, we wouldn't want to be in Somerfield's shoes. Of course, Somerfield may prove us wrong – after all, Tesco has had to climb the ladder to reach the top of the UK market – but we think the odds are heavily stacked against it.

Position not easily defended – Rentokil Initial

In case you haven't spotted it, this is the surprise new entrant in our list of companies to avoid. The reason it's a bit of a surprise is that, in the first edition of this book, we had it down as one of our Obvious Greats. Well, everyone makes mistakes and, in this regard, Fools are no different from anyone else. What we do like to think is that we're good at owning up to them and working out where we went wrong so that we might do a bit better next time. The lesson that we've learnt from Rentokil is that, no matter how good a company looks at the moment, it's of no use to you unless there is good reason to believe that it can defend its position and stay attractive – for decades.

Although the core factors that make an investment obviously great are firmly fixed, we're happy to tweak, from time to time, the tests that we use to find them. This is exactly what we've done here. This particular test, 'Is their position easily defended?' has been newly added to the list of criteria for an Obviously Great Investment as a direct response to Rentokil having slipped through the net before. Hopefully it will avoid similar occurences in the future.

We don't actually think that Rentokil is *that* bad, certainly not as bad as others on this particular list but, since it was the reason for us inserting this new test, we thought it only fair to use it as the prime example. So, we'll repeat what we said when we reviewed the company earlier in this chapter:

'The problem for Rentokil is that it is dependent on small businesses as customers for its services. These small businesses are not swayed too easily by a strong brand and they are naturally very keen to get full value for money. The services that Rentokil provides are not significantly better than can be provided by others and, as a result, when the competition moved in, there was nothing they could do but cut their own prices. The lesson that we learn from this is that, no matter how attractive a company appears now, you need to think carefully about whether it is likely to be able to fend off the competition effectively when it eventually arrives.'

So, Rentokil, we're really sorry for messing you around, but it's over, OK? Hopefully we can still be friends.

Not making a lot of money for their efforts – Acatos and Hutcheson

In the first edition of the book, we had this to say about Acatos and Hutcheson:

> *Margins dropping from 6 per cent to under 2 per cent over the last five years and heavy depreciation in earnings have not made this company a happy investment. Something, somewhere seems to have gone severely awry in edible oils and fats, the company's sphere of activity. There are always plenty of excuses for failure and in this case one of the main ones is delays in opening a new factory.*
>
> *One of the two brokers following the company rates them a buy as of early 1998, presumably on the basis that the long-awaited opening of their new facility will signal a turnaround. We prefer to let Acatos and Hutcheson's record speak for itself: today the shares are worth less than half what they were in 1987 and all this, if you remember, in the midst of one of the greatest bull markets in history. Whatever unfortunate blend of circumstances is cited for a company's poor performance, remember that nothing compels you to buy shares in that misfortune in the hope that shortly its luck will change. There are plenty of successful, market-beating companies out there – go buy them!*

Well, by halving between 1987 and 1998, the shares did quite a lot better than they have since 1998. Since then, they have halved and halved again. All this is presumably because poor old Acatos and Hutcheson (which, by the way, has now changed its name to Pura) is still struggling to make money. In fact, the low margins turned into losses for 1998 and 1999. Maybe they'll be able to turn the situation around but, then again, maybe not. We don't see any value in taking bets on the outcome.

Up to their eyebrows in debt – Eurotunnel

It took 150 years for them to get around to building the Channel Tunnel. It often seems like it'll take them another 150 for it to get out of debt. The company keeps rescheduling its debt and, eventually, it will probably be making enough money to pay the annual interest bill. When this will happen, though, is still anybody's guess. In fact, some people argue that the time has already come. The thing is, Fools, that if there is serious debate about whether a company's debt is actually covered or not by its profits or whether its debt pile is just getting bigger and bigger, then it is going to be a long way from being an Obviously Great Investment. In fact, if there is this much doubt about normally such a simple matter as a company's ongoing viability, then it would take much, much, braver Fools than us to go anywhere near it. If you want a flutter and you're bored of the horses, then have a go with Eurotunnel but we think that the time for it to be considered as a long-term investment is still some way away.

Not a success up to now – Rank Group PLC

Here, again, you can take your pick from a number of companies. In fact, many of the ones that we've already mentioned in this section wouldn't look out of place here. The thinking is simple. Good companies are generally good for a reason and, over the long term, this will (and will have) come out in the share price. If you find a company whose share price hasn't performed for years, then there's a good chance that there's something wrong with it. That doesn't mean that some investors won't make money from it: the share price goes up and down and some will be lucky. But we're looking for steady long-term growth and companies whose share prices have been yo-yoing steadily sideways, or worse still downwards, are not the best place to find it.

The company that we chose for this slot in the last edition of the book was Laura Ashley. Remember Laura Ashley? How could anyone forget? All those flowery skirts and curtains. Wonderful stuff in its day, but the company's disastrous performance (and the consequent disastrous performance of its share price) is a pretty clear indication that its day might have been and gone. It *might* make a comeback. In fact we're a pretty sentimental bunch and we'd rather like it if it did, but we're not going to be investing any of our money in the hope of it.

Rank Group is another classic example of this. It has a range of pretty interesting brands, including Mecca Bingo, Butlins and Hard Rock Café (would you believe that there are now over a hundred of these in thirty-six countries around the world?), but it looks like something's been going wrong, somewhere along the line. Having peaked at 545p in 1996, it's been pretty much one-way traffic since then and the shares have recently been finding new lows around the 140p mark. Over the years, the problems with Rank's performance have been attributed to any number of factors. For what it's worth, we'd say that it has to do with the heavy ongoing investment needed to keep their range of leisure assets looking spick and span. In the 1999 accounts, the Chairman stated that 'Capital expenditure, which peaked in 1999, is now being sharply curtailed, as the essential programme of asset modernization which began some two years ago was recently completed.' I'm afraid we consider this to be a touch optimistic. Wear and tear at places like Butlins is enormous and we'd expect this 'programme of asset modernization', which essentially just means maintenance, to be largely continuous.

Anyway, we don't really care what the problem is, although it can be instructive to think about it. The fact that the performance has been so dire demonstrates that there probably is a problem and, for that reason, we'll be focusing our attentions elsewhere. We suggest that you do too.

Buy What You Are

So, where do you look for your investments? We've already talked about buying what you know and it's hard to imagine getting much more Foolish than that. Buying shares in companies whose products and services you know to be worthwhile is an excellent start. As you become more engaged in the growth of your future wealth, however, you're going to find yourself looking more and more deeply at the way in which your own individual life is supported by the products around you. Look at what you use in your job, what your company produces, what your competitors produce, what you use in your leisure hours (you do have some, we hope), and what your family uses. If you're anything like us, you'll soon be saying to yourself: 'Hmm, this is a good product, but how would I market/manufacture/ advertise it better?' Say that to yourself about most of the products you use and you'll often come up with a great idea for how to do it better because you – the end user – are just the person to see the openings and opportunities that the company's management has overlooked. All you then have to do is send your idea off to the company, offering to enter negotiations for a licensing fee for your brainwave, sit back and let the royalties flood in. (Dream on.)

Occasionally, you'll find a product or service that you don't think can be bettered, one that is so expertly marketed and correctly targeted that you are speechless, dumbstruck with admiration. Congratulations! You have possibly just found a great investment. What you must now do is find out all you can about the company and crucially, whether it's publicly or privately owned. If it's privately owned, then tough luck: this company is going to have to go on your wish list, just in case it does one day decide to go public.

If it's a public company, then that's marvellous, but hold your horses, put the padlock back on your wallet, you have some *work* to do. First, you need their annual report and from there you want to know its history, what other products it produces, what future plans it has, its numbers (Is it growing? Is it profitable? What's its market cap?) and what other people think of it. Look up recent articles about it in the press and ask the company themselves to send you copies of any recent analysts' reports: these can be illuminating. In doing all this, you'll find that the Internet, if you have access to it, can be very useful. We've mentioned before that most companies have their accounts and a host of other useful information on their Web site. There are also a number of sites that provide financial commentaries on different markets and industry sectors and some that provide areas where you can discuss your ideas with others. There's a list of some of these sites in Appendix 5, but you do know which Web site's the best, don't you?

Anyway, after that brief commercial, let's get back to business. If you're convinced that the company you've found is the best thing since Mother's Pride, you believe its product fills a unique niche, it is expertly managed and it satisfies all the financial criteria you will have by now developed for a company you're prepared to invest in, then go ahead – put your money where your mouth is!

A(nother) word of warning, however. If you're looking at a small capitalization company, you're going to have to be much more canny and you'll have to keep a much closer eye on your investment than if you're simply choosing consumer giants of the type we've mostly been talking about here. Pizza Express is the closest to a smaller company share that we've mentioned (positively anyway) in this chapter, and you'll remember that we said we'd need to be keeping half an eye on it. As companies get smaller, then you'll probably need to spend more and more precious time keeping track of it. That said, there are real profits to be made in using the specialist knowledge you use in your daily life to invest in companies that reflect what **you are**, whether those are small growth companies or multinational conglomerates.

For now, though, congratulate yourself that you have successfully ploughed through the largest chapter in this book, take a break, stretch the legs and come back refreshed, bright-eyed and eager for the next chapter: The Foolish Operating Manual for Obviously Great Investments.

13

The Foolish Operating Manual for Obviously Great Investments

A Company for carrying on an undertaking of Great Advantage, but no one to know what it is.

— Anonymous. Company prospectus at the time of the South Sea Bubble in 1711, the greatest market crash there ever was

By now, our approach to selecting Obviously Great Investments is so deeply integrated into your soul that it is the work of just a few seconds to spot that the company quoted above doesn't quite fit the criteria. But before you go on to consider opening a brokerage account and actually *buying* some shares in your Obviously Great Investments, we'd like to run through what some of the advantages are to you of your Obviously Great Investment portfolio.

No Exhaustive Research

The most common reason people give for not investing their own money intelligently on their own behalf is lack of time. Everyone has enough time to invest in an index tracker and we would say that pretty well everyone has enough time to invest in Obviously Great Investments. Twelve hours a year, one hour a month. How much time did you spend watching television last week? One hour a month is easily within your grasp. We're not counting here, of course, the fact that you are doing your most basic company research every day as you toddle through the activities of daily life. As you become more attuned to this way of thinking, you'll find that every new product you use or pick up will raise a question mark in your mind. Is this a good product? Could I live without it? Who else provides it and do they do it better? *Does* anyone else provide it? And the crucial one: Might it be a good investment? One question we like to ask ourselves is, if *we* ran this company, how would *we* do it better? This can make a nice game for those long, tedious car journeys with the family. Either that, or they'll get so sick of you banging on about shares all the time that they'll murder you and leave your body in a lay-by. On second thoughts, be careful with this one.

The challenge for Obviously Great investors, and in fact any investor, is to sort out just which activities are crucial to your success, which aren't and then modify your actions accordingly. If you assemble the right model for choosing your investments, then you're not going to be flicking Teletext on every five minutes to catch the latest price, wading through reams of investment information and living, eating and breathing shares. What the FTSE does from one day to the next is totally irrelevant to you. You can be the anti-investor, the investor who doesn't watch the market slavishly. In fact, as long as the underlying business is good, you don't need to check on your companies more than once every month or so, perhaps even less. One of the posters at the Motley Fool's US site, a chap who signs himself Doubting Thomas, summed it up nicely when he wrote: 'In the end, I doubt that I'll look back on my life and remember the good times I had monitoring the price of a particular stock.' True enough. Investing is meant to support your ideals and dreams, not distract you from them. Despite what we've said about every minute of your life being a share research opportunity – we're tuned in to this stuff for many hours a day, so you'll have to excuse us – it will become clear to you that your challenge isn't actually to find hordes of new companies to research, or to scour the financial pages of the newspaper for investment opportunities. You won't need to subscribe to expensive newsletters, consider ten different industries and forty shares a year and try to make sense of it all. Instead, your successes will be determined by how well you can save money and how strong are the few businesses you've selected. If £1000 invested in Glaxo Wellcome shares thirty-five years ago is worth £773,000 today (and that's without taking into account all those lovely dividends that pile in twice a year), what lessons can we learn from that? Perhaps that finding just a few great companies and adding money to them each year will make for a smashingly successful investment career.

No Anxiety

Some people do genuinely believe that if they don't monitor the price of their shares twenty times every day, the company might go bust. It isn't so: staring at the screen willing your shares to go up isn't going to get you anywhere (sorry, Uri Geller, if you're reading this – you might be the exception). A friend of one of us also believes that if she doesn't concentrate every moment her flight is in the air, or if she presses down too hard with her knife and fork, it will immediately drop out of the sky. That isn't so either. The result? She takes a lot of trains and this despite the fact that trains carry *twice* the risk of aircraft, while getting there much less than half as quickly.

Obsessive checking of the share price is one thing, but what are we really, really worried about? Losing it all, of course. Everything. The lot.

'I'm sorry, darling, it's, it's . . . all gone! GONE! GONE!'

'Well, Quentin, it's your own fault and I'm afraid I shall have to leave you forthwith. I shall be taking the children and any remaining assets you have. I believe they make quite a fair wage selling the *Big Issue* these days. Farewell.'

You'll sob and tug at their coat-tails, but you'll be pushed aside, the children will be bundled into the car and the last you'll see of the little blighters is a pair of small, sad faces pressed up against the window. And all because you invested in the **stock market**! (For the full effect, you have to say this in a deep, Ben Elton-style voice, laden with dread. Try it and look around wide-eyed at the audience as you do so.)

OK, OK, this really is *not* going to happen. Well, all right, it *might* happen if you select terrible companies. What we hope to have pointed out here is that there are a lot of large, highly successful companies whose products you are probably familiar with from your everyday life and in whom you can easily invest. By sticking to things you know and understand as a consumer and picking large, quality companies to invest in over the long term, you are very unlikely to get into serious trouble. More than this, you're far more likely to see the value of your savings evaporate if you stick to the so-called risk-free investments of cash and gilts.

Finally, take a deep breath and go back to the 'Gospels of the Long-distance Investor' (see Chapter 4). The trend of shares is from the bottom left to the top right of the graph. There are blips and dips along the way, but if you selected quality companies or bought the whole market via an index tracker, a couple of sour market years are not going to hinder the long-term growth of your savings. There's no cause for stress if you take the market on your own terms. Let the short-term fluctuations horrify the rest of the investment world. You're in for the long haul.

No Foreign Languages

Here's a simple notion that works whenever you have your wallet, credit card, Switch card or brokerage account number and password handy: if you don't understand what you're hearing, walk away. In any big money transaction – from car buying to insurance to share purchases – if you can't explain entirely what you're doing, why you're doing it, and what to expect from it, don't make the investment.

So much in the traditional money world has been designed to confuse you. Before the birth of the Internet and the advent of Folly, investors using advisory brokers operated alone against corporate armies designed to extract the maximum amount of pounds from their wallet each year. For years now, your average financial salesperson has known that you are all alone, uneducated in financial matters and keen to just Get The Thing Signed. Many people we know have been so worn down by financial salespeople and so intimidated by the seeming complexity of the whole thing, that they've signed just to get rid of them so they don't have to think about it all any more: 'Look, Alan, it seems like a good idea. We'll sign, just as long as we don't lose and it's the right thing, we'll sign.' Then they often say, with a laugh: 'We trust you. We haven't got any choice, after all!' Wrong on both counts. They didn't really trust him because they didn't understand a word he said, and they did have a choice, but couldn't face going through the whole thing again.

Until you understand what you're doing, your money should be in the bank or building society walking in step with inflation. Speaking foreign languages to make money is not a fruitful long-term investment approach.

No Buy Points

There are really no buy points with these models – no magic moment when you *must* purchase your picks. The aim is to find a small group of the most financially sturdy, most profitable, best-performing, best of breed, strongest brand, most professionally-managed companies. When you find them, you can buy them and turn your eyes away from the stock market. There are other things in life and you have years, if not decades, to let the power of compounded returns work for you.

Now, if you buy and hold great shares, you will have successfully tiptoed through an industry buoyed by overpriced information and conveniently supportive jargon. Many Foolish investors believe that the most valuable financial resources out there are the ones that are free: the guides and books that sit in our public libraries, the rapidly increasing amount of information available on the Internet. With a dash of cogent research, a sprinkling of basic business principles and a heavy load of patience, investors needn't worry about what the present prices are of the shares in their portfolio.

In fact, the idea of buying 'low' and selling 'high' is essentially absurd for investors looking to make money over the next thirty years. For them, the better line is: buy intelligently, buy when you can and buy again when you have more cash you can put away for five years or more. Invest it into these cash-strong, well-managed, steadily growing, strong brand companies. And when a decade has passed, look for the next ten great companies – you'll probably find many of the same ten among them.

There are hundreds of varied and wonderful financial resources out there – expensive newsletters, hot tips in investing magazines, whisper columns in the daily newspapers, expensive computer software – all designed to tell you when precisely to BUY! and when to SELL! shares. These may be just the resources that will help you get *beaten* by the market. Once more, engage the market on your own terms and, in doing so, worry far less about the timing of your entry than the quality of your selections. Don't put off investing in a popular and successful company that looks overvalued. It will have been many times in the last ten years, and would always have been a good investment.

No Great Expense

Think back to the Miracle of Compound Interest. There we saw that costs of any kind can seriously eat into our returns. One of the easiest kinds of costs to accrue is that of frequent trading, with the consequent hits in terms of trading charges and tax that they imply. Unless you have a couple of hundred million pounds or more and are feeling generous towards stockbrokers, we don't think that furiously trading your selected investments is a good idea. Leave active trading to the unit trust managers: let them support the stockbrokers and let them underperform you and the market average as a result. Buying Obviously Great Investments is a play on market outperformance *and* minimizing associated costs.

It is fundamental to our investment methodology that you do not spend a great deal of money on research materials (The Motley Fool Online and many other resources on the Net are free), that you do not pay out large sums of money in commissions or taxes and that you do not end up paying significant opportunity costs – like missing a walk on the beach with your family next Saturday in order to stem the flow of losses from your options trading.

It's time now for a multiple choice question. As is usually the case, marks are deducted for a wrong answer, but this time a wrong answer will also cause the book to burst into flames. Good luck!

The investment philosophy of the Motley Fool may best be encapsulated by the following motto:

1   *Win at all costs!*
2   *Kill or be killed!*
3   *No guts, no glory!*
4   *No work without enduring profit.*

The answer, of course, is '4'. Unless you can show markedly improved returns by spending more time on investment, and unless you enjoy spending that additional time, a good blend of Obvious Greats and an index tracker are enough for the whole of your life.

A Caveat

In our urge to simplify matters, we are perhaps guilty of lumping together too many categories of investment under one roof. While we consider the above operating manual to be an excellent starting point, use it Foolishly, especially when investing in smaller capitalization companies. You might think that Pizza Express, or Pace Micro Technology, or Oxford Glycosciences are fantastic companies and you might be right, but you will have to keep a closer eye on them than you would, say, Unilever or Diageo. If you do wish to tuck away your investments and not look at them for a prolonged period, do not buy a smaller capitalization company, however tempting it may look. Settle instead for a nice spread of humongous, successful consumer giants. You won't be disappointed. And you won't lie awake at night worrying either.

And Finally . . .

If you're not psychologically prepared for the business of investing in shares, if you haven't rehearsed it in your mind for some time and even on paper, you may be setting yourself up for a long and painful fall. Investing profitably for the long term – a neat encapsulation of Foolishness, we think – is all about adopting an approach that is deeply contrary to the sentiments of most of us. Increasingly in our age, we have come to expect instant results and instant gratification. If something's boring us, then 'Zap!' goes the remote control again and we're on to something else. Don't like your kids/husband/wife/car? Trade 'em in! Don't like it here? Go there! Don't like it there? Come back! Doing that in the stock market will seriously damage your wealth. In 'A Foray Into Some Very foolish Futures' we saw how that kind of short-term approach to wealth accumulation can turn very sour very quickly.

Long-termism is a profitable investing creed, so read on for more of it in the next chapter.

14

The Ten Most Common Investing Mistakes

The man who makes no mistakes does not usually make anything.

— Edward John Phelps, Mansion House speech, 1889.

If you're the type who likes helpful restatements and summaries of the major portions of a book, read on. We are going to wind our way gently towards the close of this part with the ten most common investing mistakes we see people making as we wander through the online and offline worlds. There are other common ones besides these ten, but if we could all just prevent ourselves from making these, the world would be a much safer place to invest.

No. 1: Buying What You Don't Understand

Baptisms of fire are common in the stock market. Poll the investing public and you're likely to find that most of them didn't have a clue what they were buying when they made their first investments, and many of them still don't. Cousin Dennis, the chap who can't programme his video, he's starting a Web publishing business. 'Five thousand, that's all I need from start-up investors. It's a dead cert. No one's done this before. I'll double your money in six months.' And you what? You gave it to him?!

Or maybe a colleague at work has a hot tip on a biotechnology company, which he whispers to you over the coffee dispenser. 'Psst! Thunder-Box Biomedical. Hot new products. A new oscillo-proteinase inhibitor, goes like the clappers,' he says, talking in biotech-speak. 'Ripe to be bought out by one of the big pharmaceuticals, too. Get in now before the price hits the roof!' Uh-oh – you don't really understand a word of it, do you?

The pathway to superior investing is unfortunately littered with speculations in low-grade, cash-burning outfits, hyped to the heavens and with operations that are largely unfamiliar to their shareholders. But any investment that you don't understand is a mistake, even if it does beat the market for you. Allow us to make our point by going to an extreme. Would you buy Vodafone or ARM Holdings solely on the basis of what you have read here? Oh, you know the basis for our thoughts on these businesses and their great prospects for the next few decades. But hang on. We're just a bunch of Fools. Would it be particularly intelligent to rely solely on our ramblings when:

- you can come and discuss them with thousands of other investors (including ourselves for that matter) at the Motley Fool Online *right* now;
- you can phone them directly, ask for their latest company reports and any analysts' reports they happen to be giving out (for free), and run them past your investment club, mother or work colleagues for further insights;
- you can tap instantly and for free into the growing amount of information available about them over the Internet including, most likely, their own corporate Web site?

The salient point here is that the story of your epic journey into the world of savings and investing has as its antagonist anyone who tries to rush you. If you've found any useful investment principles in this book, read them again. Soak them up slow-w-w-ly. Get hold of one or two other books. Read them. Slow-w-w-ly. Becoming accustomed to this sort of approach and deliberation will benefit you as an investor; it's the direct opposite of what most people do, which is to rush to act quickly on the recommendations of others. And by 'others' we mean anybody or anything: an advisory stockbroker, an online investor, your lucky rabbit's foot, great-aunt Cicely in the middle of one of her winning streaks, or even the Chief Executive of the company in which you are about to invest.

You're responsible for your investments and so you had better verify any information or analysis you are presented with. Be canny, not gullible.

No. 2: Focusing on Your Short-term Performance

It's unfortunate that no matter how frequently the Miracle of Compound Interest is evoked, with the mightiest profits appearing at the far end of an investment life, some investors continue to believe that profits up front, profits *today*, are meaningful. Which is a shame. Because, in many cases, that impatience results in flawed logic, poor investments, frightful indigestion and pacing the floor after midnight.

It isn't worth it.

In Chapter 7, we quoted a section from Warren Buffett's 1997 Letter to Shareholders. We like it so much that we're going to repeat it:

> *A short quiz: If you plan to eat hamburgers throughout your life and are not a cattle producer, should you wish for higher or lower prices for beef? Likewise, if you are going to buy a car from time to time but are not an auto manufacturer, should you prefer higher or lower car prices? These questions, of course, answer themselves.*
>
> *But now for the final exam: if you expect to be a net saver during the next five years, should you hope for a higher or lower stock market during that period? Many investors get this one wrong. Even though they are going to be net buyers of stocks for many years to come, they are elated when stock prices rise and depressed when they fall. In effect, they rejoice because prices have risen for the 'hamburgers' they will soon be buying. This reaction makes no sense. Only those who will be sellers of equities in the near future should be happy at seeing stocks rise. Prospective purchasers should much prefer sinking prices.*

Most of us, for at least the five years to come, are going to be net purchasers of hamburgers, er, sorry, shares. So, if our investments fall in value, then that is a good thing, because it will allow us to purchase more shares that we value as long-term buys for lower prices. Our existing long-term holds may have fallen slightly in value, but it doesn't matter.

Remember that 20 per cent of £1000 is £200. And 20 per cent of £100,000 is £20,000. As time expands your base of capital, each later year of growth will provide substantially more profits. Let's hark back to Anne Scheiber, the American lawyer who started with $5000 in 1944. Back then she earned less than $1000 per year. By the time she died in the mid-90s, she was earning more than $500,000 in dividends alone and an average market year brought in more than $2 million in paper gains.

It's the tomorrows that build wealth, not the frenetic activity of the todays. What your portfolio does in the coming week is several orders of magnitude less important than what it does between the years 2005 and 2010, or better yet, 2015 and 2020. To buy and sell your shares on the back of short-term market fluctuations will mortally wound your wallet as you try to predict which way the dice is going to roll next. The trading commissions will eat into your profits and you'll become one of those sad, skeletal souls who dances to the tune of a share pager which bleeps whenever your chosen shares move more than a specified amount. Can you afford to let yourself exist on this level, a level which can only be sustained by frequent injections of caffeine, adrenalin and whisky? We say: '*Nyet!*'

Truly, Fools: 'Lift thine eyes from the dust of the short term, up, up unto the Heavens and regard the glory that is the long-term panorama!'

No. 3: Finding Yourself Becoming Enduringly Bearish

Bears, bulls – do you know them? Bears think the glass is half-empty, bulls think it's half-full. Bears think the sky is perpetually poised to fall on their investing heads, bulls fall headlong over their own two feet in their rush to invest *NOW* in this amazing market that is going to be climbing to the skies for ever. Don't miss it!

Moderation, the Middle Way. Whatever you want to call it, a long-term investor can't live without it. Excessive bearishness, though, as much as excessive bullishness, will injure your investment returns. Possibly, it will injure them mortally. There is, you see, no 'right' time to invest, no point at which the economic signs, the market sentiment and the pattern of goose entrails all come together to give you the green light. In a rising market, well, things are looking overvalued and the market may just be on the point of crashing. You'd look pretty stupid, wouldn't you, if you invested now? Best just to wait a bit. In a falling market, you're never quite sure how far it's going to fall. I mean, it might just keep going down and there's no sense in buying something that is *decreasing* in value. That would just be stupid! Then the trough comes and you're a whisker too late and the market's climbing again. You missed it, but maybe this is only a temporary rally. A friend of yours who likes to look at charts of share prices has said that this is a classical 'Double nelly, triple salco' appearance in the star – oops, FTSE 100 – chart and signifies another impending downturn. And then you decide he's wrong and that the market is on the way back up, but now you're aching at having missed your chance earlier on and . . .

And so it goes on. It's a disease. You can never be a perfect parent, only a 'good enough' parent, and so it is with investing. No one, not even Warren Buffett, can invest without regrets. They are part of the game, and trying to invest without incurring any will not move you forward. Repeat to yourself your Foolish mantra: since 1918 the London stock market has provided an annual return of 12.3 per cent on average. It has, on average, doubled investors' money every six years. Why now, at a time when our economy is growing ever faster and being propelled forward by the wonderful new technologies of our Age, should this precedent suddenly be shattered? There's no real reason why it should be. In any event, even if the returns from shares are lower over the next few decades, the evidence is overwhelming that the returns from other forms of investment are likely to lower still. Just recognize that you don't need to get it perfectly right or perfectly timed to come out the other end clutching a profit.

Remember that you are now a card-carrying contrarian. In fact, you won't be disappointed if you buy and six months later things start tumbling down, because you're a regular saver and you *like* bear markets. They give you the opportunity to pick up even more great businesses at bargain prices, or even to buy the whole market at a bargain price by sinking more of your funds into an index tracker. What a terrific business this all is!

Don't be a bear. Instead, be a 'good enough' investor, a long-term, patient bull, for this, history tells us, is the true nature of the market.

No. 4: Believing the Financial Press Is Expert

Do financial advisers have *your* best interests at heart? Is every fibre of their being dedicated to *your* long-term enrichment? Do financial journalists go to bed at night wondering if they have done the best they can by investors that day? The answer, by now, is obvious. So, what sells newspapers and gains television viewers? If you said 'Alarm, despondency, froth, short-termism', you wouldn't be far off the mark. It isn't often that you see the true power of Brother Time and Sister Logic played up in the financial press. To date, the media has shown little interest in speaking to the patient private investors who tuck money away into shares and hold them for decades. Not that there is much to say to them and that is partly the point. In the media's race to present (or design) the latest controversy and in its obsession with *today*, the business press largely ignores the variable of time. The great self-sufficient investors haven't created their wealth over the last forty years by buying on the rumour and selling on the news. They buy on the research, their own research, and often don't sell. At an investors' conference in 1997, an elderly gentleman talked with us about his decades of investing, chuckling that it seemed like everyone from investment firm to financial newspaper had tried to rock him out of his position in

Schering-Plough, one of the leading US drug companies over the past forty years. 'And, thank God, I ignored them all and held straight through.'

Thank God, indeed. He made $7 million out of that investment.

It's controversy and disaster that sell in the media business. Train crashes and terrorist bombs, estranged celebrity couples and ethnic cleansing, and . . . the collapse of the stock market. The editing process at most newspapers is heavily biased in favour of matters catastrophic.

When we return once more to Warren Buffett, who claims not to read financial papers, we're reminded of what matters. Private investors have quietly and methodically grown their savings for decades. No, they aren't half as exciting as the collapse of Barings Bank or (*sigh*) the next market collapse, so they don't often gain coverage from the press. But they do seem to be making a good deal of money this century.

Now, none of this is to imply that the market won't lean this way and that, that it won't crumble again, perhaps even soon. At some point, it will. But the average investor (median age of 34) has four decades ahead in which to invest. Whether the market drops by 30 per cent tomorrow is of supreme *inconsequence* to most individuals. Regrettably, that decline is of supreme *consequence* to the financial media, on the look-out for casualties and collision. And therein lies the inversion of interests, pitting patient reader against desperate writer. In a world where learning was prized over controversy, those financial papers whose currency is hype might become worth reading. We're not quite there yet.

No. 5: Concentrating Your Attention On Share Price

One of the frequent mistakes of the novice investor is to be overly preoccupied with share prices. Our first inclination as investors is to believe that a share trading for 150p is less expensive and holds greater potential for reward than one trading at 1500p. Seems reasonable, doesn't it? After all, we've been buying products all our lives and things that have a lower price are cheaper. Simple.

Unfortunately, this principle doesn't hold when it comes to the stock market. A share price in and of itself is meaningless. Oscar Wilde is, as he is so often, on the side of the Fools: 'Nowadays people know the price of everything and the value of nothing.'

What is the total value of a business? Let us hark back to Chapter 11, 'A Share Primer', and reiterate that the total value of a company equals the number of shares times the price of those shares. Thus, if Alan's Aardvark Adventures PLC has 100 million shares, each priced at 150p, the company is valued at £150 million (150p x 100 million = £150 million). And Ethelred's Elephant Enterprises PLC, with 5 million shares trading at 1500p a share, is priced at £75 million. In this case, the 1500p share represents a lower-priced company than the 150p share. The cheapness of a share depends on the total value of a company, not whether it is trading at 150p or 1500p.

To combat the tendency to focus on share price, imagine that all of the shares in your portfolio were trading at 1000p a share. Further, imagine that every share on the market were trading at that price. Now, which companies would you invest in? Would you buy that tin-cup-waving, self-promotional Caspian Sea oil driller, or would you buy Diageo? Would you become an owner of debt-crippled Eurotunnel or would you buy an ownership position in debt-light Glaxo Wellcome?

Shield from view the daily to-ing and fro-ing of share pricing and you will naturally bear down more rigorously on the businesses you are buying. In doing so, you will have avoided our fifth giant investing miscue. Now, on to number six.

No. 6: Buying Penny Shares

'The exception proves the rule.'

It would be so appropriate to quote this pithy saying now, as we move swiftly from telling you that share price doesn't matter to telling you that in some ways it matters a great deal. We'd love to quote it, but the fact is it's a nonsense. 'Proves' in this context has the same meaning as 'tests', as in 'proving ground'. The exception 'tests' the rule. Doesn't make sense, does it? How did this happen? How did the meaning of this ubiquitous phrase become so distorted over the years? All will be revealed in the forthcoming *Motley Fool Guide to Life*, *Loving and Comparative Etymology*. Until then, tingle at the mystery that is the English language and reflect that the following statement is indeed true:

Penny shares *will* seriously damage your wealth.

Penny shares refers to shares whose price can be measured in multiples of just a few pence and whose market capitalization can usually be measured in just a few million pounds. When companies go public, they often don't do so with an initial share price measured in multiples of just a few pence. Companies whose shares trade in pennies have often *earned* their way to the bottom of the heap.

If a share trades at 8p, then an increase in price to just 10p is a 25 per cent gain, a far easier move, you might think, for a share to make than, say, from 1000p to 1250p. 'Penny shares offer quick and easy profits.' Newsletters exist and prosper on this principle and purport to guide the naïve investor into stunning profits by offering tips on which penny shares to buy. Fellow Fools, if it were so simple, we wouldn't be writing this book and if you wanted to contact us, you'd be dialling the country code for the Seychelles first. Briefly, the rub is:

- Since the number of shares in the marketplace is so small and the amount of solid news so scanty, hype and rumour are likely to be the biggest motivators of penny share price movements.
- The small number of available shares can make them exceedingly difficult to buy or sell – remember every purchase or sale requires another party to complete the transaction. The technical term is that these shares are *illiquid*.
- The spread between buying and selling prices (the 'bid-offer spread') can be so large as to rub out any potential profits.
- Whereas the share price of Glaxo Wellcome or Unilever will never fall to zero and is highly unlikely ever to be cut in four, this kind of thing is not just possible, it is *likely* with penny shares.

There are no consistent, long-term profits to be made in penny shares. If you like to throw away money on the roulette wheel, then penny shares are for you. Our bet, though, is that if you've invested weeks of unrelenting misery to get thus far through the book, you're not the Johnny-Go-Lightly, betting type.

So, what exactly *is* a penny share? Where is the cut-off? How do you decide by price alone what is a volatile, unpredictable investment, more likely to end in tears than not and, importantly, how do you make sure you don't also end up excluding some great, up-and-coming companies with a novel product or an original idea? It's a tricky question to which there is no right answer and in the early days of the Fool UK we had quite a long discussion on this topic on our online message boards. We use the following criteria when deciding whether we are prepared to consider a company as an investment prospect:

> *Share price greater than 50p*
> *Market capitalization greater than £30 million*

Some will think this too high, perhaps others will think it too low, but it's a level at which we feel comfortable. Don't worry if you don't agree with us precisely. As long as you're discussing just where the cut-off point should be set and not the whiz-bang investment opportunities that penny shares offer, you've got the right attitude.

Having avoided six potentially fatal errors, you're in pretty good shape, but look what else is waiting to drag you down into investment hell . . .

No. 7: Not Tracking Your Investment Returns

With the Internet and with a variety of software packages available, tracking the performance of your investments is easier than ever before. If you type in your investments, then the Internet will do the rest for you, updating continuously to show you how things are going. As we've said before, you shouldn't spend all day following their movements (again, unless you're Uri Geller), but you should make a point of checking from time to time to see how you're doing both overall and against the market average. How have your 'Obviously Greats' performed over the past two years? Has your strategy to buy ownership positions in predominantly small technology companies proven fruitful? Is your financial adviser beating the market, after the deduction of all management fees?

Not knowing whether your investments are thriving or barely surviving from year to year is somewhat akin to not knowing how your favourite football team is doing, or worse: how your children are doing at school, or how old you are. The process of checking your portfolio's performance against the stock market should be painless . . . nay, joyous.

Too many investors don't know how their savings did in 1996 or in 1997 or over the past decade. There are entire investment clubs that perform wonderful research, do a top-notch job with analysis and yet, at year end, don't know how their investments have performed relative to the Footsie. Much as we enjoy the process of researching businesses and investing, measuring performance is critical. And in too many instances, our lack of attentiveness to the numbers brings good humour to the financial services industry. Not just a few unit trusts have run advertisements that read, '1995 was a great year. Our fund rose 26 per cent!' This in a year when the market climbed 35 per cent. The investor tracking returns knew to sell off that unit trust for promoting its own mediocrity.

No. 8: Not Diversifying Your Portfolio

There is a lot of discussion about how much diversification a portfolio needs. Without going into the ins and outs, the general view is that investing in somewhere between ten and fifteen different companies should be enough. Fewer than ten holdings leaves you a bit too exposed to one or two (or perhaps more) of them going wrong, whereas more than fifteen doesn't really do much to reduce your risks, but it might well increase your costs and make it harder for you to keep track of what's going on. Of course, if you got up as high as, say, thirty shares or more, it would be very hard to beat the market average (because your portfolio would now be close to mimicking it) and you'd have to ask whether you might be better off (because of things like costs) just going for an index tracker.

Don't forget, though, that buying shares in, say, twelve different companies won't spread your risk much if they're all in the same industry sector and subject to the same economic forces. You need a range of different business types. A football team is unlikely to win many matches if it is made up entirely of strikers, unless, by some freak of chance, the entire game happens to be played out in the opposition's penalty box. Instead, you need to pick a team that will cope, as well as possible, with the whole range of circumstances which might come your way, both in attack and defence. The same goes for shares – you need to build a portfolio that isn't dependent on things turning out a certain way.

Similarly, there's not much point in having twelve different shareholdings if you put £1000 in eleven of them and £11,000 in the twelfth. This twelfth company would make up 50 per cent of your portfolio and it would be more like having only two shares. Over time, some of your shares will do better than others and, gradually, one might grow to make up an uncomfortably large portion of your portfolio. You'll therefore need to sell a bit to reduce it, perhaps investing more in one of the others, or in a totally new company that you like the look of. When to do this is largely a personal matter. It has to do with how you feel about risk and taking into account the costs of making the changes. If you consistently tinkered with the holdings in your portfolio so that they remained in constant alignment, you'd end up, through dealing commission, giving the bulk of your portfolio to your stockbroker. Our recommendation is that portfolios of greater than £10,000 never have more than 15 per cent of their capital initially invested in any one share. From there, we recommend that you start to think about lightening any holdings that grow to become more than about 25 per cent of your total portfolio. Let's walk through a brief example, with a £20,000 portfolio. First, you would never invest more than £3000, or 15 per cent, in any one company. Then imagine that your portfolio took this shape two years hence:

Purchased	Number of shares	Security	In at	Now	Value
May 1998	3370	Alfie's Chip Shops	89.00	402.00	£13,547.40
Nov. 1997	450	Soup and Snails	578.00	848.00	£3816.00
May 1997	850	Happy Holidays	220.00	401.00	£3408.50
Jan. 1997	900	Eileen's Cakeshop	278.00	343.00	£3087.00
May 1995	450	New World Mining	330.00	555.00	£2497.50
Aug. 1998	550	Shaving Kits	490.00	318.00	£1749.00
Aug. 1997	2900	Pronto Pilchards	100.00	49.00	£1421.00
April 1998	1200	Motley Fool UK	250.00	68.00	£816.00
				TOTAL:	£30,342.40

In this scenario, you'll see that although no initial investment exceeded 15 per cent, one of our holdings has exploded. Alfie's Chip Shops has more than quadrupled; our holding in Alfie's has swollen to over 40 per cent of the total value of our account. Red lights should flash here. The portfolio has become overweighted in one direction. It's time to slack off on Alfie's, even though it's been our top performer. Before leaving this section, did you notice the shaggiest, smelliest, wettest dog in our portfolio? Yikes!

No. 9: Not Being Online

The financial story of the past few years has most certainly been the growth in activity on the Internet. Investors from across the planet are tapping into a network of resources that dramatically outdoes the amount of information available via any other medium.

The Motley Fool UK (**www.fool.co.uk**) services conversations between stockbrokers, analysts, consumers and private investors far removed from the City. In a few short years, we have gone from a world where only the wealthiest individuals and the largest institutional investors could gain access to valuable information and research. Today, the beginner investor with a personal computer and a modem can click into ongoing conversations about personal finance, business and investing that are educational and inclusive.

It is a profound mistake for anyone with access to the Internet – either at home, school, or via a local library – not to take advantage of the resources and the opportunities to have your individual questions answered online. A mass conversation about savings and investing is occurring even as you flip through these pages. And it's a discussion that is changing the way the money world works, an ongoing transformation that greatly works in favour of the individual.

As consumers band together and negotiate with the big boys on a far more level playing field, the balance of financial power is shifting. If you can access the Internet, you should give Fooldom a whirl, as well as a number of other financial sites which we have detailed in Appendix 5, 'Useful Web sites'. Rather than learning by passively reading, you can, with your networked computer, learn through co-operative endeavour.

No. 10: Spending Far Too Much Time on Investing

It seems only right that we close down our investing don'ts with a recognition that many of us fall into the trap of dedicating too much time to money management. If this notion seems ludicrous to you today, don't be surprised if in three years you systematically check your shares each morning and find yourself in regular conversations about the prospects of JJB Sports and the future market for Manchester United football shirts with your athletically challenged third cousin Rupert.

Studying businesses, becoming a part-owner of enterprises, and talking about your smartest and dumbest investments is actually a great deal of fun. The very brightest among us find ways to involve ourselves just enough to wallop the market's average returns, to learn much from the ongoing investigation, but never (or rarely) to compromise the other joys of life – grandchildren, a picnic lunch, handling the wheel of a sixty-year-old MG, sleeping until lunchtime one Tuesday in April.

Very few investors completely avoid at least one period in their life when they spend too much time thinking about their money, when they become consumed by their savings growth. In the very dreariest of scenarios, some even take to trading shares each day, while passing the daylight hours in torn pyjamas, bathed in the unearthly glow of a computer monitor, blindly reaching to their left and unknowingly eating a two-week-old tuna sandwich off the wrong plate. Although we find it hard to imagine a scenario where this sort of trader makes money and beats the market, even so, can you imagine this sort of living? Can you imagine eating that sandwich? Can you imagine that taste going unnoticed?

As captivating as the market can be, as much fun as the whole process of saving and investing is, verily it does not take the place of living. The blend of online services, the study of business and market-beating investing has proved nearly irresistible for some. Take heed, though, at the words of W. H. Davies in his poem 'Leisure' of 1911:

> *What is this life if, full of care,*
> *We have no time to stand and stare.*

What You've (Maybe) Already Got

It is the folly of the world, constantly, which confounds its wisdom.
— Oliver Wendell Holmes, *The Professor at the Breakfast Table*

The first step into the world of investing, for most people, is some form of product created and managed by a financial services company. This section of the book is dedicated to the most common of these, sometimes very peculiar, animals. We'll start by taking a lively stroll (we wish) through the confusing and sometimes dangerous world of pensions, then we'll leap across the disturbing abyss of endowments before arriving, safely we hope, in the tranquil paradise of the individual savings account.

Throughout the section, it's important to keep in mind that all of these things are just a form of investment wrapper. Think of them as clingfilm. Clingfilm does not change what's inside, merely the effect of the outside world on it. If the contents are good, like a slice of mature farmhouse cheddar, they stay good. If the contents are bad, like four-day-old fish pie, then they stay that way. When you hand over your hard-earned cash to some financial services company, they must invest it in order to provide the returns that you expect. Generally, they will invest your money in a range of different investments including cash, gilts, property and, of course, shares. Sometimes, they might use complicated financial instruments to guarantee a particular level of return, but these have to be paid for. Fundamentally, the underlying risks and returns that you find in the product you are buying will be the same as if you had bought those underlying investments yourself. If your product provider does the financial equivalent of serving up a slice of four-day-old fish pie, any amount of financial clingfilm isn't going to make it taste any better.

So what, you might well ask, are these wrappers all about? Well, as we said above, they're there to change the effect of the outside world on your investments. In particular, they're there to keep the taxman's greedy little fingers off them. The Government knows that it can't possibly pay to look after us all in old age, so it lines up a few tax breaks to help persuade us to look after ourselves. An added advantage of these schemes is that, by grouping together with lots of others, we can often achieve a better spread of investments than we could on our own. So, you get a good spread of investments and you might save some tax. Sounds good, doesn't it? The trouble is that none of this is achieved for free. When you give someone else your money to look after, they charge for it. So, when you are trying to find a suitable product for yourself, you need to compare the product's charges with the benefits that the particular product is designed to provide. Remember also that, as we found with actively managed unit trusts, the charges will often be the very reason that a product fails to achieve what it sets out to do.

OK, have you packed your toothbrush? Off we go.

15
The Dangerous World of Pensions

Was it a friend or foe that spread these lies?
Nay, who but infants question in such wise?
T'was one of my most intimate enemies.

— Dante Gabriel Rossetti, 'Fragments'

How many times have you heard people say: 'I really must do something about my pension, but I don't understand a word my financial adviser says.' Maybe you've said it yourself. Generally, the conversation stops there, accompanied by uncomfortable downward glances, shoe shuffling, a general feeling of unease and mutterings along the lines of 'Gosh, it's so hard to know, isn't it? I mean, I just don't understand all that stuff . . .'

It's a shame alright, but it's not surprising that people don't discuss their pensions, as they have never received any education about them, they find the whole subject intimidating in the extreme and the last thing the professionals would like is for people to be considering these investments from a knowledgeable standpoint. Just why this is, we are about to see.

You've *Got* to Have a Pension, Haven't You?

Well, yes, and then again, no. Before we answer this in a slightly more helpful manner, let's take a quick look at what pensions actually are and take a Foolish jaunt through the thorny issue of annuities. If you already have a pension yourself, our guess is that you'll be quite interested to hear what we have to say in this chapter. If you don't yet have one, then we hope it will also provide some food for thought, because sure as goldfish swim, the Pope is Catholic and the Shipping Forecast must mean something to someone somewhere, there is a financial adviser out there who is going to try and sell you one of these. Soon.

What is a pension?

A pension is an income that you receive after you've stopped work. To build up a big enough pot of money to provide that income, someone has to do some saving. What makes one pension scheme different from another is down to how this money is saved, who it is saved by and how the income is eventually generated.

As we said in the preamble to this section, to encourage us to save enough for our retirement, the Government provides a tax break. So long as a pension scheme fulfills the criteria they have set down, then the money that goes into it comes out of your *pre-tax* earnings. Think of it this way: you put some money in, then the Government chips in the tax that you have paid (or would pay) on that money. These contributions form a pension fund, which is invested over the years until your retirement. In theory all this seems dandy. In practice, life is once again about to take a shot across your bows. There are (more than) a few complications along the way.

We're going to take a look at the state pension, occupational pensions and private pensions (commonly known as Personal Pension Plans).

The State Pension

The state pension scheme basically comes in two bits — the 'basic pension' and the 'State Earnings-Related Pension Scheme' (SERPS).

Basic pension

It is slowly being abolished, as we saw in Chapter 1. Slipping in a 2 per cent drop in growth was a shrewd manoeuvre by the Thatcher Government in 1981. The Tories, in the aftermath of their 1979 landslide, realized that, since there was no investment fund out of which pensions were being paid (they are paid by the National Insurance contributions of those currently working), the rapidly ageing population was going to mean that pensions at the current levels were going to become too expensive. They therefore cut the rate at which pensions appreciated and so hastened the stranglehold on this country's old people. Whatever you think of the rights and wrongs of this, it is the case that by the time many people reading this book retire, they'll be lucky if the weekly state pension buys them a bottle of blue hair rinse and a packet of Mr Kipling's jam tarts. It's also worth bearing in mind that not everybody qualifies for it — you have to have made a minimum level of National Insurance contributions (roughly speaking, you'll be OK if you've earned at least the same amount as the basic pension for most of your working life). Do not factor the state pension into any of your retirement calculations.

SERPS and 'contracting out'

The basic pension replaces your lowest slice of income (that is, up to £66.75 per week currently). The State Earnings-Related Pension Scheme (SERPS) is designed to replace your income from £66 per week to £500 per week. It is 'earnings-related' because the more you earn (up to £500), the more you get. However, as you go from £66 to £500, less and less of your income is actually replaced. This means that someone earning, say, £200 per week will retire on a higher percentage of their pre-retirement income than someone who was earning £500 per week (although they will, of course, get less actual money). Income above the £500 per week level does not get replaced under SERPS and the scheme is only available for employees, not the self-employed.

If you want, you can choose to opt out of SERPS. This is called 'contracting out'. The effect of this is that your National Insurance payments, which would have gone towards providing your SERPS benefits, instead get paid into your occupational or personal pension. Your pension scheme then guarantees to pay out at least the SERPS benefits that you have given up. Basically, all you are doing is replacing SERPS with your own arrangements. Whether or not to contract out of SERPS is a tricky question, which depends on your view of future investment returns. One thing to remember is that SERPS is basically a defined benefit pension. Contracting out in favour of a defined contribution pension, therefore, carries risk. (Don't worry, we'll talk about this 'defined' business in the next section, 'Occupational Pension Schemes'.) As with any situation where you are taking extra risk in the hope of greater returns, the longer you have for it to come good, the better. Contracting out is therefore likely to make more sense the younger you are.

Occupational Pension Schemes

Forty years on the shop floor at Harding & Sedgewick ends with a handshake, a carriage clock and a generous pension to reflect the hard work and faithful service of a lifetime:

> *'Thank you, Higgins. Any plans for the future, my man?'*

'Well, sir, there's an allotment to dig and the cricket to watch. And may I say what a fine company this has been to work for over the years and what gentlemen you and your father before you have been. It has been an honour to work my fingers to the bone fourteen hours a day for a pittance of a weekly wage and a five shilling bonus every other Christmas. The outstanding growth in your personal wealth over that time and the way in which I was allowed to shine your shoes on my birthday have been a source of great pride to me. Truly a privilege, sir. Thank 'ee.'

Yes, those were the days, the days of Mrs Miniver and Morris Eights, of the Movietone News and good old British honesty and pluck and people jolly well knowing their place. Those days, though, are largely gone. While occupational pensions can provide a sound retirement income and should generally be opted *for* rather than against, the picture is not quite so clear as it was back then, when the sun always shone in June and we knew with such certainty who the baddies were.

The best occupational pensions are to be found in the public sector. If you are in the police force, your pension will be generous indeed and will be paid for out of the organization's budget, not an investment fund. Elsewhere, though, and especially in the private sector, pensions are paid out of an investment fund into which both employee and employer contribute. This fund will be invested in a variety of things, although generally it is heavily weighted into equities. That said, the equity investments are more likely to take the form of the underperforming unit trusts we've already talked about. There are two basic types of occupational pension scheme: defined benefit and defined contribution.

We're already getting into jargon here with 'defined benefit' and 'defined contribution', but all this boils down to is who takes the risk of the investments not performing well enough. Having an idea of who takes the risk is something well worth knowing. With a *defined benefit* pension scheme, the final benefit is what 'defines' how much the policy is worth. In effect, the final benefit – aka 'how much you get' – is guaranteed. Typically, your eventual benefits from this type of scheme are defined as a proportion of your final salary and they are often referred to as 'final salary' schemes for this reason. With these pensions, your retirement income (and any lump sum that you stand to get) simply comes out of the total pension pot that your employer has been building up over the years for all employees. If the investments have performed badly and there isn't enough in the pot, then your employer has to stump up the difference. Of course, if the investments perform well and there is extra in the pot, then the employer gets to keep the extra. (There's always a pay-off for taking risk, right?)

In a *defined contribution* pension, the value of the policy is defined by what is put into it. For this reason, they are sometimes known as 'money purchase schemes'. The level of your final benefit depends on how well the investments in your scheme perform, and are therefore not guaranteed. If the investments perform well, then you will get the extra benefit. However, if performance is poor, then you'll end up with a lower retirement income than you were hoping for. In this case, it's you that takes the risk, not your employer.

Defined benefit occupational schemes

As we've just seen, defined benefit occupational schemes pay you benefits based on your final salary (or an average of your salary for the last few years of your employment). Typically, the benefits will involve a lump sum and an income for life. There may well be a number of useful frills, such as life insurance and a pension for your spouse if they survive you.

The lump sum and income are generally expressed as a fraction of your final salary per year of service. Imagine that you are getting retirement income of $\frac{1}{60}$ of your final salary and a lump sum of $\frac{3}{80}$ of your final salary per year of service, and you have 20 years of service. You will stand to receive $\frac{1}{3}$ (that is, $\frac{20}{60}$) of your final salary as income and $\frac{3}{4}$ (that is, $\frac{60}{80}$) of your final salary as a lump sum.

Defined benefit schemes are generally pretty attractive because your employer takes the risk of things not working out on the investment front. Unfortunately, this fact is not lost on most employers and they are stampeding to change to the next option.

Defined contribution occupational schemes

The effect of a defined contribution occupational scheme is similar to having a personal pension (which we're coming to next) into which your employer makes contributions. Your benefits depend on what is put into it (and how the investments perform). At retirement you get a tax-free lump sum and the remainder of your fund must be used to purchase something called an annuity. How much of the fund you can take out as a tax-free lump sum depends on final salary and length of service.

Some schemes offer you a choice of how much to put in. For example, your employer may offer to match the amount you put into the pension by contributing the same amount again. This can make for tough choices. Your employer will work out how much to pay everyone as a salary, taking into account the average amount that it has to contribute to everyone's pension.

The effect of this is that if you are putting in less than average, then you are missing out on an employment benefit. However, just because your employer has offered to put money into a pension scheme if you do, it doesn't necessarily mean that you should. It really depends on the level of the contributions. If your employer offers to match your contributions (or better), then it would almost certainly make sense to take it. However, if your employer only puts in, say, £1 for every £9 that you put in, then the decision is more difficult: other factors about whether or not to opt for the pension will probably be more relevant.

Preserved benefits and transfers

Under an occupational scheme, if you have worked for an employer for two years you get to keep the value of any pensions benefits that have built up if you change jobs. Either you can keep the 'preserved benefits' in the old scheme, or you can get the old scheme to transfer enough money (called the 'transfer value') to the new scheme to give you the same benefits that you had already built up in the old scheme. The trouble with transferring is that it often costs you money to do it. If you have worked for less than two years with an employer, you basically just get back any contributions that you've put in.

AVCs and FSAVCs

This is an option for people who are members of an occupational scheme, but who don't think their benefits are going to be enough. An AVC scheme is run by the employer to enable people to top their pension contributions up to the maximum allowed. AVC stands for Additional Voluntary Contribution. Where your employer does not offer an AVC scheme (or even if they do, but we'll come to that), you can contribute to an FSAVC scheme (which stands for Free-Standing AVC).

As you might imagine, an AVC (or FSAVC) for a defined contribution pension just increases your contributions, although they might be in a slightly different place from your main scheme. Where an AVC scheme is available for a defined benefit pension scheme (generally only in the public sector), your contributions can purchase 'added years'. In other words, you are buying extra years to be taken into account in calculating your final salary benefits.

An AVC, sponsored by your employer, has an advantage over an FSAVC because of 'economies of scale'. In other words, by grouping together with your fellow employees, the overall charges tend to be lower. FSAVCs are very similar to the Personal Pension Plans we're shortly going to hear about.

They generally have similar, punitive charging structures, your fund will be channelled into the same kinds of underperforming investments and they are sold by the same people. Take a look at this quote from an article in the *Financial Times* of 25 April 1998:

> *Bacon & Woodrow, one of the biggest pension analysts, warned recently that the stand-alone alternative to company-sponsored AVCs — free-standing AVCs (FSAVCs) — is being sold inappropriately.*
>
> *Indeed, B&W said this week that about a quarter of pension schemes contained members who had paid commission to a salesperson, only to end up with an FSAVC identical to the in-house AVC — except for higher charges to cover the commission.*

It comes as no great surprise, then, that the Financial Sevices Authority (FSA) has launched a review into FSAVCs sold between April 1988 and August 1999. At the moment, the review is focusing on sales of FSAVCs where it has meant that the investor missed out on possible employer contributions to an available AVC scheme. But, given the way that the review of mis-selling into personal pensions has gone (don't worry, we're getting there), who knows where this may end up. In February 2000, the FSA estimated that compensation payable to investors will be between £95 million and £200 million. Anyway, the bottom line on this is that, if you have an occupational pension scheme and want to top up your contributions, an in-house AVC scheme is likely to be a far more attractive option than an FSAVC scheme.

Who puts the money in

One final thing to think about with an occupational pension is who puts the money in. In a pension scheme offered by your employer, you might put a bit in each month and so might your employer. Sometimes, in fact, your employer might offer to match your contributions. Sounds good, but let's think of it in another way. You, as an employee, are worth a certain amount to your employer and (so long as you, and/or your union, make the right noises when your pay is reviewed) hopefully this is the amount that you are paid. It makes little difference to your employer whether all your benefits come in the form of your salary or whether your salary is five per cent less and he pays five per cent into a pensions scheme for you. What matters is your overall package. If your employer offers what is generally considered to be an attractive pension scheme, then ask yourself how much more salary you could be paid if you didn't take the pension. Of course, much of this is fairly academic since few of us actually have that much control over our benefits package. Still, it's as well to think about things in this way. It helps keep the mind focused and that's what much of this book is really about.

Good and bad

Taking into account the previous section and reckoning that we don't have the option to take our employer's contribution to our occupational scheme in the form of extra salary or a tube of Smarties on our desk every morning, what makes occupational pension schemes attractive is that contribution from the employer. What makes them less attractive is the fact that they're not very portable. Since you are unlikely, these days, to be spending the whole forty years of your career at Harding & Sedgewick – the average person changes job five times in their working lives and less than 5 per cent of men and 1 per cent of women stay in the same job for thirty years – this could leave you with a number of small pensions, each paying out not very much. If it is portable, you're still likely to lose out to some extent.

There are good things, then, and bad things about company pension schemes. As throughout this book, we don't seek to tell you what you should do and what you shouldn't do – that would be pointless; what we seek to do is give you the information to make informed decisions on your own behalf. What we hope you will take away from this short section is that, for most people, an occupational pension is probably not going to provide the single, all-encompassing answer to a prosperous dotage.

Avanti!

Personal Pension Plans

The late 1980s. Thatcher's generation of self-employed entrepreneurs is busily engaged by turns in quaffing lager, racing around in Ford Escort XR3i's and revolutionizing the British economy, but none of them, of course, has access to an occupational pension scheme. We have to presume this didn't please the boss and following a gentle word in the ear of Nigel Lawson, the Chancellor of the time, an acronym was born:

> *'Unfair, Nigel! These are my children. Go and DO something about it!' Roars the 'T', eyes ablaze with fury and index finger pointing to the door of the Cabinet Room.*

'Immediately, Ma'am,' ripostes Mr Lawson and scurries off to do the
Leaderene's bidding.

PPPs, or Personal Pension Plans, give self-employed people, or those working
for small businesses without occupational schemes, a crack – as they like to
say in the Sunday newspapers – of the pensions whip. Essentially, they are
defined contribution schemes into which the PPP holder pays a percentage of
their salary (rising from a maximum of 17.5 per cent at the age of thirty-five
or below to 40 per cent at the age of sixty or above). These payments then go
into an investment fund, run by an investment or insurance company, into
which the Government also contributes the tax the investor would have paid.
In other words, they get *tax relief* on their contributions, an undoubted
advantage. The fund grows and then, on retirement, you can take 25 per cent
of your fund as a lump sum and the remainder is used to buy something called
an annuity to provide an income. Simple? No, definitely not.

First, it was with PPPs that the financial professionals got their knickers in
a very painful twist in the late 1980s and early 90s. By encouraging people to
purchase their (expensive) plans and to abandon the perfectly good occupational schemes many of them were already in, they were giving disastrous
financial advice, which would leave most of these people at a financial
disadvantage in years to come. This has become known as the 'Pensions
mis-selling scandal' and the precise reasons it arose (the companies involved
were making a killing from selling these policies) will become painfully
obvious as we consider the issue of investment charges in just one short
paragraph from here. Suffice to say that some of the biggest names in financial
services were implicated to the tune of billions of pounds of compensation,
which they are now having to pay to those they disadvantaged by their phoney
advice. The issue was supposed to be in the process of being resolved in early
1998 (with some judicious prodding from Parliament and fines for those who
were reluctant to pay compensation), when it all hit centre stage again. The
Government decreed in February of that year that the companies would have
to investigate another 1.5 *million* cases, pushing the likely compensation bill
from £5000 million to beyond £11,000 million at a single stroke. The minister
responsible referred to this as 'an awful lot of money' and we're with him on
that one.

Next comes the thorny issue of charges. Let's cast our minds back for a
moment to Chapter 2, 'The Miracle of Compound Interest'. There we saw
how important it was, nay vital, to start on the investing trail as soon as
humanly possible. Time and patience are the friends of the Foolish investor.
What think you, then, Fool, of giving up 80 per cent or more of your first two

years' contributions to a PPP in charges? This is money that will go not into your future, but into someone else's, either the financial adviser who sold you the plan, who takes it as his commission, or else the investment company itself. That's 80 per cent or more of the first two *paramount* years: also an awful lot of very important money. The process by which this money is taken from investors is called front-end loading and it's as bad for investors as it is good for the people selling the pension policies. (And are you still with us here?) It gets worse, breathtakingly so. Often, if you change the amount of your contributions, the company will *restart* the punitive charges schedule. Look at this e-mail from David Carter in 1998:

> *I increased my contribution to £300 [from £100] per month with effect from May 1st 1998. Then came the shock disclosure and here I do quote, because I was flabbergasted when I saw:*
>
> *'HOW MUCH WILL THE ADVICE COST?'*
>
> *'Company X will provide services and remuneration for arranging and servicing this increase* [sic] *to your plan amounting to £77.11 per month on average in the first year and a variable amount per month thereafter, being for example £64.50 on average in the second year, £15.28 in the third year and £24.28 in the final year. These amounts have been included in the deductions shown above and are determined by the size of the contribution increase and payment term.'*
>
> *Now, I've never been much of a jargon man myself. But to my simple thinking, this all adds up to a total of £2200 over four years just to service an increase to my premium — I even had to write the letter authorizing the increase to the company direct debit!*
>
> *I rang my Company X salesman (I've never accepted their term of 'advisor') who I've known for thirteen years. He was upset that I should question this 25 per cent (averaged over 4 years) charge. He compared it to my fees for recruiting staff for my clients (average: 20 per cent of first year's remuneration). I respectfully pointed out to him that I don't make any charges when a client increases someone's salary! (Anyway, isn't the first year's fee 40 per cent?)*
>
> *He's coming to see me tomorrow to try and sort it out. He asked me to find out whether other pension providers charge less — probably so that he can show me how well the Company X investment out-performs any other that I might choose. I don't want to play that game and told him that I shall not be doing any business with Company X again.*

Sadly, what happened to David happens to many people with personal pensions who think they're saving more and more for the future. Each time they increase their contributions, they don't realize they are paying directly into the pockets of the people who are running their policy.

Now, interesting things also happen when you stop paying into your Personal Pension Plan earlier than you'd planned. There could be a variety of reasons for this, which were nicely detailed in an article in the *Independent* on 15 November 1997: Lincoln, a PPP provider, found that 45 per cent (!) of its pension premiums lapse within three years and, to their credit, commissioned research into why this was so. This research revealed that 34 per cent lapsed due to unemployment, 23 per cent due to career breaks to raise a child and 20 per cent because people were offered a good occupational scheme – in other words 77 per cent of lapses were due to perfectly acceptable reasons, not just people jibbing out for no reason.

Let's turn again to the pages of *Money Management*, the magazine of choice for the financial services industry. Brace yourselves for the riveting story behind the paid-up value and the transfer value. If you decide to stop paying into your PPP, you can do one of two things: leave the money where it is or transfer it out. If you transfer it elsewhere you get (no great surprises here) the transfer value. If you leave it where it is, the company will credit you with a paid-up value that will then grow until the end of the term and you can take whatever benefits might be coming your way. So far, so good, but you won't be surprised to hear that some of the transfer values were truly appalling. Consider the case of a thirty-year PPP with J. Rothschild Assurance, in which contributions of £200 per month were stopped after two years. Now, um, 24 x 200 equals, um, 4800, right? No, that can't be right, let's check it again, 24 x 200 equals . . .

(Sounds of head-scratching, whistling, pencil scribbling through long multiplication sums)

. . . um, yes, 4800.

Now, in this case, the transfer value of the fund after two years is actually only £1473 – in other words 69 per cent *lower* than the contributions paid in. Just 69 per cent depreciation in two years: now, that's investment!

Fair enough, you might say (we wouldn't), they have to penalize people who decide to leave early, but take a look at their paid-up value: that's a whopping £4788. This is just about what you've paid in contributions and a definite incentive to leave the money where it is, rather than transfer it elsewhere. Not bad, you might think (we wouldn't): zero growth after two years. Leave it there and it'll grow nicely, you might think. Wrong! If we then move on to the maturity value of this £4788 at thirty years, we see that it is only £13,826, or equivalent to a paltry return of around 4 per cent per year.

Now, picture for a moment having had the misfortune of being sweet-talked into a Rothschild plan that you found you had to leave for one reason or another. The consequences are nothing short of catastrophic. For you, anyway. However, someone, somewhere is getting the benefit of all that compound interest on 4800 – 1473, or £3317 over thirty years. Nice work if you can get it, we say.

We'd like to give this as an isolated example, but it isn't. In fact, let's take a look at Lincoln itself, which commissioned the study into PPP lapses: both the two-year transfer and paid-up values of their thirty-year policies were a meagre £1346, less even than Rothschild. Now reckon that it's not just the odd person here or there who is getting hammered by these poor transfer values – according to the July 1998 edition of *Money Management*, as many as 40 per cent of pension planholders end up cancelling their contracts within five years, often as a result of what they describe as 'overzealous' selling by financial advisers.

When talking about charges, it can also be helpful to look at the effect of charges by the amount of pence in each contributed pound they eat up. This table has been taken from an article in *Money Management* in 1992, entitled 'Expenses and the Impact of Disclosure' and we think it speaks for itself:

Effect of charges on each pound paid into Personal Pension Plans

	10 yrs	25 yrs
Lowest	10p	13p
Median	17p	20p
Highest	29p	31p

Numbers like these leave us with difficulty in believing that the professionals have our best interests at heart, and little has changed since 1992. In a July 1998 survey of the cost of charges, *Money Management* still found they had a huge impact, with our old friend, Lincoln, topping the bill at a cost of a whisker under £20,000 on a 25-year policy with contributions of £200 per month. In other words, the charges amounted to almost exactly one third of the total contributions! The last sentence of the November 1997 *MM* article sums it all up nicely:

No wonder the public places such little trust in the industry.

Couldn't have put it better ourselves.

We're not finished, unfortunately, because even when investors arrive at a stage where their contributions are actually being invested in something that earns money, they don't have a great deal of say over just what those investments are. The contributions will generally be into one of the under-performing unit trusts we have already heard about, and the best the punters can hope for is to choose between the unit trusts on offer by the pension plan provider. It is possible to get PPPs these days in which the investment fund is an index-tracking unit trust and we'll take a look at these a little later on. Alternatively, there are beasts called SIPPs – Self-Invested Personal Pensions – in which the person themselves makes the investment decisions. However, these also tend to be subject to quite significant charges and you generally need a pretty big pension fund before they even begin to make any sense. However, there is one very good reason why a PPP of any kind may not be such a good idea and it has to do with the way in which you finally draw an income from your investment fund when you retire.

Annuities

The Government – and you won't be surprised to hear this – doesn't trust you a great deal. It doesn't trust you not to blow the entire amount of your retirement fund on General Montgomery at 50–1 in the 3.30 at Kempton Park. It doesn't trust you not to blow the whole caboodle on a two-week orgy of high living in a pink Rolls-Royce with personalized number plate 'FOOL 1'. It doesn't trust you not to blow the lot on a dead-cert investment in an emerald mine in the Venezuelan interior or on Russian Ministry of Finance junk bonds. You see, if they did trust you not to do any of these things and you let them down, then they would end up having to feed and house you and that's why they make you buy an annuity with the money you have accrued in your PPP or AVC fund. It's a very sensible decision on their part: they see it as just return for their generosity in giving you tax relief on your pension contributions for all those years, and it lets them avoid what could potentially be a whole lot of bother. For you, though, it may not be so good. Let's see why.

An annuity is the way in which you convert the money you have built up in your PPP or AVC fund into a regular income to see you through your retirement. It works broadly like this:

- You retire.
- You take the dosh in your PPP or AVC fund and use it to purchase an annuity, either from the company with which you already have your policy,

or another company (for the privilege of which you may be charged a penalty by your original company).
- The annuity pays you a fixed income until you die.
- The precise amount depends on how long you have left to live. Women, who live longer than men, receive less than men of the same age. Older people receive more than younger people. (And students of the macabre will note that with some companies, fat smokers can negotiate larger payments than slim non-smokers. We should have put vouchers for a large doner kebab and a packet of twenty Benson & Hedges at the back of the book. Enjoy them while you can!)
- Unless you have agreed to accept a substantially reduced initial annuity income, the amount you will receive will *not* increase with inflation.
- Unless you have agreed to accept a substantially reduced initial annuity income, your spouse may get nothing when you die.

Now, you and your spouse both die. *BIFF!*

- When you and your spouse are both dead, the annuity company keeps the money. Your relatives or favourite charity get nothing.

One of the problems with annuities is that these days we are living too long for them, and the rate of inflation is just that little bit too high to make them last. With the basic annuity, an insurance company effectively takes your money and uses it to buy some gilts. It buys gilts because it needs something that is considered to be low risk and that provides an income. But people reading this book may be looking at twenty, thirty or even more years of retirement. You'll remember from Chapter 4, 'The Bible of the Long-distance Investor', what an awful investment gilts tend to be over that sort of period. Let's do a thought experiment to look at why annuities are not powerful investments:

Hermione is fifty years old and wins the lottery: £1,000,000 in cool, gleaming pound coins. She can't be bothered with thinking about all this tiresome business of investment, she has no relatives and all she wants is a steady income with which to enjoy herself, so she uses it all to purchase an annuity. At the rates prevailing in summer 2000, this will buy her an annuity income of about £65,000 per year. Whoopee! But remember, this will not increase with inflation. Assuming that successive governments manage to achieve their inflation target of 2.5 per cent, Hermione will enter her seventieth year with an inflation-adjusted income of £39,175 (that's the real value of her intial £65,000 after it has depreciated at 2.5 per cent per year). Not bad still, but she's beginning to think hard about whether she can really afford two cruises a year. She tightens her belt and, a true warhorse, makes it to her ninetieth year. Now, her income has fallen to the equivalent of only £23,610. She can just about keep herself fed and warm in the winter, but a cruise? Forget it! In fact, things are a little worse than this when we compare the income to average earnings since, as we've seen before, this tends to increase at a rate of about 2 per cent more per year than inflation. Adjusting for this, and it seems only fair to do so, Hermione's income at ninety would be the equivalent of just £10,305. And to think she was once a millionairess.

Suppose, now, that she decides she is not going to invest in an annuity. Instead, she is going to invest £300,000 into an index tracker, £300,000 into high-yielding shares and £400,000 into gilts and high-grade (in other words, low-risk) corporate bonds, by no means an outrageous thing to do. Now, just how much income and growth each of these investments provides is a little complicated, which is why we have thoughtfully provided two different paragraphs below. 'Hermione's Income Stream Lite™' provides the bare bones of how her money will grow and provide income and is all you need to know to read further. 'Hermione's Income Stream Classic™' goes into more detail about how the numbers are derived. The choice is yours.

Hermione's Income Stream Lite™

If you don't want to get bogged down, all you really need to know is that the tracker grows at 8.5 per cent per year and gives income of 1.7 per cent, the high-yield shares grow at 5.7 per cent and give an income of 4.5 per cent and the bonds don't grow at all, but give an income of 5.5 per cent. If this is all you want to know, skip the next paragraph and go to 'Hermione's Old Age'.

Hermione's Income Stream Classic™

We're assuming that the tracker produces a total return in line with the long-term real (that is, after knocking off inflation) return from equities, which is 8.2 per cent. Adding inflation of 2.5 per cent to this gives us a total return of 10.7 per cent. However, Hermione will be taking dividend income from the tracker and so we have to take 2.2 per cent (which is the current dividend yield on the FTSE All Share index) away from our total return, leaving 8.5 per cent. The income from the tracker will be the 2.2 per cent, less 0.5 per cent in annual charges, giving the figure of 1.7 per cent per year.

We assume the same long-term returns (that is, 10.7 per cent including inflation) for the high-yield equities, but we'll take off 5 per cent this time for the dividend income. This gives the growth rate of 5.7 per cent and an income of 4.5 per cent (after 0.5 per cent for various charges).

For the gilts and corporate bonds we're using a yield of 5.5 per cent, which is a small premium to the long-term gilt yield of 4.5 per cent (the premium is to account for the slightly higher yields of corporate bonds). Got that? OK, let's move on.

Hermione's old age

If Hermione opts for the non-annuity route, her income starts at £40,600 and increases throughout her fifties to £57,032. At the age of sixty, the tracker has more than doubled to £678,295. She now removes £378,295 from the tracker and splits it evenly between the bonds and the high-yielding shares. This leaves her with the original £300,000 in the tracker, £589,148 in bonds and £711,389 in the high-yielding shares (which had grown to a value of £522,241 before the transfer from the tracker). Her income, at the age of sixty, is £69,516 – already ahead of the annuity and *she has given none of her capital away to any insurance companies*. In fact, her capital now stands at a healthy £1,600,536. At the age of seventy (and eighty and ninety), she again takes £378,295 out of her tracker and splits it between high-yield equities and bonds. You can see how the numbers pan out in the table opposite.

The key line to look at is the bottom one in each section, which shows the income and capital adjusted for both inflation and growth in average earnings. This shows the genuine value of the income (and the capital sum) at the time in question: that is, the value both in terms of inflation and also in relation to the increasing wealth of the rest of society, as measured by the increase in average earnings.

With the annuity, Hermione's income has steadily fallen away from £65,000 to just £10,305, while the capital, of course, disappeared at the beginning. With the investments, however, her income has even crept up slightly from £40,600 to £45,455 and she still has her £1,000,000 intact even after adjusting for average earnings. Now we've made a few assumptions here, about inflation and average earnings and about the returns from the various investments, but we think we've been as fair and consistent as we can be. You could also say that, by using shares, we've added to Hermione's risk a bit. We'd say that this depends on how you look at it. We saw in Chapter 4, 'The Bible of the Long-distance Investor', that shares, taken as a whole, are actually the surest way of preserving the value of your money over the long term. However you look at it, it doesn't look very good for annuities. Going the investment route, your income soon leaves the annuity miles behind and you still have your pot of money (amounting to over £6 million at the end before you adjust it for inflation and average earnings) backing you up. Why

Age	50	60	70	80	90
	£	£	£	£	£
INVESTMENT APPROACH					
Income from bonds	22,000	32,403	42,806	53,209	63,612
Income from high-yield equities	13,500	32,012	64,239	120,339	217,999
Income from tracker	5,100	5,100	5,100	5,100	5,100
Total income	40,600	69,516	112,145	178,649	286,711
Total income (inflation adjusted)	40,600	53,967	67,589	83,587	104,143
Total income (average earnings and inflation adjusted)	**40,600**	**43,865**	**44,653**	**44,885**	**45,455**
Bonds	400,000	589,148	778,295	976,443	1,156,590
High-yield equities	300,000	711,389	1,427,536	2,674,208	4,844,419
Tracker	300,000	300,000	300,000	300,000	300,000
Total fund	1,000,000	1,600,536	2,505,831	3,941,650	6,301,009
Total fund (inflation adjusted)	1,000,000	1,242,544	1,510,233	1,844,236	2,288,731
Total fund (average earnings and inflation adjusted)	**1,000,000**	**1,009,948**	**997,744**	**990,328**	**998,953**
ANNUITY APPROACH					
Annuity income	65,000	65,000	65,000	65,000	65,000
Annuity income (inflation adjusted)	65,000	50,461	39,175	30,412	23,610
Annuity income (average earnings and inflation adjusted)	**65,000**	**41,015**	**25,881**	**16,331**	**10,305**
Total fund	**0**	**0**	**0**	**0**	**0**

anyone would voluntarily choose to invest in an annuity is frankly beyond us and yet a Personal Pension Plan eventually compels you to invest 75 per cent of your fund in an annuity.

To sum up on annuities, here's *Investors' Chronicle* in 1996, waxing lyrical on the insurers who sell them:

> *Insurers take their cut by investing your capital. They expect investment gains to more than pay your income. Therein lies a cautionary tale. If insurers can make more from investing your money than the income they are prepared to offer, so can you. In other words, if you don't have to buy an annuity, they are often best avoided.*

Quite.

Stakeholder Pensions

The plan is for the much-talked-about 'stakeholder pensions' to be available from April 2001. At the time of writing, the precise detail of the proposals is still a bit unclear. However, they look as though they will be relatively attractive: certainly when compared to Personal Pension Plans and AVCs. The trouble is that the more attractive they are to us, the less attractive they are likely to be to financial services companies. There is some doubt, then, about how many of these schemes will be set up and whether they will be targeted at the people who would benefit from them most. Having said that, employers (with more than five employees) will apparently have to make a stakeholder scheme available unless they are making contributions, on behalf of their employees, of 3 per cent of salary to a group personal pension. However, this might not necessarily be such a bonus for employees, as it's quite likely that the increased pension burden on employers will simply result in slightly lower non-pension wages (or slightly lower pay rises). In other words, employers can deal with the situation simply by reshuffling the way that they pay you, rather than increasing the total amount they pay you.

Stakeholder pensions will basically be a form of defined contribution personal pension. What's worrying the financial services industry most is the proposed transparent and low-charging structure. The current plan is for charges to be limited to 1 per cent per annum. That's way below most existing pensions, and pension providers are worried that they won't be able to make them profitable enough. It is also proposed that schemes be obliged to accept single payments of as little as £20. Our Wise friends argue, with some justification it must be said, that such small contibutions would not be compatible with low ongoing charges (because of all the administrative charges that would be involved).

At this stage, it's a question of wait and see, but if stakeholder pensions can be made to work along the lines of the current proposals, then we'd say that it's a step in the right direction. There is still the problem of annuities to be wrestled with, but it is, at least, a start.

Reprise: 'You've got to have a pension, haven't you?'

We feel a little more able to answer this now and the answer is 'Nope'. While it's probably a good idea to contribute to your occupational scheme – as long as you don't switch jobs too often – in our opinion Personal Pension Plans and AVCs are overrated. Their exorbitant charges, inflexibility and the compulsion they bring to purchase an annuity counterbalance the undoubted advantage of the tax relief they attract. Bear in mind, though, that other investment wrappers provide tax relief, too: most importantly, the ISA. With a pension, you get tax relief on the money you put in, but you get taxed fully on your eventual income when you retire. With an ISA, on the other hand, you don't get any tax relief on your contributions, but the eventual income comes to you free of tax. The difference in the tax treatment of pensions and ISAs therefore comes down to when you get the tax relief and, as we'll see in the chapter on ISAs, it doesn't actually make a whole heap of difference. For the time being, just bear in mind that pensions are tax-*deferred* investments, they are not tax-*free* investments, whatever pension salespeople would like to have you believe. It's almost as though you say, 'Don't pay me that bit of salary now, pay it to me when I've retired instead.' When it is paid to you in retirement, it will still be taxed. In any event, we hope we have shown that tax advantages alone do not give sufficient reason to choose one investment over another. In our opinion, the charges alone can be enough to send you scooting away from many personal pensions and AVCs, let alone the compulsion to buy an annuity.

There is, though, one overriding reason why you might want to contribute to a pension plan and that is if you wouldn't be able to keep your grubby paws off the money otherwise. Most other types of investment will allow you to raid your funds before you really need them, before you really should. With a pension plan, you can't get any benefit from the money until retirement, no ifs ands or buts, and even then, apart perhaps from a lump sum, you can only use the money to provide you with an income. Be honest with yourself and if you haven't got the discipline to leave your savings untouched, then start looking around for some halfway decent pension provision: an index tracker-based PPP or AVC is probably going to be your best bet. Alternatively, just resolve to sit on your hands for the intervening time, as good a solution as any.

The Foolish Pension Option: An Index Tracker

You know you wouldn't be able to keep your hands off the money if there was any way you could get at it and actually, when all's said and done, you really *do* prefer the idea of having a pension. You like the feeling of security it gives you, you love the idea of the up-front tax relief and only getting 25 per cent of your invested fund as a tax-free lump sum doesn't particularly bother you. The fact that the other 75 per cent will have to go – sooner or later – into purchasing an annuity is of little interest, because since young Timothy totalled the car last Saturday night you've decided not to leave anything to your kids anyway. Also, you're a happy sixty-a-day smoker and are not planning to live long enough after retirement for inflation to eat significantly into your annuity income.

OK, Fag Ash Lil, here's what you should think about doing. It's quite simple.

Get yourself (i.e. buy it directly from the company over the telephone or on the Internet and using no intermediaries) a Personal Pension Plan in which the underlying investment fund is an index tracker. That way you pay no commission to a financial adviser, the up-front charges are peanuts, the yearly charges minimal and you'll outperform the majority of pension investments, while also benefiting from the advantage of tax relief on contributions. Easy, although you will, of course, have to end up spending most of the money on an annuity. Talking of which, you should make sure that the pension doesn't penalize you for buying the annuity from a different provider. Annuities can vary hugely in terms of value and it is always worth shopping around for the best deal.

But what if you're in an occupational pension scheme and decide you want to transfer your retirement funds into an index tracker? Well, if you're in a final salary (that is, defined benefit) scheme, you simply can't. In that case you have no say over where or how your money is invested and it's pretty well irrelevant to you anyway, since no matter how well the investments perform, your pension is fixed as a percentage of your final salary. If you're in a money purchase or defined contribution scheme on the other hand, then an index tracker may be one of the places into which you can invest your money, in which case that's great. If it isn't one of the options, then we suggest you write to the scheme manager asking why not, pointing out that the majority of actively managed unit trusts underperform the index over the long term and that as a contributor to this pension scheme you're in it for the long term, blah, blah, blah and by the way have they heard of this splendid little Web site called The Motley Fool UK . . . ? (You know it all by now – no point us repeating ourselves.)

All facetiousness aside for a millisecond and despite our stance on them as a whole, personal pensions can be made Foolish if approached in the way outlined here. The key, as ever in investment, is to avoid those two evil horsemen from the DARK SIDE: overcharging and underperformance.

16

The Disturbing Abyss of Endowments

O wombe! O bely! O stynkyng cod
Fulfilled of dong and of corrupcioun!

— Geoffrey Chaucer, *The Canterbury Tales:* 'The Pardoner's Tale'

For years and years, if you didn't have an endowment policy, you didn't have an investment. Endowment policies were the mainstay of the investment market and were commonly sold in conjunction with mortgages. You paid the interest on the mortgage and a small amount also went into an endowment policy. When the mortgage term was up, the endowment policy matured and paid off the loan on the house. Neat. Easy. So neat and easy, in fact, that by the end of the 1980s, 80 per cent of UK mortgages were backed by an endowment policy.

Before we go any further, let's hear a few comments about the life assurance industry in general (the people who sell endowments) from a former Deputy Chairman of one of the companies implicated in the pensions mis-selling scandal we've already heard about:

> . . . *for the last twenty years the big life assurance companies in this country have systematically been ripping people off* . . .

Steady on! He continues:

> . . . *the high turnover in salespeople, the commission system and the practice of front-end loading all lend weight to the accusation that there has been a massive distortion* . . . *by the life assurance companies* . . . *of the British retail savings market* . . .

Phew! Whose side is this fellow on? These comments were quoted in a book entitled *The Last Days of the Credit Culture* by Jonathan Mantle.

So, What Is an Endowment?

Endowments are a form of life assurance policy with a savings and investment mechanism built in. What happens is that the policy holder pays premiums and then, after a predetermined period of time (normally twenty-five years when linked to a mortgage) or on death, the insurance company pays out a sum to that policy holder. Sounds innocent enough, but like so many things in this deceptive ol' Wise world, it isn't. The added complexity of the products give financial services companies all the opportunity that they need to cover up what are, in most cases, indecent commissions and charges. By now, you won't be surprised to hear that our Wise friends generally don't need asking twice to take advantage of this. You also won't be surprised to hear that these commissions and charges, which come straight out of the money you pay in, are the very reason why they prove to be such lousy investments. Did you notice the words 'front-end loading' in the second of the two quotes above? We've come across that before in the chapter on pensions. Yes, the same thing happens with endowments. The salesperson largely creams off the first couple of years' contributions, pockets them and leaves you fighting to keep your head above water. Fighting so hard, in fact, that it may be as much as *seven* years before you break the surface again. The surrender value (i.e. what you'd get if you cashed the policy in) can take this long to even approach the value of the contributions paid in. In fact, let's not do our own dirty work, let's quote the industry's own magazine, *Money Management*, again. In a review of endowment mortgages in July 1997 it said:

> In most cases, even after seven years, . . . endowment surrender values do not even return premiums paid. The average yield on seven year surrender values is −0.9 per cent.

Pardon us, but haven't we been here before? It can and often does take this long for the transfer or paid-up values of PPPs and AVCs to break even. We're starting to see some common threads emerging. Low returns, massive charges, inflexibility: all these things characterize the investments that people out there want to sell you. You know, sometimes we get financial professionals coming to our site and telling us we're misleading the public, that we're giving those fellows a bad name. Well, it seems to us like they're more than capable of doing it themselves. Anyway, to understand endowments better, we need to take a little step back in history and see how they developed.

The original pure endowment

The original incarnation of endowments was the 'pure' endowment. In the finest traditions of insurance, these policies guaranteed to pay a definite sum on death or maturity. When sold alongside an interest-only mortgage, this made a good deal of sense, since it was a definite sum that would be required to pay off the mortgage at the end of the term. Essentially the effect of this would be identical to having a repayment mortgage together with pure life assurance (that is, which only pays out on death, not at the end of the term). Both approaches would guarantee that your mortgage would be repaid on death or at the end of the period of the loan. The question you then have to ask with this type of endowment is 'What's the point of it?' Why not just get a repayment mortgage together with some pure life assurance? Why bother the insurance company with the repayment part of the mortgage, since this will surely just add to costs? In the dim and distant past, there used to be some tax relief on the premiums paid into life assurance products, but after this was scrapped, it became very hard for the insurance companies to sell these products. They therefore needed to think of something to sweeten them up a little.

With-profits and unitized with-profits endowments

What insurance companies (and their salespeople) found was that it was a lot easier to sell endowments if they could suggest to prospective policy holders that there might be a 'windfall', over and above the mortgage repayment, at the end of the policy term. They therefore devised the 'with-profits' endowment. With these, they took the premiums that you paid them, took out the life assurance bit and invested the rest on your behalf, the plan being that you would get the proceeds from these investments and this would pay off your mortgage with, hopefully, a bit to spare.

What had in fact happened was that the householder, rather than the insurance company, had suddenly started to carry the risk of the investments not doing well enough to pay off the mortgage (remember how important it is to know who is taking the risk in any given situation), which effectively meant that the apparent benefit of the 'windfall' was no more than cosmetic. Householders could create the same result by channelling the money into (lower-charging) investments themselves. Of course, the sellers of endowment policies didn't really want people to realize this and, as we'll see in a moment, it is more than fair to say that, on many occasions, they were economical with the truth when selling these policies.

The investment element of with-profits endowments is added to policies in a fairly unusual manner. At the end of each year an annual or 'reversionary' bonus is added to the policy. Once added, this cannot be taken away. The effect of this is that the value of your policy won't fall (although it can still go up only very slowly). In addition to annual bonuses, a terminal bonus is added at the end of the term. Initially this seemed like a good idea. Unfortunately, the insurance companies realized that this didn't give them very much flexibility. Gradually, therefore, the terminal bonus has come to represent more and more of the investment return (at the expense of the non-removable annual bonuses) so that now terminal bonuses can account for as much as 60 per cent (or more) of the final value of a policy. So their final value is barely more reliable than if an investor had invested the money themselves without troubling the insurance company (and therefore making substantial cost savings).

In the world of PEPs and ISAs (which we look at in the next chapter), it seems odd that many people are still persuaded to pay their money into a with-profits endowment that will frequently have no value for several years, thus locking them in whether they like it or not. By contrast, should you wish to, you can get at your ISA funds at any stage. In addition, the underlying investment mix of a with-profits policy is, at best, the same as can be had from an ISA, but with higher charges. It is therefore difficult to see any reason why the investment performance of a with-profits endowment should be as good as a cheap ISA. True, the Government has only said that ISAs will be around for ten years, but it seems almost inconceivable that there would be no form of tax-free savings vehicle after that.

Unit-linked endowment policies

In order to boost the attractions of endowments further, the insurance companies decided to produce a version linked to their managed unit trusts. Instead of the complicated business of bonuses that you get on a with-profits endowment, with a unit-linked endowment the value of your investments just go up and down with the value of the unit trust that your endowment is linked to. This has the benefit of being a more transparent structure, in terms of returns as well as charges, but it makes the comparison with ISAs even more stark. Let's assume we're looking at the same unit trust. What's the point of buying it via an endowment, and possibly paying in money for years before it has any value at all, when you could pay into an ISA, a fund that will be available to you whenever you should want it? On top of this, of course, there is the fact that the vast majority of the unit trusts that these endowments are linked to will underperform a good cheap index tracker.

201

Endowment Mis-selling

It's pretty clear that endowments have come a long way from the original no-risk product. These days, their risk profile is not significantly different from the underlying investments that homeowners can buy themselves to back their mortgage. In both these cases – buying the investment yourself in the form of an ISA or buying an endowment – you are taking the risk that you will not, in fact, be able to repay your mortgage at the end of its term, in favour of what you hope will be greater return. If this is so, why would you choose to take this risk in an endowment policy which is extraordinarily costly and inflexible? As we'll see in Chapter 18, 'Be Your Own Landlord', the only way that repaying the sum at the end of the mortgage can be guaranteed is by taking a repayment mortgage, where you actually repay a bit of the capital each month until it's all gone (typically after twenty-five years). Unfortunately, in their endeavour not to miss out on the several thousand pounds of commission that selling an endowment can earn, it seems that a great number of financial advisers and salespeople have been rather slow to point this out.

This has prompted the Financial Services Authority (FSA) to undertake a review into the possible 'mis-selling' of endowments. The FSA's view is that, where the extra risks of an endowment mortgage over the repayment type have not been made clear, there 'may have been a mis-sale'. The review concludes that, because of recent strength in investment markets generally, people who were sold interest-only mortgages (with a suitable investment plan attached) rather than repayment mortgages have, as things have turned out, not suffered any loss. There is therefore no compensation payable (in almost all cases) and a full-scale review would therefore be a waste of money. This is true, as far as it goes. The trouble is that it doesn't consider whether endowments are a suitable means of saving to repay the capital on a mortgage. Whether or not a repayment mortgage should have been recommended, the extra charges on an endowment and their consequent sub-par performance means that there are very few circumstances in which an endowment can be considered a more effective means of repayment than a cheap ISA alternative.

In addition to the issue of mis-selling, the FSA has recently lowered the percentage growth figures that endowment salespeople are allowed to use to sell endowments and review existing ones. The effect is that, on the new projections, many endowments sold in recent years are now 'not on track' to pay off their mortgages. This has meant that the endowment providers have had to write to policyholders explaining this. First of all, it's important to point out that there is no great reason for panic. If the projections are lowered, then policies with insufficient leeway are bound to fall short on the new projections. The question to ask is why the projections have been lowered. The answer to this is that we are now in a lower interest rate environment than we were. Interest rates are expected to remain low and this means that the returns from all investments are now expected to be lower than they have been in the recent past. The flip side to this is that the interest rates on mortgages are also expected to be lower. The solution, then, for anyone who has an interest-only mortgage (whether it is backed by an endowment or an ISA), is to take the money that you're now saving on lower interest rates and add it to the money that you are investing (we would suggest, though, that you do this through a cheap index-tracking ISA rather than topping up the endowment). Alternatively, you could take the safe option and use the extra money to pay off a bit of the capital on the mortgage each month (in other words, convert to a 'part-repayment' mortgage).

We'll talk more about the pros and cons of different types of mortgage in Chapter 18. For the moment, suffice to say that the financial services industry has yet again failed to cover itself in glory. Unlike with pensions, though, the endowment sellers have just about got away with it because buoyant stock markets have come to their rescue. Even so it is very hard to see why an endowment should be preferred over other options.

So, Where Does This Leave Us?

Even though the proportion of mortgages being sold with endowments is now apparently down to around 10 per cent, we Fools would say that this is still 10 per cent too many. So, the first thing to say is – **don't get one**. The only possible situation that we can think of where they might be a good thing is as a savings vehicle for a higher rate taxpayer who is already making full ISA contributions. However, even in this case, we'd say that you'd be better off investing directly in the stock market and holding for a long period. Careful tax planning should remove any benefit that the endowment might have had.

What if you're one of the unlucky people who have already got an endowment? The first general suggestion that we can give for anybody worried about their endowment is to get hold of the FSA factsheet on endowment mortgages. You can get this by phoning 0800 917 3311, or you can find it on the FSA Web site, which is listed in Appendix 5. The second general pointer is to say that there is no reason to rush into anything. You should think long and hard about your situation and discuss it with others. You might even want to pop by our Web site and see what others have chosen and are choosing to do with their endowments. As you can probably imagine, it's something of a hot topic. If necessary, take professional advice. However, if you do want to do this, we'd suggest that you make sure that the adviser has no conflict of interest with your position. This will generally involve finding a financial adviser who doesn't earn commission from selling endowments.

There are a number of possible options for your endowment and you should contact your provider to find out which of these are available to you. When you have this information, think about it from first principles. Forget what has gone and think about the future. What are the costs associated with your endowment from now on? What is the likely performance of the endowment from now on? What would be the effect of selling the endowment and reinvesting the proceeds in something better? What would be the effect of stopping contributions at this stage?

The first thing to think about is whether your policy has a sale value. This might be the case if you have a with-profits endowment that is more than about seven years old. Bear in mind, though, that, if you sell, someone is buying it because they think it's cheap. They will have taken into account the effect of ongoing charges and the likely terminal bonus and they will have decided that it is a good deal. You therefore need to have some reason for thinking that it is a good deal for you too. For instance, the buyer might think that endowments are lower risk than, say, index trackers. They might therefore be prepared to accept a slightly lower future return from the endowment than you might expect to get from the tracker. You, on the other hand, might think that endowments don't significantly reduce your risk and that you'd therefore rather have the money in a tracker or you might simply want to revert to a repayment mortgage.

If you do decide to sell your endowment, you're really not giving yourself a chance of doing better unless you make absolutely sure that you get the best possible price for it. First of all, you can get a free brochure on buying and selling endowments from the Association of Policy Market Makers on 0207 739 3949. With this and the details of your policy in hand, you can go about collecting a number of quotes for your policy. Don't be afraid to tell them that you have higher quotes from elsewhere: they're bound to start low and move up. This point is amply illustrated by a post from Jonathan Teague on the Motley Fool's Endowments discussion board on 29 January 2000:

Hi all,

I'd just like to relate the happy tale of my recent endowment sale.

I had been paying into an endowment with the Pearl since Feb 89 and for the past year had been reading the Money section of the Sunday Times, listening to the various personal finance programmes on the radio and wondering if continuing with it was entirely sensible. Then, WHAM, in November I discovered the Fool. Well to cut a long story short I spent considerable time getting past performance information out of the Pearl and came to the conclusion that the future did not look rosy for the endowment and it was time to consider selling and reinvesting.

The surrender value was 9284. Amazing, a whole 3.78 per cent annualized return on the monthly investments (deducting an allowance for the life cover). Gee, was I impressed?!

Well I contacted most of the TEP [Traded Endowment Policy] traders (all online with the exception of Neville James) and the offers started to come in:

Policy Trading Company: Sorry - can't beat Life Co
Absolute Assigned Policies: 10,744
Policy Plus: 10,740
Surrenda-Link: 10,923
Beale Dobie: 11,809
Policy Portfolio: 12,200
Neville James: 12,750

An astounding range. How can one company not beat the surrender value and another give over 30 per cent more?

This is where things got interesting, basically I didn't do anything for a fortnight (the Fool does not act hastily) and the phone rang – Beale Dobie wanted to know if I liked their offer, I told them about the higher offer and they said they would 'see'.

Promptly in the post.
Beale Dobie: 13,007

Blimey, mate! Now 40 per cent more than surrender value and almost 1200 more than their original offer. But then . . . the phone rang again, Policy Portfolio this time – they too would 'see'.

Next day.
Policy Portfolio: 13,800

Sorry! Is this real, that's 48.5 per cent more than surrender and 13 per cent more than PP's original offer. Anyway, after giving some of the other offers yet another 'go' I concluded that this really was the best offer and went for it. The paperwork was dealt with very efficiently and in less than two weeks the cheque arrived.

So if you decide to sell the morals are —

1. Don't immediately accept the highest offer from the first batch — let them fight — they will!
*2. Get quotes from as many of the traders as possible (you can ask for quotes from almost all of them online). You never know which one will give the best offer for your policy. Imagine if I had only picked Policy Trading Company, Absolute Assigned Policies and Policy Plus to get quotes from — **that would have cost me £3000!***

Well I'm now well on the way to being a fully paid-up Fool. It's all going into trackers from now on.

Incidentally the 13,800 represents an annualized tax-free return of 10.73 per cent on the monthly investment, not bad so I'm not too upset. Yes, if I had invested in a tracker from day 1 I would have over 20K now but you can't regret the past — you just have to make damned sure you learn from it!

Fool on,
Jon.

We'd add just a couple of things to Jon's comments. Having got your highest offer, it could be worth putting the policy up for auction, with the offer that you've received as the 'reserve price'. If the auction beats this, then well and good; but if not, you have the other offer to fall back on. A company called H. E. Foster & Cranfield carries out weekly second-hand endowment policy auctions and, strangely enough, has done so since 1843. You can contact them on 020 7608 1941.

If your endowment policy is a unit-linked policy or is only a few years old, then you might not be able to sell it. In this case, you could think about surrendering the policy. You can get the surrender value from the endowment company and then try to work out, along the lines mentioned above, whether you think that the surrender proceeds (if any) could do better for you outside the endowment than inside it. The sums can be quite tricky, but it is well worth making the effort to look into it, rather than risk being tied into an underperforming investment for twenty years or more.

If you feel uncomfortable about selling or surrendering your endowment, you may have the opportunity to make your policy 'paid up'. The effect of this is that your accumulated pot of money stays in the endowment, but you stop making further contributions. The money that would have gone into contributions can then be used to pay into an alternative, and hopefully better, investment.

One final point to make if you are considering disposing of, or stopping contributions to, an endowment is that you will be losing your life assurance cover. If you have dependents, then the chances are that you should replace this.

In Conclusion

In the unlikely event that anyone hasn't realized that we absolutely hate and detest endowments, let's summarize by saying that endowments are inflexible, high-expense, underperforming investments that line the pockets of the Wise at the expense of the public. If you want life insurance, which, by the way, is just the same as life *as*surance, buy just that – 'term' life assurance, no more no less, and put your money for investment into real investments, Foolish investments. If you do want out, it will almost certainly pay you to sell, if you are able to, rather than surrender. Here, to end our consideration of endowments, is an editorial quote from the *Daily Telegraph* of 31 August 1991, at the height of the endowments boom:

> *It cannot be said too often that the advantages to the householder of an endowment mortgage are as nothing compared to the gain to the policy salesperson, that life assurance has nothing to do with house purchase, and that savings-related life assurance is a waste of money.*

17

The Tranquil Paradise of ISAs

For my wish . . . I desire most marvellous things; just a fine bauble and a hood garnished with long ears and bells that make a marvellous noise . . .

— Recueil de Poésies Françaises

The Government is very keen for us to save for our future and it provides tax incentives for us to do so. Unfortunately, as we saw with pensions and endowments, these tax incentives are sometimes overwhelmed by a variety of catches. Fortunately, though, every now and again, the Government hits the nail on the head and gives us exactly what we want (or very nearly anyway). This is what happened when the Personal Equity Plan (or PEP) was introduced in the late 1980s. PEPs were a means whereby any old Fool could invest money in shares while sheltering the returns from the taxman. Not surprisingly, they've proved to be extremely popular and they are still around today, although no new money can be added to them. These days, we have Individual Savings Accounts (ISAs) to put money into and, although they are a bit complicated, they remain every bit as lovely as PEPs used to be.

What? The Fools are actually endorsing a financial product?! Have they gone mad? Well, we must admit that after writing the previous couple of chapters it does feel a little strange. Perhaps this outflowing of joy is a result of the pain and sorrow of what has gone before, but we really do like ISAs a lot. The main reason for this is that, with a few reasonable limitations, you can put pretty much whatever investments you like into them. This means that we're in control. We can sit there with our ISA and say, 'Mmm . . . I'll have a bit of that and a bit of this and, oh yes, a bit of that.' It also means that they have a very transparent charging structure. You can see exactly how much it is costing you and, as a result, ISA providers are in intense competition with each other to provide them more and more cheaply. All very Foolish.

When you buy an index tracker (or an underperforming managed fund), you can generally buy it pre-wrapped in an ISA. The nice thing about doing this is that the manager of the index tracker will typically throw the ISA wrapper in for free, keeping your costs down. Alternatively, you can buy your own ISA wrapper (called a 'self-select ISA') and put what you like into it yourself. The trouble with this is that you'll have to pay for the ISA and then pay for what you put into it on top. For this reason, self-select ISAs tend to be used only where you are putting shares directly into the ISA, since, with the big exception of dealing charges when you buy and sell, shares have no additional ongoing costs.

Once you've got your money in an ISA, you won't get charged any income tax on interest received on it and you won't get charged any extra tax (in addition to what the company has already paid) on any dividends from companies (we talked about dividends in Chapter 11, 'A Share Primer'). In fact, until 2004, you get back a tiny bit of the tax that the company has paid. On top of all this, you don't get charged any capital gains tax when you sell investments within the wrapper, and you don't incur any tax when you take money out of the ISA. We'd really like to say that it's as simple as that and move on to the next section of the book. Unfortunately, as ever, the devil is in the detail. Thankfully, for once, the detail does nothing to reduce (or, for that matter, improve) the usefulness of the product. It serves only to make the head a bit sore.

The Detail

There are two basic types of ISA: the Maxi-ISA and the Mini-ISA. It's pretty important to be clear about the differences because, in each tax year, you are allowed (assuming that you're a UK resident aged eighteen or over) to invest in just one of the two types. Each type has three separate components: cash, stocks and shares, and insurance. The difference between the two is that in the Maxi, they're all mushed together into the same account, whereas with the Mini, each of the bits are in different accounts. It's perhaps easiest to think of the Maxi as being like one big teapot into which you can put up to three different types of teabag (that is, one teabag for cash, one teabag for stocks and shares and one teabag for insurance). Since it's all in one teapot, only one person can be mother. In other words, you have to pick one financial organization to run the whole Maxi-ISA for you.

Similarly, you can think of the Mini-ISA as being like three small teapots, each of which can contain a different teabag (except you can't have the same type of teabag in two different pots). So, if you like the interest rates on someone's cash Mini-ISA, but you don't like the charges on their stocks and shares Mini-ISA, then you can open the cash Mini with them, but go to someone else for the stocks and shares Mini. Before we leave our teabags analogy, we should just say that we don't much like the taste of insurance teabags. We don't like the confusion between insurance and investment at the best of times and we really can't work out who would want to put insurance policies into an ISA. It looks like we're not the only ones. Very few financial organizations offer them and, according to the Government, in the first nine months of the ISA only £44 million had been put into the insurance component compared to more than £17 billion into cash and stocks and shares. Really, then, we'd say that you can simplify matters greatly by just ignoring the insurance component and concentrating on the other bits.

Now we've got the difference between these Maxis and Minis sorted out, let's have a look at the annual limits. For the 2000/2001 tax year, you can invest up to £7000 in a Maxi-ISA. You can put as much of this into the stocks and shares component as you like, but you can only put up to £3000 into the cash component. The plan is to reduce the limit to £5000 (of which up to £1000 can be in the cash component) for the 2001/2002 tax year, although there's a fair chance that the Government will decide to extend this year's limits for at least another year. For Mini-ISAs, the limits are £3000 for a stocks and shares Mini and £3000 for a cash Mini this tax year, with the allowance for the cash Mini falling to £1000 next year (although, again, there's a fair chance that the £3000 figure will be extended for at least another year).

Each new tax year brings the opportunity to make fresh subscriptions to an existing ISA, or to open a whole new ISA. Of course, if you keep opening a new ISA each year, things are going to get pretty complicated. To simplify matters, transfers from one ISA into another are allowed. However, the components must remain the same. So, once you've gone for the stocks and shares component of a Maxi-ISA or a stocks and shares Mini, you can move it around all over the place, but it must always remain in stocks and shares. Similarly, when you've gone for a cash component, it must always stay in cash. Any transfers like this do not count for the purposes of each year's allowances.

As you can probably imagine, you can only really put cash (and one or two things that are very like cash) into a cash ISA. The fun starts when you get to the stocks and shares bit. Here you can put in most of the things that you might want to. You can put shares in it, so long as they're quoted on a major stock exchange (there's more about what that means in Chapter 11, 'A Share Primer'), you can put most unit trusts and investment trusts into it and you can put gilts and corporate bonds into it. You can even hold a bit of cash in it, but this must be for the purpose of buying the other investments that we've just mentioned. You can't hold cash in a stocks and shares component 'for the sole purpose of sheltering interest on cash deposits from tax'.

The Government has designed a scheme to help people tell which ISAs meet certain minimum standards. It's designed to reassure us a bit and it does just that. It's a voluntary code and it in no way guarantees returns, but if an ISA is CAT-marked, it does tell you that certain conditions are met. CAT stands for Charges, Access and Terms, the three areas that the standards cover. For Charges, the provisions are that cash ISAs can make no charge at all, and stocks and shares ISAs can only charge up to 1 per cent of the value of the ISA per year. For Access, you've got to be able to get at your money within seven working days. The most important part of the Terms bit is that the interest rate on cash ISAs can't be more than 2 per cent below the base rate, at least 50 per cent of stocks and shares ISAs must be invested in Europe and unit trusts must have the same buying and selling price.

Wrapping Up

Stocks and shares ISAs are very well suited to saving for retirement. You can start off with most (or all) of the investments going into shares to grow nicely over the long term, then when you get to retirement, you can switch part of the accumulated fund into gilts or corporate bonds to provide extra income. The beauty of this is that this income is received free of income tax, whereas the eventual income from a pension gets taxed. All things being equal, this amounts to the same thing. This is because we're talking about a mathematical operation called multiplication, in which it makes no difference when you do it. For example, look at the position for a higher rate taxpayer (i.e. 40 per cent) who has £1000 to invest pre-tax and gets 9 per cent growth for three years before drawing income at a rate of 5 per cent. Tax of 40 per cent before the money goes into the ISA leaves him with £600 ('1000 $\times$ 0.6'). This grows at 9 per cent a year for three years (that's the '1.09' in the equation) and is then drawn at a rate of 5 per cent (that's the '0.05'):

ISA: £1000 x 0.6 x 1.09 x 1.09 x 1.09 x 0.05 = £38.85

Meanwhile, in the pension, all the money goes in up front (i.e. there's total tax relief on it), but the income gets taxed at the end:

Pension: £1000 x 1.09 x 1.09 x 1.09 x 0.05 x 0.6 = £38.85

Each year's income is the same for the ISA and the pension: £38.85. Not a lot of people realize this. But now you do.

Unfortunately, this position is confused by a couple of factors. First of all, the tax benefits of an ISA are not quite this simple. Although the interest on bonds and cash attracts full tax relief, there is only partial relief on the income from shares, which you get in the form of dividends. In effect, because the company that you invest in pays tax on its earnings, the income from shares is automatically taxed at the basic rate (give or take a little) – even in an ISA. You therefore only really get a tax benefit on the income from shares in an ISA if you are a higher rate taxpayer in retirement (because you avoid having to pay an extra bit). Since part of the point of going along the ISA route is to keep some money in shares after retirement, this reduces their appeal somewhat, but at least you're not compelled to buy an underperforming annuity as you are with a pension. Secondly, the above example assumes that you will pay the same rate of tax in retirement as you do during your working life. In practice, your income (and therefore tax rate) in retirement is likely to be lower. Again, this might make a pension seem more attractive, but again, you're still faced with having to buy an annuity.

Other benefits of saving via the pensions route are that, if you lost your job, you'd have to use up most of your non-pension savings before you qualified for any welfare benefits. Similarly, from April 2001, any pension that you have may be protected if you are made bankrupt. The last main benefit of pensions is that the contribution limits are much higher than for ISAs. If you are already making full ISA contributions, the tax benefits of pensions become much more obvious.

One of the biggest problems with pensions is that their charging structure tends to be so much less transparent than for ISAs. Generally, those Wise financial service companies don't miss an opportunity to muddy the waters on charges and this means that they are likely to be a good deal higher than the charges on a cheap, transparent ISA. Sometimes they are very much higher. These charges have a direct and major impact on your investment returns and this, of course, has a knock-on effect on your retirement income. We've looked at charges before in the pensions and endowments chapters, but let's look at them again by playing with a few numbers. Saving £250 per month for forty years, achieving an annual return of 10 per cent per year, would get you an investment pot worth £1,398,652. Now, imagine that your pension has charges (front-end loading, annual charges, whatever) that reduce your annual return, on average, by a mere 1.5 per cent, from 10 per cent to 8.5 per cent. With growth of 8.5 per cent annually, your savings would only grow to £927,380. In other words, the lower charges route gets you a pot that is 50 per cent bigger. All things being equal, this would make your income 50 per cent greater as well. And all for a seemingly small 1.5 per cent reduction in average annual return.

The other big, humongous problem with pensions is the requirement that we keep harping on about to buy an annuity with the bulk of the fund that you build up. As we saw in the chapter on pensions, annuities leave a lot to be desired, and that's putting it politely. If you're lucky enough to have a long retirement, their real value can be considerably eroded and you don't retain the money to leave to someone in your will.

Pensions are also very inflexible. Once money has gone in, it can only come out in the form of the lump sum on retirement and your retirement income. The flip side is that this does at least impose some discipline on you. If you think you're liable to blow all your savings at the drop of a starter's flag, then a pension could well be the way to go.

All in all, there are as many different arguments about the pros and cons of pensions over ISAs as there are different types of pensions and ISAs. The important thing to take on board is that the decision, either way, is generally not clear-cut. If someone tries to tell you that a pension is unambiguously a good idea, then there is a fair chance that they have an expensive pension to sell you.

A stocks and shares ISA is also a suitable means of repaying a mortgage. You can keep paying into the fund over the term of your mortgage and then, when the time comes, cash it in free of tax and use the money to repay the loan. At any stage during the term of the mortgage, you can decide that you'd rather just use the fund that you've built up to repay part of the mortgage (or even all of it if the fund has grown big enough). We'll talk more about the pros and cons of investment-backed, or 'interest-only', mortgages in Chapter 18, 'Be Your Own Landlord'. For now, although hopefully we don't need to, we just want to reinforce the point that if you want to go down this route, a good cheap ISA investing in shares is far more likely to make sense than the dreaded endowment.

Cash ISAs are a very good way of keeping a reserve fund for emergencies. You can get at the money whenever you need it (with a CAT-marked ISA anyway) and, in the meantime, it's earning tax-free interest. The one snag with a cash ISA is that by having one, you might hit the annual contribution limits and reduce the amount that you could be paying into a stocks and shares Maxi-ISA. In this case, we'd say that the stocks and shares should take precedence (no surprises there). Still, most people aren't in a position to save this much, in which case a cash Mini-ISA to go with a stocks and shares Mini (or a cash component in a Maxi-ISA) could make a lot of sense.

All in all, ISAs are a flexible, transparent and generally pretty cheap way of saving for most things and they offer very useful tax advantages. They're a bit complicated, but we love 'em. And so should you.

What You've (Maybe) Already Got: A Pause for Thought

If all the foregoing seems complicated and you've only half grasped it, go back and read it again. Maybe not right now – you probably need a break and a stiff drink – but sometime soon, perhaps after you've read more of the book. It's important that you do it, though. The contents of this section will help you make informed choices about how you're going to save for your future and which Wise products you may – or may not – like to buy. If you understand the contents of the last three chapters and Chapter 6, 'Be Your Own Financial Adviser', no one will ever be able to pull the wool over your eyes again and you'll be in a fine position to make your own decisions about your financial future. That's pretty Foolish.

If you're happy you've ingested it all, then 'Bravo!' And onward.

Bits 'n' Bobs

18

Be Your Own Landlord

The best thing we can do is to make wherever we're lost in look as much like home as we can.

— Christopher Fry, *The Lady's not for Burning*

They do things differently in Belgium. Take Monsieur et Madame Albert Chips-Cooked-In-Lard Why *Do* They Do That-It-Really-Spoils-Them as an example. Monsieur Albert is a branch manager at a small bank in Brussels. Madame is a clerical officer at the country's (and therefore the world's) leading Cream Cake Development Institute. With sensitive documents such as '*L'éclair: crème ou chocolat?*' and '*La pâtisserie: l'avenir*' passing across her desk on a daily basis, we can see that both Monsieur et Madame occupy jobs of the greatest responsibility. Their teenage twin boys, Philippe and René, have broad interests ranging from '*le football*' to '*le football*' and back again, and there is nothing to mark this family out from the vast majority of the Belgian bourgeoisie, including the fact that they do not own their dwelling place.

The four-bedroomed apartment in a respectable part of town that they've inhabited for years is rented. Like many respectable people on the Continent, they have never felt the need or inclination to buy their own place to live. Why is this? We have no idea, but doubtless PhD theses have been written on the subject and universities are even now offering courses on 'Comparative Home Ownership: Europe and Britain in the 20th Century'. You'll tell us we should enrol for one of these and, yeah, maybe we will (read: 'When Hell freezes over'). In the meantime, though, let's do some brainstorming about property as an investment. Is it a good one? In Britain, we seem pretty convinced that it is. On the other hand, in Belgium — and in much of Europe — many people seem convinced that it is not. Someone somewhere in Europe thinks that it is, though, because that someone is Monsieur and Madame Albert Chips-Cooked-In-Lard-Why-*Do*-They-Do-That-It-Really-Spoils-Them's landlord and they clearly think it's worthwhile. We'll say more about this in a moment but, first of all, let's take a quick look at property as an investment.

Property as an Investment

The first thing to spot about property is that it is a *real* asset. 'Real' as in it is actually there. Bricks and mortar and all that. As a real asset, it is worth what people are prepared to pay for it. This is very similar to shares, but it is very unlike other types of investments, such as gilts and cash, which are worth a fixed amount of pounds. The value of gilts and cash (which you might call *nominal* assets) is defined by the value of the pounds that they represent. As we have seen, the value of pounds fluctuates and, over the long term, inflation has meant that the tendency has been for them to fall in value. In fact, since the economy (including the Government) operates by investing a large number of borrowed pounds, there are good reasons for thinking that, over the long term, if the value of the pound consistently rose, we'd all go bust. For this reason economic policy is generally organized to encourage a steady decline in the pound's value. You can see this from the Bank of England's inflation target of 2.5 per cent. The aim is not to maintain the value of the pound, but to allow it to fall. Over the long term, the interest earned on cash and gilts has been scant consolation for this. The effect of all this is that investing in real assets such as shares and property, although it introduces a certain amount of short-term risk, is the best way of maintaining or increasing the value of your money over the long term.

So property is similar to shares and Fools tend to like it as an investment. But there are some big 'buts'. The first of these is that property is a difficult thing to invest in. You can't just set up a standing order for £100 per month to buy a share in the 'property market average', as you can the 'stock market average' when you purchase an index tracker, since there is no such thing as a 'property exchange'. When you buy a property, it's like buying an entire private company (that is, one that isn't listed on any stock exchange). This means that the process of buying and selling property is fairly expensive, involving, amongst other things, surveys, legal fees and extra stamp duty. It also means that most people are really only in a position to buy one (or maybe two) of them at any one time. This doesn't do very much for spreading your risk. So in some ways, investing in property is much more inefficient than the stock market and, except for the mega-rich, it is much harder to achieve a spread of risk.

The other thing about property is that because you generally have to buy it in very big chunks and most of us can't afford to buy these big chunks outright, we tend to have to borrow big sums of money from someone else to do it.

When we borrow money to buy a house, we are borrowing a fixed (that is, nominal) sum to invest in a real asset. This is called gearing. If we buy a house for £100,000 with a £90,000 mortgage, then we have invested £10,000 ourselves. If the house then increases in value by 10 per cent to £110,000, the value of the £10,000 that we put in has actually increased by 100 per cent to £20,000. However, the flip side to this is that, if the value of the house falls by 10 per cent to £90,000, then the value of the £10,000 that we put in has fallen by 100 per cent, to zero. Our short-term risk is dramatically increased but, since we expect the value of our house to increase over the long term (if only because of inflation and increases in average earnings), our long-term returns should also be increased. This gearing effect is, for many, one of the attractive aspects to property as an investment.

Being Your Own Landlord

As we said above about our Belgian friends, just because they don't own their home does not, of course, mean that nobody does. Someone has to own every house and, if you don't own it yourself, you'll have a landlord that you rent it from (if it's council property, then the council will be the landlord). This landlord clearly thinks that it's worthwhile to own the property, otherwise they wouldn't do it. The landlord either ties up their own money, or they borrow money on a mortgage, just as you could have done. The landlord then goes and charges you just enough rent to pay for the upkeep of the property and still provide a good enough return to justify them tying up their money, or a good enough return to pay the mortgage and leave them with a profit. So, if it's profitable for your landlord to own your house (and if they've any sense then they'll fix the rent so that it is), then you have to ask yourself why you shouldn't just *be your own landlord*. That way, you can make the profit that your landlord would have been making from you. In fact, it makes even better sense, since you, yourself, are the most efficient person to be owning your home. You don't need to charge yourself a deposit, you don't need to worry that you might run off without paying rent and you don't need to worry that you might start squatting in your own home (or let anybody else do so). A landlord needs to charge a tenant just a little more than otherwise to take account of the chances of these things happening but, if you do the job yourself, you know that they're not going to happen. You therefore save yourself money.

Buy Your Home, but Do It Foolishly

All this tells Fools a few key things about buying their home. First of all, it's generally a good thing to do, if you can afford to. Secondly, though, it is a risky thing to do in the short term and, if you do take the plunge, you have to make sure that you can do it for the very long term. We've said several times in this book that you need to think of shares as investments for at least five years, and preferably more. Well, you need to think of property as an investment for at least ten years and preferably much more. As with shares, you can change properties in the meantime (although, as we've said, the costs of doing so are a lot higher than for shares), but you need to invest in property, as a class of asset, for the very long term.

Mortgages, as we'll see, tend to last for twenty-five years and you should make sure that you can stay the course. If interest rates rocket skywards in ten years' time, you should feel confident that you will be able to keep paying the interest on your mortgage. This generally happens when there is high inflation, and you'll feel the pain of that in your wallet each month. High inflation, though, also means that the amount of money you had to borrow for the mortgage in the first place will start to look more and more insignificant, which means that high interest rates are not necessarily a bad thing for the *long term* value of your property. In fact, much of the increase in house prices over the last thirty years can be put down to high inflation, despite the high interest rates that have often accompanied it.

In the *short term*, though, high interest rates can be a very bad thing for the current value of your property and, if increases in interest rates mean that you can't keep paying the interest on your mortgage, then you'll generally find that it is absolutely the worst possible time for your bank to repossess and sell your home. Apart from the possibility of some nasty 'negative equity' (where the value of your house is less than the value of your mortgage), economic conditions are likely to be bad and it may be hard to find employment.

This is beginning to sound very scary, but it isn't really meant to. We're just re-examining the old long-term/short-term perspective that we've already talked about so many times in this book. Buying your home is generally a good thing to do, but do it as a long-term investment and make sure that you don't get caught short. In other words, buy your own home, but do it Foolishly.

Which Property, When and for How Much?

The questions of which property to buy, when to buy it and how much to pay are often the questions that cause people most headaches, but if you think about things Foolishly, this needn't be the case. The answer to the first question is simple. You are buying your own house, as we've said, to be your own landlord. So, the house that you buy is the one that you want (and can afford) to live in. It really is as simple as that. Find the house with that wonderful view, that rambling garden, that short journey to work or that gentle stroll along the lane to your local pub and buy it. To buy a house and live in it just because you think it will make a good investment is putting the cart before the horse. You only have one life and to spend it living in a house that doesn't work for you is a *big* waste of time. Besides, why are you so much surer that it will be a good investment than the person you're buying it from? The better the prospects for an area, the more the property should be costing you in the first place. In any event, you should have sufficient confidence in your own taste: if you buy something that you like and you look after it, the chances are that there'll be someone who wants to buy it from you when the time comes for you to move on.

So you buy the house that you want to live in, but when do you buy it? Well, you'll be pleased to hear that the answer to this is just as Foolish. You buy it when you want to and when you're able to. Just as Fools don't try to time the short-term fluctuations of the stock market, they don't try to time the short-term fluctuations of the property market. The state of the property market should take account of people's expectations about interest rates and prices in the future and there's no point in holding off because Leo, your estate agent friend, thinks in all his Wisdom that 'the property market looks a bit high at the moment'. In our experience, people who hold off from the property market because they are expecting a big crash suffer a similar fate to those who hold off from the stock market for the same reason. There are always reasons for thinking that the market might fall in the short term, just as there are always reasons for thinking that it might rise. All that we can say with any degree of confidence is that, over the long term, investing in property is a good thing to do. So, when you can afford to buy a home, find the one that you want (and can afford) to live in and go for it.

How much should you pay for your dream home? Well, given the answers to the previous questions, you can probably work out what's coming. You pay what it costs. Here, though, there are some very important riders. First of all, you should only be buying a house that is genuinely up for sale. It's not going to make sense for you to pay twice as much as a house is worth because the current owners love it so much that they really don't want to sell. The only way that you can get a proper guide to the value of a house is if it is on the market.

Next, you look around your dream home and you're told that the asking price is £100,000. What do you do then? Well, you 'um' and you 'ah' and, making sure you don't sound too keen, you say that you want to go away and think about it. You are now in a negotiating situation and there is a large amount of money at stake. Have a look around some similar properties in the area and find out their asking price. Preferably, you should find out how much similar properties have actually sold for. Is your dream home in the same ball park? Be very careful about anything that the seller's estate agents tell you – remember whose side they're on. Another thing to do is to think about how much it would cost to rent the home. The rent that you'd have to pay should always be a good bit more than the cost of a 100 per cent mortgage (to pay for upkeep and to give the landlord his profit). When you've thought carefully about all this, you put in a tentative offer to the seller's estate agent. Don't be afraid of pitching it quite a bit below the asking price: if nothing else, you can learn a lot about the property's value from the response you get. The last thing you want is an immediate acceptance of your first offer. If you get this, you'll know you've pitched it too high. The seller will always tend to pitch the asking price higher than the price they expect to get, so you should always be very reluctant to go above this price. If someone else is interested and the bidding, as it were, gets above this level, then it's probably a good idea to walk away and start looking for another dream home. Remember that you're happy to pay what the property is worth in current market conditions, but you need to be very careful not to pay more than it's worth.

The final point to make about how much you pay is a repetition of a point that we've already made several times. Too many people fall into the trap of buying as expensive a house as they can afford. **Don't do this**. It can be very tempting – we all want somewhere nice to live and it's a very good way of impressing our friends, but it's just not very Foolish. If you can't keep up the mortgage payments, for the long term, then you can end up without anywhere to live and your friends won't be very impressed at all. Work out how much the mortgage interest is going to cost you and double it. If things got this bad, could you keep up the repayments? It's bound to be painful, but if you think they'd be too high then you perhaps need to be looking at something a bit cheaper. The bottom line is that to play the mortgage game profitably, you need to be able to play it for a long time, through good times and bad.

Mortgages

Referred to in everyday language as the 'bloody mortgage' and most commonly incorporated into the phrase 'Well, it pays the bloody mortgage, I suppose' when referring to one's job of work, the mortgage is the cheapest form of long-term loan there is. It's cheap because the lender takes your home as security for the loan and houses are unable to change their name and leave the country. If you don't keep up your repayments, then the lender steps in, sells the house for what it can get and keeps enough to repay the loan. Simple as that. When the lender sells the house, they'll only get what the house can fetch at that time, there's no obligation for them to wait 'until the market recovers'; they just go in and do it. If that means that the money *you* had put into the house goes up in a puff of smoke, then that's hard cheese. In fact, if the lender can't get enough for the house to cover the loan, you'll still owe them the difference and they can come after you to get it. No wonder we keep saying that you need to stay within your limits. Anyway, that's all the down side to mortgages.

The up side is that the rate of interest is very low. Only a percentage point or so above what the Government pays to borrow money and, since the Government prints the stuff and effectively carries no risk at all, that's a pretty good deal. It is this fact that makes mortgage debt Foolish, whereas just about all other forms of debt are distinctly unFoolish. It is, however, only Foolish if you keep well within yourself. Sorry, did we make that point before? It must be beginning to grate now. It's just that we think it is the single most important thing in this whole chapter. Anyway, we've made our point now and we promise to drop the matter, except maybe for a quick mention at the end for those readers who lost patience with all this rambling and skipped ahead. Now, where were we? Oh yes, mortgages are a good cheap way of borrowing money (can you hear the sound of tongues being bitten?).

As with any loan, there are essentially two different things that you have to do with it. You have to repay the capital on the loan and you have to pay the interest on it. It is how you do these things that makes one mortgage different from another.

Repaying the Capital on Your Mortgage

There are basically two ways of doing this. Either you pay it back bit by bit over the course of the mortgage (which we'll assume to be twenty-five years, but this can vary) or you can pay none of it back at all over the twenty-five years, and pay it all off in one go at the end. The first of these approaches is called a repayment mortgage and the second is called an interest-only mortgage. On top of these approaches, there is another, called a current account mortgage, which is essentially a hybrid of the two.

Repayment mortgages

With a repayment mortgage, you start with a large pile of debt on which you have to pay a large amount of interest. On top of this interest, you pay back a tiny bit of the capital each month. As each month goes by, the amount that you owe is reduced and the amount of interest therefore falls as well, allowing you to pay back a bit more capital. The mortgage is structured so that the payments remain broadly level (subject to fluctuating interest rates), but an increasing amount goes on repaying capital and a correspondingly decreasing amount goes on paying the interest. By the time you get to the last few years of the mortgage, most of the monthly payments are going into paying off the capital and the amount you owe starts falling more and more quickly until, at the end of the mortgage, it is all paid back. The beauty of this is that if you keep making the payments, you know that, come what may, at the end of the mortgage you'll have paid everything back. For this reason, repayment mortgages are the least risky way of repaying a mortgage. A lot of people prefer to do it like this. We can see why, since they've already taken on a fair bit of risk with the mortgage in the first place.

Interest-only mortgages

The riskier option, but the one that is potentially more profitable, is to take an interest-only mortgage. With this approach, you owe the same amount of capital and therefore have to pay the same amount of interest (subject to fluctuating interest rates) throughout the term of the mortgage. All you do each month is repay the interest. How, then, do you repay the capital? Well, in addition to repaying the interest, you put a bit aside each month into a savings plan and then, at the end of the mortgage term, you use the accumulated pot of savings to repay the mortgage. In this case, you are taking a risk as to whether you can repay the capital. If your savings plan doesn't do its job, then you might have a shortfall when the time comes. The up side is that, if your savings plan more than does its job, then you might have a fair bit left over.

A good way to think of interest-only mortgages is to think that the money you are saving is money that you are not using to repay the mortgage. If you're saving at the rate of £100 per month then, after ten years, you will have paid a total of £12,000 into your savings plan. This is £12,000 that you could have used to repay the capital on your mortgage. For it to make sense to save the money rather than use it to repay capital, the savings need to be making a greater return than the rate of interest you're being charged on your mortgage (that is, on the capital that you haven't repaid). For you to have a chance of doing this, you really need to be saving the money in the stock market and, if you do so, then there is a good chance that an interest-only mortgage will work in your favour. After all, the rate of interest that you pay on your mortgage is linked to the rate of interest on cash deposits and, as we've seen, over the long term (like twenty-five years), the returns from shares tend to leave cash deposits miles behind. With an interest-only mortgage, you are therefore effectively borrowing money at mortgage rates in order to invest in the stock market. In the past this has proved to be a very profitable thing to do and there are good reasons to think that this will remain the case, BUT there is no doubt that there is risk involved. In fact, having borrowed money to buy your house, you are now borrowing money to invest in the stock market. For many people this is too much borrowing and too much risk and they prefer to go the repayment route. One thing is for sure: if you do decide to go for an interest-only mortgage, make sure that you think long and hard about the risks involved and your tolerance for them before you do it.

If you take an interest-only mortgage, then, how do you work out how much to save? Generally, your lender will have pretty firm idea about this and they're likely to point you in the right direction. It pays to be conservative. If you end up saving a bit too much, then that's well and good. If you end up saving not enough, then you're not going to be able to repay your mortgage on time. To do the calculations yourself, we'd suggest that a good starting point would be the rates that the Financial Services Authority uses for its growth projections. Currently these are 4 per cent, 6 per cent and 8 per cent. Naturally these are conservative projections. We'd say that 4 per cent really is ridiculously conservative, but why not split the top two and use 7 per cent? Even so, this is a long way behind the stock market's long-term historical growth rate. Still, there's nothing wrong with saving too much. Once you've picked a growth rate to use, have a read of Appendix 1, 'Coping with Compound Interest', which explains how to use this to work out how much you need to save on a monthly basis to reach a particular amount. You should also bear in mind that long-term investment returns are linked to long-term interest rates (although they should amount to a bit more). Therefore, if interest rates start to fall and your monthly mortgage payments fall, you should increase the amount of your monthly savings by the difference. The flip side to this is that if interest rates rise, then you probably don't need to save quite as much, BUT remember what we said about being conservative!

The final decision to make about interest-only mortgages is which vehicle you should use to do the saving. Traditionally, this type of mortgage has been backed up by an endowment policy. We examined these in some detail in Chapter 16 – or rather we tore them limb from limb before feeding the remains to a flock of hungry vultures and exorcizing their dark spirit with a series of ancient Druidic incantations. Suffice to say here that these are an expensive, inefficient means of paying off your mortgage, whose major pay-off is to the person who sells you the policy. Back in the Dark Days of the late 1980s, well over two-thirds of British mortgages were backed by endowment policies. Following the justifiably horrendous press that they've received recently, we're pleased to say that this figure is now down to around 10 per cent. Still, in our opinion, it's about 10 per cent too many. With interest-only mortgages backed by endowments not even making it past the regional heats for Miss Mortgage Fool 2000, who is going to win the cruise to Barbados, the modelling contract and the free year's liposuction? (You're going to think it's fixed, we know you are, but it honestly isn't.) And the winner is …

> *'Oh, Ladies and Gentlemen, the tension here at Fool Central is unbearable and I just can't seem to get this envelope open . . . Ah, here we are! . . . I can't believe it! It's so wonderful! It's so marvellous! She's so beautiful! Step up onto the podium, Miss Mortgage Fool of 2000, Miss Agnes Index-Tra-a-a-acker!'*
>
> *'Well, Agnes (sotto voce: 'That's right, stand here, luv, and flash yer gnashers into the camera with the light on'). It's a great honour. You've done so well and against such strong competition. What does winning here tonight mean to you?'*
>
> *'I weell use my poseeshun as Meess Mortgage Fool to work for world peace, spread ze Folliculitis and I love all children and ze animals. I love you all so much! Mwwoooh, my darleengs!'*
>
> *'Thank you, Agnes! I think you meant "Folly" there. "Folliculitis" is a nasty skin infection, as we all know! Har! Har! Isn't she wonderful, Ladies 'n Gennulmen?'*

Having read this book this far, this should come as no great surprise. Shares are the best way of saving for the long term and index trackers are the best way to get a good spread of shares with regular savings. Very experienced Fools might say that they prefer to choose their own shares and that's OK, so long as they bear in mind that they are betting their ability to repay their mortgage on their ability to choose good enough shares. We're confident that buying great shares for the long term, as we suggested in Chapter 12, 'Obviously Great Investments', would do the job as well or even better, but the task of repaying your mortgage is probably best left to the simplest, safest, yes we'll say most boring option. A good cheap index tracker it is then. If you were paying attention when we talked about ISAs in Chapter 17, then you'll know it goes without saying that this index tracker should be in the form of an Individual Savings Account (ISA).

And now for some numbers

Having looked at the difference between repayment and interest-only mortgages, let's have a look at how this might all pan out in practice. To take one mortgage as an example, we'll look at the Standard Life 'Future Perfect' mortgage and imagine we wish to borrow £100,000 to repay over twenty-five years. The Future Perfect mortgage is, in fact, no longer available, but it seemed like a good product to use as an illustration since it has a 'capped' rate of 6.25 per cent for the full twenty-five years of the mortgage. For sake of argument, let's assume that interest rates don't drop during the whole term, so the 6.25 per cent remains constant too.

For a repayment mortgage, our monthly payments on the £100,000 loan would be £659.67. If you keep paying this for twenty-five years, then the debt will be gone by then. At the beginning of the mortgage, £520.83 of the £659.67 monthly repayment relates to interest (the remaining £138.84 going in repayments of capital). If we didn't pay down any of the capital, our monthly interest charge would stick at £520.83 for the life of the mortgage. BUT, we can use the remaining £138.84 that we save on the monthly payments to put into an index tracker. Over twenty-five years, this would need to grow at 6.4 per cent for us to end up with the £100,000 to repay the mortgage. If it did this, then you'd have made the same overall monthly payments as with the repayment mortgage, and you'd have the same end result. However, if your tracker grew at more than this 6.4 per cent, then you'd end up doing better with the interest-only approach. For instance, if we assume a rate of growth of 10 per cent (conservative by historical standards), then you'd end up with £172,600 after twenty-five years. With this you could pay off the mortgage and still have £72,600 in your pocket.

Of course you can't necessarily rely on getting a return of greater than 6.4 per cent, even if that's what has happened in the past. This is where the risk comes in. For instance, if over twenty-five years your tracker grew at only 5 per cent, you'd end up with just £81,655; that is, £18,345 shy of repaying your mortgage. Again, there's more about doing this type of calculation in Appendix 1, 'Coping with Compound Interest'.

Current account mortgages

These are new. They effectively allow you to carry the mortgage debt in a bank account. Your lender sets a limit on how much you can borrow and then, so long as you keep below this, you can let the total amount of your mortgage debt fluctuate, upwards or downwards. This means you can treat it like an interest-only mortgage if you want, where you just pay the interest each month, or like a repayment mortgage where you pay back a bit of the actual loan each month. You can repay the loan more quickly than in the traditional twenty-five years or, if you like, you can pay it back more slowly.

If all this is sounding as though current account mortgages are supremely flexible, then that's because they are. Be careful, though, because with flexibility comes responsibility. If you don't make the effort to reduce the mortgage, then it won't reduce. In fact, if you're allowed to skip a few interest payments and do, then the mortgage will actually increase. If you're the interest-only mortgage sort of person and you're using the money saved to invest, then you might not see this as a problem. But you need to make sure that what you are doing is a conscious and well-considered decision and not just a bit of financial slackness.

Another benefit of current account mortgages is that you can effectively use them to save cash tax free. However much your current account is in credit, then that sum is effectively knocked off the outstanding amount to repay on your mortgage. Imagine that you have £10,000 that you want to save in cash. With a normal mortgage, the interest payments that you make will not be affected, as your mortgage and your bank accounts are completely separate. This means that, ISAs aside, you'll pay tax on the interest that you're getting on the £10,000 in a deposit account. With the current account mortgage, on the other hand, the cash that you save goes directly into paying off your mortgage. You can get the cash back out at any stage but, in the meantime, you're not paying tax on any interest that you've earned, because you haven't earned any. Sounds bad, hey? £10,000 saved and not earning any interest. What's the point of that? Well, by reducing the amount of your mortgage by £10,000, you've reduced the amount of interest that you have to pay on it, which more than corresponds to the interest you would have earned on the money in a deposit account. The current account mortgage lets you have your cake and eat it. Because your overall borrowing can go up and down, you can effectively have a cash reserve without actually having any cash. Neat, hey?! Not only this, the sums don't have to be as high as £10,000 to work in your favour. With the interest on the loan calculated on a daily basis, the few days (as long as that?) that your bank account is in credit at the beginning of the month after your salary has been paid will also count and save you money on your mortgage. Over time, this could add up to a very significant saving on your mortgage payments.

Before we get carried away, we should say that, at the moment, the market for this type of mortgage is relatively young and there are only a few of them around. This means that the competition among the providers is fairly limited and you might have to pay a slightly higher rate of interest than you would for a more conventional mortgage. Still, you might well feel that it's worth it for the advantages and, as these things prove more popular, so the interest rates should become more competitive.

Paying the Interest on Your Mortgage

The first question to ask here is where do interest rates actually come from? Knowing the answer certainly won't make you sparkle at parties, but it is one of those things worth knowing anyway. The answer is that they are set by the Monetary Policy Committee (MPC) of the Bank of England. If the MPC thinks that the economy is doing rather too well, potentially setting off a nasty bout of inflation, then it will put up interest rates to slow things down. On the other hand, if the MPC thinks that the economy is going too slowly, and that inflation is not a real threat, then it will bring interest rates down to try to get things going again. The MPC tries to make small adjustments well ahead of events (about eighteen months ahead), so as to avoid the need to make big adjustments later. If it fails to put up interest rates when it should, then the chances are that inflation will increase and, ultimately, rates will have to go much higher than they otherwise would in order to bring it back under control. It's a case of a stitch in time saving nine.

The base rate is effectively the rate of interest at which the Government borrows money in the very short term. The Government has the best credit rating there is, so if it is prepared to pay 6 per cent to borrow money, then everyone else will have to pay a bit more. After all, why would a bank take only

5 per cent from you and me if it can get 6 per cent from the Government? How much more everyone else has to pay depends on how good a risk they are. If you put your house up as security, then you're a pretty good risk and you should only have to pay slightly more than base rates, perhaps 0.5 per cent to 1 per cent more.

Tracking and variable rate mortgages

When you get a tracking mortgage, your interest rate 'tracks' the base rate. Say you get a tracking mortgage on which you pay the base rate plus 0.75 per cent. This means that if base rates are 5.75 per cent, then you will be paying 6.5 per cent. If base rates go up by 0.5 per cent then you'd be paying 7.0 per cent. Fair enough.

Variable rate mortgages are similar to this, but perhaps not quite so good since they are slightly less predictable. In this case, your mortgage provider sets rates pretty much how it likes. It has savers to whom it must pay interest and it wants to make a profit, so it would like to charge you as much as possible. However, it can't charge too much or all its borrowers will simply move to someone else who's charging less and then where will it be? Taking all this into account, each lender's variable rate is likely to float around a bit above the base rate. In fact, it is likely to float around at about the same sort of premium to base rates as a tracking mortgage. The difference, and the reason for preferring the tracker, is that with the tracker you know exactly what the deal is and it's not subject to the fickleness of your mortgage provider. (By the way, don't get confused with index trackers here – we're talking about something different. A tracking mortgage simply refers to the way the interest rate is calculated. An index tracker is a type of investment you may or may not be using to pay off the mortgage in the end.)

Fixed rate mortgages

With a fixed rate mortgage, as the name suggests, your interest payments are fixed for a certain period. This period is typically anything from a year to ten years. So, if you have a mortgage with the interest rate fixed at 7 per cent for five years, your monthly interest payments on the outstanding capital will be set at that rate for five years.

To understand properly how fixed rate mortgages work, you need to think about the gilt market. In just the same way that the base rate determines what interest rate the Government pays on its short-term debt, the 'redemption yield' on gilts determines the interest rate that the Government pays on its medium- and long-term borrowings. The redemption yield on gilts therefore also dictates the interest rate of fixed rate mortgages. Most broadsheet newspapers will have a list of gilts, together with their yields, somewhere in the business section. If you are looking at a five-year fixed rate mortgage, then you want to compare it to the redemption yield on gilts with a maturity date five years from now. In other words, if it's now 2001, then you want to look at a gilt called something like Treas 5% 2006. Make sure you're looking at the column for redemption yields, rather than the column for the interest yield or flat yield (which are different).

As with variable rates and trackers, you will generally pay a small premium (of perhaps 0.5 to 1 per cent) on the rate that the Government pays (that is, the redemption yield on the relevant gilt). So, if you are offered a five-year fixed rate mortgage at 6 per cent and you see that the redemption yield on a five-year dated gilt is 5.5 per cent, then you know that it's a pretty good deal. Sometimes you might see a deal where the interest rate is less than the gilt yield. If this is the case, then there is often a catch in the form of a lengthy tie-in period or something similar. If not, then the provider is probably relying on enough borrowers being too lazy to move when the rate eventually goes up. If you go for something like this, then make sure you're not the lazy type because it could end up costing a lot more in the long run.

The effect of a fixed rate deal is, of course, that your repayments will stay the same for the period of the fix. This provides a bit of certainty for your budgeting. However, once you have fixed the deal you are, to a greater or a lesser extent, committed to it for that period. If interest rates go up, then you'll sit back smugly, thanking your lucky stars that you decided to fix your interest rate and congratulating yourself on your vision and perspicacity. On the other hand, if interest rates fall, then you will have to watch enviously as variable rate mortgages get cheaper and cheaper, while blaming your spouse for talking you into a fixed rate mortgage in the first place. In this situation, it will cost you to get out of the deal. This is entirely reasonable, since you wouldn't let the bank back out of the fixed rate deal if the rates went up, and you can't have it both ways. Different mortgage deals have different penalties for copping out early. There is no such thing as a free lunch and, where the penalties for early redemption are slack, the borrower will have to pay for this with a higher interest rate. So, if you hunt around for the cheapest five-year fixed rate deal on the market, don't be surprised if it also contains the toughest redemption penalties. If you want the cheapest interest rate, then you'll have to accept the least flexibility. If you don't like the idea of being tied in, then rather than looking around for slack redemption penalties, you should probably be looking at a tracking or variable rate deal instead.

The final point that we want to make about fixed rate mortgages is that the longer the period of your fixed rate, the more risky the thing becomes. This is because if it goes wrong for you and interest rates fall, it will be longer before your fixed period ends and you can go back to the lower rate. We would say that fixed deals of more than five years are too risky for most people. There are plenty of people who took out ten-year fixed rate deals in the early 1990s (when rates were much higher) who have been kicking themselves for a long time now.

Bells and whistles

What we've done here is try to simplify the important elements of a mortgage. However, there are literally thousands of different types of mortgage on the market. They are littered with extra frills like 'cash-back' deals and 'discounted rates'. It is safe to say that we don't much like this sort of thing. They are generally just a way of muddying the waters so that the providers can end up charging us more. They know we love a discount and they know that dangling some cash before our eyes (to buy that washing machine) is going to get us right where they want us. Remember that there is no such thing as a free lunch and the more unnecessary bells and whistles that attach to a mortgage, the less likely it is to be the best value. Remember to keep things simple.

A word on the different types of mortgage

The way the interest is calculated on your mortgage is an entirely separate issue from whether the mortgage is a repayment type or an interest-only type. This means you can have a repayment fixed rate, variable or tracking mortgage or an interest-only fixed rate, variable or tracking mortgage. Sorry if by now this seems ridiculously obvious to you, but it is a point of confusion for quite a few people so we just wanted to make sure it was all completely clear.

Summing Up on Mortgages

First of all, decide how you want to repay the capital. If you want the least risky option, then this will mean a repayment mortgage. If you can stomach a bit of risk, then there's a very good chance that an interest-only mortgage will work out better in the end. If you want the maximum flexibility over your repayments, then one of the new current account type mortgages might suit.

As far as paying the interest is concerned, bear in mind that no one, despite what they might want you to believe, knows where interest rates are headed. If anyone really knew what was going to happen, they'd be busy making a fortune on the gilt market. They certainly wouldn't be trying to sell you a mortgage. The gilt market takes into account the market's best guesses, and is therefore the best guide as to where interest rates are heading. Fixed rate mortgages are dictated by yields in the gilt market. The yields in the gilt market, in turn, are dictated by the market's best guess as to where the base rate is headed and the base rate dictates the interest rates on variable rates and tracker mortgages. Phew! Anyway, the effect of all this is that, all things being equal, a fixed rate mortgage should reflect what the market expects a variable rate or tracking mortgage to cost you over the same period. In other words, it should make no real difference which type of mortgage you go for (so long as you get the cheapest available of the type you're looking at) and you shouldn't get too het up about it. However, for peace of mind, there's a lot to be said for a straightforward five-year fixed rate deal. At least that way you know where you are for five years and can budget accordingly. The choice is yours, and now that you have all the facts you're in the best position to make it.

Finally, we just want to return to that point that we made several times at the beginning of this chapter. The best mortgage is one that you can easily afford – even if interest rates rocket. For the whole homeowning thing to work well, you must make sure that you can stick it out for the long term, through good times and bad. That really is the last time we'll mention it. Now let's move on and see how we might get our hands on one of these, how you say, mortgages?

The Five Steps to a Successful Mortgage

It's always been our personal experience, and people have been telling us over the last few years, that there is a yawning chasm between knowing the theory and feeling able and confident enough to put that theory into practice. That's why here we'd like to include some practical steps on how to get the mortgage you want. Your mortgage is going to be with you for a long time and it's worth putting just a little effort into getting it right.

Step One: Do not buy a mortgage from anyone who spontaneously offers to sell you a mortgage

These people should be approached with the greatest caution, as they can be very convincing. They are, however, looking at you as a potential gold mine and will almost certainly try to sell you an endowment as well. On no account let them get between you and the exit: instead speak soothing, polite words, avoid eye contact (this can be dangerous) and back slowly out of the door. If you do this skilfully enough, they will still be talking to an empty room as you turn the key in the door of No. 1 Fleapit Mansions, your current, luxury residence.

Step Two: Also do not buy a mortgage during a face-to-face encounter

You know what you want. You do not have to be 'sold' to. Agreeing to a face-to-face encounter with a mortgage salesperson is agreeing to the possibility that the salesperson may be able to change your mind and sell you what he/she wants. If this is the case, then you are not ready to buy a mortgage.

Step Three: You're the customer, so act like one. Go out and shop!

It's easy to think that the people who lend you the money to buy your house are being kind to you, that they are doing you a favour. This is wrong. You are doing them a favour by gracing them with your custom. Try not to forget this, as it helps in the game of psychological one-upmanship on which you are about to embark. *They* have to earn *your* business; you do not have to prove yourself worthy to them. Be upfront, pushy even. If the person on the other end of the line is starting to sound exasperated or is even putting on mock offence, then go elsewhere. The likelihood of your causing real offence with your polite questions is small and remember this Foolish law of personal finance:

> *It's your life and it's only their job.*

Step Four: Log on and/or pop down the newsagent's

In the first edition of this book we said:

> 'We'd love to be able to say to you that you can do all the shopping you need
> for a mortgage on the Internet, but it just isn't true. There is certainly a lot
> of information there but, to make sure you've seen everything that's available,

you'll end up falling back on the telephone and that's where the magazines come in. They have listings of all the mortgages and mortgage companies and also large glossy advertisements with telephone numbers and, occasionally, Web site addresses.'

Well, times have moved on a lot. These days there are a number of sites online that offer comparative lists of mortgages and which allow you to search according to location, how large a mortgage you need, what type you're after, etc. You may still want to buy a copy of *What Mortgage* or *Your Mortgage* or anything with 'mortgage' in the title from the newsagent's to give you an overall perspective, but it's by no means as necessary as it was just two short years ago.

Step Five: The chase

Park yourself by the computer and/or the telephone with the Foolish mortgage-hunter's survival kit: pen, reams of paper, cup of tea and one box of Jaffa Cakes, comfort-eating for the use of. By now you've decided what you want. Let's assume you've decided on the Foolish combination of a five-year fixed rate interest-only mortgage, backed by an index tracker. You either log on and start searching various Web sites to find a mortgage (useful Web site addresses are listed in Appendix 5) or start phoning likely-looking organizations on your list. To help you through the potential trauma of such a phone call (and you may still have to resort to the phone even if you find what you want on the Internet), here's an example of how it might go:

DIRECT MORTGAGES FOR FOOLS. Hello, Direct Mortgages for Fools, how can I be of Foolish assistance today?

YOU. Hello. I'm interested in a five-year fixed rate interest-only mortgage, which I will back with an index tracker. I'm wondering what you've got to offer me.

(This is a good start. You're confident and you've shown you know a little bit about the subject. The person on the other end is already saying to themselves: 'For this is a Fool!')

DIRECT MORTGAGES FOR FOOLS. Certainly, we have the blah, blah . . .

(If you're lucky at this point, they will indeed give you the information you ask for. If you're not, you may find yourself giving away a load of demographic information designed to ensure that you and your family unto the seventh generation shall receive direct mail from these people. If that is the case, then you may want to ask them to cut through the malarkey and get to the point.)

DIRECT MORTGAGES FOR FOOLS. . . . and then we have the ValuePlan Five-Year Fixed Rate Mortgage.

(You're going to be faced with a bewildering array of superficially enticing schemes designed to make you buy one of DMF's mortgages. We go into some of the permutations below — you'll figure them out pretty quickly and it doesn't make for the most exciting of reading — but just remember that if it looks too good to be true, it definitely is.)

YOU. Sounds interesting. I wonder if you'd send me some details?

(You're for it now. They really are going to ask you a whole lot of questions about your income, spouse's income, other debts, etc. They need this to make up a proposal for you which they will then send out. Despite the rigour of this interrogation and the professional, personalized nature of the proposal when it arrives, be reassured that this commits you to nothing.)

DIRECT MORTGAGES FOR FOOLS. No problem. May I just ask how you are planning to pay off the amount of the loan at the end of the mortgage term?

(At this point, you say either that you're going to link it to an index tracker as you pointed out at the beginning and you already have one in mind, thank you very much, or else that you will be making regular contributions into a self-select ISA and building up an equity portfolio. If you plump for the latter, sound very confident and knowledgeable. In fact, if you plump for the former, be very confident and knowledgeable.)

DIRECT MORTGAGES FOR FOOLS. That sounds interesting, sir/madam. I wonder if you've considered one of our endowment policies? They have quite impressive bonuses at the end of the policy, they provide life assurance as well and they are portable.

(You didn't sound confident enough, did you? DMF thought there was just the minutest chance that they could flog you an endowment policy. Remember, it means a lot to them and they're going to try very hard. They always use the life assurance thing, because you generally need to have life assurance to cover your mortgage and they always plug the fact that you can keep the same endowment policy if you move house — i.e. they're 'portable'. Luckily, you were ahead of them and you reply:)

YOU. Thanks very much, but I'm not all that impressed with endowments in general. I'll be shopping around for the best deal I can find in level term life assurance and the index tracker's portable in any case.

(Way to go, Fool! [Sorry, that was the Americans in this writing team getting a little out of hand. Normal service will now be resumed.] Yes, you've done really well. Level term life assurance is what you will need and unless DMF is willing to offer you the best deal, don't buy it from them. Level term simply means that you will be insured for the whole sum of the loan for the whole period. If the credits start to roll before your time — or what you thought ought to be your time — then the insurance company

pays out on the policy. If you survive until the end of the policy and pay off the mortgage as planned, the insurance cover finishes and you get nothing. Except the satisfaction of having survived, that is. If DMF can't sell you an endowment policy, they may push their life assurance pretty hard and if they do, it may well be a 'with-profits' policy in which there is an investment component (and an even larger charges component) to it. Decline it. You have the information you want, it is now time to make your excuses and leave.)

DIRECT MORTGAGES FOR FOOLS. Thank you very much, I'll get that proposal out in the post to you today.

YOU. Thanks a lot, I appreciate it. Byeee.

There, it wasn't too bad, was it? And the reason is that you knew what you wanted beforehand and were in control throughout. Granted you've had to expend five weeks of unremitting misery to get to this point in the book, but it's starting to pay off. You now move on to the next likely-looking candidate in the magazine:

GERBILS PROVIDENT. Hello, Gerbils Provident – two hundred years of faithful service to rodents and other small mammals – how can I help?

We'll be honest here. This is going to take you a couple of hours one Saturday morning to sort out. Perhaps even a bit more by the time you've sorted through all the paperwork you're going to get sent and made your decision. But it'll be worth it.

The MIG and Life Assurance

One more sting in the tail for house purchasers that it's worth knowing about is the Mortgage Indemnity Guarantee premium, or MIG. It can have other names, too, but whatever it's called, it's a one-off premium that can amount to £1500 or more, which you generally have to pay if you are taking out a loan of more than 75 per cent of the property value. You see, the statistics tell the mortgage companies that loans of this kind of size are more likely to be defaulted on. Hmm, so that means the MIG insures you against not being able to repay the loan and you won't lose your house …? Sorry, it insures *them* against your not being able to repay the loan. They'll still repossess it, you'll still lose it and they'll still sell it on for whatever they can get for it. What's the point of it for the buyer, then? Good question. At the time of writing some

239

companies are starting to abolish the MIG and it's a trend that we hope will continue. Good riddance!

Generally, people assume that they will need some life assurance to go with their mortgage. In fact, this isn't necessarily the case at all. If you can keep your mortgage down to 75 per cent or so of the value of your property, then there's a good chance the mortgage company won't require you to have any. Sure, people will try to sell it to you, but think about whether you really need it. If you don't have any dependents, you almost certainly don't need it. If your mortgage outlasts you, then the lender can get its money back when the house is sold. That is, after all, one reason why it took security in the first place. By avoiding superfluous life assurance, you can save yourself sizeable sums which you can add to your savings – a far better use for the money. If you do have dependents, then you still might not need *more* life assurance. While providing for your family in the unlikely event of your demise is something that everyone should think about and this will generally mean taking on some life assurance, if you've already got this sorted out then there is no definite reason why you should increase it just because you've got a mortgage. Maybe you should, maybe you shouldn't. It depends on the particular situation – the point to bear in mind is that it is a separate issue.

Be Your Own Landlord – The End

Sounding a bit complicated? Starting to wonder if it's all worth it? Don't! It's actually not all that complicated when you get into it and it's too late, anyway. You see, you may want to give all this over to someone else to manage, but you've ruined it. You now know too much. You've passed the point of no return and should have put this book back on the shelf in the shop immediately after you picked it up, silly Fool! For you now know that many of the people who are trying to sell you a mortgage are trying to make a fast buck, that some mortgages are far worse for your health than others and that these are the ones that will be pushed hardest at you. You can't unlearn any of this stuff and while some say that ignorance is bliss, we say that when it comes to investment it carries a pretty hefty price tag and actually isn't all that blissful anyway.

Being ignorant and having to rely on others to make *your* financial decisions on *their* behalf is a little like one of those falling dreams when you tumble off a cliff and can see the ground coming towards you, but can't do anything about it. Sometimes you actually go on and hit the ground, but at other times you manage to wake yourself up with a start before you do, and that's what happened to you when you picked up this book on that fateful Tuesday afternoon in Bromsgrove. There's no going back and while that may feel a little burdensome at times, on the other hand the financial benefits are potentially enormous and the 'feelgood' factor is pretty strong too. You are now a fully-fledged, card-carrying Fool, managing his or her own investments, captain of your fate and mistress of your soul. It's exhilarating, so savour it. After all, anyone who has got this far through a book on investment has earned it.

19

Where Else *to Invest*

They change their clime, not their frame of mind, who rush
across the sea.

— Horace, *Epistles*

In his excellent book *Mother Tongue – The English Language* Bill Bryson reveals that in the 1920s a US novel published in Britain required a glossary to apprise readers of the meaning of words like *grapevine*, *fan* (in the sense of a sports enthusiast), *gimmick* and *phoney*. In the 1940s an article in the *Daily Mail* proposed that British readers would be confounded by the use of words such as *commuter*, *seafood*, *rare* (as applied to meat), *mean* (in the sense of nasty), *dumb* (in the sense of stupid), *dirt road* and *living room*. As Bryson points out, it does seem an unjustified slight on *Daily Mail* readers that they would not be able to deduce the meaning of at least some of these words, but it does show just how close our countries have become in the last fifty years. There are still major, major differences, as both sides would admit, but in investment terms – and let's pinch ourselves to remind us that we are meant to be talking about investing here – there are many more similarities than differences.

The fact is that what happens on the US markets, on Wall Street, is very shortly mirrored in the UK market and others around the world. We don't believe in monitoring short-term market hiccups as a route to successful investing, but it is extraordinary the way the UK market will hang on news of the decision of the US Federal Reserve Board (their equivalent of the Bank of England) chairman on US interest rates, or be propelled upwards by confidence in US stocks. The one does not move without the other. Or rather, the UK market mirrors its transatlantic partner.

In researching this book and looking at the topic of great consumer brands, we came across a report published by the international brand consultancy Interbrand, listing the world's top 75 brands in order of financial value. Of those, forty-two were associated with American companies, including nine out of the top ten. We're pleased (and a little surprised) to say that the UK makes the second largest contribution to the list, with a total of nine brands, even though the biggest of these, Reuters, only makes it in at forty-ninth on the list. The two tables below list the world's top ten brands (because that's what we're talking about) and the nine from the UK that make it into the list (because we knew you wanted to know):

The ten most valuable brands in the world

Global rank	Brand	Value ($bn)	Country	Annual share price growth over last ten years
1	Coca-Cola	72.5	US	16.8%
2	Microsoft	70.2	US	36.3%
3	IBM	53.2	US	13.5%
4	Intel	39.0	US	45.9%
5	Nokia	38.5	Finland	50.0%
6	General Electric	38.1	US	24.6%
7	Ford	36.4	US	12.3%
8	Disney	33.6	US	14.6%
9	McDonald's	27.9	US	14.8%
10	AT&T	25.5	US	5.8%

The nine most valuable brands from the UK

Global rank	Brand	Value ($bn)
49	Reuters	4.9
58	BP	3.1
60	Shell	2.8
61	Burger King	2.7
62	Smirnoff	2.4
67	Johnnie Walker	1.5
68	Hilton	1.5
73	Guinness	1.2
74	Financial Times	1.1

Source: Interbrand Annual Survey 2000

We've seen four of these top UK brands before, when we discussed Diageo in Chapter 12. But even if Diageo helps the UK to sneak nine companies into the list, there really is no contest. However you look at it, if you want to invest in the biggest and most powerful brands in the world, then you can't ignore America. What's more, many, many of the companies over there are just as familiar to us, or more so, than our own. Going beyond the table that we showed above, have you ever heard of Marlboro, Hewlett-Packard, Gillette, American Express, Kodak, Nike, Kelloggs, Wrigley's? OK, we're boring you now, but it's hard to imagine that British consumers are much less familiar with the products of these worldwide giants than are their US cousins.

It's no surprise, then, that many investors like to wander across the pond in their search for great investments. You can see from the first table that these powerful US brands have performed well in share price terms over the last ten years as well (compared to the S&P 500 index which has risen at a rate of 14.8 per cent per year) – and it's not as if most of them weren't great brands for a long time before that. Companies like these have made the US stock market one of the strongest performers in the world over the years. Take a look at this graph, which shows the progress of the Dow-Jones Industrial Average (a US index of thirty of the most important industrial stocks) since 1918:

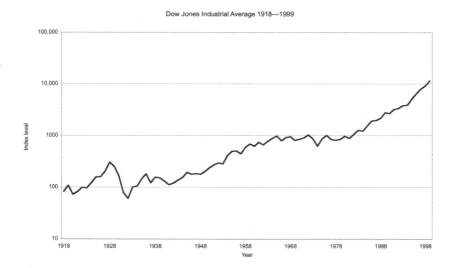

Dow Jones Industrial Average 1918—1999

Looks suspiciously familiar, doesn't it? That's because you saw almost exactly the same thing when you looked at the performance graph of shares on the London Stock Exchange earlier in this Foolish tome. Where they dip, we dip, where they peak, we peak and just as ours does, their graph zigs more than it zags and soars more than it sags. Although the shape is very similar, in absolute terms, the Dow Jones doesn't really show a fair comparison with the earlier graph, since it does not include re-invested dividends and therefore does not reflect *total* returns. It also doesn't remove the effects of inflation, which has been much greater in the UK. The best comparison of the underlying picture that we can find is our old friend the CSFB Equity-Gilt Study. This finds that, since 1920, the US total real returns from equities has averaged 8.5%, whereas bonds have achieved only 2.7%. In the UK, these figures are remarkably similar at 8.6% and 2.8% respectively.

Starting from the Motley Fool's US site (**www.fool.com**), it is in fact easier for a UK-based investor to research US companies than it is to research UK companies. The resources at the Fool make a great start, of course, and there are people available twenty-four hours a day to give you a helping hand, but beyond that US companies tend to have more informative and wide-ranging Web sites than their UK counterparts; they also have to file an official report on how they're doing to the investment authorities every *three* months. In the UK, this is required only every six months and there is no requirement to file it online, unlike in the US where every financial report from every listed company is available on the Net, in its entirety, for everyone to see (**www. edgar-online.com**). Now, *that* we like. One day it will be the norm here, too, and the Motley Fool UK won't stop pushing until that happens. Other facilities you will find easily accessible and far more comprehensive than on the UK Internet are share quotes, graphs, earnings estimates and company news.

Buying and selling US shares over the Internet from the UK is as easy and cheaper than buying and selling UK shares. Using a US-based (or indeed UK-based), Internet 'deep discount' brokerage, you can expect to be able to buy and sell shares for as little as a flat rate charge of £6, no matter how large the transaction. And you can expect the trade to be carried through within under a minute, too. Some people get a little anxious at the thought of sending their money across the world and then trading it via the Internet. Just a few years ago this was science fiction and so it's not surprising that we feel wary. However, the Internet really has shrunk the world and with the opportunities that exist on the US market it seems perverse not to take advantage of them just because you're dealing with something new.

As we've just seen, the financial regulations concerning public companies are stricter than any in the UK – including four times a year company reporting – and any broker you choose should be indemnified up to at least $500,000 by the Securities Investor Protection Corporation (SIPC). Many carry far higher indemnity provisions than this (this is the US, land of litigation, remember) and one we know of carries provision as high as $57 *million*. Your friends and neighbours might look at you a little strangely because you're now buying a stake in some of the world's greatest businesses via your computer, but let them! You're a Fool now, you're making use of the communication revolution to invest sensibly and profitably for your long-term future and nothing's going to stop you.

The first step is often the most difficult. Good places to start are with the US book by David and Tom Gardner, *Rule Breakers, Rule Makers*. Actually, what we really suggest is that you don't go out and start spending more money right away. Spend some time at the Motley Fool US site before you make any decisions about whether or not you want to invest in the US. There are some terrific investment ideas over there and first-time investors might want to pay particular attention to the Rule Breaker, Rule Maker and DRiP portfolios, each of which focuses on investments in great American companies. Then there is the Foolish Four portfolio with its mechanical approach to investment in certain of the Dow-Jones heavies (we say more about this type of investing in Chapter 20, 'Mechanical Investing'). The possibilities are limitless, links to resources for further research are easily accessible and help is readily at hand on the discussion boards.

If you do make the decision that you want to invest in the United States, then you have a number of options, including:

1. Doing so via a UK-based stockbroker. You'll find there are a number now that offer cheap, efficient Internet-based trading in US stocks. The basic series of steps to go through is the same as in Option 2 below.
2. Setting up a US Internet 'deep discount' brokerage account. Simply stop by the Fool's deep discount brokerage centre (**www.fool.com/dbc/dbc2.htm**), then:
    * Fire off a series of e-mails to likely candidates asking whether it's possible to open an account from the UK;
    * Ask your selected broker to mail you an application form and US W8 tax form. They use the normal post to send you the forms to make sure you're who you say you are, living where you say you do;
    * Count off the days until they arrive and then fill out the forms and send them back;
    * Await e-mail confirmation that your account is open;
    * Transfer your pile of Foolishly saved cash by bank transfer to your new brokerage account;
    * Await the e-mail saying that your money has arrived;
    * Reflect that you are now an international Internet tycoon and investor, surfing the crest of the global investment wave. Feel good? You should!
3. Doing so via your Individual Savings Account. The details of how this works will vary and although there will be an obvious tax advantage, transaction charges may be hefty.

By logging onto the site using your username and password, you will be able to access the details of your portfolio, updated in real time according to the latest share prices, as well as buying and selling shares with the utmost ease. Of course, you're not going to let the ease and cheapness of the service tempt you into becoming a day trader, are you? As you do with your UK investments, you buy and hold quality companies on the basis of their fundamental performance, not on the whims of the marketplace or the hype of a hypester.

One useful place to visit for those with an interest in the US is the Nasdaq Web site specially dedicated to UK investors: **www.nasdaq.co.uk**. The Nasdaq is a US stock exchange that tends to cater for high-tech companies and which has a large number of foreign companies listed on it. Microsoft, Intel, Ericsson and ARM Holdings are all listed on the Nasdaq.

What about currency fluctuations over the years? Currently, the pound is very strong, meaning it will buy a lot of US dollars. What if it gets even stronger in thirty years' time when you want to bring your dollars back to live in the UK? It might happen that way, yes, or the pound may be weaker then than it is now. In our opinion, there is risk inherent in any enterprise, but there's idiotic risk and there's Foolish risk. With the kinds of returns that great American companies have provided over decades (Coca-Cola: 17 per cent every year since 1918) and with the general strength of both our economies, this is a Foolish risk and not one which we think will figure hugely in your financial equations a few decades from now. In any event, many of the best US investment opportunites, like their UK counterparts, are dominant *global* companies, which earn their money all over the world in many different currencies. Although their shares are quoted in dollars and their dividends are paid in dollars, their fortunes are not solely linked to the fortunes of that currency.

Where *Else* to Invest: EuroFool

So that's it, is it? America and Britain. There are no other countries in the world worth investing in. The 300 million or so people on the other side of the English Channel are all living in an economic and investment wasteland where mangy dogs roam the streets and the occasional burst of gunfire breaks the tense silence of a sultry afternoon.

Er, no. Keen-eyed readers of this book will have noticed that one of our Obviously Great Investments is in fact Ericsson, a Swedish mobile telecommunications company, although it is listed both in Stockholm and on the Nasdaq exchange in the US. There are many great investment opportunities in Europe, but to be honest most of us don't know a huge amount about them. We don't like to speak foreign languages when it comes to investing and we mean that in the nicest possible way. Actually, we *love* to speak foreign languages, but like to know what we're investing in. If we don't understand an investment, or don't feel comfortable with it, we don't invest. Our lack of familiarity, though, with Europe and the European markets is something that is going to change rapidly with the advent of the euro and the Internet. In fact, we already have a German Motley Fool site up and running (**www.fool.de**). The only potential snag for UK users, of course, is that it's in German.

However, the ease with which the new currency, the euro, will allow trading across borders is likely to open up the stock markets of Europe to such an extent that this book, largely confined as it is to dealing with investment in the UK, will seem like a laughable anachronism in just a few years. Already, the London Stock Exchange is discussing the possibility of merging with Frankfurt's equivalent to produce an exchange to be called, provisionally, iX. Whereas today we talk about the FTSE 100, tomorrow we'll almost certainly be talking about the iX Euro 100 or something similar. If what we're primarily worried about in investment is total return on our money, then we wish to invest in the best businesses we can, whether they're French, Dutch, British, American or Italian and, so long as there's no serious currency hit to be reckoned with, it seems ludicrous not to invest in a company simply because it's foreign. In a very few years, you will likely be able to trade almost instantaneously via the Internet on any of the exchanges of Europe, using your single pan-European stockbroker, and frankly we think this is going to be one hell of a market. Currently the US – the largest market in the world – has companies adding up to a market capitalization of $12.5 trillion. The Bloomberg Europe 500 companies are currently worth $6.9 trillion.

Of course, if the standards of financial regulation aren't up to scratch in the country in which a company is listed, then that isn't much good, no matter what you think of the company itself. That's why we're so attracted to the soon-to-be-united countries of Western Europe with their high standards of financial reporting and some very well-known brand name companies. What would make us drown our grandmothers before investing in some of the other countries of Europe is precisely the lack of any of those things. Entry into some of the emerging markets of Eastern Europe, or indeed emerging economies anywhere else in the world, is to lay yourself open to precisely the kinds of currency fluctuations that could prove disastrous to your investments and to the possibility of outrageous scams or accounting 'irregularities' over which neither you nor anyone else has any control. There is real money to be made in the stable economies of the Western world. Don't spoil your investment returns by throwing money into a cauldron of economic turmoil.

If you do have special knowledge of a particular European market or some European companies, please come and tell us about it at the Fool online. If you do decide to invest in any foreign companies, please be sure that the market you are investing in has acceptable financial reporting standards.

20
Mechanical Investing

'The game,' said he, 'is never lost till won.'

— George Crabbe, *Tales of the Hall*

Different people have different temperaments. Some will wish to stick with an index tracker for the whole of their lives, others will look for Obviously Great Investments, yet others will invest in more speculative small-cap. shares and some will always feel safest and happiest handing their money over to someone else to manage. There are also some people who are fascinated by odds, people who like to stake their money on the winning side, even if that winning side doesn't win every time. They know that you don't have to win *every* time to win over the long term, simply more of the time than you lose. These people probably appreciate the elegant simplicity of the index tracker; they smile ruefully as they reflect that this philosophy is exactly how casinos turn in huge profits over the long term and they are almost certainly not regular players of the National Lottery, for such an activity would be an intolerable affront to their sensibilities.

Mechanical investing is a process by which you select shares according to pre-set, rigid and objective criteria. You don't worry about whether one company has a better brand than another or whether one company has a more sustainable market position because these are subjective assessments – you could be right and you could be wrong. Instead, the shares that you buy depend on hard and fast numbers and these numbers will generally be backed up by some degree of backtesting, in other words a look back into history to check to see what would have happened had you followed the strategy in the past. As an example, depending on which strategy you chose to follow, you might buy the five shares that have the highest dividend yield (remember this from Chapter 11, 'A Share Primer'?) or the ten shares that have gone up the most in the last six months.

Why should anyone want to do this? Well, it's all about trying to swing the odds in your favour. The most well-known form of mechanical investing is actually the humble index tracker. An index tracker buys the shares in a particular index, in direct proportion to their 'weightings' in that index (as measured by their market capitalization divided by the total market capitalization of the entire index). In effect, when you buy an index tracker, you buy a portfolio whose constituents exactly match the index and, as a result, your portfolio exactly matches the performance of that index (or at least it would in a perfect world and before the deduction of charges – have a look at Appendix 2 for more about all this). As we've already seen, the point of doing this is that by keeping your charges lower than the average fund manager you give yourself superior odds. Hardcore mechanical investors believe that by focusing on particular criteria they can weight the odds more firmly in their favour.

Mechanical Investing and the Fool Online

There are a large variety of mechanical investment strategies that people follow and an extremely active community of investors talking and writing about them every day at the Motley Fool's UK and US Web sites. Which one you choose – if at all – depends on your temperament, tolerance for risk and volatility, and degree of interest in the subject. In this chapter, we'll touch briefly on one so-called 'value' strategy, Beating the Footsie, and also a 'relative strength' strategy. Each is quite different, but with common threads binding them. A unifying factor for all mechanical strategies is that to follow them requires a good deal of faith in the particular system you have chosen, because you need to commit to it through thick and thin. While the actual mechanics of running a mechanical investment strategy need take up only thirty minutes of your time a year (or less), this must be backed up by a sound understanding of – and high level of comfort with – both the principles underlying mechanical strategies in general and the ins and outs of the particular strategy you have chosen. You'll find the depth of information and expertise necessary to give you this at the Motley Fool's online areas devoted to mechanical investing. We'd urge you, therefore, not to embark on a long-term mechanical strategy without stopping by the Foolish Workshop areas of the UK Web site (and also the US Web site, hey, why not?) to check out the discussion and share ideas with other investors. This kind of opportunity is what the Web is all about, so if mechanical investing tickles your fancy, make use of it.

Beating the Footsie

In the early 1990s a US money manager by the name of Michael O'Higgins published a landmark book entitled *Beating the Dow*. In it he outlined a mechanical investment strategy that involved buying those five of the thirty members of the Dow-Jones Industrial Average which he considered had been 'excessively' penalized by the market, holding them for a year and then at the end of that time rebalancing the portfolio into the next five laggards, or 'Dogs' as they are often referred to. During the course of that year, the Dogs tended to move up as the market's 'excessive' marking-down of these shares bled away and they came closer to what might be termed a fairer valuation. Over the years, this strategy brought in astonishing market-beating returns and required no share-picking skill at all to follow. It was also totally and utterly objective, not allowing for any subjectivity in which shares to buy, which shares to sell and when to do it. It depended on the fact that *often enough* the market overreacted to bad news about particular companies, only to change its mind later. Buy the companies when they're feeling the full heat of their market disgrace, hold them until tempers have cooled, sell them at a profit and, hey presto, you have a market-beating strategy.

Let's take a couple of graphic, though extremely unpleasant, examples to make the point. Union Carbide poisoned the entire Indian city of Bhopal in 1984 with clouds of poison gas, killing thousands. Union Carbide is a massive industrial conglomerate and was never going to go out of business as a result of this. It was going to be expensive, yes, but the company was always going to recover. The public, however, and the market were so shocked that the shares dived sharply at the time, to recover later when all the *brouhaha* had died down. The same thing happened when the Exxon Valdez oil tanker was driven onto a reef and polluted hundreds of miles of pristine Alaskan coastline. Again, Exxon, a massive oil company, garnered adverse publicity from this, but the cost was never going to be paralysing. The market, however, marked the shares down, making them a potential bargain. We're very pleased to say that O'Higgins's strategy isn't, for the most part, founded on such tragedies as these, but more commonplace ones such as temporary interruptions in profit flow, or adverse trading conditions. An important part of the strategy, though, is that the selections are limited to the thirty companies in the Dow-Jones, the theory being that these huge companies have the might to withstand what are essentially gnat bites on their elephant hides and come back fighting a little later.

That's all fine, but how do you identify these companies? The answer, for O'Higgins, is in the dividend yield. Remember this? Share prices fluctuate according to the whims of the market. Dividends, however, are set by the companies themselves twice a year (or four times in the US) and there is tremendous pressure on them not to cut them. For one thing, it looks very, very bad indeed and the implication it brings that the company is in real trouble is only going to hammer the share price even more. For another, shareholders, both private and institutional, reckon on the dividend for at least part of their income. Cutting it is going to make a lot of people very angry. So, as the share price drops and the dividend stays the same, the yield (the dividend divided by the share price and expressed as a percentage) goes . . .

Can you see which way it goes? Yes, it goes *up*. So, high yielders are more likely to be shares in trouble, or at least shares currently in disfavour for whatever reason. O'Higgins evolved a system of taking the ten highest yielders from the thirty shares of the Dow-Jones Industrial Average – some of the largest companies in the US – taking the five *cheapest* of those (purely in terms of the actual share price), buying them in equal dollar amounts and holding them for exactly a year, before reallocating to the next 'Dow Dividend Five', or 'DD5'. At the Motley Fool, we did some of our own backtesting calculations on this strategy, from 1961 to 1999. Here's the result:

	Yearly average	Total return
Dow 30	12.39%	9,521.18%
DD5	15.61%	2,8621.35%

Isn't it interesting that with just over three percentage points between the index and the DD5 strategy, the total return over the thirty-six years should be so different? It is, of course, the power of compound interest once more laying its gentle hand upon our shoulders. And the thing to remember is that these world-beating returns are being obtained by investing, once a year, in a selection from some of the largest, most successful companies in the world, including American Express, Boeing, Coca-Cola, IBM, McDonald's, Procter and Gamble and Walt Disney.

Since 1997, however, the Dow Dividend strategies have not been performing very well, returning just 6.95 per cent from 1997 to 1999, against a return of 19.42 per cent for the Dow 30. One reason for this may be the phenomenal performance of the stock market since then, largely driven by newer technology-based stocks, which has really left other shares such as the old world giants of the Dow 30 out in the cold. Of course, it's impossible to say for sure and if you take a long-term perspective, several years of under-performance barely dents the statistics. If you believe in the strategy, you'll stick with it through thick and thin, but as we said earlier that kind of resolve takes a thorough understanding of the principles underlying the strategy.

So that's Beating the Dow, asks you, but what about Beating the *Footsie*, which is what we're supposed to be talking about here? Well spotted. Back in 1935 the FT 30 index was invented as an equivalent to the Dow-Jones Industrial Average index in the United States and most of the backtesting of the high-yielding strategy in the UK has been done on this index. From 1970–96, anyway, Johnson Fry, a unit trust company, did some backtesting and the results look like this:

	Yearly average	Total return
FTSE All-Share Index	15.6%	5,028%
Footsie 5	20.5%	15,370%

Pretty impressive numbers for a strategy that requires no thought and no skill to implement. An investment of £10,000 in the Footsie Five back in 1970 would have been worth £1,537,000 by 1996. Unfortunately, like the DD5, the recent returns have been poor. By June 2000, the Footsie 5 strategy which we started on our website in October 1997 had returned a yearly average of just 3.3% compared to 12.4% for the FTSE All-Share. It's periods like this that are sent to try mechanical investors and you need to be very comfortable with the strategy to sit it out patiently.

Like the Dow Jones in America, the FT30 is designed to give a broad representation of the great and the good of the UK stockmarket. It is currently made up of the following companies:

Allied Domecq	ICI
BAE Systems	Invensys
BG	Lloyds TSB
Blue Circle	Marconi
BOC	Marks & Spencer
Boots	P&O
BP Amoco	Prudential
British Airways	Reuters
British Telecom	Royal & Sun Alliance
Cadbury Schweppes	Royal Bank of Scotland

Diageo	Scottish Power
EMI	SmithKline Beecham
GKN	Tate & Lyle
Glaxo Wellcome	Tesco
Granada	Vodafone AirTouch

One question you might ask is why use the FT 30 index as a starting point? It's the first time this index has been mentioned in this book, it's rarely quoted elsewhere and seems to have been superseded by the FTSE 100 and FTSE All-Share Index. Wouldn't it make more sense to use one of these? Further, you say – warming to your theme now – there are some members of the FT 30 whose market capitalization has slipped so far they are no longer even included in the FTSE 100, Tate & Lyle being a case in point. This index is ridiculous, you say. We admit it. You're spot-on: all this is true. However, it makes for a circumscribed group of well-known, large capitalization shares and, importantly, it contains representatives from all the main industrial sectors. The 800 shares of the FTSE All Share Index are clearly too many to sort by yield and, in any case, this strategy depends for its success on using very large capitalization shares that have the resilience to withstand a touch of market disfavour. A company with a market capitalization of only £100 million that disappoints the market will get *killed* and may never rise again. One with a market capitalization of £5000 million, on the other hand, has the momentum to surge through to the other side and emerge victorious once more. As for the FTSE 100, yes, that would be a possibility, but again, 100 shares is rather a lot to sort through, although limited backtesting has been done on the FTSE 100 and has revealed that the strategy works reasonably well. One argument against using the FTSE 100 is that it may be possible to end up with a selection of high yielders in which several may be from the same sector – banking, say. This potential lack of diversity in share selections from year to year makes the FTSE 100 less appealing as an index and this isn't nearly as much of an issue with the FT 30.

Relative Strength Strategies

While Beating the Footsie could be looked on as a 'contrarian' strategy, one that buys the shares no one else loves, relative strength strategies buy the shares every one else adores. These strategies involve some variant of buying the best-performing shares in the FTSE 100 over the last six months (i.e. those whose share price has gone up most) and holding onto them for a time period (a year, say), before rebalancing the portfolio. The idea is that you are catching a wave of enthusiasm for a particular share which you then ride, for a short while, hopefully getting off before the wave fades away. One difficulty with this is that you often end up buying some of the most volatile shares on the market.

Backtesting in the UK has only been carried out as far as 1994, but in that period the overall returns have been spectacular. Of course, this also coincides with a remarkable period of growth in the stock market as a whole; it's been a phase in which shares that have gone up have, in many cases, just tended to keep on going. The cynics would therefore say that over the last few years this type of strategy was bound to have worked well; and it did. Whether this means that it has a good chance of working consistently in the future, or whether you can predict the conditions in which it will work, depends on your point of view. This is the sort of argument that mechanical investing is all about and, as we've said, before getting involved with a particular scheme, you need to understand exactly how and why it is supposed to work. Backing out halfway through, just when things aren't working, isn't likely to do you many favours.

Why does Mechanical Investing Work?

First of all, it's important to recognize that mechanical systems aren't going to pick out winning companies every time. What they are trying to do is find a set of criteria that will find companies which have a better than average chance of increasing in share price during the time that they are held. It's all a matter of playing the odds, and mechanical investors are trying to weight the odds in their favour so that, over the long term, they'll come up smiling. It's a similar situation to that of the casino boss, who knows that fifty-one times out of a hundred he will win at the blackjack table. The casino punter, meanwhile, knows (or should know) that the long-term odds are against him, but hopes for a bit of luck on the day. Of the two, the casino boss will indubitably win in the long term but will miss out on the short-term excitement, while the punter will ultimately lose if he keeps coming back but will certainly have had an exciting time. Rather like the casino punter, though, many people want a more hands-on approach to stock-picking. Quite simply, they want a bit more excitement from their investments.

Let's be honest about this: mechanical investing is DULL. In between once-yearly bursts of activity lasting precisely one half hour, there is nothing for a restless investor to do (apart from playing around with spreadsheets and trying to devise more mechanical investment strategies), not even keep an eye on the market. Funnily enough, this may be one good reason for mechanical strategies to continue to work. The Wise men of the market are forever pointing out that, once a system is known to work, everybody will start doing it. This will push the price of the undervalued shares up before you can pick them out, thus scuppering the whole plan. Well, this sounds logical, but the thing is that very little of the money in the market is ever likely to be managed this way. It's unlikely to appeal to most professional investors: they need to pretend that they have some mystical expertise so they can charge us lots of money. Mechanical investing, by contrast is very, very simple in essence. The industry has finally brought us the index tracker, but it took an extremely long time for it to get around to this and we can't see the pros welcoming other mechanical schemes.

Of course, you don't need to operate a mechanical scheme to decide that some high-yielding shares are undervalued. But it is a fair argument that you need the discipline of a mechanical scheme to keep finding the ones that are, on average, consistently undervalued. Certainly it requires a steely nerve to continue to hold that absolute Dog of a share that just keeps going down. Many investors find that they can't stop themselves from tampering: 'Oh, it won't matter if I sell this one and buy that one instead.' Well, it does matter, Fool! The casino boss won't close the roulette table after a string of bad losses because he knows that the odds are still in his favour. In the same way, the dedicated mechanical investor will stick rigidly to his or her guns, at least while there remain good reasons for thinking that the long-term odds remain on their side.

Don't get us wrong, Fools, we are not saying that this approach to investing will always work: clearly it depends a great deal on the criteria that you use to pick the shares. We are just saying that from the backtesting that we and others have done, it appears that some mechanical strategies would have served you very well over the last thirty-odd years. We also think it's possible to put forward a strong argument as to why some systems have done well and why they might well carry on doing so. There are no guarantees, but there are no guarantees for anything and the mechanical investor is just working on the basis that the past can provide a decent enough guide. This leads us to one final point, without which this chapter won't be complete.

Probabilities, Randomness and Data-mining

You have to be more than a little bit careful about thinking of the past as concrete evidence of anything. Of course, it has some relevance. Indeed it is how we all lead our lives. We turn right out of our front door to walk to the shops because that has served us well in the past (when we turned left we ended up in the neighbour's garden being chased by Harry, their cuddly Rottweiler). We carry an umbrella when the sky looks grey because, in the past, doing so has helped us to avoid a good soaking. However, just because there is a pattern to past events, it doesn't necessarily mean that those events are anything other than random. In fact, the laws of probability work in such a way that a series of entirely random events will almost invariably have some sort of vague pattern to them. After all, what are the chances of there being no pattern at all?! Finding patterns in random data and attributing meaning to them is called 'data-mining' and, for obvious reasons, it's something that mechanical investors discuss until the ends of the earth.

We can see a basic example of data-mining in action by looking at the National Lottery. In the first year, there were a total of fifty-two prize draws and, excluding the bonus balls, a total of 312 (52 times 6) numbers were drawn. This means that, on average, each number should have been drawn 6.37 times (312 divided by the 49 balls). The probability of every number being drawn exactly six or seven times is fantastically small. Of course, as things turned out, some were drawn quite a bit more than this and some were drawn quite a bit less. The actual number of times that each number was drawn is set out in the opposite table.

The number 5, for instance, was drawn an impressive ten times in fifty-two draws and the number 39 was only drawn once, yet it would be very wrong to conclude from this that the number 5 is any more likely than 39 to be drawn the next time. We can also see that seven out of the ten least common numbers contained a 3, whereas of the ten most common numbers there is only one that contains a 3. But, no matter how tempting it may be to ascribe some relevance to this, it doesn't mean for a moment that a number containing a 3 is somehow less likely to come up. The numbers drawn in the National Lottery are entirely random, whether or not you can find a pattern in them.

All this is intended to show that you have to be careful about relying on past-performance data. If you look at a set of data, you will always be able to find some sort of pattern, but it doesn't prove that the data is anything other than random. A far better approach is to think about how the data is generated and

Number	How many times drawn	Number	How many times drawn	Number	How many times drawn
5	10	29	7	6	5
22	10	32	7	8	5
44	10	33	7	9	5
25	10	40	7	11	5
17	9	42	7	12	5
30	9	7	6	20	5
41	9	10	6	23	5
16	8	18	6	35	5
21	8	26	6	36	5
28	8	27	6	19	4
31	8	43	6	24	4
38	8	45	6	37	4
48	8	46	6	13	3
1	7	47	6	34	3
2	7	49	6	39	1
14	7	3	5		
15	7	4	5		

ask yourself whether there is a particular pattern that you would expect to see. If you decide on a pattern that you would expect to see and then, by examining the data, you find that it is there, then you may be on to something.

So, if you're thinking about developing a mechanical investment strategy, start by asking yourself which set of criteria might single out companies that do well. Only after doing this should you examine the past data and see if that pattern is, in fact, there. The further you look back and the wider the range of market conditions that this encompasses, the more confidence you can have in what you find. Above all, don't look at historical data, winkle out a pattern and then try to construct a rationale as to why this represents a coherent mechanical investment strategy.

Aspirant constructors of mechanical strategies should buy a book entitled *What Works on Wall Street*, by James O'Shaughnessy. This looks in detail at a variety of investment strategies, successful and unsuccessful, backtested since the early 1950s in the US. It's exhaustive, well written and thought provoking.

Where do Mechanical Strategies Fit?

Having thought about all of this, you might now be wondering whether (and how) to integrate a mechanical strategy into your investment portfolio. As with much in life, it is down to temperament. Some people will swear that this method of investing – in which a knowledge of the fundamentals of the company is not only irrelevant, but can be counter-productive – is strictly for the insane. Others will be charmed by its apparent elegance and simplicity. So, first of all you have to decide whether the approach suits you. If you think it does, then the next thing to think about is which type of strategy. Of course, the aim of all of them is to provide market-beating returns, but some have other benefits as well. For instance, the high-yielding strategies naturally generate a high level of income. Some strategies go even further than this and try to find, by objective measures, companies with both a high dividend yield and a dividend that is unlikely to be reduced. For people in need of income from their equity portfolios, this type of system can be particularly useful.

There are any number of different mechanical schemes that different people have thought up. In the Workshop areas of our Web sites, Fools are constantly working on testing and improving their various systems. If this type of investing interests you, we strongly suggest you pop along and see what's going on for yourself.

Mechanically, then, and with our heads reeling with investment strategies, it's time to move on to the next chapter, on ethical Fooling.

21
The Ethical Fool

A custom loathsome to the eye, hateful to the nose, harmful to the brain, dangerous to the lungs, and in the black, stinking fume thereof, nearest resembling the horrible Stygian smoke of the pit that is bottomless.

— James I (James VI of Scotland), *A Counterblast to Tobacco*

Agree or disagree with him, King James certainly had one or two strong thoughts on the smoking weed that had so recently been introduced from the Americas. So, certainly, will many of the people reading this. Whether you're pro or anti the free marketing of tobacco, there is no escaping the issue that there is an issue here, as there is with many other activities in the business world. What about arms manufacturing, or mining, or paper manufacturing and its consequent effect on deforestation? Depending on your outlook, this stuff can be tricky.

So what are we going to call this subject, about which the passions run so high? 'Socially responsible investing'? 'Ethical investing'? 'Green investing', even? The choice, ultimately, is yours, but what we're trying to get at is a self-imposed, selective approach to investing, one which has ultimately kept millions of potential investors around the globe from buying into certain public companies, whose corporate activities they deem immoral, damaging or exploitative.

If we lived in Utopia (from the ancient Greek *ou topos* meaning 'no place'), we could simply tell you to invest without concern. You'd be living in a perfect society with perfect laws and no need for regulatory bodies. You would know, in every moment you spent investing, that your company was maximizing the growth of well-being for every constituency: customers, employees, shareholders, management and society. If ever one group was temporarily over- or under-compensated, the whole structure would tilt immediately to correct it (probably slightly too far in the other direction, briefly, to create total equity). Doesn't it sound great?

Look at the name again. *Ou topos* — no place.

No such world has ever yet existed, unless Thomas More's legendary traveller was telling the truth. And most importantly, no single life has ever been continually, uncompromisingly painless. With no Utopia in our personal or professional lives, we certainly shouldn't expect one in our investing life. At the most basic level, we all just have to do our best, make the best of things.

The whole concept of ethics in investing has had much ink spilled over it, with many zealots beating each other around the head with their own moral codes and a number of very bad and highly-charging unit trusts springing up to meet the need for people to feel wholesome about their investing endeavours. It's a deadly serious issue and that's why we're touching on it here. Our approach is very simple, so simple in fact that we're in danger of being called naive:

Buy what you are; buy **only** *what you are.*

If you don't like British American Tobacco, don't invest in it. If you think companies that manufacture and export arms are immoral, don't invest in them. Never lose sleep over an investment that you made tentatively in an enterprise you don't wholeheartedly support. Flog it. Buy something else. Ultimately, when you buy a share in a business, you are providing it with capital so that it can further what it does. If you buy a share in a uranium mining company, then you are providing capital so that it can mine more uranium. If you don't approve of the mining of uranium, then you shouldn't be doing that, should you?! In fact, if enough people thought like this, it would be much harder for the companies doing things that people don't approve of to raise funds for what they do. Perhaps you can think of it as a grand global economic democracy. If everyone does their bit according to their values, then the world may become a better place. We can dream, can't we?

Buying what you are, what informs your daily life, what sits snugly with your beliefs and values about the world is the only way to feel comfortable with the investments you hold. No one else can tell you what you are and especially not the fund manager of an 'ethical' unit trust. When you buy one of these – and why would you, because their long-term returns have been abysmal – are you buying what you are or what someone else is? When you buy a unit trust, you're consigning the destiny of your money to a stranger you'll most likely never meet. Social responsibility? If you take ethics in investing at all seriously, then we fervently argue that you're being most *irresponsible* by saying, 'I'll buy that pleasingly-named unit trust.'

Let's go a little further. You don't like Hilton Group because you don't approve of gambling (and Hilton owns Ladbrokes and a string of casinos), but you stay in a Hilton hotel from time to time when on holiday. Whoops! Let's say you avoid investing in SmithKline Beecham because you don't like animal testing. Then you fall ill and are prescribed a medicine by your doctor. Three days later, you look at the name on the packet . . . If you're going to avoid investing in a particular company, then make sure you're not helping them more directly by buying their products. Make your investment pounds work in harmony with your consumption pounds and you'll feel right about what you're doing. You'll be in sync. You'll be a Fool.

The Active Shareholder

There's no way we can dictate the moral choices that you alone must decide for yourself. The history of the world is full to busting with people moralizing to others and we have no intention of joining their ranks. Decide for yourself what is acceptable, decide if your investing philosophy sits easily with your life philosophy and if it does, then that's fine. There may well come a time, though, when a company you bought into, and which you thought you knew well, goes off on a tangent with which you don't feel comfortable. Alternatively, perhaps you disapprove only mildly of the activities of a company and would like to invest in it, but at the same time would like to do what you can to modify their behaviour. The answer is to become an active shareholder.

Quite apart from the purely financial reasons not to own more than ten to fifteen companies at a time, there are good reasons from an ethical point of view not to hold more than this number. Not only can you not follow the details of their business if you own many more than this, but you can't follow their ethical activities either. As an active shareholder – a part-owner, remember – of whatever business you're invested in, you are uniquely placed to make your views heard. You can attend shareholder meetings, bombard who you like with letters, faxes and e-mails and generally make a nuisance of yourself (polite or otherwise) and at all times your views will have to be heard and answered courteously. Working from the inside to change the face of business is likely to be much more effective than standing on the outside knocking on a large smoked glass door.

Investing in this way in a company whose business you essentially deem worthy of respect, but which has one or two practices of which you disapprove, can be very positive. What about the business, though, that you think is an absolute shocker? How can you justify to yourself making money out of that company and using it for your own personal gain? That, we're afraid, is an issue between you and your bathroom mirror. However, one rather elegant line of approach that you might want to consider is to only invest the money in Evil Activities PLC that you would otherwise donate to charity. Then, as an active shareholder you keep up your barrage from the side of morality and probity, but channel the profits from your investment – it's a sad fact that 'nasty' companies are often very profitable – into activities or charities that seek to counteract the damaging effects of the actions of your evil company. It's quite a neat way of changing the world, but won't do anything for your investment returns. Don't, therefore, take this money from the funds you are allocating for your retirement nest egg. This is strictly hobby money, but using part of your investment life to try and put things right can be an attractive idea for many people who are turned off the very idea of stock market investing by the dirty corporate world they feel they're buying into. Bear in mind, though, that simply by holding the shares, you are effectively providing the company with the capital it needs to pursue its activities.

One thing to note is that it is worth asking your stockbroker just what shareholder rights you are entitled to if you are holding your shares in a nominee account. (These are the types of accounts that many execution-only stockbrokers use to hold clients' shares communally, thus making dealing easier.) It's no good planning to be an active shareholder if you then find you don't have an easily exercisable voting right at meetings. A useful resource for the active shareholder is *The Shareholder Action Handbook*, written by Craig Mackenzie, which is crammed full of information. The paperback version is cheap and can be ordered from your local bookshop, quoting ISBN number 1897806000. There is also a great deal of useful information online – try typing 'shareholder action' into an Internet search engine.

Conclusion

We live in a dirty world. (You didn't need us to tell you that.) As an investor – if you wish to use this opportunity – you have much scope to shape that world for the better. Do debate and discuss this issue with others, for down that path lies greater understanding and tolerance. Don't, however, let others bully you into a course of action with which you feel uncomfortable: you won't stick with it and the sum of resentment and ill-feeling will have been increased in the world, surely the very opposite of what we all hope will occur.

Rounding Up

22

Welcome to the End of the Beginning!

Now this is not the end. It is not even the beginning of the end. But it is, perhaps, the end of the beginning.

— Winston Churchill, Mansion House speech following the first major German defeat of the war at El Alamein, 1942

Congratulations. If this is the first time you have dipped your toe in the murky waters of investment, you have now reached the end of the very beginning of your life as a Foolish, savvy, active investor. From now on, you can start to put your critical skills to good use in building for your financial future. To celebrate this new phase, we're going to take the opportunity to have one last shot at the world of Wisdom, and believe us, it's a real cracker.

When the Motley Fool UK was launched in September 1997, we started off by sending one or two (250, actually) press releases out to the great and the good of the world of British financial journalism. In it we made one or two Foolish observations including the fact that, according to research from the *Investor's Chronicle* in March 1996, more than 90 per cent of managed unit trusts had underperformed their index over the preceding five- and ten-year periods. We believe that most of these press releases were filed straight into the paper shredder but just a few elicited some interest. In fact, David B. received a phone call from one of the worthies of financial writing at one of the UK's most respected newspapers. The encounter was so remarkable that he wrote about it later that day in an article on our Web site. Here's an extract:

This afternoon, I found myself talking on the telephone to a senior City journalist on one of the national newspapers. It was an education in Wisdom and went something like this.
ME (*SQUEAKILY*). Erm, hello, it's David Berger of the Motley Fool UK here.
HE (*FOR HE IT WAS*). Ah yes. I'm most concerned about this little scheme of yours.
ME. Oh yes.

HE. Yes, all this guff about index trackers. I've written a lot about them myself and I don't know where you get this figure of 90 per cent underperforming the market. I am very concerned [that word again] about this. It's not true, you know.

ME. Oh. It does come from a reputable source. In fact, I've read a lot about index trackers in your newspaper, I'm sure. Although I think this is from a different source.

HE (*BREAST PUFFING AUDIBLY OVER THE PHONE*). Yes, what you've read in my paper was almost certainly written by me. I write a lot about them and I'm very concerned [again] about this 90 per cent figure.

(D.B. flicks through past copies of the *Investor's Chronicle*.)

ME. Here we are, March 22nd, 1996, page 16. Of 203 UK unit trusts in existence for ten years, only fifteen outperformed the market over that period and that is even giving them an unfair advantage by disregarding initial charges. The source of the data is Micropal.

HE (*FOLLOWING A SHORT SILENCE*). Good God!

(I kid you not, he really said 'Good God!' I have filed this as one of my lifetime Golden Moments.)

HE (*SLIGHTLY OFF BALANCE, BUT RECOVERING QUICKLY*). Yes, well, I can see what they've done. But I'm very concerned about these message boards of yours. Won't people be able to cause a buying panic by posting unfounded rumours on your message boards? What's to stop that happening?

ME. Nothing, but we don't advocate buying on the basis of a single, hysterical tip. We stress buying on the basis of a sound analysis of a company's fundamentals. And anyway, anyone who believes an outrageous story on the basis of no obvious evidence merely because they want to, deserves everything they get. That's just stupid!

HE. Still, I am very concerned about this.

ME. Well, why don't you come and visit the site, or even better the American site where they have over 2000 message boards … ?

HE (*INTERJECTING, A TRIFLE IRRITADO NOW*). Oh, don't talk to me about computers. I don't know anything about computers!

ME. More Foolish stuff.

HE. More Wise stuff.

ME. More Foolish stuff.

HE. Etc., etc.

And so it went on for a few more desultory minutes. Later, he talked to a fellow Fool in the USA and came out with this:

HE. But your information is quite simple, isn't it? It's not very sophisticated.

THE FELLOW FOOL. Exactly.

It's hard to imagine a more succinct illustration than this snapshot for why there is a need for a sane, understandable alternative to the stuffy blather you so often find being purveyed as financial information these days. Of course, we hope that this book and the daily to-ings and fro-ings at our online areas go some way to meeting this need, but as of now it's in your hands, those of the reader, to judge.

Our aspiration is that even if you don't agree with everything written here and even if some of it seems incomprehensible – for which we blame no one but ourselves – you will at least put the book down with the belief that it is *possible* for you to understand enough about investment to manage your own financial affairs. We don't expect everyone to rush off and suddenly become self-sufficient amateur stock market investors. The process of learning and understanding simply doesn't work like that. We do hope, though, that with a small chink of light showing at the end of a long black tunnel you may now be starting to question any and everything that is being sold to you in the financial world and scheming about how *you* can do it better.

Hurry Up and Slow Down

Inspiration and panic make dangerous bedfellows and it's quite possible that by turns both of these will have accompanied you on your journey through these pages. Talk of endowments and other Wise investment plans may have caused you to fear that your best years are behind you, squandered on wastrel investments with huge charges and underperformance by way of return. Combine this with the exciting possibilities open to you in the stock market – from index trackers to the Obviously Great Investments and beyond– and you may be inspired to rush out and transform all your investments into Foolish ones. Now. Right now.

But stop!

Go back.

Don't do it.

Precipitate, unthinking action is not the way to set yourself up for a lifetime of secure, profitable investment. Similarly, precipitate, unthinking *inaction* is not the right way either. Interestingly, one evening in May 1998 we asked a selection of visiting Fools, at our Fool UK focus group meeting/Pizza Express field study trip, what the hardest thing had been about starting in investment. Simultaneously, two answers were shot back. The first was: 'The hardest thing was buying my first share.' The second was: 'The hardest thing was *not* buying my first share.' Whichever of these categories you fall into, you need to think incrementally.

The only way you will be able to set up the habits of a lifetime of sensible investment is by approaching the whole subject cautiously, yet steadily. Don't rush out and cancel your endowment policy, AVC or Personal Pension Plan. It is entirely possible that you will have passed the point where you were paying 80 per cent or more of your contributions in charges and it may make more sense to hold onto it. You may decide not to increase the amount you put into it and instead divert those extra savings elsewhere, but that's another story entirely.

We suggest that the first thing you do is put down this book and have a good old think about your investment goals, the amount you can realistically save and where your interests lie. Where they really lie. It is easy to be inspired (which is a good thing) but inspiration alone is not going to carry you through a lifetime of investing. It requires persistence, too. Ask yourself if you're going to want to be the type of person who keeps an eye on their shares every few weeks and is prepared to put in a fair amount of graft to choose them in the first place. No? You're not? Then you don't want to be investing in a relatively small company like Pizza Express, or an up-and-coming chip designer (the silicon variety). Some solid long-term, might we say Obviously Great, investments are more likely to suit. If you think you'll just be able to muster enough interest to read this book and then forget about investment for the next twenty or so years, then an index tracker is most likely what you're after. Take a good hard look, too, at the investments you already have. Learn about them, about how well they've done for you and how much they might have cost you. If you decide to ditch one or any of them, make sure you do so after having weighed up the pros and cons carefully. From now on, you have no one to blame but yourself. Similarly, when things go well, as they most assuredly should, if you approach investment sensibly and realistically, then no one else will be standing in line to take the credit which will rightly fall to you.

Oh yes, debt. Almost forgot about that. That comes before any of the above. Pay off any non-mortgage debt as quickly as you can before you start investing, and also aim to refinance any large chunks of credit card debt with a personal loan from your bank at a lower rate as quickly as you can. You knew that anyway.

When you've decided what strategy you might like to follow, then immediately do nothing. Nothing, that is, except track the progress of your strategy on paper, or on a Web site with portfolio tracking facilities. After three months, six months, a year — yes, as long as that, or even longer — think about committing a small amount of your funds to your chosen strategy. Start with 5 per cent and work up as you feel comfortable. You're in it for the long haul and there's no sense in rushing into something you don't feel comfortable with and which you're going to bail out of at the first sign of market volatility. If you get yourself bitten badly in the stock market at the start, it'll be a long time, if ever, before you're back.

The Bottom Line

Several years ago, one of us (D.B.) spent a year working with a Frenchman: '*Mais*, Daveed, explain once more, what ees ze "Bottom Line"?' It does seem as if there is no equivalent expression in French (if you're a French scholar and you think there is, then you know where to e-mail us) and he never quite grasped the concept to his satisfaction. Of course, we know what it means and the expression we use in our daily lives ('Yeah, Snodbury United may have played well, but the bottom line is they lost twelve-nil') probably comes from company accounting, where the bottom line means after-tax profits. This is the money that remains to be divvied up between the company and its shareholders after all the froth and fury of the annual accounts has been played out. Often, it's the whole reason that investors have bought into the company and some would say the whole reason a public company exists.

'What's the bottom line?' is a question we should always ask, whatever endeavour we're about to embark upon. Of course, we hope that the process of reading this Foolish volume has encouraged you, nay, converted you, into a fanatical devotee of the bottom line when it comes to your investments and your financial future, but since you've now come to the end of it, it seems reasonable to ask what's the bottom line of the book itself and the Motley Fool as a whole? What have we been trying to say here? What are the crucial points we hope you'll take away from this book and which, in our opinion anyway, make it worth the purchase price? Okay, we think it's all pretty well encapsulated like this:

- Investment is not inherently difficult to understand.
- The average person is not as stupid as they are made out to be.
- Many types of investment on sale today overcharge and underperform.
- The people selling you those investments have interests diametrically opposed to your own.
- Investors should understand and have faith in the supremacy of shares as the long-term route to growing wealth.

- An understanding of the awesome power of compound interest is a prerequisite for any successful investor.
- The application of simple, common-sense rules and a small amount of knowledge can produce returns far exceeding those of the professionals.
- The Internet facilitates the spread of knowledge and information in a revolutionary and unprecedented fashion.
- Shareholders are uniquely placed to play an active role in modifying corporate behaviour for the greater good of society and of the world as a whole.
- Taking responsibility for your own investments and financial future need not be onerous and is one of the most lucrative, enjoyable and fulfilling activities open to you.
- The emphasis is on enjoyable.

That's it. That's our bottom line. The end of the beginning. We hope it pleaseth you.

Be Foolish, one and all!

DAVID BERGER
DAVID GARDNER
TOM GARDNER

Acknowledgements

In most of mankind, gratitude is merely a secret hope for greater favours.

— Duc de la Rochefoucauld, *Maximes*

Permission Acknowledgements

Permission to use existing material

We thank PanMacmillan for permission to quote from the *Hitch Hiker's Guide to the Galaxy*. And we are very grateful to Brian Martin of Barclays for permission to use that marvellously sloped graph, along with incredibly compelling numbers from the Barclays Capital Gilt-Equity Study. And finally, thanks to Gartmore.

Acknowledgements for the second edition

Thanks first and foremost must go to James 'Jimmy C' Carlisle, personal finance writer here at the Motley Fool, whose hand has been in all the revisions for this second edition. He worked tirelessly, and with lamentably little support, to help put this edition together. Jimmy was originally hired off the back of a job advert we put on our site which seemed to have an extraordinarily long and superhuman list of required skills and qualities. So ridiculous did this list seem that we threw in another two for the hell of it: 'Eats with mouth closed', and 'Possession of British Association of Gymnastics Award level 4 or above'. Back came Jimmy's job application with a copy of his BAGA level 4 certificate from his schooldays and we have to say that to date Jimmy's table manners have proved *impeccable*. He also managed to meet all the other requirements on the list and has been an outstanding writer, with great skills and knowledge, both in personal finance and equity investing. So, thanks, Jimmy for hard work, relentless good humour, excellent counsel and the energy with which we have been able to produce what I think is an even more solid work than the first edition.

David and Tom Gardner, founders of the Motley Fool and co-authors, thanks to you for two things. Firstly, the cerebral short circuit you both possess which came up with an idea as crazy as the Fool in the first place. Secondly, for having the vision, passion and humanity to have steered it thus far and thus well.

My thanks also go to my long-suffering wife Carol, our two impish boys Max and Tom and my irreplaceable parents Gerry and Maurice. Also, to Benoit and Otti Zurkinden, good friends, for the loan of their apartment in the Swiss Alps to complete the manuscript.

Finally, a word to the staff and the ever-increasing number of users of the Motley Fool UK. The Fool seems to have taken on a life of its own in the last couple of years. Special thanks to all those who sent in feedback on the first edition of this book. And thanks to you all for contributing so wholeheartedly to this tremendous endeavour and keeping it moving inexorably on the right course, that of a path to greater financial freedom for the ordinary people of the UK.

DAVID BERGER
LANGTREE, DEVON
SUMMER 2000

Foolish Glossary of Investment Terms

'When I use a word,' Humpty Dumpty said in a rather scornful tone, 'it means just what I choose it to mean – neither more nor less.'

— Lewis Carroll, *Through the Looking Glass*

None of us likes complicated words and many of us are distinctly allergic to them. Often it seems as if they are bandied about simply to confuse. However, like most things in life, it's not quite that simple. Using specialist terminology can be a useful aid to communication and means that you don't have to go into long-winded explanations every time you want to explain a particular concept.

But don't take it from us, take it from Sir David Attenborough:

> *The first time I travelled in the forests of Borneo, I knew no Malay. My guide, a Dyak hunter who, with his blowpipe, regularly collected birds for the local museum, knew no English. So, to begin with, we had some difficulty — to put it mildly — in sorting out where we should go and what we should do. On our first day out together, we were paddling up a river in a canoe, when I heard a sonorous* tok-tok-tok-tok *call echoing through the trees. I cupped my hand round my ear and raised my eyebrows towards my guide. He then, for the very first time in our acquaintance, spoke words that I precisely understood. 'Caprimulgus macrurus,' he said and I knew immediately that I was listening to the voice of the long-tailed nightjar. It was a nice demonstration that those cumbersome Latin names, sometimes mocked by the ignorant as pretentious obfuscations invented by scientists to prevent others understanding what they are talking about, do indeed constitute a truly international lingua franca.*
>
> (Foreword, *Oxford Dictionary of Natural History*)

To the accompaniment of a gentle 'lap, lap, lapping' along the side of the canoe, the ever-present 'drip, drip, dripping' of huge droplets from the dark, forest canopy overhead, eerie shrieks from the impenetrable green tangle on the banks and the occasional 'Thwoop!' as your Dyak guide spits another wad of betel nut into the river, please feel free to consult our Foolish glossary of investment terms.

Additional Voluntary Contributions (AVCs) Many try and enhance their OCCUPATIONAL PENSION schemes by paying into one of these plans. Watch out for the hefty charges and dismal underperformance, though. Like PERSONAL PENSION PLANS, they attract tax relief.

Advisory Stockbroker Stockbrokers who offer advice on which shares to buy and sell. We don't favour using them. See EXECUTION-ONLY STOCKBROKER and CHURNING.

Alternative Investment Market (AIM) AIM opened in 1995 for small, growing companies. It's less difficult to be listed here than on the LONDON STOCK EXCHANGE and shares are higher risk and more likely to be difficult to buy and sell. See LIQUIDITY.

Analyst A financial professional who analyses securities to determine a 'fair' or 'intrinsic' value for those securities. The term is generally applied to almost any professional investor who does research of some kind.

Annualize To take an item measured over a certain period and restate it on an annual basis. For instance, if it costs £10 million every month to run a factory, the annualized cost is £10 million x 12, or £120 million, since there are twelve months in a year.

Annual Percentage Rate (APR) When you borrow money, this rate should always be quoted to you. It's the percentage rate that your loan will cost you each year, *including* all charges. Incredibly, APRs for credit cards can reach around 20 per cent.

Annual Report A yearly statement of a public company's operating and financial performance punctuated by pictures of families enjoying the firm's products and/or services.

Annuity The investment you purchase with your pension fund, which will provide you with a regular income in your retirement. They are intrinsically poor investments.

Appreciation Increase in the price (or value) of a share or other asset. Appreciation is one component of total return.

Balance Sheet Part of the ANNUAL REPORT. It provides a look at a company's assets, debts and shareholder equity at one particular point in time. See also CASH FLOW STATEMENT and PROFIT AND LOSS ACCOUNT.

Bank of England Set up in 1649, the 'Old Lady of Threadneedle Street' is the 'lender of last resort', which means that it shores up the banking system if there is a liquidity crisis. To put it another way, it lends us money when everyone else has run out. At a more mundane level, it sets interest rates to help the Government meet its inflation targets. The stock market often gets very excited about these short-term interest rate movements.

Bankruptcy When a company owes more than it can pay, or when its debts exceed its assets, it's bankrupt.

Bear So you think that the market is headed south? You're bracing yourself for a crash or correction? You feel that share XYZ will soon be taking a tumble? Guess what – you're a bear! Bears are investors with pessimistic outlooks, as opposed to BULLS.

Beating the Dow The US grand-daddy of our very own BEATING THE FOOTSIE.

Beating the Footsie A mechanical investment strategy, based on buying large-cap. shares with a high DIVIDEND YIELD on a regular, rotational basis. Like BEATING THE DOW, it has been very successful historically.

Bid-offer Spread The difference between the bid price (at which the holder can sell shares) and the offer price (at which the holder can buy shares). On occasion this can be quite large and depends on the equity's underlying price, LIQUIDITY, volatility and a number of other factors. Many UNIT TRUSTS also have a bid-offer spread and effectively this amounts to an EXIT CHARGE when the investor sells.

Big Bang The first big shake-up of the stock market in October 1986, when computers were introduced into the trading process for the first time. This was followed in 1996 by the introduction of CREST and then in 1997 by BIG BANG II.

Big Bang II 20 October 1997. The use of a computer-driven trading system to cut out the middlemen in share trading, who match buyers and sellers. Initially, this was just for FTSE 100 shares, but is likely to be extended.

Blue Chip A share in a large, safe, prestigious company. Unilever is a blue chip, so is Lloyds TSB and so is Tesco. Many of the other shares making up the FTSE 100 would also be considered blue chips. The small mining company Minmet is not a blue chip. Neither is Fortune Oil.

Bond A bond is essentially a loan. Bondholders lend money to governments or companies and are promised a certain rate of interest in return. Interest rates vary depending on the quality or reliability of the bond issuer. UK Government bonds, or gilts, for example, carry no risk and thus offer the lowest sterling interest rates. Company bonds offer higher interest rates, with the riskiest companies' bonds offering the highest of all and being called junk bonds.

Bonus Issue Not to be confused with a SHARE SPLIT. If a company believes that its share price has risen to a point where it might affect liquidity, they may have a bonus issue or a share split. This reduces the share price but increases the number of shares outstanding. With a bonus issue, you get issued with new shares on top of your existing shares. By contrast, with a share split, your shares actually get split into smaller chunks. So, if you start with ten shares and the company does a 3 for 1 bonus issue, you'd be given three more shares for each share that you already hold. You'd therefore end up with forty shares. This would be equivalent to a 4 for 1 share split, in which each of your ten shares gets split into four. The difference between the two approaches means something to accountants but not to anyone else.

Broker One who sells financial products. Be it in insurance, pensions or shares, most brokers work under compensation structures that are at direct odds with the greatest good of their clients. (Also see INDEPENDENT FINANCIAL ADVISER, EXECUTION-ONLY STOCKBROKER, ADVISORY STOCKBROKER, STOCKBROKER.)

Building Society A mutual organization, owned by the people saving money in it and borrowing money from it. Increasing numbers have converted to banks in recent years, paying windfall profits to the owners. See DEMUTUALIZATION.

Bull Are your glasses rose-coloured? Do you see nothing but blue skies ahead for the stock market or a particular share? Then you're a bull – an optimistic investor – as opposed to a BEAR.

CAC 40 French INDEX of – wait for it – the 40 major French companies.

Capital The overall pile of assets which a company uses to carry on its business, or an investor's pot of cash and investments.

Capital Gain You bought a share and later sold it. If you made a profit, then you'll have a capital gain. If you lost money, you'll have a capital loss. Too much in the way of capital gains and you might have to pay capital gains tax.

Capped Rate Mortgage The mortgage interest rate cannot go above a certain level if mortgage rates rise, but can fall as rates drop. Ain't no free lunches, though, and, for various reasons, the interest rate may fall more slowly than otherwise.

Cash Flow Statement The part of a company's ANNUAL REPORT that tells you how much money a company really is making, rather than what an accountant thinks the company is making (as in the PROFIT AND LOSS ACCOUNT). See also BALANCE SHEET.

Chief Executive The Chief Executive is the highest executive officer in a company, rather like the captain of a ship. He or she is accountable to the company's Board of Directors and will be a member of that Board. The Chief Executive participates in setting strategy with the Board and other officers and is responsible for developing strategies to meet the company's goals.

Churning The unconscious or conscious overtrading by a STOCKBROKER in a customer's account. Since stockbrokers are generally compensated by the number of transactions made on a customer's behalf, there is a temptation to trade for the sake of it. It's illegal, but hard to prove.

The City London's financial district, which encompasses the square mile of the old City of London, bounded to the south by the Thames, to the west by the Law Courts, to the east by the Tower of London and to the north by Billingsgate Market. It's full of banks, sandwich shops and wine bars.

Commission The way a STOCKBROKER or an INDEPENDENT FINANCIAL ADVISER is compensated. When he or she makes a transaction for a customer, the customer pays a commission.

Common Stock A US term for SHARES.

Compound Interest The investor's best friend. One hundred pounds invested in the stock market in 1869 would be worth nearly £20,000,000 today. Now, *that's* compound interest!

Correction A decline, usually short and steep, in the prevailing price of shares traded in the market or in an individual share. Any time that commentators cannot find a reason for an individual stock or the entire market falling, they call it a correction. A really big correction gets called a CRASH.

Coupon The interest paid by a bond or gilt as a percentage of the nominal value.

Crash A really big CORRECTION. The worst crashes in modern times were in 1929 and 1974. We're still waiting for the next one. Plenty of people have been predicting it for years and, as a result, have missed out on a period of very strong stock market growth.

CREST Introduced in 1996, this is a computerized system to settle up share purchases. No more bits of paper changing hands.

Cum-dividend *Cum* means 'with' in Latin. If you buy shares cum-dividend, you are buying them at a time when you will be entitled to receive the next dividend. This is as opposed to EX-DIVIDEND, where you buy the share without that entitlement.

Current Account Mortgage A type of mortgage in which your debt is effectively held in a current account. Interest due is calculated daily as opposed to yearly, which can make a significant difference to the cost for those on a REPAYMENT MORTGAGE. Also more flexible and allows periods of both under- and overpayment of the mortgage to suit the borrower's changing financial circumstances.

Dax An index of major German companies.

Day Trader Day traders are in and out of the market many times during the course of one trading session and may not even hold a position in any securities overnight. This approach tends to make your broker rich at your expense. By losing so much of your returns in trading costs, day traders deny themselves the opportunity of participating in the long-term creation of wealth generated by business over the long term.

Defined Benefit Scheme A type of pension. See FINAL SALARY SCHEME.

Defined Contribution Scheme Another type of pension. See MONEY PURCHASE SCHEME.

Demutualization The process building societies go through when they convert to banks and thus go from being owned by their members (the borrowers and savers of the society) to being a PUBLIC LIMITED COMPANY owned by shareholders. There are pros and cons and the arguments rage on . . .

Derivatives Derivatives represent contracts conferring rights and obligations to do something with a security at a particular point in time. OPTIONS and FUTURES are derivatives. They can be used to lessen investment risk, but often their main attraction is that they are highly geared (see GEARING) and can thus offer spectacular profits ... and spectacular losses. They generally have substantial associated costs and we do not advocate their use.

Disclosure Since 1995 INDEPENDENT FINANCIAL ADVISERS and TIED AGENTS have been forced to disclose the level of commission they will earn from selling financial products to clients. It's a good thing, but the investor still isn't able to compare the levels of commission between investments. STOCKBROKERS also have to tell you of any financial interests they have in SECURITIES they are recommending.

Discount Broker The US term for EXECUTION-ONLY BROKER.

Discounted Rate Mortgage A mortgage with a guaranteed reduction in the variable mortgage rate (say, 2 per cent below the variable, whatever it may be). Generally the variable rate that you'll switch to when the discount ends will be higher than otherwise so that the bank can afford all the enticing discounts in the first place. Even if you're not tied into the variable rate by a REDEMPTION PENALTY, borrowers often forget to switch to a better rate. We'd generally suggest finding a cheap, non-discounted rate in the first place.

Dividend A distribution from a company to a shareholder in the form of cash, shares, or other assets. The most common kind of dividend is a distribution of cash out of a company's earnings. See DIVIDEND YIELD.

Dividend Yield The dividend divided by the current share price, expressed as a percentage. Different companies have different policies on the size of their dividend payouts. See BEATING THE FOOTSIE.

Dow Dividend Approach Another name for BEATING THE DOW.

Dow-Jones Industrial Average The thirty companies chosen by editors of Dow-Jones & Company that are supposed to epitomize the very best American corporations and reflect the landscape of corporate America.

Earnings The after-tax profit that a company makes after all of costs of delivering a product or service have been accounted for. See EARNINGS PER SHARE.

Earnings Per Share (EPS) EARNINGS divided by the current number of shares outstanding. This is one of the principal elements used in determining at what value the shares should trade. See also PRICE/EARNINGS RATIO.

Endowment A life assurance and savings and investment policy, classically sold to back an INTEREST-ONLY MORTGAGE. The key word here is 'sold'. No one in their right minds would 'buy' one of these overcharging and underperforming abominations these days. See WITH-PROFITS INSURANCE and SURRENDER VALUE.

EPIC Stands for Electronic Price Information Code. Also known as 'Ticker Symbol', it is an abbreviation for a company's name that is used as shorthand by share quote reporting services and various online sites.

Equities A concept that comes from 'equitable claims'. Equities are essentially shares in a company. Because they represent a proportional share in the business, they are equitable claims on the business itself.

Ex-dividend A share sold without the right to receive the dividend payment which is marked as due to those shareholders who are on the share register at a pre-announced date. These shares have 'xd' next to their price listings in the *Financial Times*.

Execution-only Stockbroker Stockbrokers who offer fewer of the services championed by ADVISORY STOCKBROKERS, but charge cheaper transaction fees. Basically, you tell them to buy or sell a particular share and they get on and do it with no frills and no hassles. Often they hold your shares in a NOMINEE ACCOUNT. Execution-only brokers are ideal for do-it-yourself investors – that's you. They are called discount brokers in the USA.

Exit Charge A sales charge paid for redeeming a unit trust or other investment. See FRONT-END LOADING.

Final Salary Scheme An occupational pension scheme where the benefits are calculated as a percentage of final salary (maximum ^{40}⁄₆₀ths). Also known as a DEFINED BENEFIT scheme, they mean that the employer takes the risk of things not working out on the investment front. Employers don't like this very much and many are changing over to MONEY PURCHASE SCHEMES.

Financial Services Authority (FSA) The top investment watchdog. If you have a problem with a financial adviser, stockbroker, bank or other financial institution, contact them on 0845 606 1234 and they should be able to tell you what to do.

Fixed Rate Mortgage The interest rate on the mortgage is pegged at a set level for an agreed number of months or years. Pull out before the end of that period and you'll end up paying a REDEMPTION PENALTY.

Flotation See NEW ISSUE.

Fool One who exhibits a high degree of FOOLISHNESS.

Foolishness The state of being wry, contrary, canny and capable of looking after your own investments. Fools believe in shares as the long-term path to wealth creation and believe that this is best achieved by investing in INDEX TRACKERs and buying and holding good companies for the long haul based on their fundamental financial and business strengths. This sort of behaviour does little to support the salaries of those in the financial services industry. See WISDOM.

Front-end Loading A sales charge paid when a PPP, AVC, ENDOWMENT or other investment is purchased. It can amount to the bulk of the first few years' contributions. The sellers of financial products are very keen on it. We're not.

FTSE All Share Index An INDEX containing around 800 of the largest companies on the LONDON STOCK EXCHANGE. The FTSE All Share Index (also known as the FTSE-ASI or, simply, the All Share) and the FTSE 100 are the indices generally tracked by index trackers (see INDEX TRACKER).

FTSE 100 An INDEX containing the 100 largest companies by MARKET CAPITALIZATION on the LONDON STOCK EXCHANGE. Came into being in 1984 and largely superseded the FT 30.

FTSE 250 An INDEX containing the 250 largest companies by MARKET CAPITALIZATION on the London Stock Exchange, created in 1992.

FT 30 For many years, the FT 30 was the INDEX most often quoted in relation to the LONDON STOCK EXCHANGE. It was originally conceived as being the UK equivalent to the DOW-JONES INDUSTRIAL AVERAGE, but is little quoted now. (Except by Fools intent on BEATING THE FOOTSIE.)

Full-service Broker The US name for an ADVISORY STOCKBROKER.

Futures A type of DERIVATIVE that allows people to buy or sell, for a price today, securities to be delivered some time in the future. Futures are a great way to lose your money because, for instance, if the security rises in value before you must deliver it, you might not be able to buy enough to fulfil your part of the bargain.

Gearing Buy a house for £100,000 with a deposit of £10,000 and the rest as a mortgage. Six months later, sell it for £150,000 and you've made 500 per cent profit on your original deposit – that's gearing. Of course, it can work the other way too (see NEGATIVE EQUITY). Gearing can be expressed as the ratio of debt to assets and is used by companies and investing individuals to enhance their profits, as well as homeowners to allow them to buy a home.

Gilts When the Government needs to borrow money, it sells you these. They are very safe and their US equivalent is the Treasury bill, or 'T-Bill'.

Gross The payment of any form of taxable income without the prior deduction of tax.

Independent Financial Adviser A financial adviser who is not employed by a particular company to market their products. They may be paid by COMMISSION, which in our view amounts to a conflict of interest, or else by agreed fee. We like to call these people Independent Financial Advisers (salespeople).

Index Groups of shares mathematically reworked to be representative of the current level of the market or of different subgroups of companies within the market. See FTSE 100, FTSE-ASI, FTSE 250, FTSE 30.

Index-linking Something that increases at the rate of inflation is index-linked. Some gilts are index-linked and the old age pension is index-linked.

Index Tracker The only type of unit trust that makes sense to us. While most unit trusts are actively (mis-) managed, index trackers are computer-driven and designed to mimic the performance of a given stock market index such as the FTSE 100 or the FTSE ALL SHARE INDEX. Over the long term, they outperform the vast majority of actively managed unit trusts.

Individual Savings Account (ISA) ISAs started in April 1999 and have replaced PEPs and TESSAs. This year you can invest £7000 and thereafter £5000 per year into a wide variety of investments. They are very attractive to FOOLs.

Inflation The process by which the real value of money is eroded over time. Inflation rates vary over the years and indirectly cause the direction of interest rate movements. The worst rate of inflation in modern times was in Hungary in the 1930s and 40s. By 1946, the 1931 gold pengo was valued at 130 million trillion paper pengos. You would not have wanted to retire in 1931 on an annuity of 100 pengos a month.

Initial Public Offering (IPO) The US name for a company's first sale of SHAREs to the public. In the UK we call it a NEW ISSUE or FLOTATION.

Inland Revenue Come on, you know who these people are! You probably don't know their very helpful Web site, though, which is at **www.inland revenue.gov.uk/**.

Insider Dealing This is when you buy or sell a share and at the same time possess privileged information that would move the price if it were widely known. It's illegal, but is also widespread and there are few prosecutions for it.

Institutions Institutional investors include pension funds and unit trusts. These are the big players in the stock market as they have a lot of money to invest. As major shareholders, they often have a say in company decisions.

Interest-only Mortgage Monthly payments to the lender are made up simply of interest. You don't pay off any of the CAPITAL of the mortgage during the term of the mortgage, but do so at the end, having – hopefully! – accrued a large enough amount of money in an investment fund. In the past, ENDOWMENTS were sold to back this type of mortgage. They didn't do it very well and we're pleased to say that INDIVIDUAL SAVINGS ACCOUNTs are more commonly used for this purpose these days.

Investment Club Group of investors that meets regularly to discuss which shares to buy and sell out of a common fund. See PROSHARE.

Investment Trust A public limited company that makes investments into a variety of other companies. Like actively managed UNIT TRUSTs, these are pooled investment funds and they tend to underperform the stock market average. However, investment trusts (particularly the very large ones) tend to do better than unit trusts since they tend to have lower charges.

ISEQ The Irish stock market INDEX.

Large-cap. See MARKET CAPITALIZATION.

Leverage The US term for GEARING.

Life Insurance See TERM LIFE INSURANCE and WHOLE OF LIFE INSURANCE. (By the way, life *in*surance means the same as life *as*surance.)

Liquidity The easier it is to turn an asset into cash, the more liquid it is. Shares in LISTED COMPANIES are very liquid as they can be sold at any time during normal market hours. Works of art and homes are not nearly as liquid because you need to find an interested buyer. Since every buyer needs a seller and vice versa, PENNY SHARES, which are very thinly traded, are more *illiquid* than larger capitalization shares.

Listed Company A company whose shares are listed on a STOCK EXCHANGE.

London Stock Exchange The place where shares in the 2000 or so UK public companies are bought and sold. It is in the CITY.

Margin 1. Borrowing money to use specifically for buying securities of any kind in a broking account. Buying shares on margin is very risky. 2. A measure of profitability of a company, like profit margin, operating margin or gross margin.

Market Capitalization The total market value of all of a firm's outstanding shares. Market capitalization is calculated by multiplying a firm's share price by the number of shares outstanding. Large-cap., medium-cap., small-cap. refer to shares in decreasing order of market capitalization.

Medium-cap. See MARKET CAPITALIZATION.

MIG Mortgage Indemnity Guarantee. If you borrow more than 75 per cent of the value of your house, you may get stung with one of these. It insures the lender against you being unable to pay. Even though it's you that pays this premium, it still won't stop you ending up at the Salvation Army soup kitchen. Do your best to avoid them, they're a rip-off.

Money Purchase Scheme Pension schemes where you build up a pot of cash, out of which your pension will be generated, also known as a DEFINED CONTRIBUTION scheme. The effect is that you take the risk of the investments not doing their job. PPPs and AVCs work on this kind of system, as do an increasing number of OCCUPATIONAL PENSION SCHEMES.

Mortgage A loan to buy a home, where you put up the property as a security against your paying back the loan.

Mutual Fund The US equivalent of a UNIT TRUST.

Nasdaq A national US stock market where trades are made exclusively via computers. The second largest market in the country, the Nasdaq is home to many high-tech and newer firms, including Microsoft. It now has its own Web site for UK investors, **www.nasdaq.co.uk**.

Negative Equity Bought a house for £80,000 and now it's only worth £60,000? Bad luck – that's £20k of negative equity you're sitting on there. See GEARING.

New Issue The first time a company is floated on the stock market. Selling your company, or a part of it, to outside investors is a way to raise money for expansion plans.

New York Stock Exchange (NYSE) The largest and oldest stock exchange in the United States, this Wall Street haunt is the one frequently featured on television, with hundreds of traders on the floor staring up at screens and answering phones, ready to trade stocks upon command from their firms.

Nil-paid Rights See RIGHTS ISSUE.

Nominee Account A type of account in which STOCKBROKERS tend to hold shares belonging to clients, to make buying and selling those shares easier. It does mean, however, that it might be difficult to get the benefit of any shareholders' perks.

Occupational Pension Scheme A form of pension scheme set up by employers. See FINAL SALARY SCHEME and MONEY PURCHASE SCHEME.

OEIC See OPEN ENDED INVESTMENT COMPANY.

Open Ended Investment Company These are similar to unit trusts. In fact, many UNIT TRUSTS are already converting to them. Ostensibly, they will be simpler for investors to understand and the charges will be lower as there will not be a BID-OFFER SPREAD between the buying and selling prices. In practice this will likely be replaced by a 'Dilution levy'. *Plus ça change* . . .

Options Contracts that give a person the right to buy or sell an underlying share or commodity at a set price within a set amount of time. They're a risky and expensive way of investing in shares. The majority of options expire worthless.

Paid-up Value If you stop paying into your AVC or PPP, but leave the money where it is, this is the amount of money that will be left to grow in the investment fund. In the first years of the plan, this is generally much less than the amount you have put in. See TRANSFER VALUE.

Penny Share A share of very low MARKET CAPITALIZATION (often a few million pounds) trading in multiples of just a few pence. They are very volatile, subject to extreme price fluctuations on the flimsiest of rumours and not at all the thing for the long-distance FOOL. See LIQUIDITY.

Personal Equity Plan (PEP) Started in 1987. They've been superseded by ISAs and you can no longer pay money into them. Existing PEPs, though, are still sitting there, growing away free of tax.

Personal Pension Plan (PPP) A private (i.e. non-state, non-occupational) pension. Charges can eat dramatically into what is often, in any case, poor investment performance. You then have to spend the bulk of your fund on an annuity. PPPs receive tax relief on contributions. See also AVC.

Portfolio Management Give all your money over to the STOCKBROKER and say, 'Here, go manage this.' It's one step up even from an advisory service. See ADVISORY STOCKBROKER.

Price/Earnings Ratio (P/E) A measure of a company's share price calculated by dividing the share price by the EARNINGS PER SHARE. Generally, the more future growth investors expect from a company, the higher its price/earnings ratio.

Profit and Loss Account Part of a company's ANNUAL REPORT, in which accountants try to explain to investors how much money the company is making. See also BALANCE SHEET and CASH FLOW STATEMENT.

ProShare A pressure group representing the interests of the private investor. They publish a magazine called *The Investor*, and also have a useful information pack on how to set up an INVESTMENT CLUB. Contact them on 0207 220 1750 or at their Web site – **www.proshare.org.uk/**.

Public Limited Company (PLC) As opposed to private (ltd.) companies, PLCs have a few extra legal requirements to go through to demonstrate, amongst other things, their creditworthiness. Only PLCs can be listed on the LONDON STOCK EXCHANGE or the ALTERNATIVE INVESTMENT MARKET.

Quarterly Reporting In the US after each quarter-year a company is required to file a report providing investors with juicy details on how the company is doing. In the UK equivalent reports are generally seen only every six months.

Redemption Penalty If you try and bow out of a CAPPED RATE, DISCOUNTED RATE or FIXED RATE MORTGAGE early, you may well be liable for one of these.

Repayment Mortgage As well as paying the interest, the monthly repayments on this type of mortgage repay part of the CAPITAL. Early on, the majority of the monthly payment goes towards the interest. See also CURRENT ACCOUNT MORTGAGE and INTEREST-ONLY MORTGAGE.

Revenue See SALES.

Rights Issue When a company raises money from SHAREHOLDERS by issuing new shares. Existing shareholders are given the right to purchase a certain number of new shares for each existing share that they hold at a discount to the market value. Each shareholder can either take up this right to buy the discounted shares or sell the right (known as NIL-PAID RIGHTS) to others.

Sales The money a company collects from a customer for a product or service. It generally forms the top line in a company's profit and loss account. Also known as TURNOVER or (in the US) REVENUE.

Securities Securities is just a blanket way to refer to any kind of financial asset that can be traded.

Security & Exchange Commission (SEC) The United States agency charged with ensuring that the US stock market is a free and open market. All companies with stock registered in the United States must comply with SEC rules and regulations, which include filing quarterly reports on how well the company is doing.

Share A SECURITY that represents part ownership of a company.

Shareholder If you buy even one SHARE in a company, you can proudly call yourself a shareholder. As a shareholder you get an invitation to the company's annual meeting, and you have the right to vote on the members of the Board of Directors and other company matters.

Share Split See BONUS ISSUE.

SIPP Self Invested Pension Plan. Like a PERSONAL PENSION PLAN, but the plan holder calls the shots in terms of which investments fill the plan.

Small-cap. See MARKET CAPITALIZATION.

Stakeholder Pension A new form of private pension to be introduced in April 2001. They are designed for people who do not have access to OCCUPATIONAL PENSION SCHEMES and will have lower costs than most PERSONAL PENSION PLANS. You will still have to spend the bulk of your investment fund on an ANNUITY, but the enforced low charges are a step in the right direction.

Stamp Duty A tax you pay on buying shares (0.5 per cent). For property, it starts at 1 per cent for properties worth over £60,000, increasing to 4 per cent for properties worth £500,000 or more.

Standard and Poor's 500 Stock Index (S&P 500) An index of 500 of the biggest and bestest companies in American industry.

Stock The same as a SHARE and used more commonly in the US. A share of stock (confusing, yes – just use the two interchangeably; everyone else does) represents a proportional ownership stake in a corporation. Investors purchase stock as a way to own a part of a publicly traded business.

Stockbroker A middleman who buys and sells shares on your behalf and earns commission on the transactions. Considered by many to be the fifth-oldest profession after prostitutes, pimps, tax collectors and accountants. See ADVISORY STOCKBROKER, EXECUTION-ONLY STOCKBROKER and PORTFOLIO MANAGEMENT.

Stock Exchange A place where stocks and shares are bought and sold. The LONDON STOCK EXCHANGE serves this function in the UK.

Surrender Value If you cash in your ENDOWMENT before its time, this is what you'll get. On average, it takes more than *seven* years for the surrender value to equal the money you've put in.

Tax-deferred When you invest in something like an AVC or PPP, you receive an initial tax refund from the Government and are then deferring taxes until you withdraw money in the form of ANNUITY payments, when you will be liable to income tax.

Tax-efficient AVCs, PPPs, TESSAs, ISAs – we have many, many ways in this country to invest with a minimum tax penalty. Some are far better than others.

Term Life Insurance A no-nonsense life insurance plan where you pay low annual payments (premiums) in return for a payment to be paid to your dependents if you die during the term. See WHOLE OF LIFE INSURANCE.

Ticker symbol See EPIC.

Tied Agent Less independent even than an INDEPENDENT FINANCIAL ADVISER. These are company salespersons, trying to sell you the products of the company they work for. Buying from them is a fool's, not a FOOL's game.

Transfer Value If you stop paying into your AVC or PPP, and decide to take the money out, this is what you'll be left with. In the first years of the plan, this is generally much less than the amount you have put in. See PAID-UP VALUE.

Treasury The Government's finance department. They have a natty little Web site: **www.hm-treasury.gov.uk/**.

Turnover See SALES.

Underwriters The STOCKBROKERS who help a company raise money by issuing new shares. They get paid a fee in return for promising to take up the shares if others don't. There is generally a let-out if the market is going haywire, so most people regard it as money for old rope.

Unit Trust Your money is invested with thousands of others in one pooled fund. Presiding over the fund is a manager or managers responsible for achieving the fund's stated investment objective. Most unit trusts under-perform the INDEX and have high charges. INDEX TRACKERS are the only form of unit trusts we advocate.

Valuation The determination of a fair value for a security. If you don't use some reasonable method, then you have what is technically called a 'guess' or a 'hope'.

Wall Street Also known as 'The Street' in US cocktail-party patter, this is the main drag in New York City's financial district.

Whole of Life Insurance This will cover you until you die, whenever that may be, unlike TERM LIFE INSURANCE. Don't think, though, that you'll pay the same premiums for the rest of your life – they'll be revised upwards every ten years or so!

Wisdom The state of being Wise. These are the people who seek to sell you inherently underperforming investments, hobbled even further by heavy charges. See ENDOWMENTS, FOOLISHNESS, INDEPENDENT FINANCIAL ADVISER and TIED AGENT.

With-profits Insurance Insurance policies that have both an insurance cover element and an investment element. Some ENDOWMENTS are 'with-profits' insurance policies. Remember that quote in the pensions chapter from the *Daily Telegraph* about endowment mortgages? It goes well here: 'It cannot be said too often that the advantages to the householder of an endowment mortgage are as nothing compared to the gain to the policy salesperson, that life assurance has nothing to do with house purchase, and that savings-related life assurance is a waste of money.'

Yield See DIVIDEND YIELD.

Zymurgy The pre-epileptic state a non-Foolish investor enters when the market drops 10 per cent in a day.

Appendices

Appendix 1
Coping with Compound Interest: The Mathematics

I shall light a candle of understanding in thine heart, which shall not be put out.

— 2 Esdras 14: 25

In Chapter 2, we looked at the awesome power of compound interest and, in the first edition of this book, we left it at that. It turned out, though, that this was not enough for some people. 'Tell us more about this compound interest,' some Fools cried. 'How does it actually work? Remove this cloak of magic and give it to us straight.'

This is what we shall be attempting to do in this appendix. We hope the first bit, which is the important bit, is relatively easy to follow. Unfortunately, the sums get a little hairy towards the end but it certainly looks pretty fancy on paper. If you don't follow it all, don't worry. This is about as hard as the sums ever get in investment (actually no harder than GCSE mathematics) and, anyway, to be a successful investor you don't need to understand all this stuff. It's strictly for those who are interested. People who want to know how to compound regular payments, however, but don't want to go through all the derivation of the formula can skip to the section 'The Magic Formula' on page 303. Alternatively, you could try our natty little online calculator at **www. fool.co.uk/compoundinterest**.

Let's start with some good news. Compound interest is not really mathematics, it's just arithmetic and, for us anyway, arithmetic is a lot less scary. Arithmetic just involves adding things together and taking them away. If you add a lot of the same thing together it becomes multiplication, it's just like addition gone a bit mad. Compound interest is just like multiplication gone mad. It's like adding a lot of things together and then adding all those together lots of times. Because there are a lot of sums to do, a calculator will come in very handy, but don't worry too much about this — the most important thing is to follow along and get a feeling for how it all works.

Compound Interest on Lump Sums

Let's start with a simple example. Imagine that you lend someone £100 and they agree to pay you an annual rate of interest of 10 per cent.

After one year

How much will they owe you after one year? Well, first of all, they still owe you the original £100. Then, on top of this, they owe you 10 per cent of £100 in interest. For anyone who has difficulty with percentages, 10 per cent can be thought of as 'ten hundredths', so 10 per cent of £100 is '£100 divided by 100 and multiplied by 10', which equals £10. So you are owed £100 plus £10, which equals £110.

After two years

At the beginning of year two (that is, the end of year one), you are owed £110. So, at the end of the second year, you are still owed the £110 but, on top of this, you are owed your interest for year two. This interest amounts to 10 per cent of £110 or '£110 divided by 100 and times 10', which equals £11. So, at the end of year two, you are owed £110 plus £11, which equals £121.

After three years

At the beginning of year three (that is, the end of year two), you are owed £121. So, at the end of the third year, you are still owed the £121 but, on top of this, you are also owed your interest for year three. This interest amounts to 10 per cent of £121 or '£121 divided by 100 and times 10', which equals £12.10. So, at the end of year three, you are owed £121 plus £12.10, which equals £133.10.

All three years together

Opposite is a table that breaks it all down into its components.

Don't worry if the table doesn't make sense. We just thought that it might help for some people. What we're trying to get across is that, after year one, you have your original sum (the £100), plus your interest (the £10). After year two, you have your original sum (the £100), plus your interest (the two £10s), plus your interest on your interest (the £1). By the time we get to year three, we have your original sum (the £100), plus your interest (the three £10s), plus your interest on your interest (the £1s), plus your interest on your interest on your interest (the 10p). Phew.

	Year 1		**Year 2**		**Year 3**	
	Start	Int.	Start	Int.	Start	Int.
	100	10	100	10	100	10
			10	1	10	1
					10	1
					1	0.1
Total	100	10	110	11	121	12.1
End Yr Total	**110**		**121**		**133.1**	

Int. = interest

It is because you are getting interest on your interest (and interest on your interest on your interest . . .), that it is described as 'compound interest' and this is what causes the seemingly miraculous results.

A quicker way to work it out

If we want to say, 'Keep what you had and add another 10 per cent,' it's the same as saying, 'Multiply what you had by 1.10 (or, simply, 1.1).' The 0.1 is equivalent to the 10 per cent and the 1 is there so you keep what you had. Now, remember that each year we want to 'keep what we had and add another 10 per cent'. So, each year we want to multiply by 1.1. After each year we end up with the following amounts:

After Year 1	£100 x 1.1	which equals £110
After Year 2	£100 x 1.1 x 1.1	which equals £121
After Year 3	£100 x 1.1 x 1.1 x 1.1	which equals £133.10

So, if we put £1000 in a bank and it earns annual interest of 10 per cent, how much will we have after three years? The answer is
£1000 x 1.1 x 1.1 x 1.1 (which comes to £1331).

If our £1000 was only earning 8 per cent in interest but we had it for four years, we would have
£1000 x 1.08 x 1.08 x 1.08 x 1.08 (which comes to £1360.49).

Now, hopefully this is all clear. If it's not, then go back and reread it up to here, because now things are going to get a little bit more tricky.

The shorthand approach

Well, it's not that hard really. And in fact the only reason this bit is here is to save you a bit of wear and tear on your keyboard or calculator.

We can reduce the number of buttons that you need to push by thinking of '1.1 x 1.1 x 1.1' as '1.1 to the power of 3'. So, '1.1 to the power of 3' means three 1.1s multiplied together.

If we have £1000 earning interest at 10 per cent for three years, we have '£1000 times 1.1 to the power of 3', which is equivalent to '£1000 times 1.1 x 1.1 x 1.1', which equals £1331.

If we had £1000 earning interest at 8 per cent for four years, we would end up with '£1000 times 1.08 to the power of 4', which is equivalent to '£1000 x 1.08 x 1.08 x 1.08 x 1.08', which equals £1360,49.

The words '1.1 to the power of 3' can also be written in shorthand as 1.1, with a little 3 slightly above and to the right of it – like this: 1.1^3. Computers aren't very good at putting in the little 3 so you may sometimes see it written as '1.1^3'. 1.1^3 is the same as 1.1^3.

Doing the sums

There are several ways of doing '1.1 to the power of 3' on a calculator. The first and simplest way is just to do 1.1 x 1.1 x 1.1. This is nice and easy and simple enough to get your head around. The trouble is that when the sums get a bit bigger it becomes a little bit boring. Imagine doing 1.0835 to the power of 30.

The second and third ways depend (very slightly) on what sort of calculator you have. So, if your numbers are coming out a bit funny, it might be that you need to get your calculator's instruction booklet out. What? Of course you kept it. It's in the bottom of THAT drawer (or maybe that other one).

Anyway, the second way is to type in 1.1, then hit the multiplication button (marked with an X) TWICE. A little 'k' (or something) should come up on the calculator's screen. This has told the calculator to multiply the number you put in (in this case 1.1) by itself every time you press 'equals'. So, the first time you press 'equals', it comes up with 1.21 (that is, 1.1 times 1.1). The second time you press 'equals', it should come up with 1.331 (that is, 1.1 times 1.1 times 1.1). Notice that you are actually pressing the equals sign one less time than the number you are going to the power of. This is because you had already put the number in to the calculator (representing the first power in the process). So, if you start with £1000 and earn interest at 8 per cent for four years, you could type 1.08 into your calculator, press 'X' twice and press 'equals' three times. The screen should now show 1.36048896. You now multiply this by the £1000 that you started with and you get the answer – £1360.49 (I know, it's actually £1360.48896 but I'm rounding to the nearest penny, OK?).

The third way to work it out involves using the 'X to the power of Y' button. Basically this means using a 'scientific calculator'. The button you want will be marked with an X, with a little Y slightly above and to the right of it – like this: χ^γ. On the calculator on a computer, it will probably be marked 'X^Y'. To work out '1.1 to the power of 3' on a typical scientific calculator, what you do is this. Put in the 1.1, then press the 'χ^γ' button, then press 3, then press = and, hey presto, it comes up with 1.331. If you start with £1000 and it earns interest at 8 per cent per year for four years and you want to know what you end up with, you do this. Put in the 1.08, then press the 'χ^γ' button, then press 4, then press 'equals'. The screen should now show 1.36048896. You now multiply this by the £1000 that you started with and you get the answer – £1360.49.

Now try doing it backwards

If you've got a calculator with an 'χ^γ' button, we can have a go at doing it backwards. For instance, if we know that we want £1500 in five years' time and we have £1000 now, how do we work out the annual return that we need to achieve? Well, to get to £1500 from £1000 means we need to multiply our money by 1.5 times. This is calculated by dividing the end money by the start money (that is, £1500 divided by £1000). What we need, then, is a number which, when we 'put it to the power of 5' gives us 1.5. We get this by using the same 'χ^γ' button on the calculator. But, this time, we have to press 'inv' or 'shift' beforehand so that the calculator knows we are doing it backwards.

So, we put 1.5 into the calculator, press 'inv' or 'shift', then press the 'χ^γ' button, then press 5, then press = and we get 1.08447. What this basically means is that £1000 x 1.08447 x 1.08447 x 1.08447 x 1.08447 x 1.08447 equals £1500.

You can check the answer by 'putting it to the power of 5' and making sure that it comes out as 1.5 again.

So, what does the number 1.08447 mean? It is a growth rate in disguise. Remember that when we wanted to 'keep what we had and add another 10 per cent', we had to multiply by 1.10? So, 1.08447 is the number that we would multiply by if we wanted to 'keep what we had and add another 8.447 per cent'. To turn £1000 into £1500 over five years, we would therefore need an annual rate of return (or, growth) of 8.447 per cent.

Compound Interest – Regular Payments

OK, did you manage to follow all that stuff on lump sums? If not, you might want to go through it again, because now things are going to get a little harder still. We are now going to look at compound interest on regular payments. In normal language, this means answering the following question. If I save £100 per month for ten years and my annual rate of growth is 12.6825 per cent, how much money will I have?

First of all, we should issue a maths warning. This is going to be a bit more complicated than basic compound interest and will even involve a bit of mathematical smoke and mirrors. But the smoke is quite fine and the mirrors are quite shiny and hopefully you will at least sort of follow what we're saying. It has been said before and it will be said again but – DON'T PANIC.

Undressing regular payments

At the beginning of this appendix, we said that compound interest was just an example of addition gone mad. It is a matter of adding a lot of things together and then adding all those together a lot of times. The good news is that regular payments are no different. Regular, let's say monthly, payments are just a series of lump sums. We just have to work out what each monthly lump sum is worth at the end and add them all up. This is the key to understanding it. Unfortunately, it can also lead to an awful, awful lot of adding up. This is what all the smoke and mirrors are about. They're just a way of condensing all the adding up so that it can be done in a matter of minutes. If you don't follow everything in this section, then it doesn't really matter, because the formula is at the end. The reason for going through it all is just that Fools never like putting their faith in mystery and it is nice to have at least a vague grasp of where the numbers are coming from.

A simple example

Imagine that you save £100 at the beginning of each month with a monthly rate of interest of 1 per cent. At the end of three months, you have invested three lump sums. One has been invested for three months, one for two months and the last one for only one month.

The first lump sum is now worth £100 x 1.01 x 1.01 x 1.01. That is, £100 x 1.01^3. This comes out as £103.0301. To the nearest penny, it's £103.03.

The second lump sum is now worth £100 x 1.01 x 1.01. That is, £100 x 1.01^2. This comes out as £102.01.

The third lump sum is now worth £100 x 1.01. This comes out as £101.

Adding these together, after three months we would have

£103.03 + £102.01 + £101 = £306.04

So, if after three months we have

£100 x 1.01^3 + £100 x 1.01^2 + £100 x 1.01,

what do you reckon we'll have after, say, five months? How about

£100 x 1.01^5 + £100 x 1.01^4 + £100 x 1.01^3 + £100 x 1.10^2 + £100 x 1.01

This comes out as

£105.10 + £104.06 + £103.03 + £102.01 + £101 = £515.20

If we saved like this for ten years (that is, 120 months), we would end up with

£100 x 1.01^{120} + £100 x 1.01^{119} + ... + £100 x 1.01^2 + £100 x 1.01

The problem we have is that, without the aid of a spreadsheet or a special calculator, working this out involves doing 120 separate sums and then adding them all up. Unless you're Carol Vorderman, that's not going to be much fun! What we need is a way of condensing the sum. This is where the smoke and mirrors come in.

Here's the smoke

Let's start by adding some mathematical smoke. We will call the amount of each monthly payment 'a' and our monthly rate of interest will be called 'r'. After three months, we have

$a(1+r)^3$ + $a(1+r)^2$ + a(1+r)

DON'T PANIC! We know there are some multiplication signs missing. You're allowed to do that. By putting a number immediately in front of brackets, you are saying that you are multiplying everything in the brackets by that number. It's just mathematical shorthand. We're going to have some big sums to do and we're not going to make them look messy (and even more confusing) by putting in Xs everywhere. They're surplus to requirements because we know what we mean.

Another point to make is about the order you do the sums in. That's why we need brackets in the first place. Brackets come first so, before doing anything else, we have to do the sums that are inside the brackets (that is add the 1 and the 'r' together). After brackets come indices ('indices' is just a posh way of saying 'to the power of'), so the next thing we do is put the contents of the brackets to the power of whatever. Next comes multiplication (so we multiply by the 'a') and, finally, we have addition, so we add the three separate sums together. In fact you can remember the full list by the mnemonic 'BIODMAS'. It stands for 'brackets', 'indices', 'of', 'division', 'multiplication', 'addition', 'subtraction'. If you don't believe that the order you do things in makes a big difference, then write down some sums and try doing them in different orders. You'll soon get the point.

There is nothing sneaky about this order thing. It is just a convention, whereby mathematicians can explain to people reading what order they should do the sums in. If you want to move something to the top of the list, you just put it in brackets (as we have with the '1+r').

Still with us? OK, the next thing to notice is that each of the bits of the equation is multiplied by 'a'. So, we can put it all in brackets and multiply the contents of the brackets by 'a'. What we mean is that

$$a(1+r)^3 + a(1+r)^2 + a(1+r)$$

is the same as

$$a((1+r)^3 + (1+r)^2 + (1+r))$$

In fact, each of the bits is also multiplied by a '1+r', so we can take one of these outside the brackets too. Don't forget that $(1+r)^3$ is the same as $(1+r)$ $(1+r)(1+r)$, which is the same as $(1+r)(1+r)^2$. So:

$$a((1+r)^3 + (1+r)^2 + (1+r))$$

is the same as

$$a(1+r)((1+r)^2 + (1+r) + 1)$$

And now come the mirrors

There was an article about all this that went up in the personal finance section of the Motley Fool's UK Web site in January 2000. This part of it was unbearably confusing and it is a testament to the power of the Motley Fool community that it is now a lot simpler. You see, a kind Fool sent in an e-mail explaining how it could be done so much more simply. He really buffed up the mirrors, if you like. So, if you think this is bad, just be glad you weren't exposed to the murky mirrors from before. Anyway ... We were trying to find the answer to the following sum without actually having to add it all up.

£100 x 1.01^120 + £100 x 1.01^{119} + . . . + £100 x 1.01^2 + £100 x 1.01

As we have seen, this can be written as

$100(1.01)(1.01^{119} + 1.01^{118} + \ldots + 1.01 + 1)$

If we replace the hundreds and the 0.01s by 'a' and 'r', we get

$a(1+r)((1+r)^{119} + (1+r)^{118} + \ldots + (1+r) + 1)$

In fact, if we replace the 120 by 'n', we get

$a(1+r)((1+r)^{n-1} + (1+r)^{n-2} + \ldots + (1+r) + 1)$

It makes sense to reduce the sum to this, because then we can use the compressed formula for any periodic amount, for any periodic rate of growth and for any number of periods. What we need to do now is to compress this unwieldy sum. To do this, we need to get rid of the + . . . + bit.

For the moment, let's leave the a(1+r) to one side and just concentrate on adding up what's in the big bracket, since this is where the problems are. We can come back and multiply by a(1+r) at the end. We're also going to replace all the other (1+r)s with 'R', to make things look a little nicer. Again, don't worry, we can put the (1+r)s back in at the end. So, we're trying to compress the following (V just stands for 'Value' – that is, the answer we're trying to get):

$V = R^{n-1} + R^{n-2} + \ldots + R + 1$

Are you ready for this? What you do is multiply both sides of the sum by R. We can do this because, if one thing equals another, then that thing multiplied by R will equal the other thing also multiplied by R. That's what equals signs are all about. So long as you do the same to both sides, then they're both still equal (just a bit different to what they were before). So, you get

$VR = R(R^{n-1} + R^{n-2} + \ldots + R + 1)$

Multiplying what's in the big bracket by the R outside, we get

$VR = R^n + R^{n-1} + \ldots + R^2 + R$

Notice that R^n is R^{n-1} times R in just the same way as 1.01^{120} is 1.01^{119} times another 1.01.

Now, we can subtract V from the left-hand side of the equation and $R^{n-1} + R^{n-2} + \ldots + R + 1$ from the right-hand side. Remember that, since these two things are equal, we are taking the same amount from each side which is therefore allowed. This leaves us with

$$VR-V = R^n + R^{n-1} + R^{n-2} + \ldots + R^2 + R$$

minus

$$R^{n-1} + R^{n-2} + \ldots + R^2 + R + 1$$

To make it a bit easier to spot what's about to happen, we've pulled some bits out of the $+ \ldots +$ bit and put some of them in **bold**. You see the classy thing is that all the stuff in the middle cancels out. For instance, we're taking R^{n-1} away from R^{n-1} and this gives us, you've guessed it, nought – not a thing. So, after all the dust settles, all we're left with is

$$VR-V = R^n - 1$$

How about that!! Of course, that's not quite what we want (we're after V), but we're nearly there. We can put a bracket in the left-hand side so it looks like this:

$$V(R-1) = R^n - 1$$

And then we just divide both sides by $(R-1)$ and we get

$$V = \frac{(R^n - 1)}{(R - 1)}$$

Now, we've got our V, but we need to replace our R's with $(1+r)$s and multiply everything by $a(1+r)$ and this gives us

$$V = \frac{a(1+r)((1+r)^n - 1)}{r}$$

We can now work out the answer to our original question. It seems a long time ago now, so I'll repeat it. If you save £100 per month for ten years with a monthly rate of interest of 1 per cent (which is the same as an annual rate of 12.6825 per cent), you will end up with

$$\frac{(£100 \,(1.01)(1.01^{120} - 1))}{0.01}$$

Remember that you have to do everything in the right order. To start off with, work out what's in the big bracket on the top. Within that bracket, you must do the smaller brackets first. So, do 1.01^{120} first, take the 1 away (giving you 2.300387 on your calculator screen) before multiplying by 100 and 1.01 (giving you 232.3391). Finally, you can divide this by 0.01 and you get £23,233.91 and that's the answer. Not bad for ten years' saving.

Of course, we know from the Miracle of Compound Interest that the longer you save for, the more it takes off. If we were saving £100 per month for twenty years, we'd have:

$$\frac{(£100\,(1.01)(1.01^{240}-1))}{0.01}$$

Now we're really talking. This comes to £99,914.79. If we did it for thirty years, we'd have £352,991.38 and after forty years, we'd have £1,188,242.02.

The magic formula

So the magic formula for compounding regular payments is this:

$$V = \frac{a\,(1+r)((1+r)^{n}-1)}{r}$$

Where
V = future value
a = periodic amount
r = interest rate for a period
n = the total number of periods

Remember that if you are saving monthly, your monthly rate on interest (or growth) is the number (less 1) which, when you put it to the power of 12, gives you your annual rate of return (plus 1). Similarly, the daily rate of interest is the number (less 1) which, when you put it to the power of 30 (in fact, more like 30.4375: that is, the average month), gives you your monthly rate and when you put it to the power of 365 (or rather 365.24: that is, the average year) gives you your annual rate.

So, imagine that you are saving £200 per month in an index tracker. The tracker has costs of 0.5 per cent (charged annually) and you expect the index to rise by 12 per cent per annum. How much will you have after twenty-five years?

Since our annual costs are 0.5 per cent, our actual annual return is only 11.5 per cent (12 per cent less 0.5 per cent). To get the monthly rate of interest, we need to find the number which, when we put it to the power of 12, gives us 1.115. In other words, the monthly interest rate is $1.115^{1/12}-1$. This comes to 0.00911247 and is our 'r'. Our monthly amount, or 'a', is £200. The number of periods is 'n' and comes to 25 x 12, or 300. So, we get,

$$V = \frac{£200(1.00911247)(1.00911247^{300}-1)}{0.009911247}$$

This comes to £289,174.44.

So, there it is, Fools, it's as simple as that — we wish. Anyway, if you want to save yourself a lot of trouble, you could simply use our online calculator to work these things out, at **www.fool.co.uk/compoundinterest**.

Appendix 2
What Makes A Good Index Tracker?

Give a man horse he can ride,
Give a man a boat he can sail.

— James Thompson, *Sunday up the River*

As you may have gathered from our various mutterings in this book, there are few subjects as close to a Fool's heart as index trackers. It seems only fair, then, that we put these creatures under the microscope and see what makes them tick. In fact, we'll try and go a step further than this and see what goes into making a good one. It's worth noting, though, that you don't have to read this appendix to invest in index trackers. What we've written elsewhere in the book is enough. This appendix is strictly for the interested, which is why it's just an appendix. Anyway, let's start at the beginning.

What Is an Index Tracker?

An index tracker attempts to match the performance of a particular 'index' of shares. In other words, it attempts to grow as closely as possible to the growth rate of that index of shares. It does this by exposing itself to the performance of the shares in that index. To keep things simple, let's imagine that the table on page 306 shows the biggest five companies on a theoretical stock market and that we want to create an index of them.

The *market cap* or *market capitalization* is the figure for the total value of all the shares in each company. It is therefore the sum of the value of every shareholder's shareholdings, the sum total of every pound invested in each company. £400 billion is therefore the sum total of every pound invested in these five companies.

There are basically two types of index that people might try to make out of this: *weighted* and *unweighted*. An unweighted index would give equal weight to the movements of each company. Each company would make up one fifth

305

Company	Share price	Shares in issue (millions)	Market capitalization (£m)
Allied Pharma	1600p	10,000	160,000
British Banking	500p	20,000	100,000
Cable Telecoms	800p	10,000	80,000
Deep Hole Mining	100p	40,000	40,000
Exploration Oil	500p	2,000	20,000
Total			**400,000**

of the index. So, one fifth of the index's percentage movement is accounted for by each share. If Allied Pharma goes up 10 per cent, then the index will rise 2 per cent. If Exploration Oil moves up 10 per cent, then the index will also rise 2 per cent. If both Allied and Exploration rise 10 per cent, then the index will rise 4 per cent. If one rises 10 per cent and the other falls 10 per cent, then the index will be unchanged. Of course, if all the shares in the index rose 10 per cent, then the index would rise 10 per cent.

A weighted index gives different weights to the effect of each share's movement on the index according to how big the company is (by market cap. or total money invested). Allied Pharma, with a market cap. of £160 billion, makes up 40 per cent of the index (that is, 160 divided by 400). So, if its shares rise 10 per cent, the index will rise by 4 per cent. Exploration Oil, on the other hand, only accounts for 5 per cent of the index. A 10 per cent rise by Exploration therefore only has a 0.5 per cent effect on the index. In other words, movements in Exploration Oil's share price only have an eighth of the effect on the index that movements in Allied Pharma's have. This is because Exploration is only an eighth of the size, and only has an eighth as much money invested in it.

The important thing about weighted indices is that they reflect the average performance of every pound in the index. You can think of a weighted index as being like a portfolio, which owns all the shares in all the companies. Whatever happens to the share price of the companies in the index, a weighted index matches the performance of the average pound invested in it.

Anyway, the point of all this is that if we want a tracker that gives us the average performance of the market as a whole (which we do) then, for starters, we need to be tracking a weighted index. For this reason, the majority of indices are weighted. Examples from the UK include the FTSE 100, the

FTSE 250, the FTSE 350 and the FTSE All Share. In the US, there is the S&P 500. Perhaps the most famous index in the world, the Dow-Jones Industrial Average, is an unweighted index. Other unweighted indices are the FT 30 in the UK and the Nikkei 225 in Japan. Tracking these (unweighted) indices would not (necessarily) give you anything like the average performance of the US, UK and Japanese stock markets and would therefore be a fairly pointless exercise.

Going back to the weighted indices, the good news is that there are plenty of these to track. However, before trying to work out which one is best, we need to consider how trackers actually go about tracking their various indices.

How Does a Tracker Track?

There are three basic ways that a tracker tracks an index: **Full Replication**, **Statistical Sampling** and **Use of Derivatives**.

Full replication

This is the most straightforward method of tracking an index. It involves simply creating a portfolio including all the shares in the index at their relevant weights. So, if you were setting up a tracker fund with £4 million to track the performance of the theoretical weighted index that we looked at above (which we'll call the TMF 5, standing for 'The Motley Fool 5'), then we would need to buy 0.001 per cent of each company (that is, our fund of £4 million divided by the total value of the index of £400 billion). So, we'd buy the following:

Company	Share price	Shares purchased	Value
Allied Pharma	1600p	100,000	£1,600,000
British Banking	500p	200,000	£1,000,000
Cable Telecoms	800p	100,000	£800,000
Deep Hole Mining	100p	400,000	£400,000
Exploration Oil	500p	20,000	£200,000
Total			**£4,000,000**

Once we've bought these shares, then all things being equal, we can just leave the tracker to do its job. We basically only have to buy and sell the shares in three situations.

Index changes

The TMF 5 is designed to follow the performance of the average pound invested in the five biggest companies on our theoretical stock market. So, if Exploration Oil shares did badly and it was overtaken, in terms of market capitalization, by Future Technologies plc whose shares have recently been doing well, then Future Technologies would replace it in the TMF 5 Index. We would therefore have to sell all our shares in Exploration Oil and buy, instead, shares in Future Technologies (we might also have to tinker with the overall weightings of all the stocks if our correctly weighted stake in Future costs more than we get for our Exploration shares).

Share capital changes

This is when the member companies issue new shares or cancel any of their existing shares. Imagine that Deep Hole Mining issued one new share for every four of its existing shares to buy the Australian company Gold Diggers Pty Ltd. The TMF 5 would have to reconstitute itself to take account of this. Assuming that the market was ambivalent towards the deal and the share price of Deep Hole didn't move, the new index would look like this:

Company	Share price	Shares in issue (millions)	Market capitalization (£m)
Allied Pharma	1600p	10,000	160,000
British Banking	500p	20,000	100,000
Cable Telecoms	800p	10,000	80,000
Deep Hole Mining	100p	*50,000*	*50,000*
Exploration Oil	500p	2,000	20,000
Total			***410,000***

So all the other companies' weightings have fallen (Allied Pharma's weighting has fallen from 40 per cent (160/400) to 39.0 per cent (160/410)), while Deep Hole's weighting has increased (from 10 per cent (40/400) to 12.2 per cent (50/410)). As a result, a little of each of the other companies will need to be sold and the money used to buy extra shares in Deep Hole.

New money from investors

The third reason for buying and selling would be if a new investor came along and asked to invest £100,000 in the tracker fund (or if an existing investor decided to withdraw £100,000 from the tracker). In this case, we would have to add 2.5 per cent to (or sell 2.5 per cent of) the value of each of our holdings.

This is what is happening all the time with unit trusts. Every day, people are coming along to put more money in or to take money out. If there is a pound put in for every pound that gets taken out, the balance is maintained. However, if, overall, money is flowing into the fund, then it will need to be buying shares in each company each day to maintain its correct exposures. If there is net money flowing out, then it needs to be selling shares in each company each day to maintain the balance. All this buying and selling costs money and it is mostly borne by the new or departing investors.

The main advantage of the full replication tracking approach is that you can expect to match the index very closely. The disadvantage is that it can be expensive and it is only really very practical where you have a small number of shares in an index. The FTSE 100, with its 100 member companies, lends itself reasonably well to this.

Statistical sampling

With an index like the FTSE All Share (which has around 800 member companies), full replication is likely to be extremely costly to achieve. To track these larger indices, most fund management companies will therefore use a process called statistical sampling. The fund doesn't try to hold every share in the index, but it analyses the index and works out its investments so that it is very confident of achieving a performance very close to it.

So, at a basic level with the TMF 5 we might decide that since Exploration Oil only accounts for 5 per cent of the index's value, then we don't actually need to hold it to ensure a performance very close to the index. We do, though, have to keep a close eye on it. If it increases by 20 per cent relative to the rest of the index, then we will underperform by 1 per cent and we don't want to risk underperforming by more than that. We might therefore decide that we can afford to save costs by not holding Exploration unless and until it increases to a level where it accounts for 6 per cent of the index. Of course, if Exploration underperformed the rest of the index then we would benefit from not holding it.

Statistical sampling is a bit of a fudge. If money flows into the fund from new investors, shares of one sort or another will certainly have to be bought, but we might be able to save a bit on costs by not sticking rigidly to buying exactly the right amount of every single company. With a large index such as the FTSE All Share, the relationships between the different shares will be examined, so that the tracker's manager can be very confident of not departing very far from the index. Of course, some companies will be good at this and others bad. To have the same range of likely performance compared to the index, it might cost one company less than another. Unfortunately, few trackers have a long enough track for us to work out who's good and who's bad. It's probably not a bad idea, then, to stick with the more established fund management companies who have good experience of this sort of thing. Pound for pound, it is also probably cheaper for the larger funds to do all the sums needed for this method.

Use of derivatives

Finally, a tracker might use things called 'derivatives' to match the performance of an index. For instance, it might leave all its investors' cash in the bank and use it as the collateral for a futures contract on the performance on the relevant index. By buying the right derivatives, a fund can organize things so that its performance will reflect the performance of an index very closely.

One advantage of doing things this way is that money coming into the fund just goes into the bank. In the same way, when people take their cash out, it can simply be paid out of the bank. This might be a lot simpler than having to buy or sell all of the shares every day (or a representative sample of them). However, the fund manager would still need to increase or reduce the level of exposure the fund has to the index each day, and there will be costs associated with this.

A fund might combine using derivatives with some form of statistical sampling. By buying an underlying level of derivatives exposure, the fund might be able to reduce costs in the buying and selling of the actual stocks that it needs to top up its exposure.

Call us old fashioned but, despite some potential for cost savings, we Fools don't really like the sound of trackers using derivatives. We're sure they're all very careful, but everyone was sure that Barings Bank was very careful until it went bust. Insuring against problems would just increase costs and, to us, it looks like yet another case of it being best to keep things simple.

Which Index?

Choosing the market or index that you want to track is obviously of primary importance. Fools living in the UK are most likely to want to be exposed to the UK stock market. On the whole, this means choosing between the FTSE 100 and the FTSE All Share. We're therefore going to limit the comments here to these two indices. However, it should generally be pretty relevant to choices between other indices.

The FTSE 100 is an index of the UK's biggest 100 companies. The FTSE All Share is designed to follow the whole of the stock market. To do this it contains about 800 companies. These are mostly, but not necessarily, the 800 biggest companies. However, even the FTSE All Share avoids around a thousand or so of the real tiddlers. Still, as soon as the tiddlers start getting big, they tend to get included, so the FTSE All Share should never be far away from the average performance of the whole market (to a lesser extent, the same can be said about the FTSE 100). The FTSE 100 companies make up about 80 per cent by value of the FTSE All Share so the differences between them are fairly small. Even so, the FTSE All Share has a slightly better spread of investments than the FTSE 100 and it therefore represents the overall UK market that little bit better.

As far as the returns from the FTSE 100 and the FTSE All Share themselves (that is, not necessarily the trackers) are concerned, history has things very slightly in favour of the FTSE All Share. The argument goes that smaller companies are more risky and, over the long term, the market prices them to compensate you for taking this risk on. However, recent history (perhaps the last ten years or so) has things on the side of the FTSE 100. The argument for this is that, in the modern globalizing economy, big is best (because of things like 'economies of scale'). If any threat is posed by the smaller companies then, the story goes, they just get taken over or crushed by the big boys.

All in all, there is probably not much to choose between the two indices (although this is not necessarily so for the trackers following them). Other factors are more likely to make a difference.

Deviating from the Index

On top of the performance of the underlying index, you also need to consider the amount by which a tracker misses its index. Tracking an index is not as straightforward as it sounds (or, rather, tracking an index cheaply isn't very easy). So, we need to look at the reasons why certain types of tracker might deviate from the index they're tracking.

One reason for a deviation is dividends. Most indices, including the FTSE 100 and the FTSE All Share, do not include reinvested dividends. As a result, any tracker that includes reinvested income (often called 'accumulation units') will look better than its index (or it should do anyway) because it's getting an extra couple of per cent or so per year. This difference is purely artificial and, as long as you are comparing like with like, it can be ignored.

When companies describe other deviations in the performance of their trackers, they seem to use the words 'tracking error' to describe any departure from the performance of the underlying index. However, to get to the bottom of things, we need to look at things a little more closely.

Charges

The number one reason for a tracker not performing in line with its index is its charges. It's the number one reason because it is easily quantifiable, operates in one direction (that is, downwards) and is relatively visible. If the index manages an annual rise of 12 per cent and your tracker charges 1 per cent per annum then, all other things being equal, your return will only be 11 per cent. It's as simple as that.

Well, not quite. You have to be careful that you've picked up all the charges. First of all, there is the annual management fee, which is frequently described (incorrectly) as the total charges. In addition, there will generally be some 'admin and trustees fees' or something like that.

Also, don't forget the effect of any 'initial charge' and/or 'bid-offer spread'. On the whole, very few trackers have an initial charge these days and it therefore makes sense just to avoid any that do. The bid-offer spread reflects the tracker's costs in buying (or selling) the underlying shares in the particular index when you put money in (or finally take it out). The difference between the bid and offer price of units should be a very small percentage (certainly less than 1 per cent and probably less than 0.5 per cent) of the actual cost of the units.

On top of all this, there are the dealing charges involved in buying and selling shares to keep the tracker in line with its index. Generally, the dealing charges that relate to new money coming into the fund (or old money leaving) will come through in the 'bid-offer spread'. Where there is no bid-offer spread, the costs will be reflected in the annual fees. Overall it probably makes little difference how it is done, except that you need to be aware of it and include it in any comparison.

There will also be the costs of buying and selling shares to keep the tracker properly weighted. All trackers will suffer a little from this, but statistical samplers will suffer less, since they have more flexibility about which shares they buy and in what volume. This should enable them to save on dealing costs.

Tracking error

There are basically two types of tracking error. In the first type, the error is as likely to be towards the up side as the down side, whereas in the second it is weighted in one particular direction. For want of better expressions, we'll call these unbiased error and biased error. Not surprisingly, an error biased to the down side is much worse than an unbiased error of the same amount, since it has definitely gone against you.

Biased tracking error

Biased tracking error has a tendency to be in one particular direction. In this way, it actually tends to make the tracker perform above or below its index. Unfortunately, biased tracking error will tend to be towards the down side (otherwise everybody would be doing it). Charges, which are so important that they got their own little section above, are the most obvious form of down side weighted tracking error.

Other forms of biased tracking error should have a much smaller effect. All the time, a unit trust tracker has people putting money into it and taking money out. It therefore has to buy and sell shares to maintain its weightings in the index. However, in amongst all this buying and selling, the fund may, for instance, tend to have a very small permanent cash balance. In a rising market, this will tend to cause the tracker to fall behind its index whereas, in a falling market, it would tend to cause the tracker to beat its index. Since, as we saw in Chapter 4, markets tend to go up over the longer term, then this would be an error biased towards the down side. This type of error is a problem for unit trust trackers since these are the ones that accept new money into the fund and let old money leave, but we needn't worry about it too much, since the effects should be pretty small. Investment trust trackers avoid this problem because they are structured so that they don't have money flowing into and out of them. Unfortunately, partly as a result of this, it can make it more expensive to put investment trust trackers into an ISA.

Unbiased tracking error

There are two main sources of unbiased tracking error. The first is when new companies come into and leave the index. The tracker generally has some flexibility to decide when to sell the old companies and buy the new ones. Sometimes it will get it right, sometimes it will get it wrong. On the whole it won't make much difference over the long term. Having said that, it could be argued that shares that are about to join the index are heavily in demand and that trackers always have to pay too much for them. This would turn part of this error into an error biased to the down side. However, since we are talking about the shares joining the index, we are generally talking about very small weightings and the effect should be small. This will mainly be a problem for the FTSE 100 trackers, since the relative weighting of the shares coming into and leaving the index is much greater for the FTSE 100 than for the FTSE All Share. It will also be more of a problem for full replication trackers than statistical sampling trackers, since the latter have much more flexibility about when to buy the new entries.

A second form of unbiased tracking error is almost entirely a problem for the statistical samplers. This makes it more of a problem for the more widely-spread indices like the FTSE All Share (which are more likely to use this approach). It simply comes down to the fact that they do not actually own (or attempt to own) all the shares in the relevant index. So, if the shares they don't own happen to do very well, then the tracker will do a bit worse than its index. Of course, it works both ways and if the shares that the tracker doesn't own do relatively badly, then the tracker will beat its index. The effects should be fairly small and, over many years, they should all even out.

How big a variation you might get here from year to year depends on the index tracked, how good the manager is at tracking it and how much (of your) money the manager throws at the problem. If you were prepared to pay the extra, then you could fully replicate the FTSE All Share index. However, it almost certainly wouldn't be worth it because the extra charges would drag the performance down. It would be a self-defeating strategy because, by paying more to try to reduce a small error that might as easily work in your favour as work against you, you turn it into an error, in the form of charges, which you know will work against you. In the end, it will always be a bit of a balance but, the longer you are invested for, the more likely the cheapest method of tracking is to come out on top.

The Moral of the Tale

The trouble with all this tracking error stuff is that you need a very long performance history to have any real confidence about the level of overall tracking error. You'd need longer still to have any confidence about how much of this was simple error and how much was biased against you. Of course, the beauty of investing in trackers is that so long as you follow a few fairly obvious fundamentals it isn't going to make a great deal of difference which one you go for.

First and foremost, as with all investments, you want to avoid high (apparent and hidden) charges. Secondly, you want something that isn't likely to vary too far from the index (within reason). Finally, if there is to be any variation, then you'd obviously prefer it to be even-handed. The second and third points are likely to come down to thinking about the index that you're tracking, thinking about how it is being tracked and thinking about the reputation of the company doing the tracking. As trackers get a longer and longer history (they're a relatively new breed), we'll be able to make better and better judgments about who's any good at making them work. For the time being we'll have to feel our way a bit. Still, we can be sure that, over the long term, our performance is going to be better than the vast majority of actively managed funds.

Appendix 3
Major UK Index Trackers

Acquaintance I would have, but when't depends
Not on the number, but the choice of friends.

— Abraham Cowley, *Of Myself*

Information at 1 June 2000

Dresdner RCM UK Index
Index: FTSE All Share
Initial: 0%
Annual: 0.57% (0.5% management plus 0.07% trustee fees etc.)
Bid/offer spread: 0.5%
Web site: **www.dresdnerrcm.co.uk**
Tel: 0345 127128

Edinburgh UK Tracker (Investment Trust – EPIC Symbol: EUK)
Index: FTSE All Share
Initial: 0%
Annual: 0.35%
Bid/offer spread: 0.4% (estimated)
Web site: **www.edfd.com/**
Tel: 0131 313 1000
Other: They operate a savings scheme that accepts a minimum of £30 per month or £250 as an initial lump sum.

Fidelity Moneybuilder
Index: FTSE All Share
Initial: 0%
Annual: 0.75% (0.5% management charge plus 0.25%)
Bid/offer spread: 0%

Web site: **www.fidelity.co.uk**
Tel: 0800 414161
Other: Minimum of £50 per month.

Gartmore UK Index

Index: FTSE All Share
Initial: 0%
Annual: 0.5%
Bid/offer spread: 0.5% (estimated)
Web site: **www.gartmore.co.uk**
Tel: 0800 289336
Other: Minimum investment is £2500 lump sum or £100 a month in a
regular savings scheme.

HSBC UK Index Fund

Index: FTSE All Share
Initial: 0%
Annual: 0.5%
Bid/offer spread: 0.5% (estimated)
Tel: 0800 289505
Other: Minimum investment is £1000 lump sum or £50 a month in a
regular savings scheme.

iShares FTSE 100 (Exchange Traded Fund – EPIC Symbol: ISF)

Index: FTSE 100
Initial: 0%
Annual: 0.4% (0.35% management plus 0.05% other)
Bid/offer spread: 0.5% (estimated)
Web site: **www.ishares.net/**

Legal & General UK Index

Index: FTSE All Share
Initial: 0%
Annual: 0.53% (0.5% management plus custodian and registrar fee)
Bid/offer spread: 0%
Web site: **www.landg.com**
Tel: 01222 448412
Other: Minimum £500. There are withdrawal charges if you invest outside
of an ISA, starting at 3 per cent, in the first five years.

M&G Index Tracker
Index: FTSE All Share
Within an ISA
Initial: 0%
Annual: 0.439% (0.3% management plus custodian and registrar fees)
Bid/offer spread: None
Outside an ISA
Initial: 0%
Annual: 0.439% (0.3% management plus custodian and registrar fees)
Bid/offer spread: 0.53%
Web site: **www.mgisa.co.uk**
Tel: 0800 390390
Other: Using the M&G savings scheme, you can invest an initial lump sum
(min. £500) or invest on a monthly basis (min. £10).

Scottish Widows UK Tracker
Index: FTSE 100
Initial: 0%
Annual: 0.5%
Bid/offer spread: 0%
Web site: **www.scottishwidows.co.uk/**
Tel: 0345 678910
Other: Minimum lump sum of £500. Monthly minimum of £50. Note that
all the figures for this fund are for within an ISA only.

Virgin UK Index Tracker
Index: FTSE All Share
Initial: 0%
Annual: 1%
Bid/offer spread: 0%
Web site: **www.virgin-direct.co.uk/**
Tel: 08456 10 20 30
Other: Minimum £1 for lump sums or monthly investments.

Appendix 4
How to Open a Broking Account

We demand that big business give the people a square deal;
in return we must insist that when anyone engaged in big business
honestly endeavours to do right he shall himself be given a square
deal.

— Theodore Roosevelt, *Autobiography*

You've decided you want to do your own research and invest in some shares for the long term, but how do you go about it? In our experience it's this kind of mundane detail that puts people off investing in shares most of all. Don't worry, it can be simple, unlike the experience Neil Fletcher from Liverpool described when he wrote to us at our Web site in early 1998:

I've always had a somewhat ambivalent attitude to the stocks and shares scene, slightly in awe of it but at the same time secretly wishing to be involved.

Until November 1997 I had never bought a share in my life. But having just received the proceeds of an endowment policy, I decided more or less on the spur of the moment to have a go. The only drawback was I knew absolutely nothing about how to do it. So on a wet Monday morning I went to my bank, one of the larger branches of NatWest in Liverpool city centre, eager to shell out £2000 on some shares I'd seen tipped by Paul Kavanagh in the Sunday Times *and which were in a field I knew something about – education. I was told that I'd have to go to an even larger branch, one that did all the share dealing.*

I traipsed through the rain to the branch in question where I was informed the dealing charge would be 1.5 per cent. I asked the girl to arrange it for me, but she couldn't find the company listed anywhere on her monitor (and we're not talking AIM or penny shares here, by the way). I would have to return to my own branch where they would buy the shares for me over the phone but with somewhat higher charges. Another trudge through wet Liverpool back to my own branch where I had to explain the whole rigmarole all over again – by which time I just wanted to buy the damn things and go home. The deal was finally done. I had become a shareholder, but only by paying a hefty 1.75 per cent for the privilege.

Because I was even greener then than I am now, I paid up without hesitation. I just wanted to buy them, for heaven's sake, before they went up in price (they've subsequently done quite well, incidentally). It's only since reading the various Fool UK postings that I've discovered there are easier and cheaper ways of buying shares. So I hope this anecdote will be helpful to those entering the share buying jungle for the first time and prevent exhausting and expensive safaris through wet streets.

Neil, we won't let you down.

Shares can only be bought and sold on your behalf by stockbrokers, who naturally charge for the privilege. Those are the rules. How much they charge depends on a number of things, but primarily on whether they provide an advisory service or are 'execution-only' brokers. Advisory brokers do just that – they advise you what to buy and sell, often with a fairly short-term perspective. They'll say things like: 'Zelda's Zips is looking good at the moment and it's ripe for a takeover bid.' Or: 'The market's bearish on banks at the moment. Let's move out of Lloyds for a while.' The first problem with this is that the current market price of Lloyds represents the sum total of all these people's thinking on the matter. The chances are that for each broker saying that the market is bearish on Lloyds, another is saying 'banks look as if they've bottomed out, so it's time to move back in'. In each case, one is likely to be right and one is likely to be wrong, but working out in advance which camp a particular advisory broker falls into is as hard as picking the right unit trust and we saw in Chapter 7 that there is no reliable way of doing it. If you are in a position to decide whether your broker is right, then you don't need the advice anyway.

The other problem with advisory brokers is that they are getting paid by commission for *each* trade. That's how they make money. How they make *more* money is to induce you to trade more frequently. It's against the rules for them to trade on your account simply to make themselves money but, as so often in the murky world of finance, there is a storming, stonking conflict of interest here. While independent financial advisers (salespeople) have strong incentives to sell you high-commission investments, advisory brokers have a similar incentive to trade you in and out of shares on a regular basis.

Here's a salutary tale of advisory broking from a Motley Fool reader posted at the end of May 1998:

My wife and I have experienced stockbrokers. They persuaded us to sell good stock to buy not so good, netting huge commissions in the process. We were advised to sell 3500 Prudential shares at £3.03 and buy BTR at £3.34.

Weeks later, the Pru was at £5.00 and BTR at £3.00. They then advised us to buy more of the Pru at £5.00 and sell Unilever for consolidation purposes.

Another time, we were advised to buy De la Rue at £9.60. They fell and fell, but we thought, 'Well, the professional knows what he's doing,' and waited for a rise. At £3.70 they wrote and said we ought to consider selling them. These are 'active fund managers'.

Professional advice? Never again.

I have in the past worked for an insurance company, and seen some of the dirty tricks they play on customers, but that's another story.

Best wishes,

Adrian Gill

PS We eventually sacked them two months ago and sold BTR at £1.60, while the Pru were over £9.00. The only ones to make money in all this were the brokers who received our commission. We are now invested in a Legal and General index tracker and to my mind these so-called fund managers are in the main not competent.

As long as everyone believes the fiction that this kind of frequent trading is beneficial to your financial health, then it looks like everyone is having their cake and eating it. However, introduce a subversive into the equation (sorry, we meant 'Fool') and pretty soon things start to fall apart. It's especially undermining when that subversive threatens the very foundations of the belief system they are challenging. Remember that chap Galileo we mentioned earlier in the book? The one who said that the Earth moved around the sun? His revolutionary ideas, which fitted the observable facts so neatly, caused consternation in his era (in fact, they were originally the ideas of a Pole named Copernicus, but this didn't stop Galileo launching himself into the debate with a gusto that would have made a hawker in Marrakesh blush). Anyway, the Pope wasn't quite so impressed with the notion of a sun-centred solar system and Galileo was lucky not to have his head neatly disengaged at the neck and served up to him on a platter.

Times have moved on, but as a Fool you're going to come up against similar antagonism as you strike at the roots of a rotten system and challenge not only a set of deeply held beliefs, but – let's face it – the means of earning a livelihood for very many people. Does that make you feel bad or guilty? Do you feel that you must continue to support a flawed system which has provided the daily bread for so many people for so many years? You do? That's lovely and so thoughtful. Why, you Fool! We didn't know you had it in you! In that case, you need an advisory stockbroker, charging the highest fees per transaction possible, the fattest yearly portfolio management fee and pursuing a policy of 'active management of a client's portfolio, based on the most up-to-date stock market trends'. And while you're at it, enlist your favourite group of rock stars to put on a benefits concert: BrokerAid. And don't forget the Web site: www.brokeraid.co.uk. Or the adoption programme: 'Adopt a broker today.'

The rest of you hardhearted fiends should avoid these people as if they carried the Black Death. Which, in financial terms, they generally do. What you need to find is an execution-only broker who will buy and sell shares on your behalf when you ask them to. Nothing more, nothing less.

Choosing an Execution-Only Stockbroker

So, you're a Fool and you want to set up an account with an execution-only stockbroker. How do you go about doing this? As with anything, the first step is to decide what level of service you want and what you are prepared to pay for it. You then need to work out a balance between these two things. If you want the cheapest possible dealing, then you will probably have to settle for a no-frills service. If, on the other hand, you want the highest level of service, then you will probably need to pay a bit more for it.

All this first becomes relevant when you are choosing how you want to place your buy and sell orders. Do you want to do it only over the Internet, do you want to do it only over the telephone or would you prefer to do be able to do both? The advantage of dealing over the Internet is that, since the costs to the broker are lower, it's likely to be cheaper. However, many people don't have sufficient access to the Internet and those that do will be aware that occasionally they can't make a connection with their service provider. Even if you're dealing over the phone, some brokers will have more people taking orders than others and these, while being easier to get through to, are likely to be more expensive. If you're really Foolish, you'll know that trying to time the market, and therefore your buys and your sells, is pretty futile. On this basis, it might not matter if it takes an hour or two to place your order: in the meantime the shares that you want to deal in are as likely to go up as they are to go down. More important, you think to yourself, is getting the cheapest deal possible when you do get through. However, some people, once they've made a decision, might find it frustrating if they can't put it into action immediately, even if being certain of this is likely to cost them more. None of this is meant to sound alarmist: most execution-only brokers are highly efficient, but to decide which to go with you need to consider carefully the level of service that you are looking for.

The next thing to think about is charges. Different brokers have different commission structures and to decide which one suits you best, you need to decide how often, and in what amount, you are likely to trade. Typically, a broker will charge you a percentage of the value of each trade as commission, with a minimum level. Let's look at an example where the commission is 1 per cent and the minimum is £15. This would mean that, since £15 is 1 per cent of £1500, any deal with a value of less than £1500 would cost you more than 1 per cent. For instance a deal involving shares worth only £1000 would cost you £15, and this comes to 1.5 per cent. So, one broker might be the best value for deals worth up to £2000, another might be best value for deals between £2000 and £4000 and yet another might be better for deals worth more than £4000. Some brokers might offer special deals for people who deal a lot. You might pay 1 per cent for your first ten deals in a year and then only 0.5 per cent after that. Trading frequently is a very costly way of achieving little or no benefit and it's not very Foolish at all. But, if that's your bag, then this sort of deal might interest you. Some brokers might also charge you an annual account charge. This might be a flat fee of, say, £40, or it might be £6 for each individual shareholding that you have. Obviously you will need to factor this into any calculations as well. All this sounds very confusing, but really it isn't. You just need to estimate what might happen in a year's worth of investing. Be honest with yourself! You might estimate that in an average year you will do four trades of £2000 each. Having worked that out, you just need to work out how much this will cost with each of the brokers on your shortlist.

Shortlist? Sorry, we haven't mentioned this yet. You need to start off with one of these. Speak to your friends, look out for adverts in the back of investment magazines and in the financial sections of newpapers, maybe even have a look in the Yellow Pages. If you have Internet access, you might want to have a look at the Motley Fool's Broker Area at **www.fool.co.uk/ brokers** or visit our Brokers discussion board to see who others use and what they think of them. Once you've done all this, you should have a list of a number of brokers that you like the sound of. Contact each of them and get them to send you their bumf.

With your shortlist and your bumf in hand, you're in a position to start crossing some off the list. If they don't send you the bumf within a week, you might decide that they're not going to deal with your dealing very efficiently and cross them off straight away. Do you want to deal in foreign markets? If you want to be able to do this, then cross off anybody who doesn't offer this.

Do you want to be able to reinvest dividends automatically in the shares of the companies that produce them? If you absolutely do, then you need to cross off the brokers who don't allow this. However, if it would just be quite nice and you're not really prepared to pay much more for it, then just put a black mark against those who don't offer it. Do you want to be able to ask for a valuation of your portfolio to be sent to you whenever you like? How much are you prepared to pay for this? There might well be a number of other criteria that matter to you but, whatever they are, you get the general idea. After a while, you should have a very messy piece of paper and several names that seem to fit the bill. Now work out how much you'd have to pay each of these brokers in your average year of investing. Taking these costs into account and looking at the black marks, you should be able to narrow things down to a choice between two. Now take a coin and . . . (only kidding).

Once you've decided who to go with, contact them again, tell them the good news and ask them to send you an account application form (if it didn't come with the bumf). Even if you're going for an Internet broker, you'll have to do this bit by post since they like to make sure you're who you say you are. Fill in the application form, send it in with a cheque to get yourself started, and Bob's your auntie's husband.

Of course, you're still not quite home and dry. Now comes the tricky business of working out which shares to buy. We've already said a fair bit about this, but if your still thirsting for more, why not have a look at the *Motley Fool UK Investment Workbook*, or come to our Web site to chew things over with other Fools. Once you've made a decision (and don't rush it!), you are ready to do your first deal.

Before you place an order, check the morning paper to see that the shares are still at a level that you're prepared to pay for them. Even better, check Ceefax or a financial site on the Internet. It's also worth checking to make sure that there hasn't been any major news announced which might affect your decision. In this respect, the Internet takes a lot of beating. Next, check that it's after about 10.00am and before about 3.00pm. Stockbrokers and other Wise 'market professionals' are a funny lot and they can send prices flying around first thing in the morning or last thing at night. Remember that we're not trying to be clever. We are not traders, we are Foolish investors. We've decided on a share to buy and we're happy to pay the going rate. What we don't want is to get a funny deal (good or bad) because some Wise guy somewhere is doing something Wise. Having thought about all this, it's time to get on the phone or the Internet.

On the phone, you should get another chance to check the current price. Don't be afraid to say that this is your first time. If your broker isn't prepared to take the time to explain things clearly, then it might be an idea to get that shortlist out again. Your broker may well be able to do the deal there and then, while you're on the phone, in which case you can put down the phone knowing exactly how many shares you've bought and for how much. Sometimes, though, this might not be possible. In which case, you might want to set a limit above which you're not prepared to go through with it. If you do this, remember that you're just trying to guard against things going very funny, so be happy to set a limit a couple of per cent higher than the current price. You can then phone back later to see whether, and at what price, the deal has been executed. A few days later, you should receive something called a contract note in the post, detailing the transaction that took place. This should be checked before being filed away for future reference.

If you're on the Internet, use the various resources to check the current price and make sure there hasn't been any bad news. The actual share-buying process should be explained clearly in the bumf or on the Web site. Depending on the broker, you might even be able to do a dummy run. Generally, you'll be offered a price to trade at and then you'll be given about fifteen seconds to decide whether to accept. Don't panic! If you don't feel comfortable, then you don't have to go through with it. You can step back and wait a bit until you do. Once you've completed your trade, something should appear on the Web site saying exactly what has been done. Print it out if you can or, at the very least, note down the details. It's very unlikely that anything will go wrong but, if it does, then it's a good idea to have this piece of paper as evidence. As with telephone dealing, after a few days you should receive a contract note in the post. Check it and file it away. If you are happy for your broker to hold the shares on your behalf, in something called a nominee account, then that's pretty much the end of it. However, some people like the feeling of having their actual share certificate with their name on it, tucked away in a drawer. If you want this, then you will need a broker that will issue 'own-name certificates'. But beware, it is an administrative hassle for them and they're likely to charge for it. It also makes it awkward to sell when the time comes, since you will need to send your certificate in and complete something called a stock transfer form.

After doing a few deals, you'll really start to get the hang of it. Be careful, it can be easy to get carried away: 'Sell Rentokil! Buy low! Sell high! Short Vodafone! Get me BP! I wanna kick some ass and I wanna kick it now, goddammit!' This sort of behaviour will make your broker rich instead of you. Dealing is not like basket-weaving. You don't get better at it the more you practise, and the practice is very much more expensive.

Appendix 5
Useful Web Sites

With as little a web as this I will ensnare as great a fly as Cassio.

— William Shakespeare, *Othello* (I, i)

As we've already pointed out on a number of occasions, the Internet represents a fantastic resource for the private investor. So much so that it's hard to make a case for not getting on the Internet and making use of it. We wouldn't really be doing our duty if we didn't give you a list of the addresses of a few Web sites to get you started. The only problem with lists like this is that they can be a real pain to use. Things change and they change very rapidly. All of these links were valid at the time of writing, but some of them will have ceased to exist by the time it reaches the bookshops. Don't worry, because we have created a Foolish Resources section at **www.fool.co.uk/community/ resource/** where you can find all these links online. Most of them refer to sites beyond the Motley Fool, for which we can take no responsibility.

Government and regulation
Association of British Insurers – **www.abi.org.uk**
Bank of England – **www.bankofengland.co.uk**
Companies House – **www.companieshouse.gov.uk**
Department of Social Security – **www.dss.gov.uk**
Department of Trade and Industry – **www.dti.gov.uk**
Financial Services Authority – **www.fsa.gov.uk**
HM Treasury – **www.hm-treasury.gov.uk**
Inland Revenue – **www.inlandrevenue.gov.uk**
Occupational Pensions Advisory Service – **www.opas.org.uk**
Occupational Pensions Regulatory Authority – **www.opra.gov.uk**
Office for National Statistics – **www.statistics.gov.uk**
Office of Fair Trading – **www.oft.gov.uk**

News and weather
BBC News – **news.bbc.co.uk**
BBC Weather Centre – **www.bbc.co.uk/weather**
Bloomberg UK – **www.bloomberg.com/uk/ukhome.html**
Daily Express – **www.express.co.uk**
The Economist – **www.economist.com/**
Financial Times – **www.ft.com**
The Guardian – **www.guardianunlimited.co.uk**
The Independent – **www.independent.co.uk/www**
Met Office – **www.met-office.gov.uk**
The Mirror – **www.mirror.co.uk**
Reuters – **www.reuters.com/news/**
Sky News – **www.sky.com/news**
The Sun – **www.the-sun.co.uk**
The Telegraph – **www.telegraph.co.uk**
The Times – **www.the-times.co.uk**

Personal finance
Moneyextra – **www.moneyextra.com/personal**
Moneynet – **www.moneynet.co.uk**
Motley Fool UK – **www.fool.co.uk/personalfinance/personal finance.htm**
FT Your Money – **www.ftyourmoney.com**
This is Money – **www.thisismoney.com**
Trustnet – **www.trustnet.com**

Search engines
Excite – **www.excite.com**
Go – **www.go.com**
Google – **www.google.com**
Lycos – **www.lycos.co.uk**
Yahoo – **www.yahoo.com**

Stocks and shares
Citywire – **www.citywire.co.uk**
Company Annual Reports Online – **www.carol.co.uk**
FTSE International – **www.ftse.com**
Hemscott – **www.hemscott.net**
Interactive Investor International – **www.iii.co.uk**
Market Eye – **www.marketeye.co.uk**

Motley Fool UK – **www.fool.co.uk**
Motley Fool US – **www.fool.com**
ProShare – **www.proshare.org.uk**
The Street – **www.thestreet.co.uk**
UK-Invest – **www.uk-invest.com**

Other

Association of Investment Trust Companies – **www.aitc.co.uk**
Association of Unit Trusts and Investment Funds – **www.investment
 funds.org.uk**
Barclays Capital Equity-Gilt Study – **www.barcap.com/egs**
CSFB Equity-Gilt Study – **www.csfb.com/eqres/eqres_gilt.html**

Appendix 6
The Pan-galactic Gargle Blaster

For those of you who are wondering just what is in the Pan-galactic Gargle Blaster, the 'best drink in existence' to which we alluded in the Introduction, then read on:

> Here's what the Encyclopaedia Galactica *has to say about alcohol. It says that alcohol is a colourless volatile liquid formed by the fermentation of sugars and also notes its intoxicating effect on certain carbon-based life forms.*
>
> *The* Hitch Hiker's Guide to the Galaxy *also mentions alcohol. It says that the best drink in existence is the Pan-galactic Gargle Blaster.*
>
> *It says that the effect of drinking a Pan-galactic Gargle Blaster is like having your brains smashed out by a slice of lemon wrapped around a large gold brick.*
>
> *The* Guide *also tells you on which planets the best Pan-galactic Gargle Blasters are mixed, how much you can expect to pay for one and what voluntary organisations exist to help you rehabilitate afterwards.*
>
> *The* Guide *even tells you how you can mix one yourself.*
>
> *Take the juice from one bottle of that Ol' Janx Spirit, it says.*
>
> *Pour into it one measure of water from the seas of Santraginous V – Oh, that Santraginean sea water, it says. Oh, those Santraginean fish!!!*
>
> *Allow three cubes of Arcturan Mega-gin to melt into the mixture (it must be properly iced or the benzine is lost).*
>
> *Allow four litres of Fallian marsh gas to bubble through it, in memory of all those happy Hikers who have died of pleasure in the Marshes of Fallia.*
>
> *Over the back of a silver spoon float a measure of Qualactin Hypermint extract, redolent of all the heady odours of the dark Qualactin Zones, subtle, sweet and mystic.*
>
> *Drop in a tooth of an Algolian Suntiger. Watch it dissolve, spreading the fires of the Algolian Suns deep into the heart of the drink.*

Sprinkle Zamphuor.

Add an olive.

Drink . . . but . . . very carefully . . .

The Hitch Hiker's Guide to the Galaxy *sells rather better than the* Encyclopaedia Galactica.

From The Hitch Hiker's Guide to the Galaxy *by Douglas Adams (Pan, 1979).*

The Motley Fool UK would like to add that it accepts no liability for anyone following the directions above. All claims to be addressed to Douglas Adams.

Index

THE MOTLEY FOOL

TM

OTHER MOTLEY FOOL BOOKS AVAILABLE

RULE BREAKERS, RULE MAKERS

The best selling US Motley Fool guide to picking market-beating companies.
David & Tom Gardner
£12.99

THE MOTLEY FOOL UK INVESTMENT WORKBOOK

A practical workbook where The Motley Fool takes the novice investor through the basics of investing. *David Berger & Bruce Jackson*
£9.99

THE FOOL'S GUIDE SERIES:

MAKE YOUR CHILD A MILLIONAIRE

With of a bit of careful investing, plan for your child's future. *Alan Oscroft* £5.99

THE OLD FOOL'S RETIREMENT GUIDE

A no-nonsense guide to long-term investment decisions and making the best of your retirement. *Rob Davies*
Available November 2000   £5.99

HOW TO INVEST WHEN YOU DON'T HAVE ANY MONEY

If you're in debt, just graduated, or started your first job (or are still earning a pittance), this is the essential guide for you. *Christopher Spink*   £5.99

ONLINE INVESTING

Want to invest using the internet, but don't know where to start? Let The Motley Fool help you untangle the World Wide Web.
Nigel Roberts with David Berger   £5.99

INVESTMENT CLUBS

Get together with your friends, neighbours and colleagues and form an investment club – a great way to learn about investing. *Mark Goodson with David Berger*
£5.99

*All **Motley Fool** books are available from Boxtree: please call the 24-hour hotline order number – Tel: 01624 836000 (p&p FREE in the UK) or direct from The Motley Fool UK www.fool.co.uk*

www.fool.co.uk